B.A.O.R: BRITISH ARMY ON THE RAMPAGE

B.A.O.R: BRITISH ARMY ON THE RAMPAGE

SEAN CONNOLLY

Matador
9 Priory Business Park
Kibworth Beauchamp
Leicestershire LE8 0RX, UK
Tel: (+44) 116 279 2299
Fax: (+44) 116 279 2277
Email: books@troubador.co.uk
Web: www.troubador.co.uk/matador

ISBN 978 1783062 928

British Library Cataloguing in Publication Data.
A catalogue record for this book is available from the British Library.

Typeset in Aldine401 BT Roman by Troubador Publishing Ltd
Printed and bound in the UK by TJ International, Padstow, Cornwall

Matador is an imprint of Troubador Publishing Ltd

www.armynovels.com
infor@armynovels.com

In memory of Bombardier 'Goulash' Tommy Harta, Royal Regiment of Artillery. One of the best non commissioned officers (N.C.O's) the British army had the fortune to hold in its ranks.

We miss you mate and thanks for the introduction to Apfel Korn.

FOREWORD

This is the first autobiographical and humorous book detailing the exploits of Bombardier Sean Connolly. The Country of Belize forms the amazingly colourful landscape to his novels. Why the British Army were and still are there, stretches credulity – but then why the British Army are anywhere can be a little confusing. Let's just say that for a young 'squaddie' – the idea of a posting to this Caribbean Country seemed like a dream come true – '…for like many soldiers I saw it for what it was – one long wild holiday – Club 18-30 with guns… but it was more than that!'

The indigenous Belize Defence Force was too few in number to control the Belize & Guatemala border. They were ill equipped and proved to be no match for the Guatemalans storming the borders and attacking Belize. The terror they spread throughout this small Central American country was nothing in comparison to the anguish that their drugs brought. It proved too much for this British colony.

As a result of this the British government were left little choice but to intervene and support the former British Honduras.

And so, British Army Belize, was formed consisting of one of Her Majesty's best infantry regiments, a detachment of harrier jump jets, a team of England's finest Special Forces and a six gun Battery of support artillery, the latter being made up of myself and a bunch of uncontrollable psychopaths known as the British Army on the Rampage (B.A.O.R).

A 'warning order' for a six-month fully operational tour of the Caribbean was issued by the Battery Commander and the training began. With the journey leading up to the beginning of April 1982 came the misery of training in freezing conditions for a deployment in a very hot climate. This was typical of the British army and so was the decision to send their wildest bunch of 'squaddies' for the deployment to Belize.

One hundred trained lunatics running around under the canopies of dense jungle, armed with live ammunition. And they called this the solution…

PREFACE

I was born in Preston on the 5 October 1961. As a young boy I grew up in Southport, in the North West of England. For as far back as I can remember I wanted only to serve as a soldier in the British Army.

My childhood days were mainly spent fighting, either with my two brothers or with my 'so called' mates. We lived in a small house along with my two sisters and my father. He was a hard man both physically and mentally and an ex-Burma campaign soldier who took no prisoners. My father had to work full time to keep us, we would often be up to mischief, which would inevitably lead to us being caught. This was not good if you had MY father!

At the age of twelve, I joined army cadets, although I did have to tell a 'little white lie' because the official age for joining was thirteen. I attended Army cadets every Tuesday and Friday night without being found out until I needed written permission from my parents so I could fly in a Wessex helicopter. Then my true age was found out for which I subsequently received a 'telling off' from the sergeant. I continued in the cadets until I joined up, knowing that these years would prove to be so valuable in the early stages of my army career.

My life as a teenager was more dysfunctional than my younger life. Being the second youngest child my sisters had now grown up and left home. My eldest brother had gone to live with another relative, but, perhaps more significant, my mum had left too and some months were spent in foster care. This left me and my younger brother to do all the chores! By the time I joined the army at sixteen years old I was hard and unemotional. I had left school with hardly any academic qualifications, but I *had* achieved what I had set out to do all those years before.

I spent my last five weeks of freedom working in a ice-cream shop and further realising there was nothing for me in Southport, and so I went and signed on the dotted line to earn the Queen's shilling.

On 12 September 1978, I joined Junior Leaders Regiment Royal Artillery in Nuneaton. This was the proudest day of my life. The transition into this 'hard' life was quite easy for me as I felt I had trained for it; not only in cadets, but in my life so far, thus I could not understand why so many new soldiers were getting upset about leaving home. I was thinking, this is what it's all about, away from dad, living a cushy life. I was wrong!

I left Junior Leaders after one year and joined my regiment in Gutersloh, West Germany, where I served for a further two years before being posted to Colchester, Essex. Throughout my next years, we were sent to some far off and exotic places and some REAL dumps that would NEVER be talked about in books.

Then, at twenty years old my crew and our gun battery deployed to Belize, Central America, where I achieved the rank of Bombardier and carried out the role of a gun commander, these duties normally held for a sergeant. Had it not been for my service in the army I dread to think how I may have ended up due to being so easily led, but after over a decade of service, I left feeling very proud of my achievements but also proud of what the British Army had done for me as a person.

My military service record reads as exemplary, although sometimes I wonder how!

It was announced in July 2011 that my regiment (The Lowland Gunners) would disband along with some of the Brigade that it supports. June 22 2012 would see the end of one of the finest regiments in the British Army.

Her Majesty, Queen Elizabeth sent a letter to the regiment and its contents were read during a farewell function at Murrayfield on the evening of June 23 2012. She expressed her sincere thanks to all who had served in the regiment.

It is with pride and honour that I write this book for all the soldiers from my regiment who did or did not make it, and indeed for all the troops I had the privilege to serve with.

'Ubique' (Everywhere).
'Quo Fas Et Gloria Ducunt' (Where Right and Glory Lead)

CHAPTER ONE

WARNING ORDER BELIZE

Colchester March 1982

Colchester was a huge garrison town, which was home to a number of regular army regiments. What was more significant was the fact that a couple of them were of special interest to me.

Colchester was home to the infamous Military Corrective Training Centre (M.C.T.C) or better known to ALL British squaddies as, 'Colly Nick'. The hallowed ground of Colly Nick was also a place that NO British soldier wanted to end up. I remember bringing a prisoner from Gutersloh in West Germany to Colly Nick and the permanent staff (P.S) gave me as much a hard time as they did the prisoner! I was only delivering him and I couldn't get out of the place fast enough. It frightened me to death.

Putting that aside and the fact that the town was full of coppers, the troops reckoned that being posted in Colly was the best UK posting going. Each regiment had its own barracks in Colchester.

My regiment was 41 Field Regiment Royal Artillery, we lived in Kirkee Barracks, which were okay but very dated. The rooms were like something out of the 'Carry on Matron' film, only our Regimental Sergeant Major (R.S.M) was no Sid James and the girls working in the N.A.A.F.I were no Barbara Windsor.

The four-one regiment Royal Artillery was a part of the seven armoured division and our operational role was to provide artillery support for the infantry. One of the regiments that interested me, no frightened me, was the Military Police (M.P). Their presence was massive within the town, with an arm of the Special Investigation Branch (S.I.B) attached for good measure. The M.Ps were not what we wanted to see

1

when we were having inter-regimental pub scraps at the weekend. They were always the bringer of bad news and the rest of the British Army treated them, 'like the common cold'. Unwanted and always left the taste of snot in your throat! If you had the choice though, you would prefer the attention of the M.Ps as opposed to the S.I.B any day of the week.

Those S.I.B. were out and out animals and made civvy coppers look like Teletubbies. When those boys investigated you, there was no doubt about it, you were in deep shit. In 1980 I had the misfortune to cross their path in Gutersloh, West Germany, when I gave an old mate from my Junior Leaders days a smoke grenade to get rid of, for me. He was up visiting me from Paderborn

He had thrown it out of his car window on the Autobahn on his way back to his regiment. Fantastic idea, until he saw the blue flashing lights of the unmarked car behind him. Its occupants, who happened to be the S.I.B, had witnessed first hand his criminal activity and the aftermath, which now looked like a scorched field to the left of his car.

Now one would be excused into thinking that us squaddies are as 'thick as thieves' and would never grass on a mate. You would be dead wrong. When he was questioned at the side of the road by the investigating sergeant, my mate sang like a grey parrot having just made it through to the finals of 'X Factor'! He furnished the sergeant with the full details of the grenade, its origin, and as if that wasn't enough, he then informed them how long I had kept it in my locker. I don't think there was any other information that he could have offered up at this time. Fuck me, when I was a kid, I was in a foster home, he could have told him about that too. Mind you, I did wonder why the sergeant called me '245024773 Bombardier orphan boy' later on in Mansergh Barracks when he was interviewing me under caution.

Now there are two things extremely relevant at this time.

Firstly, whenever you leave a military firing range, or where arms or ammunitions are handled, you must issue a declaration which goes something like this. 'I have no live rounds or empty cartridge cases in my possession sir'. It was a very serious declaration that every individual screamed out loud to an officer or senior non-commissioned officer (N.C.O.) prior to leaving the ranges. The troops however added a little squaddie humour and changed it to 'We have no Live Rockets in our Pockets'.

The second being was the fact that I was an N.C.O. at the time and should have been enforcing this law and not breaking it.

Anyway, this was a serious issue for which the S.I.B was pegging me. I was charged and, luckily, only got commanding officer's (C.O.'s) orders. It could have been a Court Martial, this was like the equivalent of Crown Court in Civvy Street. It was very serious and normally the punishment from it was severe if found guilty, you could even find yourself serving six months in Colly Nick.

Ninety quid it cost me in the end, but at least it was done and finished with.

I had gone from being the youngest soldier in the Royal Artillery to have been promoted, to having a stain on my military record. This was my one and only brush with the S.I.B. and from this moment on, I would break out in a red rash and develop an instant bout of alopecia every time I heard the words 'Special Investigation Bureau' or S.I.B.

An episode of my military career I didn't wish to repeat.

As well as the infantry and military police, Colchester boasted one of the largest Royal Electrical and Mechanical Engineers (R.E.M.E) detachments anywhere in the country. I had a particular interest in these too and always found myself watching this regiment while I was stationed here. This was the outfit that I initially wanted to join throughout my early teenage years, but unfortunately my academic level was below what was expected to allow me into the R.E.M.E This regiment was responsible for fixing, maintaining, calibrating and when necessary replacing any piece of machinery that we cared to break. That could be anything from a large artillery gun to a small arms rifle, Land Rover to a push bike.

The R.E.M.E were respected in one sense, but hated in another. They were known by the real fighting men as (R.E.M.F) Rear Echelon Mother-Fuckers (an Americanism I believe!) or (F.U.M.P) Fat Useless Mountain of Piss (the British Version). The hatred was only out of jealousy though, as the gunners weren't clever enough to make it into the R.E.M.E. and it was always perceived that they had a cushy time when we were deployed on exercise.

In all fairness though, they were very good at what they did and looking back, they were very proficient soldiers. Bastards!

On Friday 5 March 1982, the Battery Commander (B.C) Major Mark

Moran, had warned us for Belize. What this meant was that our Field Gun Battery, which consisted of approximately one hundred and three serving soldiers which formed less than one quarter of our regiment, was to be sent to Belize. We all stood on parade in front of the Battery Head Quarters (B.H.Q) while the Battery Sergeant Major (B.S.M) brought us up to attention, saluted and then handed us over to the B.C. There was no one within the Battery (Bty) that held as high a rank, as the B.C. Major Moran was a top officer. Better than most of the Rodneys we were getting through in those days.

"This is a warning order; you are now all warned for Belize. You will be deployed at the beginning of April 1982 until 1 October 1982. A Six Months Tour," he said

I immediately knew what most of the troops were thinking.

Where the fuck is Belize? How do you spell it? Do they sell beer? Why the fuck are we going there?

The warning order came right out of the blue. Right between the eyes. We knew one thing though. This was not a regimental adventure training playground or a holiday. We had just received a 'warning order' so we knew it was an operational tour. Would we get a chance to kill someone at long last? Shit. Twenty years old and taking my own crew on an operational tour. This was a buzz for me.

As a result of this warning order, something immediately sprang to the front of my mind. Not accepting this and the thoughts of 'doing a runner' would have been going through the minds of a few of these troops stood on parade at this time.

I must explain that under normal circumstances when a 'squaddie' goes 'Absent without Leave' (A.W.O.L). He is classed as 'Absent'. When the same guy does a runner when he has received a 'Warning Order' he is known as a 'Deserter'. Serious shit. You used to get shot for less.

The B.C. asked us if we had any questions. Although there were probably hundreds, we looked at the B.S.M who gave us the look which said 'let the B.C. dismiss'. He would answer our questions afterwards.

"Where is it, Sir?" Mick McCarthy asked the B.S.M

"Central America," he replied.

I looked at the rest of the troop, I could see the look of a group of children as they were about to depart for Disneyland on the faces of some of the less intelligent soldiers!

"A six month holiday in the Caribbean, it doesn't get any better than this," I heard Teukter say.

That's what he thought!

There were a number of married soldiers in our battery who were now left with the job of going home to their wives to inform them that they were going absent for six months. I knew in my head that for a number of them, this would go down like a lead balloon. There would be some tears in the married quarters that particular evening, that was for sure.

For some of the single soldiers who had been in long-term relationships or had strong family ties back in their home towns, this was going to be equally as hard. (At this moment, I was fortunate, as I had recently broken up with my girlfriend of twelve months. I'd finished with Julie six weeks ago and although it wasn't a serious relationship it appeared even less serious for her as she'd met a private from the Anglian Regiment and had been seeing him behind my back. The decision to part was an easy one for me and I was over her in 'oh let's say eleven minutes'.)

It wasn't going to be difficult for me to travel up the M6 and say a quick goodbye to my mother and father. It would also provide me the opportunity to have a goodbye drink with my mates.

I put the thoughts of the other soldiers' emotions behind me.

Anyway, there was something more important I needed to do.

Before we knocked off work for a long weekend, I ran straight to the phone box on Layer Road and rang my mate Kev Doolan who I had served with in Junior Soldiers in Nuneaton. He was now serving with 77 heavy regiment, Royal Artillery in Catterick and had returned from this six month operational tour of Belize the previous October.

"It's the shit hole of the world, it's the boil on the Earth's core, listen mate, it doesn't get any worse than Belize," he said.

"No way, Kev. You're joking aren't you?"

"No mate! Seriously, be careful. It's not funny. Oh and one more thing, No birds."

With that my ten pence ran out and even if I had more I wouldn't have put any in. I didn't want to hear anymore. What the hell was I letting myself in for?

As it was now Friday night, and in the light of what Kev had told me, I was now on a mission to get arseholed.

"A pint of Brown Bitter please?" I asked the Barmaid in The Robin's Head.

I think her name was Pat, but she was known to us as Juanita (pronounced 'one eater ') because she had one tooth right in the middle of her mouth.

"Oh and a burger and chips please," I added.

This was my fifth pint. It is never a good idea to start a session on an empty stomach I thought. The trough here was legendary, one meal and that was it for forty-eight hours, the portions were that big. It would be enough to fill three men let alone one. There was an old saying in the army 'An army marches on its belly'. Well we read this as the belly not being full of food, but beer and we would make sure we marched into battle as pissed as farts. We had decided that in this preferred state, we would easily cause more disruption and confuse the enemy. We would give them a sound slapping (if they were German we were at war with) and win the war with less casualties and loss of life. We saw this as a win, win situation.

Oh sorry. Let me explain. The Germans would be easy to beat as they don't punch or kick when engaged in the art of 'weekend scrapping'. I have been fortunate enough to engage with the German Civvies most weekends when we served in Germany and I was relieved to find that they only slap with the flat inside palm of their hand when in combat unlike us who preferred the more aggressive, non Queensbury Rules approach (name Calling, Hair Pulling and such like).

I looked over towards the pool table and saw five of our Bty having a pint with three of the gunners from Four Eight Battery (48Bty). 48Bty always thought they were the 'Senior Bty' within our regiment, but it was a fact that we held the senior battle honours, so we were top dogs. Not only that, but my gun crew had come first in the recent 'Regimental Best Gun Competition', so I was buzzing and untouchable. Number one, out of eighteen guns. These lads were only having a laugh though. It was good inter-Bty banter. I sat down next to three of our lads, in front of Tommy (Bombardier Bamber), and Sergeant Taff Terry on the outer edge of the large table. Tommy was a full Bombardier in our battery, he was a fantastic non-commissioned officer (N.C.O.) and knew how to get the best out of a gun crew without beasting them until their legs fell off. I admired his methods and his man management skills and had often wished that I had some of his qualities and experience. His crew both admired and respected him. The Rodneys (officers) on the other hand were not one hundred percent behind his methods as they were not always carried out in accordance with the gunnery drill book (an artilleryman's Bible), but he got his results, quicker better and with a lot less fuss. I put a lot of the officers dislike for his ways down to jealousy. When an officer comes through the other end of Sandhurst Officer Training College where they carry out their basic training, their brain is removed to an extent that they really believe that there is only one way of achieving a goal and that's the 'army way'. Experience taught the Non-Commissioned Officers (N.C.O.s) that there was always, always more than one way of skinning a cat and the cat didn't always have to be wearing a camouflage jacket.

Tommy and I hated each other years previous when I first joined the regiment. He must have thought I was cheeky, arrogant, cocky, full of myself and full of shit… He was a good judge of character and he was right. Within a few months I had attended, passed and come first on my Cadre Course (Promotions course) and had been given my first stripe. This pissed Tommy off, and also the other troops who had been in for years and were unable to reach the dizzy heights of lance Bombardier. A lance Bombardier is one stripe. The same as a lance corporal in an infantry regiment. A Bombardier in the Royal Artillery (R.A) was two stripes, this being a full corporal in the infantry. We were considered too posh to be called corporals. Bombardier was much cooler. I made many American soldiers double (run) around the gun position with an artillery shell above his head for calling me Corporal. We hated anyone calling us corporal.

Things had changed over the following years. Tommy and I had begun to understand each other so much more and because we lived opposite each other, we had become best friends. Things progressed even further and we became inseparable. He knew me and my methods and respected them as I did his. We had reached the same rank and were both Gun Detachment Number Ones. We spent a lot of time watching each others' backs.

A Gun N01 normally holds the rank of sergeant and has a Bombardier (Bdr) for his 2ic (second in command), dependant on which artillery gun you worked on or which artillery regiment you were serving in. There would normally be a further four crew members on a gun detachment and two drivers.

"What do you reckon Sean? Six months in the sun eh," Tommy said.

"Well mate, I hate to piss on your Cornflakes, but it's the shits."

Tommy took his mouth away from his pint of lager and looked over at me.

"I just looked at it on the map see and it looks fantastic. Right in the heart of the Caribbean sea..."

"Tommy," I said. "Firstly, when have the British Army ever sent us anywhere nice? And secondly, I have a mate who I served in Brats (Junior Soldiers) with and he has just come back from this so called Belize. He told me that it was the shits, so much so that as he slides down the banister of his life in the Royal Artillery, he sees Belize as the rather large splinter in his arse." He hadn't said that really, but I did, just to labour the point.

Tommy said exactly what I knew he was going to say, "Trust you, you miserable bastard. You could have told us after battery parade on Monday. That's the weekend fucked up then isn't it?"

"Not quite," I said. Cheap fags, beer and L.O.A. (Local Overseas Allowance), for six months, but guess what? No women. L.O.A was the allowance the British Army paid us whilst serving anywhere abroad to enable us to meet the cost of living in a particular country. Fuck me, you could buy a house for thirty-seven pence in Belize, but I wasn't complaining. It would be extra wedge in our pockets anyway. Superb! My interpretation for the reason for L.O.A was somewhat different. It was the army's way of saying 'sorry troops, we fucked up, again. The sovereignty has found another shit hole in the world, called it a British Colony and put a picture of three lions on it. Unfortunately now though we need some plebs to go and guard it for us and seeing you are doing jack shit at the moment, you can go out there for six months. Oh it's not all bad news though because while you are there, here's seven-hundred quid to help you get pissed for your troubles'.

All right, so I was a little bitter. Does it show?

"Sorry lads. Let's leave it until Monday then." I necked the last half of my pint and remembered that feeling I always got when I was about to engage in a heavy session.

We had another two pints in the Robin's Head and I just couldn't get the thought of our new operational posting out of my head. The one thing I wanted to do that weekend was to get that shit hole out of my head. I hated the place already and I didn't even know exactly where it was. I think I could just about spell it.

"Anyone fancy the Clarrett after trough?" I said. No shortage of takers then. Typical squaddies, the mention of another pub and they are out the door before you can say 'free beer'.

That was going to be me then. My plan was to stay in the Clarrett until closing, last orders in those days was about eleven o'clock. After that I would make my way back to the Robin's Head to be thrown onto the Bellwood Bus.

Please let me tell you about 'The Bellwood', it was the shittiest night club you could ever imagine. The den of depravity and it stunk like a lavatory. It was a rundown ex truck-stop out on the A12, in the middle of nowhere, so as a means of getting punters out to the club ten miles away, they used to run a Mk1 Ford Transit panel van from the Robin's Head. There was no charge for this service, asking for a bus fare would have been as insulting as slipping a bag of Richmond sausages into the Christmas buffet at the Colchester Synagogue. There was a piss ridden mattress thrown in the back of this van that would make Rab C Nesbitt smell like a chip supper. It was disgusting and it was only due to the onslaught of a heavy lashing of cheap Brown and bitter that you would even contemplate going anywhere near it, but it saved you fifteen dabs in a Joe Baxi. I think I counted twenty three people in the back of it one weekend. It was a bastard of a ride though, ten miles along winding country roads stood up in the back trying to keep our balance while standing on the piss ridden mattress.

When you got to the Bellwood, you stunk as far away as your Brut aftershave you could possibly get. The Bellwood staff were very clever because they had got you by the short and curlies. They had been successful in getting you out there and then charged what they called a 'nominal fee' to cover your entrance. A Fiver! nominal fee? You are having a laugh! A fiver was a lot of money back then. They also had a training shoe policy at this gaff, if you had no trainers; it was fine; you could enter in your bare feet! The big worry there was that there was that much glass on the floor; you would have torn your feet apart. On top of all these delights, the beer was like piss, like sucking on a pair of

9

wet swimming trunks. Then, when you were pissed, you had to fork out for a return taxi to get you back to Colly. There was no walking this distance, not in that condition. In addition to this there were no pavements on either side of the road for miles, not good for a pissed up squaddie. We wouldn't have made it one hundred metres down the road.

The Bellwood was chocker that night, I already had a fuzzy head and couldn't even remember tonight's trip in the back of the Bellwood Bus. I don't think it had much to do with the copious amounts of beer I had just consumed, more likely, there not being anything memorable about the journey. All I remember clearly was that Taff Terry was with me. As I looked up from the sticky floor I noticed Teuchter standing in front of me, he was wearing his heavy, black leather biker's jacket, which was not unusual but Teuchter owned a Yamaha PE 175, a monster of a trail bike and he had ridden it to the Bellwood this particular night. I couldn't believe it! He was definitely arseholed. If he came off that thing on those country roads, the late night truckers tramping along the A12 would have made short work of his 'Big Boys Toy'. I wouldn't imagine they would even know that they had just run over him and his bike. I was a little pissed off with him at the time and told him so. He was more than mental on the bike without a drink inside him. One night as I was driving around a roundabout in my Hillman Imp, he had used the sloped paving flag on the roundabout as a ramp and hit it at speed. He had flown at least eight feet in the air, straight over the top of my car and in the direction we were headed. No wonder they called him Teuchter.

Taff got the ale in and mine was ghastly. When I was young the taste of beer used to make me pull a face much like a bulldog sucking a wasp. I hated the taste of it until just before joining the army. It was around this time that I started, for whatever reason to enjoy the taste of the hops. Drinking in the Bellwood was like returning to my pre-army days. Now at twenty years old, I would often wake up on a Saturday or Sunday morning with a throat like a Swiss Anglers Maggot Box and wishing I had stayed at home watching 'Fawlty Towers'.

We had only been in the Bellwood for about fifteen minutes when I looked over at the bar. Samantha and Sheila were sat right on the end by the D.J. They had been in the Robin's Head earlier and had definitely been giving us the eye then. I gave Taff the nod and we made our way over to them. They were two sisters who were roughly my age and lived in Colchester town centre. We had known them since the regiment arrived in the garrison. They were always up for a good laugh, and more than a bit flirty with Taff and I, but more importantly they were two fit birds. By the time we got to them, I can remember feeling very horny and really not bothered at all as to which one I wanted to bed. It would have been like picking between Debby Harry and Olivia Newton John. Taff followed like a lap dog and it was customary for only one of us to take the lead while the other one acted as the 'lost soul'.

"How you doin girls?" I shouted. The noise was deafening in the club. It didn't help that they were sat near the biggest speakers I had ever seen in a disco. The girls seemed happy to engage in conversation with us.

Within minutes, it became obvious that I was chatting up Samantha and Taff was doing well with Sheila. I turned around to ask him what he was drinking, but he was unable to reply as his tongue had chosen an alternative exercise. Neither of them heard my comment about 'getting a room'. Taff wasn't hanging about and was necking this girl in record time. So much for the lost soul routine.

Before I moved up the bar to be served, Sam, as she wanted me to call her, was very receptive to a big smacker I had just planted on her lips. By the time I returned to where they were sitting some minutes later, she was keen to repay the compliment with one of her own. This girl could kiss, I thought to myself as her tongue was pushing down my throat. This had more than confirmed that I had to get her back to the barracks or somewhere or anywhere. I didn't care.

The destination agreed by all, the journey back to the barracks was in an old London hackney cab. I was happy as Larry on the back seat with Sam. We were all over each other. Taff on the other hand wasn't having as much luck. He was constantly trying to reach over from one of the single fold down seats to the one on the other side to get at Sheila and the winding country roads were not helping his cause.

I lived in a room on my own in the barracks. Being an N.C.O did have some minor privileges. There were two single army beds in the room, the one to the right behind the door which was mine and the second being directly in front as you walked in, some twelve feet into the room.

When the army issued a mattress it came with a thick plastic mattress cover on it and you were told to keep it on. Mine was straight off as it made me sweat in the night. The cover had its good points and its bad points. If there was one tiny stain on a mattress when you were handing it back to the stores on leaving the camp, then you had to pay the full price for its replacement. The main down side to the plastic mattress cover was about to come clear.

We burst through my door like something out of a 'Starsky and Hutch' film. The room was in total darkness. Like a military operation, I peeled off to the right dragging Sam by both hands and as for Taff, he knew where my spare bed was as this wasn't the first time we had invited female company into the barracks so he carried on ahead.

When the back of my legs hit the steel bed frame, I sat at first then immediately laid down, pulling Sam on top of me. I kicked my shoes off and then sat up while I leaned forward, reached down and removed her ankle boots. I could hear something similar occurring to my right as four shoes hit the floor boards. Thud, thud, thud, thud.

The giggling in the room suddenly stopped and this was replaced by a number of quiet moans as both couples were kissing passionately. I remember feeling horny and thankfully only half-pissed at this time. I wasted no time in removing her top followed swiftly by her bra. She had a gorgeous figure and although I didn't know what her perfume was, she smelt fantastic. This in itself made me want her even more.

As I removed the last of her clothes she practically ripped the shirt off my back. We were both stark bollock naked and ready to go for it. I was thinking about my next moves and I had to stop briefly when I heard a noise that could only be described as someone fucking a bag of crisps.

Taff would have had no grounds to deny that he was now banging away like a steam train. The noise from the plastic mattress cover was horrendous and at times quite off-putting. However by the time Sam had redirected my tongue down her throat it was as if there was no one else in the room, and we were soon doing the same.

After some time, (okay probably a little time), Taff's side of the room went quiet and not long after so did ours. When Sam and I had finished, I needed the toilet so I made my excuses. I had just left the room when Taff came chasing after me. He had a smile upon his face as big as the parade ground.

"Fucking Hell, she's good," Taff said.

"Sam's not bad either," I replied.

"Okay, here's the plan. When we get back in the room, you walk straight ahead and I will go to your bed," he said.

"What. Are you fucking mad?" I answered.

The big smile reappeared on his face and although this was crazy, this could be a laugh. Even though the room was totally dark, we would never get away with this surely?

My room was still in total darkness, neither of us spoke a word and before I knew it I was touching the bed in front of me and groping a new body. I lay down on the bed and Sheila's hands started groping me all over. I tried my hardest not to groan and give the game away. There was no resistance from the other side of the room, but just when I started feeling horny again, I heard a loud slap.

"You dirty bastards," Sam screamed. And then another loud slap.

Sheila quickly realised what was happening and reached down and produced a clipper lighter which she was now sparking up right in front of my face.

"You pair of Wankers," she shouted as she was removing her naked body off the bed.

She turned as she picked up her clothes and slapped me really hard on the left side of my face.

"You pair of shits," Sam shouted.

They were now both getting dressed as quickly as they could and in the blink of an eye the door opened and they were gone.

I was more than pissed off with Taff.

"You fucking idiot! What kind of an idea was that?" I asked.

Taff was laughing his head off and made up that we had nearly managed to swap girls without them knowing. He hadn't yet realised that he had lost us both a night of passion. What a dipstick.

I woke to the smell of bacon from the cookhouse the next morning. The thought of the stunt we had tried to pull the night before brought a smirk to my face. My wallet was on the floor next to my bed, fair enough it was empty, but it was all present and correct. What a night. There was no way I wasn't doing brekky this morning with that smell of bacon wafting from the cookhouse under my door.

As I sat down to eat my breakfast, I looked over at the chefs behind

13

the hotplate. The A.C.C (Army Catering Corps) were very touchy when you called them by their usual name, 'The Aldershot Concrete Company', or if you called one of the chefs 'a cook'. If you were caught firing out either of these insults, there were no seconds on the cards for you, but if you stretched this even further and made the mistake of calling them 'slop jockeys' you were in for the 'lump end' of the soup ladle right on the crown of your head.

My dad who had been twenty-two years in the marines and served his time in Burma had taught me a valuable lesson.

"Son," he had said, "before you join the army, remember these words, never upset a store man or a cook." It was the one piece of advice I took with me when I joined up. I never forgot his words and always went out of my way to get on with both of them.

The rest of the weekend came and went, and as I had blown the best part of my monthly wages the previous night, I decided that two pints in the Pads N.A.A.F.I was all I could stretch to. The 'Pads' was the name given to the married soldiers who lived in the military quarters on the military estates. To us, it was just another location for us to purchase cheap beer. 'Navy, Army and Air Force Institute'. That's what they told us. 'No ambition and fuck all interest'. That's what we told them. Who was right? If a Naafi had a café attached to it then we would call it 'The Gag and Puke'…. As we did in Canada. A little bit disrespectful maybe, but we were well pissed off because Navy was the first letter and with the Army being the senior of the three services, we found it a bitter pill to swallow. To think that they were before us in the word N.A.A.F.I.

I spent Sunday night bulling my boots ready for Battery Parade on Monday Morning 07.30 hrs. This was a serious affair with the full compliment of men, *One-hundred and three*. You had to be dead or dead to be excused Bty Parade! The Battery Commander (B.C.) Major Moran loved the sight of shiny boots. Well now! One thing I could do is bull boots. What I couldn't do very well was iron my lightweights (army trousers) or my KF shirt, this was something that Tommy and I had sussed though. He would iron my kit to a standard where he would make it stand up on its own, whilst I would spend the time bulling his boots until they were looking like black glass. Even if I say so myself, we were a smart pair of bastards.

"BATTERY SHUN," the B.S.M screamed. With that, everyone

came to attention. "Keep still you shit heads." He turned to the right, saluted the B.C. and screamed, "Three eight Imperial Field Battery ready for your inspection, Sir." The B.C. returned the salute and ordered the B.S.M to fall in. Now this was not normal practice, the B.S.M always accompanied the B.C. while he carried out his inspection ready to rip another hole in the arses of the mingers that the B.C. identified. The B.C. started with me. I was the 'Right hand marker' the tallest man in the BTY. Everyone fell in and dressed off me. This was the way the British Army ensured that the three ranks were always lined up straight, by falling in on and dressing off the right hand marker. It meant that you were also the first one that the B.C. inspected.

"Good Turn Out, Bombardier," the B.C. said to me. I never moved a muscle. Tommy next to me got the same. We all heard the B.C. mumble some more compliments as he hurried his inspection and moved quickly along the ranks. He never once throughout the inspection picked anyone up for a poor turnout. What was happening? This was alien to us, the B.C. was no push over if you had so much as a hair out of place or a twisted bootlace, you could guarantee at least ten extras (ten extra guard duties). The B.S.M. would have been pissed off at this unusual inspection technique as he loved nothing better than a good old Monday morning scream at the mingers. The B.S.M, (Yorkie Davenport), was a controlled psycho. He was one of the biggest and hardest men I had ever met and well known throughout the whole Royal Artillery. You really did not want to cross this man. We were all frightened to death of him, regardless of our size or rank. He was an out and out nutter. He would disappear for weeks on end leaving us all wondering where he had gone then you would be watching the news some ten weeks later and who would be body guarding Margaret Thatcher? Yes the man himself. I suppose we were proud of him in some respects.

There were not many men who pushed the B.S.M but Gunner Sayville (A Gunner is the lowest rank and is equivalent to a private soldier in the Infantry) once decided, against his better judgement and our sound advice, to approach the B.S.M and ask him to go guarantor for his new motorbike. The B.S.M had agreed to this, but it came with a stark warning that should he default on a payment then he would beat him to within an inch of his life. The deal was done; Sayville got his bike and subsequently missed the second payment on it. Yorkie was witnessed by two senior N.C.O.s beating him about the crown of his cranium profusely with a heavy brass ended parade stick. Needless to say, he never missed another payment after that.

Personally I wouldn't have missed the second or any other payment for that matter and saved myself severe pain at the hands of a masochist and a future life of blackouts and migraine. I felt a little sorry for Sayville, because he had already suffered beatings about the head from his father which had caused him to be dim witted and these were now being superseded by the B.S.M out of their joint respect for the word 'stupidity'. There was a plus to his thrashings though. I had worked out, that by the time he was thirty-two, he wouldn't feel any pain on his head. How good was that? No toothache ever again. Wow. What a bonus.....

The B.C. had completed his inspection within ten minutes, a record I had never seen before. What's going on? I thought to myself. It soon became abundantly clear. The B.C. wanted to carry on with delivering the information pertaining to Belize. I think we were all made up because for the first time in years no one was getting so much as a cracked pair of boots or their beret being flung across the parade ground.

"Belize is the only country of the English-speaking Caribbean in which armed forces are used, primarily for defence and attack. This is to deter the Guatemalan army from marching into Belize and also to control the infiltration of its borders by illegal immigrants. Moreover, with Belize being dubbed as one of the largest producers of marijuana, the BDF 'Belize Defence force' has become increasingly involved in 'police' operations, including the combating of drugs and maintaining order, thus leading to a blurring of the roles of the police and the military. Finally, Belize's military are engaged in self-help programs and performs tasks normally carried out by civil organisations and is used in civil military defence roles. Truth be known, the Belizeans are losing the battle and it is reported that a number, above three, British soldiers have been reported as 'missing in action'. There was also the battle of keeping Guatemalan tyrants and rebels away from the border areas, where they had been active in staking claims on Belize territorial rights and causing unrest between factions of rioters and Belizean authorities. Reported deaths have been brutal with torture always part of the Guat

M.O. This army is gathering intelligence and are getting cleverer by the day. The head honchos must be sniffed out and stopped.

"You are all going to the heart of the Caribbean basin. The most Northern country of Central America. You will assist in preventing a Guatemalan invasion into the country and assisting five (5) Royal Anglian Infantry Regiment. There is a detachment of Harriers based in the north of the country to react to such invasions. A team of SAS are also present in, and will be on hand should the shit hit the fan. Gentlemen, this is a serious operational tour not a holiday. The road ahead will be very difficult. You will be deployed for six months in a hot, humid and dry country, of which a large percentage is thick jungle. When I fall you out now, I want you all to join your relevant troop sergeant majors (T.S.M's) who will issue you the next stage of information which you will need going forward. I will remind you now that what has been spoken here today is 'secret' and must not be repeated anywhere."

The British Army were good at telling you the information at the last moment. 'Loose lips sink ships' and all that jazz.

The T.S.M of 'C' Troop was an old guy called Mick Mayers. We knew him as Chindit. This guy had attempted SAS selection on two separate occasions and had failed both times. He had been RTU'd (Return to Unit) twice, a broken man and on the last occasion it was reported that someone had actually seen him crying in the toilets of the sergeants mess. If you fail SAS selection in any regiment in the British Army you are never considered a failure, you are still considered a hero and respected immensely. To put your mind and soul through torture to that level once in an attempt to be the best commands total respect but to pick yourself up and do it all again makes you a very special and dedicated person. He failed the second time because he arrived at a check point two minutes early on a twenty five mile tab (speed march carrying 70lb), so they binned him off the course. What this meant for us though, was that we gained all his soldiering knowledge and experience, knowledge of jungle warfare was what we needed and that's exactly what we had. All my mates agreed with me when I said that the SAS lost a good soldier when they sent this fellow packing.

Chindit bimbled on, and after three hours of having Belize rammed down our throats, we knocked off for a welcome fifteen minute Naafi

17

break. Chindit had been to Belize before and had given us a much more detailed account of what we should expect and about the hierarchy and the structure of the Battery we would be working to when we arrived out there. What became clear now was that for the last five months the regiment had had us running our legs off. Completing ten mile runs every day, seven days a week and now we knew the reasons for it. The 'reality penny' had finally dropped. We were about to deploy to one of the hottest, driest operational theatres in the British Army map case and we needed to be in tip-top condition. When we returned from Naafi break Tommy and I sat apart from each other on the grass outside the BTY office. March was a cold time to be sitting on the damp grass, but when Chindit said sit, you sat.

We were going to be deploying as a six gun battery. Three guns would stay up in the north of Belize. This would be 'D' Troop. 'C' Troop, which was us, would deploy in the south of the country. D Troop contained the three guns of 'G Sub' 'H Sub' and 'I Sub'. Our troop had J, K and L Subs. 'L Sub' was my gun. The three guns up north were to be stationed in a place called Holdfast Camp. An area of the country we now know only occupied by the R.E.M.F (Rear echelon Mother Fuckers), whereby we in the south were going to have two guns in a place called Rideau Camp one mile outside of a little fishing village called Punta Gorda and the third gun at a place close to the Guatemalan border called Salamanca. The three south guns would rotate serving four months in Rideau and the two months in Salamanca, right in the middle of dense jungle and closest to the Guat border. I didn't like the sound of Salamanca at all, but hey ho, such was life.

Chapter Two

Thumbs Away

Our regiment in Colchester was issued with the Field Howitzer 70 or
F.H70. This was a tri-national gun which was a partnership between
France, Italy and Britain. It entered service in Britain around 1978-1980
and was clearly the worse disaster the British Army had ever been a part
of and the hardest piece of equipment to get used to. What a pile of junk.
It beggared belief that the G.W.C's (Great White Chiefs) had never even
consulted the lowest of the gunners when considering developing
artillery guns. The 'Development Rodneys' must have been more stupid
than we gave them credit for. There were the voices of experience
available to these boffins who could have warned them that this gun fell
well below what the British Royal Artillery aspired to. It was out and
out crap. The gun only had two things going for it and that was its
nuclear capabilities (and I will say no more on that front) and its range.
I cannot remember the exact range of this piece, but it was a
considerable distance. A 155mm 103lb H.E (high explosive) shell could
be winging its way over your village in Wiltshire while you were eating
your tea and you wouldn't have had any idea! The downside of it was
that it was too heavy, the hydraulics was constantly becoming
unserviceable, it was useless in cold weather, it was useless in wet
weather and so were its crew. There was no protection from the
elements and no protection from effective enemy small arms fire or
exploding shrapnel. It was impracticable in that it was cumbersome,
lumpy and slow to bring into action as opposed to a tracked gun. It was
supposed to be self-mobile once it was unhooked from the back of the
Foden Gun Tractor, but it wasn't. The front mounted VW engine
suggested that you would be able to drive the gun from a hard standing
or a road onto a grassed area. The engine drove at only 8mph and the

second you drove it off road it sank. It was far too heavy and had the worse 'off road' tyres you could put on any vehicle. It was deemed so dangerous for the crew that this gun was guilty of claiming many a thumb or fingertip as the troops were constantly trapping them in the breach. I lost count of the broken feet that had been received due to short-staffed gun crews forcing one man to remove the giant spades of the side of the gun. As a result of the weight of the spades and without a second team member, they were always dropping them on their feet. The F.H70 horded shit more than any other artillery piece in service and was a bastard to clean, it had so many nooks and crannies it was untrue. At the testing stage of this gun, how had the gun crew, namely Stevie Wonder, Roy Orbison, Ray Charles, Bochelli and Mr Magoo not spotted all these faults?

Our chosen artillery piece for Belize was the Light Gun, there was fuck all light about it. In fact it came in at about two tons if I remember rightly. The 105 mm Light Gun had been in service with the Royal Artillery for about thirty years and had served the troops well all over the world. This weapon was a fantastic asset for British Artillery Regiments as it would go anywhere. I think we must have sent an advance shit stirrer before all of our conflicts kicked off and his job was to say 'Yes we will fight you. We can get a Light Gun in your country'. He then reported these findings back to the War office and the scrap began…. The Light Gun is also very air portable meaning it can be carried around the battlefield underslung on a Puma or Chinook. This gun replaced the 105mm Pack Howitzer. Another robust 105mm system that proved its worth on many occasions. It was often found to be firing up to four hundred rounds per day. Since taking it to Belize the gun has seen operational service in Kuwait, Bosnia, Afghanistan, the Falklands and Iraq. The 105mm Light Gun had a crew of six men and was towed by a V8 one tonne Land Rover and was very rapid out the blocks. This gun was everything the F.H70 wasn't. It couldn't have the devastation of a long range 103lb shell, but this little gem of the Royal Artillery left the F.H70 standing in every other respect. It was a cracker. The F.H70 had cost the British tax Payer millions upon millions to develop and introduce into service, whereas the Light Gun must have cost all of seventeen quid. It was a no brainer for us.

The following Monday (15th March), we were to deploy, with our new toy to Sennybridge in Wales for a two week tactical exercise, that gave us only seven days to convert from the F.H70 to the Light Gun in order for us to be able to hit the ground running in Sennybridge and knock the shit out of the welsh countryside. It was the Head Hunters way of confirming to them that we were proficient enough to use the Light Gun in Belize when the time came.

Every artilleryman's dream was to knock the crap out of open countryside causing utter destruction *and* get paid for it. The downside of this was that we had to be ready in seven days and that was a bit of a tall order. Failure could potentially mean death or serious injury to one of my gun crew. I knew that the harder I pushed them the easier it would be for them when they got to Sennybridge and on to Belize. The Gun Number Ones and the Coverers, (the second in command) were to go with the S.M.I.G, no not the Stig, the Sergeant Major Instructor Gunnery. This was a warrant officer second class, a sergeant major that had gone away for years to learn everything there possibly is to know about artillery guns and the deployment of them, returns back to a regiment and hammers gun drill into a group of senior ranks before they in turn go away and train their own gun crews. A bit like 'train the trainer'. He was going to beast us for the remainder of that day; there was nothing new there then. We had gone through this many times before when we were converting onto a new gun and we knew what was to come. More importantly we knew the reasons behind it. Mind you that wasn't at the forefront of your mind when you were calling him a 'Wanker' under your breath as he was making you run around the parade ground with an artillery shell above your head. It's really not funny when your arms can't take anymore and you drop 35lb on the top of your bonce (head). The reasons why became insignificant at this point and you emphasised and repeated the word 'Wanker' in your head a thousand times. What you also had to remember is that at the end of this day when you returned back to your gun crew, you were going to put them through the same paces. In your quest to make them 'war ready', they would call you a 'Wanker' a thousand times too…

It was after these sessions with the S.M.I.G, that he would then oversee the training you gave to your troops in Colchester. Once he was happy you wouldn't see him after this until the 'live firing' part of your final exercise up at Sennybridge, after that we had one week back in sunny Colly to clean up and pack up and then that was it we were to deploy to the heart of the 'Caribbean basin'. I'll tell you what wasn't funny about this whole ordeal though, we were about to be deployed to Sennybridge in the depths of Welsh Wales in March when it was fucking freezing and wet, then we would be returned to Colly for a week and then on to Belize which was hot, dry and humid. How does that work?

The S.M.I.G knocked us off for some food. The lads were starving after running around like idiots all morning.

The food was good in our cookhouse. It's amazing what the threat of outside caterers can do to a regiment of 'slop jockeys'… Harry the Bastard The Regimental Sergeant major (R.S.M) or Raz man as he was known, had segregated and cordoned off a part of the cookhouse for the N.C.O's to eat behind, but none of the N.C.O's I knew used it. There was talk though that he came into the cookhouse once at lunchtime and caught a lance Bombardier eating on the same table as a gunner. That's a lance corporal eating on the same table as a private soldier. Remember we are in the Royal Artillery. The R.S.M bust him down (demoted him) to gunner saying that if he wanted to eat with the gunners then he could be one again. What a horrible man he was, I know stories about this evil being that would make your toes curl. All you need to know is that he was hated by everyone in the regiment including his wife… I always said that if ever there was a foot battle and he was leading us into the charge, the post-mortem would be asking why there were nine hundred S.L.R (self loading rifle) bullet holes in his back. We would just say that he was running away in an act of cowardice and the enemy shot him.

He carried out a particular cruel stunt on me In 1980, when I was eighteen years old, I had been doing a twenty-four hour guard duty on a Saturday, I was well pissed off because I was serving the last of my ten extra duties when on the Monday morning I went to present the Daily Occurrence Book (DOB) to the Raz Man. Now let me tell you, this D.O.B had to be written like nothing you had compiled before. Talk about neat, with every punctuation and the recording of every occurrence during your twenty-four hour duty. Guard commanders used to stay up all night making sure the entries in this book were spot on and grammatically correct. I marched into the R.S.M's office, slammed my feet together.

"245024773 Bombardier Connolly completed duty, Sir'," I screamed. He looked up at me with eyes that could kill.

"Book," he said. I leaned forward and handed him the DOB and then returned to attention. He opened the page where my entries were made. "Take forty extra duties," he said.

"Yes sir," I answered.

"Do you know what for?"

"No sir."

"Well, take another ten then."

I racked my brain thinking what the hell I had done or not done as the case was.

"Look Dickhead," he said. 'No full stop." He had awarded me a year's worth of extra twenty-four hour duties for missing a full stop. Twelve hundred hours extra work for nothing. Fifty extra duties. What a complete Wanker. I remember thinking the worst thought a man could think about another human being just before I wished death on him. I hoped his kids walked backwards. I wasn't to know at the time he didn't have any. I hope his next shit was a Christmas tree. God I had nothing but pure hatred for him as a result of this stunt.

"Right Fuck off," he said.

"Yes Sir," I shouted and marched out of his office. This was the kind of man we were dealing with here. He did nothing for our regiment and nothing for the morale of the troops. I had met no man in our regiment who showed any respect for him. They say that an R.S.M is put on earth to be hated and if he is not hated then he is not doing his job. Harry the Bastard was very good at his job.

Fortunately for us the R.S.M didn't visit the cookhouse and as soon as we had finished lunch we returned to the parade square and decided to have a quick fag while we waited for the S.M.I.G. We (the gun commanders) were feeling pleased with ourselves and all agreed that the training for that morning had gone really well. The simplicity of the gun, the experience of the troops and the knowledge of the S.M.I.G proved to be a good recipe for our achievements.

However, the feeling was short lived when the scream of, "FIRE MISSION BATTERY," came from behind a six foot brick windbreak where the S.M.I.G had been hiding, just waiting for us to spark up. Fire mission battery were the words which brought every artillery gunner running to man their guns and commence with a fire mission. An example of this in wartime could be if the infantry had come under heavy fire and needed some artillery cover and they needed it now, then we would be called in to throw some artillery into the mix. The importance of reacting very quickly was most important. If you could imagine that every second your shells are not raining down onto the battlefield one or more of our own troops could lose a life. This is why these words were taken so seriously by everyone in an artillery regiment. Each gun crew always left one man on the gun to man the communications in case the order came over the net, even when taking a rest or break.

He would then shout to the remaining members of the gun crew, "Fire Mission Battery," who in turn would come sprinting back to the gun. 'Fire mission battery' or 'fire mission' was never used in jest. It was a serious order and was always treated as such.

We stood to attention behind the two guns on the regimental square with the S.M.I.G behind us. He must have been laughing his nuts off at the fact that we had just lit up and now we had legged it back to the gun with our fags still burning away on the ground. We didn't mind the S.M.I.Gs as we felt they had earned the respect of all artillery troops. To take yourself away from all the good things in life and then bury your head in 'Gun Drill' and 'Gunnery' for two years was very commendable. They would return to the regiment as very knowledgeable individuals.

The S.M.I.G ,(Warrant officer Tony Catterham) commented on how well we had done that particular morning and he would only need to keep us for an hour that afternoon before we went back to our own crew to start the training with them. We were going to have a gun race as the final part of our training whereby the two crews would bring their guns into action as fast as we could. This meant that the Light Gun would be hooked up to the one tonne Land Rover with the six man crew onboard. The S.M.I.G would blow his whistle and we would have to de-bus as quickly as possible, bring the gun into action by making it ready for firing by the quickest means. We had to be careful here, because it was a known fact by all artillerymen, that should you hear short sharp whistle blasts on a gun position then you had to freeze exactly where you were. It meant 'STAND FAST'. This was another artillery term, if someone spotted something dangerous which could mean imminent danger to persons or property, he would shout 'Stand Fast' or do the whistle thingy. Only the person who initiated 'Stand Fast' could then cancel it. (Unless he was dead!).

I was the 'number two' for this particular race. I always got the shitty end of the stick in these situations. The S.M.I.G blew a long blast on his whistle and off we went. Side by side the two guns raced into action. Within a flash we were now pointing in the right direction and before we knew it the gun was in action. We all fell in at the rear of the gun, finished. I looked over to 'G'Sub and they were still struggling with the wheel nut. It turned out that their man had nearly cross-threaded the wheel nut, thus costing them valuable seconds and losing them the race.

"Well done 'H' sub. 'G' sub, give me twenty." At that, our opposition crew all hit the deck and pushed out twenty press-ups. This was funny on two counts. Firstly, it wasn't our crew doing the press ups and secondly, I could hear Taff Terry calling out his words of obscenities to his crew every time he was at the lowest part of the press up.

"You-Wankers-I-hate-losing.   Cant-even-take-off-a-wheel-you-Tosser." All within the space of twenty press ups. I was well impressed. I remember seeing the nylon hammer still lying on the ground at the side of his gun and thinking that this hammer needed to be moved out of sight while Taff was pissed off like this. It would be too easy for Taff to use it on the Number 2's head.

"That's it," shouted the S.M.I.G "Let's knock it on the head. Well done lads close it up and back to your crews." We took our time taking the gun 'out of action' and discussed some of the finer points on bringing the gun into action even quicker than we had just done. The use of a block of wood for underneath the jack if we were on a wet field would improve our timings. You could guarantee that most of the areas where we went when live firing were very wet and boggy, so taking a block was well worth it. It wasn't needed when on the regimental square though. We were quite impressed at the speed at which we brought the gun into action, but if there were other areas where we could shave off a few seconds of time to assist us getting our first round down the range then we wanted to know now where that was going to come from.

We looked over to the left hand edge of the regimental square and there was a lot of movement occurring. There was a steady stream of F.H70 guns driving onto the parade ground. I had remembered that the

G.R.A (General of the Royal Artillery) was visiting shortly, but I was under the impression that it was Tuesday of the following week; if that was the case then we would miss his visit as we were in sunny Sennybridge on exercise. I was wrong, it was that day. That's all we needed. A visit from the GRA when all we wanted to do was concentrate on training our own gun crews on the Light Gun. Directly in front of our parade square stood the single soldier accommodation blocks, three storeys high and two hundred yards long. They were huge. I wouldn't like to hazard a guess as to how big these accommodation blocks were, but they were home to three or four hundred single soldiers. As it was an old barracks, there were approximately one hundred and eighty windows in view with twenty-four individual single glazed windows within each frame. Each piece of glass measured approximately eight inch by ten inch. My calculations worked out to be four thousand and twenty pieces of glass! Now you may be wondering why I am furnishing you with this useless information. Well there is a point to my madness, I had pleaded and begged with Lt Jordan from 66 Battery when he was asking my advice regarding the G.R.A's visit, not to fire large blank rounds down the barrels of the F.H70. We had never fired blank ammunition from the F.H70 before, so we were dealing with an unknown and to fire eighteen guns, all at the same time in such a confined area was sheer lunacy. Unfortunately though, he didn't see it that way and was certain that all would be fine.

"Do we really need to fire blank rounds off, Sir?" I said.

"Of course we do. It's the GRA and I am organising his visit," he replied.

"Sir, I really don't think it's a good idea. I don't think the windows will take it."

"Nonsense man. They are only blanks."

"Sir, it's not the ammunition that's the issue, it's the crack it will make when they all go off together. I am sure it will smash some of the windows."

"Unfortunately Bombardier, you are wrong."

"Ok sir." What a twat. Ever since we hung him by his feet when we lynched him on exercise from a stalwart Hiab and greased his balls with XG279 grease, his mind had never worked the same. The guns lined up with our battery tucking in first. Ours was the senior battery so whenever it came to lining up as a regiment, we were always the first in. Lt Jordan carefully lined each gun up before making them bring it into action. I was well pissed off now as we had just trained on the Light Gun and now we had to return to working on the F.H70. What a bastard. It got worse.

When we had finished hammering the Light Gun into our crews and deployed to Sennybridge for a live firing exercise we had to take the F.H70 up there as well, because a group of Rodneys (young officers) wanted to see the F.H70 live firing. This was stupid and was going to cost the British tax payer a hell of a lot of money. It meant that all six gun crews were going to have to take one large Foden wagon, a one tonne Land Rover, an F.H70 and a Light Gun. Now this was not good because working at great speed on a heavy artillery gun that you were not fully conversant with was dangerous, and also, working on two guns was madness and high risk. We were having to fire the F.H70 for two days on Sennybridge Live Firing Ranges because Rodney wasn't satisfied with 'little bang' and wanted to see and hear 'big bang'. If that's what it was going to take for Rodney to get a little stiffy on, then so say all of us. Ours was not to reason why, ours was to eat shit!

For the rest of this day though we had to concentrate on F.H70 and the G.R.A's visit. I screamed to my crew to get the one tonne Lanny and the Light Gun out of the way and hidden in the garages. Once they had done that, they had to sprint back over to our F.H70 on the main parade ground so we could get the gun in action and wiped clean again before the GRA pitched up. It was obvious that the crew had been cleaning the gun that morning while we were gun training with the S.M.I.G. We had a bit of a cheat to be fair, but we weren't telling the British Army. The reason for this was that the I.R (Infra red paint) on the gun, was being destroyed by the OM20 we were using to clean the guns with. If the enemy were to look at our gun through an Infra Red or night sight, providing the I.R capability of the paintwork wasn't damaged, they wouldn't be able to see the gun. If the I.R paint has been damaged you will see it no problem. O.M20 was army oil which when wiped on painted metallic surfaces made it look like new. O.M stood for Oils Minerals. There was also O.M.D 80, no not Orchestral Manoeuvres in the Dark: Oils, Minerals, Detergents. This was engine oil. A little like 20/40w that you stick in your car engine. In fact, I don't know many troops who didn't stick it in their own car engines! It was free. So was the petrol to some people, but that's another story.

There was a couple of draw backs with using oil to make your gun look new, the first being that if you were then going to be climbing on the gun, you were guaranteed to fall off it with potentially serious implications. I had seen many gunners sitting with the gun trails between their legs as they had slipped off. The pitiful look of excruciating agony as their balls were coated in olive drab gun paint was enough to make a glass eye weep. The second problem was that as soon as you hooked the gun up and dragged it down the road it was covered in shite and debris again. Hey ho, it worked at the time. If we had to go to war with them we would be up shit creak without a paddle. Paul O'Neil was the first of my crew to return to the F.H70.

"What took you?"

"Sorry Bomb, I got back as soon as I could."

"Where are the rest of them?"

"On their way bomb."

"Let's get the gun into action and get the barrel up to three-hundred mils," I said. What that meant was that all eighteen gun barrels were being raised to the same height so they were all uniformal. Within minutes the gun was deployed and the barrel was up. Sods law, that's when the rest of my crew arrived.

"Where the fuck have you lot been, you skiving little shits?"

"Sorry Bomb, we got back as soon as we could," Joe Smiley said.

"Well where the fuck is Rab Somerville?"

"He has been sapped for battery runner."

"Ahhhh you are having me on, aren't you?" Battery runner was as it says on the tin, one man that was chosen on a daily basis to be the B.S.M's whipping boy. He would run messages for the battery clerk or any of the officers' sergeant majors (W.O's) or sergeants who were up in the battery offices at the time. When he wasn't running errands he was making them all cups of tea. Remember, nineteen eighty two was the days of typewriters and not computers and emails. The internal mail systems were like something out of the Wild West and the battery runners would often meet each other in corridors around the barracks and pass letters over to each other. What a shit life a battery runner had. If you were sick, lame and lazy, you could end up on battery runner for weeks on end. As I wasn't a gunner (private) for long, it was a duty I never had to endure. Anyone who was a lance Bombardier upwards didn't get suckered with this duty. You had to be very careful as you were up in the heavens with the gods so your 'turn out' had to be immaculate at all times. The last thing you wanted was for the B.S.M ripping you to pieces because you looked like something out of Rab C Nesbitt.

The B.S.M would stick his head out of the window while we were all out on parade and shout, "Can anyone out there ride a motorbike?" And of course you always got one who stuck his hand up… (Mug).

"Me, Sir," one would shout.

"Good, get your arse up here, you are battery runner for the day." One born every minute…

We had ten minutes before the General was arriving with his cronies and I was now one man down. Where the fuck was I going to get another man from at such short notice and for the duration of the big cheese visit? Everyone had a full compliment of men on their guns except me. I searched the garages and the accommodation block for a man to stand by the breach of the gun and go through the motions whilst the General was in attendance. I couldn't find anyone. I told my gun crew to 'stand to' (take up their positions on the gun), it looked dreadful. I only had one man at the breach instead of two. I was going to be in the shit if I didn't find someone and quick. On the other side of the parade square I could see the regimental photographer and his helper screwing the tripod to a mount on the wall. They had fitted this mount so that the photograper could get some really good high up shots of any action on the regimental parade ground. You knew at this point that the visit was close as you could set your watch by the regimental photographer.

Shit, I thought, five minutes and I am fucked. The gun was immaculate, the blank charge was lying on a small tarpaulin behind the gun and all the troops for eighteen guns were in position, all except mine.

I was dreading it, then it came, the voice screaming from the C.P.O (command post officer), "FIRE MISSION REGIMENT." That was it, all of our eighteen guns at the ready… all except me. I was going to get my balls chewed off by the Raz man if he saw this. Fifty extra duties would be the least of my worries if he turned up to my gun and I was one man down. I would be living at the kitchen sink peeling spuds for the rest of my army career. I couldn't believe the B.S.M stuck one of my crew on battery runner knowing that this visit was today. What kind of planning was this? Why didn't he stick a R.E.M.F (rear echelon mother fucker) on it? The 'six Ps' sprang to mind: 'Poor Planning and Preparation makes for Piss Poor Performance'. Someone with a shiny arse who wasn't a gun bunny should have been on it. Gun bunny was the name given to the troops who worked on the guns. What was I going to do when General Blenkington Smyth pitches up and I had to salute him and then introduce him to my reduced crew? The entourage would see right away that I was missing one man and I would be in a lot of trouble. At that point, I looked up and saw Barry Brunn coming out of the accommodation block. Barry Brunn was command post assistance (C.P.A), so he knew nothing about guns. I didn't give two hoots about that, I just wanted a body to stand at the side of the breach and look pretty. I didn't even care if he was dead as long as we could stand him up, Brunn was that body.

I screamed at the top of my voice, "BRUNN, get your arse here now." Brunn looked up and looked straight at me, he sprinted over to me at the rear end of the gun. "Go and stand at the breach and listen to what O'Neil has to say to you," I said.

"But Bomb, I don't know anything about gunnery."

"Shut the fuck up and just do as I tell you."

The C.P.O screamed at the top of his voice to all eighteen guns. "Elevation 350 mils."

With that, all the guns elevated the barrels by another fifty mils. In the artillery we work in mils and not degrees. A circle has 360 degrees which is 6400 mils. This had little significance on what was about to happen, but it all looked extremely smart and very professional for the General. As I looked over to the corner of the building, I saw a party of at least ten high ranking officers including our Commanding Officer and some younger Rodneys appear. Behind them was a bigger group with all of the Battery Sergeant Majors (B.S.M's) and some of the senior ranks bringing up the rear. I remember thinking to myself, thank god Brunn was crossing the square when he was, I would have ended up in Colly nick by one of these head hunters if I had got this wrong.

The C.P.O shouted, "All guns, with a blank charge, LOAD."

As the number one at the time, I shouted, "Number 3 gun load." My Number Five, bent down and lifted the blank charge from the canvas. He walked to where I was standing took the end of the charge bag off and presented the opening of the charge to me. The previous week the S.M.I.G had taken all the gun number ones and showed us what the blank charge for an F.H70 looked like, so we knew what we were checking. It was all bollocks and show for the General anyway, because we had checked them ten times previous to him arriving. I went through the motions of having a look at the two salmon coloured charge increments before he returned the cap and it was then passed to the Number Two at the breach. The Number Five marched back to the rear of the gun, while the Number Two waited for O'Neil (Number Four) to open the breach. Paul O'Neil looked at Brunn as if to say, 'I have just told you what to do now open the fucking breach'. It finally dawned on Brunn that we couldn't load the charge without the breach being opened. This was the switch in his brain that told him that that was his job. He opened the breach lever and the 308lb solid steel breach lifted and the barrel was open. Where I was standing, I could see right through the 155mm of the rifled barrel. They both went through the motions of loading an imaginary shell at this stage and then rammed the two man manual rammer into the barrel and pushed it home. They removed the rammer and Brunn placed the charge into the mouth of the barrel. It was at this stage I had a sly look around to see where the General was and to compare my timing with the other guns. In a split second, I had heard probably two or three of the eighteen breaches closing and then my own gun.

What instantly followed was a scream that still lives with me many years after the event. Brunn turned round at the same time as I was turning towards him; he stared right into my eyes with a look of sheer terror on his face. It quickly became apparent that Barry Brunn had left his thumb in the mouth of the breach while it closed and was now one thumb deficient. I can remember thinking to myself, what the fuck else can happen today? I really shouldn't have asked.

I looked back at Brunn and as calm as you like said to him, 'Fuck off to the medical centre you Tosser,' with that he ran to the rear of the gun and beyond until he was out of sight. Everyone had just witnessed what had just happened to Brunn and I knew that I was going to be quizzed over his well being. What a Wanker, I thought.

The C.P.O shouted, "All guns down safety, all guns FIRE."

What followed next was the biggest 'see I told you so' I have ever said. Now, if you have never heard 4320 pieces of glass break at the same time, you would have been in for a right royal treat as every single piece of glass in every window frame shattered. The noise was like we were on a 'live firing' exercise in Larkhill, not with eighteen guns firing, but one hundred. It was tremendous, it must have shook Colchester to a 7 on the Richter scale. I noticed something fall from the loading tray of our gun, so while everyone was still suffering traumatic shock at the thought of sleeping with Heinz boxes taped all over their windows I took the liberty of investigating. I thought it was a mouse at first glance, but as I looked on the ground directly under the breach I saw a thumb! Yes it was Brunn's thumb. I made my way to the gun barrel as everyone was starting to whinge at the destruction of the broken glass. I quickly bent down, picked the thumb up and thought to myself, where does one put a thumb? I remembered my matchbox in my pocket and wondered if the thumb would fit.... I removed the few remaining matches and replaced them with the thumb, it fitted like a glove. Pardon the pun. If I didn't know better, I would have said it was made to measure. Brunn may not have shared my excitement though. I remember thinking that the thumb may have been re-attached if it hadn't been detached for so long and wasn't covered in oil, dust and detritus. I knew from the word go that I was going to have some fun with this. Barry Brunn losing his thumb wasn't so important anymore. Everyone was looking, no, staring, at the glass strewn all over the ground. Lt Jordan was in deep shit, I begged him not to do this. It was completely obvious to anyone with half a brain cell that this was going to be the outcome of a world war three explosion. What the fuck was he thinking? A Regimental Rodney Cluster fuck of the highest magnitude. Well done sir, I thought.

The whole of Essex heard a scream like just after a football team scoring in a cup final. "Lieutenant Jordan, my fucking office now."

It wasn't all my years of constant big bangs in the Royal Artillery that destroyed my ears; it was this one scream from the battery commander.

"Yes sir," came the reply. I thought that my name would be next as

I was attached to this little cluster fuck by association, but it never came. Lt Jordan sprinted up to the B.C.'s office double quick.

There was no way of telling what the B.C. would have said to this nugget, but I can remember seeing him on duty officer every other night for a year! What a plank, a bad advertisement for Sandhurst Officer Training College.

I got back to my room in the accommodation that night and went straight to my chest freezer. I opened the lid and dug out a few well-frozen loaves of white bread. I removed the matchbox from my pocket and gave myself a little smile. I was quite proud of my secret assignment. 'Operation cooling thumb'. I didn't want anyone else to know about it for now as I had a plan! If anyone else knew I had a thumb in my freezer, I would have been in the shit again.

We only had a few days left before we deployed to Sennybridge and I was dying to give Brunn his thumb back. I knew when I had found it, how and when it was going to be returned. It was going to be so funny.

Two days later and we were running ten miles at 6 a.m. around the fields of Colchester. I was getting pissed off with this running lark now, it was getting boring. Seventy miles a week we were clocking up, with this ten miler every morning and playing sports most afternoons. The Battery and Troop Sergeant Majors couldn't stress how hot it was going to be out in Belize so it was paramount that we went through this process to get ourselves as fit as we possibly could. Yeah right, we thought. We knew the senior ranks just took great pleasure in beasting us. Fair play to them though, they always attended the run, no matter what was happening in the barracks or how busy they were. The R.S.M had given special permission for junior non-commissioned officers (N.C.O..s') to leave their duties early in the morning to ensure that they made it for the early morning run. I have to admit though; I was super fit and was really proud of that fact. I was carrying out the second part of my battle fitness test (BFT) in seven minutes forty seconds. That's some going for a 1.5 mile run dressed in Lightweight Trousers and Boots, it would have probably been even better had I not a smoker.

After the run, we all showered and then met in Barry Brunn's room for a brew before we went on parade. Troop parade was at nine o'clock that morning, it was now only half past eight, so we had plenty of time. I had left it two days as Brunn was in the British Medical Hospital

(BMH) Colchester. His room was packed with about ten other troops by the time I got there. It's a good job I had my pint mug in my webbing as there was no chance of a proper cup, they'd beaten me to it.

"Help yourself Bomb," Brunn said pointing to the kettle on a table at the side of his bed.

"Cheers Brunn," I replied. As I turned to the table with my back to the lads, I heard the magic words I had been waiting for from Brunn.

"Has any of you lot got a light". Oh my God, I thought. I distinctly remember thinking, it was brilliant. I had waited for this moment since I found his thumb. I just didn't think the opportunity would come so easily.

"Yes mate," I said as I turned back to him. Just like a magician producing the named playing card swiftly from his trouser pocket, I pulled out the matchbox and threw it over to him. I didn't want anyone else to beat me to it; all I wanted now was for Tommy to keep quiet. I looked over at Tommy and he dropped both eyebrows as if to say 'what the hell are you up to?'. I gave him the 'it's ok mate, just leave it and all will become clear' look and he lowered his head a little.

As I was turning back towards Barry, I heard his voice say, "You sick fucker." Everybody stopped what they were doing and looked over at Brunn. There he stood, with his cigarette in his mouth, a matchbox in his right hand and his thumb in the other. "You sick fucker," he repeated. "I can't believe you've got my fucking thumb."

"I haven't, you have it now, it's a present from me to you," I replied. Everyone in the room had now realised what had happened and were laughing uncontrollably. "You heartless bunch of bastards," he shouted above the laughter. "I hope your kids walk backwards," he said.

Sergeant Taff Terry burst into the room and said, "What the fuck's going on you lot?" Phew, I thought. Taff was as crazy as I was, so this was going to be a breeze.

"Brunn has just come across his thumb sarge," I answered.

"Oh that's brilliant," Taff said, "He can use it this weekend when he is polishing the mess silver for making all the fucking noise can't he?" The whole room just exploded into laughter and Brunn's jaw hit the floor. "I'm only joking Brunn, just keep the fucking noise down".

"Yes Sarge," he replied with great relief in his tone.

Artillery regiments were known for troops losing fingers in the barrels of the guns and there were reoccurring incidents reported on a daily basis. Due to the nature of the job injuries to fellow soldiers was not uncommon. I was no stranger to feeling pain in my finger myself, as six weeks after joining the army in 1978; I suffered a terrible injury to my trigger finger.

I was just seventeen when I passed out after six weeks basic training. We were now permitted to go out at night, but we were warned that if we dared return to camp late we would be jailed immediately. Eleven p.m. was the deadline and for every minute you were late, you were awarded one week in jail, no questions asked. Believe me when I say that one week in an army jail is the worst nightmare you will ever encounter in your life. Knowing all this information I decided to return to camp two minutes late that night. I was thrown into the guardroom then into the nearest cell. In the morning, the provost sergeant came into my cell and verbally destroyed me. He screamed at me like I have never been screamed at before. He told me what he was going to do to me within this two-week period. He was a complete bastard this bloke. Hated by everyone, even his own Provo staff. He had been sent to Bramcote Barracks to run the guardroom, because he was a failure at everything in his own regiment and they had run out of shit postings to send him to. Just my luck, I had to remember that this predicament was entirely my own fault.

This sergeant thrived on more than just punishing soldiers; he also got a big kick out of breaking them. He was nothing more than a bully and a nasty piece of work, but just like basic training he wasn't going to beat me. I would just turn the 'pain switch' in my head to off. I was seventeen years of age and although I was not physically strong enough to tackle this bloke, I felt that I could beat him mentally. I knew I frustrated him because I wouldn't crack under his pressure.

The days in a military guardroom were hard labour. Everything that a prisoner had to do was designed to crack his spirit. From the P.T session at four thirty each morning until the end of the cleaning parade at twenty three hundred hours each night, a soldier was worked until he was fit to drop.

On the sixth day of my sentence, all was quiet in the Guardroom. The Provo sergeant was on duty as the camp orderly sergeant, but had decided that as the camp was very quiet; he was going to the sergeant's mess for a few pints. He was making me finger bull the whole floor of the guardroom with a bulling rag that we used to bull our boots, and a tin of wax polish. I wasn't allowed to use the floor buffer, just my finger. A ridiculous task, but hey ho, I didn't care.

It was approximately four-thirty when the door of the guardroom burst open. "Where's that Wanker?" I heard him call to one of his staff.

"Er bulling the floor in the cells, Sarge," he replied. I kept my head down as I could now hear the steel soles of his boots getting louder and louder as he marched closer to me.

There was a pause before his drunken voice shouted, "You've missed a bit ,Wanker." At this point I felt this rush of agony in my right hand. I looked down as he was removing his right foot. He had stamped down on my hand with all his force while he was wearing his best ammo boots. For those who don't know, Ammo boots have a steel studded sole that makes a loud noise as you march on the square. They are not designed for stamping on the hands of your work colleagues. He instantly drew blood in a number of areas, but more importantly he had broken my index finger. This bloke had crossed the line. He had not only broken my index finger, but my trigger finger. Picture this, we are suddenly called to war and I am in a position where I am called upon to defend this bastard. Not only would I have shot him in the back of the head, but had the need arisen to defend him, I wouldn't now be able to pull my trigger as he had damaged my finger after stamping on it.

I was fuming; I looked up from the ground, stared right into his eyes and remembered the smirk he had on his face. I stared at him for a good five seconds and thought to myself that I would repay him for this. One day I would avenge this act of bullying. I couldn't believe we were in the same army. I wouldn't give him the satisfaction of hearing me screaming, although inside that's exactly what I wanted to do. The pain was immense.

Then he walked out of the guardroom laughing loudly. Once he had gone, I picked up the yellow bulling rag from the floor and wrapped it around my hand. The blood seeped through in seconds, which didn't bother me too much, but my broken finger did. I shouted for the Bombardier to come to my cell. He didn't come alone, the gunner came too.

I heard the Bombardier say to the lance Bombardier, "He's gone too fucking far this time."

The Lance Bombardier replied, "Listen mate, I am off back to my regiment next Monday, leave me out of it." 'What a shit house' I thought.

I asked the Bombardier to let me put my hand in cold water. After the relief from the cold water, I got the Gunner to tie my fingers together. I was then given some painkillers, which one of the guard staff got from the medical centre. I asked all the staff in the guardroom to leave the issue and not report it. This was for two reasons. Firstly, I didn't want them to get into any trouble and secondly, our intake into the artillery this summer had been the biggest ever with nine hundred men signing up. The staff had been ordered to give us as hard a time as possible because they had to whittle this number down to two hundred in just six weeks. Actually there was also a third reason; I really wanted him to believe he had got away with it. He hadn't though.

The remaining time in the nick was made easier by the other Provo staff. The sergeant thought they were giving me hell while he wasn't about, but they weren't. They were helping me get over the nasty injury he had given me by giving me an easy time.

When the time had come for me to leave the guardroom, he just looked up from his desk and said, "Don't ever come back Wanker."

"No, Sergeant," I replied. Oh, I forgot to inform him that I would be seeing him again sometime in the future.

Nine years later, I had just come out of the Clarence pub after two or three pints. I was heading to the Robin's Head where I was meeting Tommy for a good Saturday session. The entrance of the pub was on a corner, to the right of that was an alleyway where the deliveries were made. There was always the smell of piss coming from down there as it was frequently used by the troops as a toilet at 'throwing out time'. It was still daylight on this particular day and I was approximately three feet away from the door, when a guy came out. I looked at his face and my heart sank, then became excited within the same minute. It was Sergeant Bully Boy, who had stamped on my fingers all that time ago. Guess what? He was half cut and I was as sober as a judge. My reactions were lightning fast and immediately the direction of my hand changed from going to grab the door handle to grabbing this Tosser by the scruff of the neck.

I manhandled him with a speed and ferocity that gave him little

37

chance to react as I dragged him down the alleyway. I could hear him whimpering like a little boy right up to the point of me standing him up and throwing him hard against the side of the brick building. The back of his head cannoned into the brickwork before he managed to look forward at who was causing him this grief. I grabbed him tightly by the throat and moved my head closer to his. I didn't want him to make any visual mistake when he spoke his next words.

"Do you remember this face Wanker and do you remember this hand?" I said lifting my hand up to his face.

He looked at my hand and then deep into my eyes and muttered the words, "Oh fuck." That's all I wanted to hear. The fact that he remembered was the trigger for my subsequent actions. As he turned back to look at me, I hammered my forehead into the bridge of his nose. I heard his nose crumble and tear like a chicken bone being torn away from the carcass. A head butt on the bridge of the nose can do a number of things. Not only will it make the eyes fill up affecting the vision, but it can cause severe bleeding and pain when delivered correctly. He was now squealing like a baby and he fell forward holding his nose. I punched him in the jaw as hard as I could and then in the kidneys. His jaw was definitely broken. He screamed again and fell to the floor. I saw his hand come away from his face, I seized the moment and stamped as hard as I could on it with my right foot. The damage was a lot more than what he had caused me as his hand was laying side down.

I started to walk away but remembered something. I turned round and shouted back at him, "Don't come back now will you Wanker." He didn't answer.

Tommy was standing at the bar, looking at his watch. "I thought we said four o'clock?"

"Sorry mate. I thought I had a migraine coming on, but I took something for it and it appears to have gone now."

He looked at me puzzled. He didn't need to know. Funny old thing, I never bumped into the sergeant again!

CHAPTER THREE

CHIPS WITH CHIPS PLEASE

Thursday 11th March 1982, we stood on parade and the T.S.M inspected us. It was a quick inspection, like the one with the B.C. a few days previous; we could sense that he wanted to fill us in on some information about Belize and we were right. He allowed us to break ranks to make a note in our books as to what he was telling us. The store man was told to 'fall out' and go fetch 'The Box'. What was the box? I thought. Anyway, Dave the store man returned with this box and opened it for the Troop Sergeant Major (T.S.M). The T.S.M took out packets of tablets and passed them to the sergeants who then handed them out to the troops.

"Right you miserable toe rags," he started. "Welcome to the world of Paludrine."

"Can anyone tell me what Paludrine is for?"

Teukter raised his hand and immediately shouted, "Is it a tablet to stop us getting a 'hard on' while we are in Belize, Sir?"

The T.S.M looked at Sergeant Terry and said, "Is he for real?"

"Unfortunately, he is, Sir."

"Thank fuck there's a Navy," he answered. "Right, I am going to tell you this only once, so pin back your ears. You take one of these every morning from now until one month after we return to the UK." He went on, "If you don't take it, you will catch malaria and die and that way Teukter, you won't have to worry about your fucking 'hard on' will you?"

"No, Sir," came back the reply.

I think it's worth mentioning that if you failed to attend a parade in the army, you would have missed the 'Queen's parade'. Our T.S.M said that if we missed taking our Paludrine tablets you may as well have missed a Queen's parade and you would be in deep shit. It was one of those old customs that no one ever dared challenge. If you missed a parade then it was deemed as an insult to her majesty. It's a bit like the saluting thing. You are not saluting the officer; you are saluting the Queen's commission.

With the briefing of the Paludrine and the remainder of the Belize information for the day out of the way we were herded into the main corridor in the office block, where one of the nurses from the Medical Reception Station (MRS) was sat. She had a table in front of her with hundreds of syringes on it. If you asked me, I would have said that the whole operation looked about as sterile as a fucking cow shed and we were about to let nurse pointaprick, stick needles into us for a laugh. The best of it was, we didn't have a clue what we were being injected for. Had we objected however, we may have been persuaded by Chindits size twelve ammo boots. Best not to say anything then.

Lance Bombardier Chandler was in front of me as we all lined up in alphabetical order for our jabs. The problem with this and every single time we went for jabs prior to this, was that the guy hated needles. Every time he saw one, he collapsed. Fainted on the spot. I always tried to catch him when he fell and today would be no different. The nurse stuck the first needle in his arm and he hit the deck like a sack of spuds. When he fell, the nurse would always give him a quick once over and then spear the remaining needles into his arm while he was out! He would always come round within a few minutes, with no problems. I felt a little sorry for the guy as this clearly was a serious phobia that the army didn't recognise.

Once we had all received the wrath of 'Doctor Death' we were dismissed and made our way over to the garages. I sent two of my gun crew to the F.H70 to give it a final dust off before we deployed to Sennybridge. The remainder of the crew started packing up the one tonne Land Rover and making sure the Light Gun was ready for the same exercise deployment on Monday.

I remember it being a very cold day in Colchester with a good eight inches of snow still on the ground from the recent snow storms that the South East had suffered over the previous week. There were also problems with really cold winds that dropped the chill factor to a very big minus. While I was walking over to the garages where the guns were parked, I was thinking to myself, What the hell are we doing going on exercise in Sennybridge with a minus ten or fifteen and then returning to Colly for a short time before deploying to a part of the world where it can reach temperatures over 130 degrees? If that was 'character building', I wasn't showing any characteristics of a comedian, that's for sure. This was ridiculous.

I climbed out of the one tonny and walked over to the gun. It was bitterly cold, but my crew were doing really well working through it. They were wiping the gun down before tying the tarpaulin over it and hooking it up to the Land Rover. Once we did that we were done. We could park the gun and the Land Rover up in the garage and before we knew it we would be on our way to lunch.

"Come on lads, let's get a move on." They all looked over at me knowing full well that I was happy about their performance of late, but they also knew that I had to be heard. Tam shouted that they had been over to get a five gallon drum of OMD 80 engine oil, but the R.E.M.E corporal had told them that he would dig one out and send it over in half an hour as he couldn't spare anyone at the moment to get one out of the oil store. I thought that was fair enough. At least we didn't have to go over again.

There was a considerable amount of kit which needed storing away in the one tonny, so to save a bit of time, I lent a hand. This was always dodgy ground, if a senior rank came past and saw you grafting with the crew when you should be supervising you were in the shit. They would always beat you with, 'If you want to work with the lower ranks we can always bust you back down to gunner again you know'. That always seemed to do the job and make you think about your position on the crew.

I looked to the rear of the gun and there was a three foot by three foot bundle of rags scattered on the ground in a heap, I was about to approach the rags, when I looked to the front of the gun and noticed that Smudge Smith, who was a craftsman in the R.E.M.E was approaching. Now Smudge was a good lad for a R.E.M.F (Rear Echelon Mother Fucker) and played a mean game of football too. I was sure he could have turned professional had he not joined the army. He had thrown this five gallon drum of oil on his shoulders and had trudged through the snow to deliver it to us. Even though it was only a short journey he had come out of his building without a coat on and surely must have been freezing.

"How you doing Sean?" he shouted through the wind.

"Fine mate. Yes, we're all sound as a pound."

"Brilliant mate, where do you want the oil."

"Just throw it on the bag of rags over there," I said, pointing to the rear of the gun. As I finished pointing, he leaned forward and threw the large drum directly from his shoulder towards the rags. This looked very impressive but the palm of his and had nearly stuck to the side of the five gallon drum due to the cold. I looked over at Smudge and although His hand was sore the injury was not severe.

We finished packing the gun away and did a double check of all the equipment that remained in our gun cage. The gun cage was as it says a secure cage inside the gun garages where we stored all the expensive equipment that belonged to the gun. That included not only the specialist items, but also the ancillary equipment. When we checked the gun cage, we applied the theory that if there was hardly anything left in it then we knew it was now stored on one of the two guns we were taking to Sennybridge or packed on one of the two towing vehicles. We were leaving for exercise at 04.00hrs on Monday 15th March, so there was only time for us to collect our small arms and nothing else. Our small arms consisted of an L.M.G (light machine gun), a few S.L.Rs (self-loading rifles) and a couple of sterling sub machine guns.

The Battery Commander knocked us all off for a long weekend before the final exercise in Sennybridge, he had just told us that we had all worked very hard over the last six months in preparation for this operational tour (even though we knew nothing about it) and for that he was giving us all a long weekend. Well done the B.C. Three days on the beer. Happy days!

I pulled my crew to one side and spoke to them in my official capacity. "Right you shower, listen to me. Do not get so pissed on Sunday night that you forget where the barracks are at 4 a.m. on Monday morning, right. Remember if you fail to turn up, it's not A.W.O.L (absent without leave), it's desertion. Secondly," I said, "don't forget all your personal equipment. It's very cold and wet where we are going so you will need your waterproofs. Lastly, go and get shit faced and if no one has any questions for me, then I will see you all on

Monday." Silence ensued. "Right go on then, fall out." They turned away and as I watched them march off, I saw the B.S.M walking towards me.

"Bombardiers' Connolly and Moran. On me," he screamed. That's military terminology for 'get your arse here now'. What the hell have I done? I thought to myself. I sprinted over to him and slammed my foot in, coming up to attention. I was joined by Taff Moran a second later.

"Yes, Sir," we both shouted.

"Stand at ease, stand easy," he said. "You two up for going home early in the morning then? I am orderly officer tonight so can't leave until the morning," he added. The B.S.M lived in Liverpool, as did Taff Moran's' family. I lived in Southport a few miles away. When the B.S.M drove from Colchester to Liverpool on leave, he would always try to take us with him. Not because he was kind hearted and loving family man, not a chance. We chipped in a fiver each for petrol for his Capri and although a fiver was a few quid in nineteen eighty-two, it was better than paying for the whole journey myself. I had also half planned going home this weekend to say my goodbyes to my family before we deployed to Belize and collect a hundred quid a mate owed me. Even if we didn't wish to make the trip up north, it would be hard saying no to the B.S.M. Taff was up for it too. Leaving early Friday morning wasn't too bad and we could be home by Friday lunchtime, it was normally a five to six hour journey to Liverpool.

"Car park behind the block, 0600hrs, okay?" the B.S.M said as he was turning away.

"Yes sir, six it is," I answered for both of us. The B.S.M had his own car parking space behind the office block with B.S.M painted in six foot letters on the ground. In fact, now I come to think about it, it may as well have read GOD. The B.S.M had a 2.0ltr Burgundy Ford Capri Laser.

The 'Laser' came during 1980 and 1981 when The Ford motor company and its manufacturing plants had produced far too many cars. The reason for the 'over production' was quite admirable as it happens. Amongst other things they were trying not to reduce production in order to retain jobs. However the problem came to a head, when one of the bosses at Ford opened the blinds in his office one fine and sunny morning and it suddenly dawned upon him that he had *five hundred thousand* brand new Ford cars all parked up in fields at various plants across the UK.

In a blind panic, he called an emergency board meeting at The Halewood Plant in Liverpool and started with, "Oh dear, we are in the shit. We have made far too many cars, which are now clogging up countless fields all over the UK. What the fuck are we going to do?"

Scouse John stands up and shouts, "No worries boss, I have a plan."

At this moment the boss thinks to himself; Oh God, not Scouse John he's about as much use as an ashtray on a motorbike, but we must hear him out if nothing else... "Go on then John, how the hell do you plan to solve this problem and save all of our jobs?" he says.

"No problem, it's easy," he replies. "Paint the word 'Laser' after the name of the car. It doesn't matter if it's a Capri, Escort, and Fiesta. Reduce the price by one hundred pound and then sell them to anyone who thinks they are getting a good deal but I was thinking possibly H.M forces personnel? They will sell like hot cakes." Where the hell did that come from? This man is a genius thinks the top man.

This is exactly what Ford UK did and they did fly out like hot cakes. Everyone in the Army, Navy and Air Force, suddenly had a 'Ford Whatever Laser', and truly believed they'd got a good deal that was exclusive to them. I was gutted at first as I thought I had missed out having just purchased a used BMW, but when all this came to light, I suddenly wasn't that bothered.

The problem for tonight though, was that I couldn't go and get pissed with my mates down the Robin's Head. If I was riding shotgun in the morning with the B.S.M, this may prove *not* to be the brightest of ideas.

"Taff, do you fancy a quick visit to Baileys," I said.

"Sounds like a decent plan," he replied.

Baileys was a chip shop on the High Street in Colchester, it was one that I will never forget for the rest of my life. We had pitched up at this chippie for the first time a couple of years ago. Tommy and I were walking along Colly High Street when Tommy pointed to a queue of people standing outside this chip shop. There must have been twenty or more people waiting to be served.

"Oh, I fancy some real chips," he said.

"Look at the fucking people waiting to be served," I replied.

"Ah, what does that tell you then?" he said.

"I'll tell you what it tells me, there's a fucking big queue," I said.

"Let's wait, just think real chips," he answered.

We joined the queue as it was entering the shop. I was actually looking forward to some real chips. I was sick to death of the fast food crap that we were always eating because everyone else was! It was as we were entering the door and I was using my highly trained military skills when a couple of things didn't seem quite right. Number one; there was no menu on the facing wall or on the counter. Number two; I couldn't see the big shiny food display that is normally situated directly on top of the counter showing off the establishment's fine and freshly cooked food, you know the one you burn your arm on? By the time it was our turn to be served, the shop had filled up again behind us. I remember thinking that the food must be good here as there are tons of people waiting to get it. I was before Tommy in the queue and quite right too, I was the hungrier one out of the two of us and I knew exactly what I wanted.

That was my selfish conclusion anyway, and the next thing I heard myself saying was, "Chips, Jumbo Sausage, Mushy Peas and gravy in a tray please mate." I noticed a smile appear on this chaps face after I had placed my order, but I soon discovered that it wasn't as a result of him being friendly.

"It's a chip shop mate, we don't sell all that rubbish here," came my answer.

"Oh okay, I will have a meat and potato pie and chips please."

"No, you are not listening are you pal? This is a chip shop, we sell chips."

I couldn't believe what I was hearing. I looked at him, then to Tommy, and back to this guy and said to him, "Fine mate, but other than chips what else do you sell?"

"CHIPS!" he said through clenched teeth. "Listen to what I am saying to you, I will say it one more time, THIS IS A CHIP SHOP, GET IT? A CHIP SHOP! We sell CHIPS! Oh, we have recently started to sell gravy as well, but other than that, we sell nothing but chips."

I couldn't believe this and found it all very amusing. I looked at Tommy again and he was equally as shocked as I was. Unbelievable! The chippie was also full of people listening to this shopkeeper making a complete fool of me. Mind you I didn't need the shopkeeper's help as I was doing a sterling job on my own. I bought two bags of chips without my frigging sausage or anything else for that matter and funnily enough Tommy ordered the same. I have to say though, the chips were glorious and as much as I felt a right arse I would definitely be going back. I passed the details of this find to many of the troops in our regiment and all of a sudden, this chap had another nine hundred customers. Within a couple of months of my first visit, I had become quite friendly with the owner Tony and he was made up for the extra custom. (Not that he needed it). I was on for cheap chips for the rest of my time in Colchester and believe me I took every available opportunity to collect.

We had arrived at Baileys this evening before the 'tea time' rush. Tony wasn't in the shop yet so we said our hellos grabbed our chips and got out of Colly town centre before the silly traffic built up.

When we arrived back at the barracks I dropped Taff off at the front of the accommodation block before parking my car up on the main car park. My plan was to get my chips down me, sort my kit ready for Monday and then get an early night. My last job was to ring the Guard Room and book an early call for the morning. There was no way I was going to be late meeting the B.S.M, fiver or no fiver, it wasn't a good idea.

I arrived at the B.S.M's car at 05.45hrs the next morning, Taff was already there having a smoke.

"Morning Sean," he said. "It's bloody freezing mate."

"Yes, I know mate. I can't remember it being this cold in Colly," I replied. The temperature must have been at best minus ten degrees. The roads within the confines of the camp were a little icy, but out on the main roads leading into the town centre, they were now wet and greasy. I wondered what the A12 and motorways would be like. The B.S.M arrived shortly afterwards still dressed in his best uniform and apologised for being late. Firstly, he was never late and secondly, the B.S.M doesn't apologise to anyone! Taff and I both looked at each other puzzled and I shrugged my shoulders.

The car was frozen over, so the B.S.M set about the normal routine of starting up and turning the heater on full blast. Taff and I threw our overnight bags into the boot of the Capri; I then tilted the passenger seat forward so Taff could climb into the back of the car. I remember thinking again how cold it was as I was getting into the front seat. I knew though that this car had a brilliant heater so it wouldn't be long before it was toasty warm. A good heater in a Capri was unusual at this time and you would have been quicker blowing on the windscreen in some of the other models. Fords were renowned for having really bad heaters, it was a fact. It took ten minutes for the B.S.M to scrape his car, check the lights and do what we in the army called 'First Parade'. This is just a simple term for when a driver is carrying out his daily vehicle checks: water, oil, tyres, lights etc. I could see him now through the side window and I was thinking what a giant of a man this is. He truly was a hard man the B.S.M. I would worry if ever I had to tackle this man in the future.

As he climbed into the driver's seat and took off his gloves I heard him say, "Four-eight battery tossers." Had I been taking a drink at that point, I would have probably choked and spat it all over the inside of the windscreen.

"Sir?" I said with a 'please explain' voice.

"If I catch either of you two nicking flagpoles from down town, I will lock you up for a long time, got it?" What was he suggesting? I looked at Taff and wondered if he had been pissed in the last couple of weeks.

Before I had time to reply, he went on. "No, I don't mean you." He explained, "Donahue, four-eight battery what an idiot. I told the guardroom not to wake me during the night unless it was important. So, what did they do at half three?" Again, before we could answer. "The Civvy Police had spotted a man marching down Layer Road with a full sized flag pole on his shoulder and when they questioned him he said that he had just bought if from Tesco. Of course they got the Mod Plod (M.O.D. Police) who, in turn notified the Military Police." It is worth mentioning at this time that the MOD Plod had the authority of a primary school class attendant, hence the reason for the MP intervention. "Fucking brilliant! Two hours kip all night," he finished.

"Sir, do you want me to drive?" I asked not giving it a thought. I was only trying to help the situation, and the last thing we wanted was for him to fall asleep at the wheel. The journey was going to take it out of him with his tiredness, never mind the conditions of the roads with the recent inclement weather. I thought he would blast me for offering my assistance, but he didn't. I was shocked to say the least.

"No Bomb, it's okay, I will be fine. I will let you know if I start to feel tired," he answered. Yeah right, I thought. I remembered this guy's background. He was trained by the SAS and that training would have been really intense. This man wouldn't sleep at the wheel; his mind would be trained to do exactly what he wanted it to do, when he wanted it to do it. The 'falling asleep at the wheel' feeling which most drivers would feel would have been recognised, acknowledged and binned within the blink of an eye. The SAS were trained to stay awake for a week at a time with no sleep. I am not just saying it, but this man was special soldier. A no nonsense, take no shit Sergeant Major. He was feared by all, but well respected by everyone too.

He was often heard saying, "I can be your best friend, or your worst enemy." Should the time come to choose a mucker to go into battle with, then this man would have been top of my list. A few years ago when we were out in Gutersloh in Germany, The B.S.M had occasion to dish out some of his own military, 'not so by the book' justice. It was a Monday morning and we had just finished battery parade, it was a good inspection as inspections go. The B.S.M threw one lad in the nick for a week for a double crease in his trousers, but on the whole not bad. It was noticed by all at the role call that two gunners were missing, Anthony Hall and Bob Masters. It is not the done thing in the British Army to miss a parade, A.W.O.L was not funny. Once you started this caper, you were on the slippery slope to ruin but to do it while this B.S.M was taking it was both suicidal and stupid. Anthony and Bob were a right pair of Jack the lads, being the handsome dudes they were, they would bed anything female that came within a twenty-mile radius of them. We all knew in our hearts what had happened with these two. Although they were technically A.W.O.L, they weren't, if you know what I mean. There was a small section missing from the Disciplinary Procedure of the Army's Act, section sixty nine and that was the bit which said 'if you were out getting your proverbial rocks off with some innocent, unknowing N.A.A.F.I girls the night before Battery Parade, you had better make sure your rocks can get you up out of bed and back to camp, *well* before parade starts'.

The B.S.M was doing his nut. "When that pair of idiots return to camp, I want them in this fucking office before they do anything, is that clear?" he screamed down the office block corridor. I was walking past his office at this time and I heard the battery clerk scream back.

"Yes, Sir! I will see to it." What a mug, I thought. Mick, the battery clerk has just put his name on the line just by even answering the B.S.M.

I had checked the mail and looked at what courses I was on in the near future. I was over the moon, they were about to send me to Aldershot to do a six week R.M.A (Regimental Medical Assistants) course. This was a course I had been after for a long time. Brilliant I thought. I quickly checked the personal mail for my gun crew and then started to leave the Battery Office complex. I was looking at the front of a letter which was addressed to me, it read B.F.P.O 40. (British Forces Post Office) and as I looked up to see where I was going, Anthony and Bob sneaked into the corridor with their heads down. Eleven o'clock in the morning, Oh my God, I thought. Bob looked up and over at me and I screwed my face up as if to say 'what have you done? You know you are in the shit' he sort of acknowledged but they both knew what was coming. As I passed the B.S.M's office he looked up from his desk and directly at me.

"Morning, Sir," I said.

"Good Morning Bomb Connolly," he replied. "Just wait there a minute; I need to talk to you about Aldershot."

"Yes, Sir," I answered. As the current security state was 'high' he wanted to impress the need for my personal safety while I was back in the U.K.

Just then, he spotted Twit and Twat (Bob and Anthony). "You two! In here now." At this point in time, I was stood at ease directly outside his office staring right at his desk. Bob and Anthony marched into his office and stood to attention. The B.S.M in his anger never closed the door. He then unleashed what was one of the most severe bollockings I have ever heard. He touched on everything from military conduct to us all being worried that they may have been taken out by the Baader-Meinhof (an active German Terrorist Group).

After a while, he came from behind his desk and walked over to Anthony, he stared right into his eyes and said to him, "Hall, I was going to ask you where the fuck you have been and why you saw fit to miss the Queen's Parade, but I won't. Do you know why I am not asking you

Hall?" Before Anthony could even answer him, the B.S.M screamed at the top of his voice, "Because you are a lying little shit! That's why not." The B.S.M then snapped his head to the left and stared into Bob's eyes. "I am going to ask you this once Masters and once only, so do think carefully about your answer, but before I do ask you; any thoughts of presenting me with that brilliant story that you two twats will have concocted on your way back to the barracks this morning will now have disappeared far from your head wont it Masters?"

Bob looked at the B.S.M and then over to his left, where Anthony was stood to attention. "Yes, Sir," he said quietly.

"Well where the fuck have you been until now then?" roared the B.S.M.

"We met these two N.A.A.F.I birds yesterday Sir and went back to their flat, got pissed and ended up doing the business. The plan was to stay awake all night and then come back to camp early, but we fell asleep, Sir."

The B.S.M turned to Anthony. "Is that true Hall?" he said. After confirmation of this version of events, the B.S.M paused for what seemed like five minutes. I now feared for the lives of these two, as we all knew what the B.S.M was capable of doing. Mick the Battery Clerk had now joined me outside the B.S.M's office with a brew for his boss, but at least he was out of sight of him. I was in the direct line of sight of the B.S.M and Twit and Twat. From time to time the B.S.M looked over at me. Oh shit, I thought to myself. Just like a coward, I remember thinking to myself, Oh please not me Sir, I haven't done anything, hit them. They are the guilty ones and they have admitted it.

"Right," said the B.S.M. I knew what was coming next. This is what we all liked about the B.S.M. "I am going to give you a choice," he went on. "My way or the military way?" This was a massive question of choice though and I think it's where the term 'No Brainer' originated from. Everyone in our battery had heard this at some stage coming from the B.S.M. The choices were as follows. Choice one, Bob and Anthony would be charged under section sixty-nine of the army act for missing the Queen's Parade, Absent without Leave, Bringing the Army into disrepute and being a Twat. For this, you would be subject to Commanding Officer's Orders and end up in jail or M.C.T.C for six months of hard labour or a fine of up to five hundred quid. Either way, you would have a stain on your army record which would be looked at and nearly always prove detrimental when it came time for senior officers to award the promotions! Oh, I forgot to mention that throughout this process, the Regimental Sergeant Major (R.S.M) would take frequent opportunities to beat you about the head with the brass end of his parade stick. Choice two and the preferred choice of men, the B.S.M would hit you very hard rendering you completely incapable of anything other than breathing (even that was debatable) for the next fifteen to twenty minutes. This choice had a number of benefits attached to it. He, (the B.S.M) would subject you to some form of violence, but unlike choice one, this was over in a much shorter period. Although at the time of assault you may not agree, later you would still have great respect for this man. For me and many others though, the two best reasons for opting for choice two were that there was no financial penalty nor was there any stain on your military record at the end of it. The matter was completely forgotten and the B.S.M would not hold this against you at any time in the future, unless of course, you were that brain dead you repeated the offence. Both options had the same effect in the end though. You never repeated the same offence. Job done.

Like a well rehearsed school play Bob and Anthony both piped up, "Your way sir."

"Good, no paperwork," came the reply from the B.S.M by which time, Bob was writhing around on the floor clutching his chest and groaning loudly. Anthony was in the process of turning his head to the right to look at his best mate when the B.S.M dealt him a similar blow. The B.S.M had punched him once in the base of the sternum with an almighty blow which came from his right shoulder, and all the way down to what looked like an Accrington brick on the end of his wrist. I witnessed Anthony drop like a sack of potatoes.

"Get up, fuck off and don't let it happen again," he said as calm as you like. Bob was on his feet first, fair play to him. Tough man, how he got up from this I will never know. "Masters," the B.S.M called.

"Yes, Sir," Tony croaked. "Were these two girls worth it?"

"Fuck, yes Sir," he replied.

"Good, go and get changed and get to work," the B.S.M finished.

"Thank you," he said as he practically crawled out of his office closely followed by Anthony. Anthony couldn't speak and still looked in a pretty bad way; I think the twenty minute recovery period was going to have to be extended after what I had just witnessed. I couldn't believe I had just heard Bob say 'thank you' for that. Oh my God, I think I wanted to cry on their behalf. The B.S.M obviously knew how and where he was striking them, and boy did it have the desired effect! I realised no problem at the time, but I now often contemplate how the UK's current workplace H.R regulations would interpret such effective disciplinary measures.

It would have been at this point that I would have said that these two lads got off lightly, but in reflection, I don't think they did.

I would have thought no one in their right mind would attempt to go A.W.O.L while this man was the B.S.M, but one man did.

It is said to be really difficult to break borders once the Military Police had informed the German Police and Border Agencies or an absence by a British squaddie. In 1980 Troffer Graham we all called him, absconded from Germany and somehow made it back to UK. It was a mystery to all involved in tracking him down but they didn't find him. I am the only man who can confirm that (okay maybe not the only person whilst you are reading this).

Four years later in eighty-four I was posted to Edinburgh along with thirty other troops to take part in the Military Tattoo, we would be there for one month. It was the second time I had done the Tattoo. I had taken part once before in the P.T Display team when I was in Junior Leaders. I knew Edinburgh well and felt honoured to be returning again to take part in the gun race at the Edinburgh Tattoo years later. During the Tattoo month your services are required mainly at night when the show takes place. The next day however, once the artillery guns are cleaned up and made ready for the next show, you generally get the afternoon to yourself. I got changed into my civvies and got into the back of the four tonner. I was getting a lift into town with the 'slop jockeys' (Army Cooks).

The weather was glorious, and before I knew it I found myself enjoying a slow walk along Princess Street. It was amazing because as I was walking, I could smell that fantastic smell you get as you walk past the butcher's shop. I don't know why but I had always loved that smell when I was a little lad and I loved it even more as an adult. As I drew level with the shop, I could see through the window. There must have been ten people waiting to be served and three behind the counter, two lads and a girl. I remember that they were working frantically to get through the queue. I was intrigued by one of the men as he was cutting meat with a cleaver on a butcher's table. I used to love watching this process, and wonder when a finger would fly into the air! It must have taken years of practice though. As the butcher turned round to show the customer a piece of steak I had to do a double take. I can't believe it, no, it can't be, I thought. Fuck me. It's Troffer Graham. I had to take another look, this man had a big black bushy beard, but this didn't disguise his ugly mush. It was him, it was definitely Troffer. I stepped back from the shop window to gather my thoughts and think about what I was going to do next. I had to think about this and make sure I didn't rush into anything. After some time and much deliberation, I decided that I needed to sit down and apply some logic. I like the easy life but if logic also meant responsibility, I had to be sure in my mind that what I was doing was right.

I concluded that there were a number of things I needed to do here. Firstly, I had to look more closely at his face to confirm it was him even though I felt sure beyond belief that it was. I wanted him to realise that he had been caught. I thought back to the time I knew him and although he wasn't a close mate, he had helped me tremendously when I was seventeen and had arrived in the regiment at Mansergh Barracks in Gutersloh. I remember him having some family problems and the military not permitting him to 'buy himself out' of the army at the time. I am not saying the army did this out of spite, I think there was more of an operational reason at the time. Either way, I felt really sorry for him as he was a good soldier and to have taken these measures was a sign of desperation on his part. With these last thoughts rattling around my head, I knew what I was going to do. If he was returned to the Army now, he would serve six months hard labour in MCTC (Military Corrective Training Centre) and then he would be binned out with a D.D. (Dishonourable Discharge). What good was that for anyone? Had he been absent for less than a year, then maybe I would have shown more responsibility and he would have soldiered on after his punishment. Okay I hear you say, who was I to make that call? Well I did and I have no problem living with it.

I headed for the shop entrance, this had to be short and sweet, then

I had to leave and never return. Edinburgh was a big military city, if anyone witnessed what was about to happen, we would be both in the shit. The queue in the shop was now down to two people, but I walked round to the side of the counter, I was two feet away from where my suspect was cutting meat, at the end of the block where I had seen him a few minutes previous.

"Troffer," I said. He turned his head so fast I thought he would have got whiplash and was now staring at me, he knew, that I knew and on that there was no mistake. He looked frightened for his life.

"Sean," he answered. I had to say what I needed to say and be gone quickly, but I needed him to know that his secret was safe and I wasn't going to grass him up.

"Troffer, listen to me carefully and trust me. It's okay. Relax, this meeting hasn't happened. You are safe! Go and enjoy the rest of your life". His shoulders which were initially raised and tense then dropped and he gave me half a smile.

"Thanks Sean," he replied in pure relief. I looked at him one last time and then turned and walked to the door. As soon as I got outside, I picked up my pace a little to put some distance between me and the shop, I was glad that I had convinced him that I wasn't going to grass him up.

The B.S.M stopped his car at the rear door of the mess where one of the 'slop jockeys' appeared, he was carrying one of the large thirty egg trays full of fresh, large eggs. The B.S.M climbed out of his car, tilted the driver's seat forward and placed the tray on the floor behind the driver's seat.

He turned to Taff and said, "Look after them Bomber."

"Yes, Sir," came the reply from the back. How the hell, are they going to come to any harm on the floor behind the driver's seat I thought to myself. Little did I know. The B.S.M placed his parade stick on the back seat next to Taff, threw his hat next to it and off we set. It only took us a short time and we were bombing down the A12. The B.S.M was known as a bit of a psycho but this Ford Capri was really quick, even with us three lumps in it. Mind you, there was very little traffic on the road at this time of the day. A lot of the snow and ice had cleared off the main drag, leaving a lot of white salty grease. We hit the M25 and made it to the M1. Phew, we had made it past this bottleneck before the rush hour. There were alternative routes by road to Liverpool and we had tried them all over the years, but we always came back to this one though. It was a few miles longer on paper, but always turned out to be the quickest.

"So what will happen to this nugget from four-eight battery sir? Mr Flagpole I mean," I asked.

"C.O's orders for that," he replied. "Definitely," he added.

I remember thinking, that had he been serving in our battery and belonged to our B.S.M, the lad would now be sleeping off the effects of the beer in the nick and meeting up with our B.S.M on his return. There would be no C.O's' orders that's for sure. I could see that the B.S.M wasn't pissed off at the offence this lad had committed, more so at the fact that the guards had woken him up and ruined his sleep. This lad would have been bounced had he been one of ours.

"Newport Pagnell services you two?" the B.S.M said.

"Yes please, Sir. Are we having a brew?" I asked.

"Yes, why not, we're making good time," he answered. He pulled off the motorway and into the service's car park. Luckily, a Rover was reversing out so he slotted the car into the space which was directly adjacent to the main entrance. We got out of the car and started off towards the door. The B.S.M locked the car doors and followed Taff and myself as we made our way through the entrance. I headed straight to the toilet and splashed some cold water on my face to wake myself up. I turned to look at Taff and it looked as if he had been dragged through a hedge backwards, but I soon learnt that he had been asleep in the car for ages. I was sitting directly in front of him and never even realised. This would be a good man to take on stag with you, if he fell asleep, he wouldn't alert the enemy. I on the other hand had a snoring problem I assure you the enemy wouldn't need trackers to find me.

The B.S.M had got the brews in and was sat with his back to the wall, scouring the café looking for suspicious people. Taff and I joined him and tried to sit in front of him, to hide the fact that he was still in uniform. The early eighties saw a considerable amount of mainland terrorist activity and travelling around the U.K in military uniform was a big no no. However, he was wearing a civilian mack with the zip fastened up to the top to hide his military shirt and tie. Truth be known, all that could be seen were his dark green barrack room trousers and his brown officer's shoes. You would have to be seriously looking for this specific attire to notice he was army.

We took our time with our brews, the B.S.M doing most of the talking. It was always awkward in these situations as we knew that there was a lot of information that someone in his rank and position couldn't talk about. This was ongoing, but you respected it. The B.S.M would have known about us deploying on an operational tour to Belize a long time ago, but he was sworn to secrecy. We knew this. He did ask us how the morale was within the battery as this was of great concern to him. If the troops are happy then they will do a good job and perform to the best of their ability should the shit hit the fan and we had to stick together. He wanted reassurance that this would be the case. I reassured the B.S.M by telling him that we weren't just a *good* battery, we were the *best* in the Royal Artillery. Morale was high. The training we received was second to none, delivered by our own staff. The personnel within the battery were the most experienced and the best I had seen. We had one hundred and three men in our Battery and I don't know one man who wouldn't die for another within the battery if it came to it. Everything in our battery was superb and I don't mind saying, we were a professional and very highly skilled team of troops. I also told the B.S.M that should there be any problem within the battery in the future, I would tell him and that I didn't want it to change in any way. This was a good group of people to be going to Belize with and I wouldn't change one individual.

The B.S.M smiled at me and I could see a look of contentment on his face. A lot of the praise I had just spoken about was down to him, but being the rough arsed, low emotioned squaddie that I was at that time, I couldn't bring myself to say it. Here sat a great man. We left the services and hit the M1 to the sound of Reo Speedwagon on Radio one. I knew this song well. 'Keep on Loving You' was one of the only songs I liked, that didn't belong to the Rock and Roll genre. It had come out a couple of years earlier and I couldn't stop singing it in my head. I looked out of the window and noticed the sky had turned really dark. Maybe it's going to rain, I thought to myself. How wrong I was, by the time we had gone another twenty or thirty miles, the sky had changed again and this time it was full of snow.

By the time we had reached the M6, the sleet had started to fall. We had been listening to the weather forecast on our journey but there was nothing about sleet or snow in the north or northwest. There was no problem at this time and we could see the road clearly up ahead. The surface conditions were okay but the roads were wet. Our speed remained unchanged and we were still on par for making it up north before lunchtime. Hopefully, before the crappy weather set in. Unfortunately, by the time we reached Staffordshire, the heavens opened and we suddenly found ourselves driving through a total 'white out' snow blizzard. Our visibility had been massively reduced and our speed was down to about sixty miles per hour. The windscreen wipers were now working overtime and they still weren't quick enough to clear the windscreen. We reached a point where we were bombing along in the third lane when I noticed a long line of brake lights in front of us. The traffic had now come to a stand still but I was convinced the B.S.M hadn't seen it. He travelled on another hundred yards and spotted the traffic jam just as I was about to inform him that the traffic had stopped ahead. I immediately felt the front of the car dip as he stamped on the brake pedal, the car did really well to grip the surface in these conditions and I was convinced that the car would stop before we ploughed into the rear end of a stationary car in front. It was touch and go but we missed it. There must have been six inches from the front of our car and the rear of the car in front of us when we stopped. Oh my god, I thought to myself. Then suddenly, I heard the B.S.M.

"No, please. No," he said, as he glared into his rear view mirror. Being a driver myself, I knew what was coming. The car behind us had also not realised the traffic jam but added to this I think, where we had really good brakes on our car, the one behind us didn't. This time, I heard him shout. "Oh no, fuck NOOOOO," and with that I pushed the soles of my feet into the floor pan in front of me and my arse against the back of the seat. At that point, I heard a loud bang and felt the rear of the car jump up into the air, it slammed back down to the ground with another bang.

Shit, I thought, "What the fuck was that?" before I could finish my words the B.S.M was out of the car, his stick had been taken from the back seat and he was gone. I went to open the passenger door which was stuck on my first attempt. I then hit my shoulder really hard against it, and it opened. As I climbed out I looked behind us and noticed the

B.S.M leaning over the driver's side of the car behind us. He had opened the driver's door and was hauling a middle-aged woman from her seat.

"You stupid fucking bitch," he screamed. "What the fuck do you think you are doing you blind bastard?" Oh shit, I thought.

"Taff, give me a hand," I shouted. Taff came running over to the back of the car where I was now frantically tugging at the B.S.M. "Sir, Sir, Sir. Let go," I shouted. All at once, he snapped out of it and released the woman. He walked away from her car and headed straight back to his own, then I noticed that the husband had climbed out of the passenger seat and was eyeing up the B.S.M. He started to walk over towards him when I turned to the husband and called towards him, "I apologise mate but leave it. Shock, you know."

"Fucking Shock, I'll give him fucking shock," he replied.

"Listen mate, you won't give him anything, just get back in your car and stay warm," I advised. Taff looked at me, and instantly knowing what I was thinking he walked over to the irate husband. After a little word in his ear, the bloke reluctantly climbed back into his car and started to comfort his wife, who by this time, was a gibbering wreck and was going to take some consoling. I knew if this guy had confronted the B.S.M at this moment, he would have regretted every second it took for the B.S.M to put him on the ground with something broken. I wanted to save the guy the pain, after all the B.S.M had just nearly chinned his missus so I did feel a little sorry for them both.

The B.S.M was still sitting in his car and I surveyed the damage to the back of his Capri. It wasn't as bad as what the bang had first suggested. All right, it would need a bit of cosmetics but hey ho, it was very driveable. The eggs on the other hand were all up the back of the seat and fortunately the B.S.M hadn't spotted them. I walked further down the line for approximately six cars. The weather was really bad and the sleet was hammering down. I could see the blue sirens approaching in the distance, so I started to make my way back to the B.S.M's' car. I looked at the damage at the rear of all six vehicles as I was walking. Unlike ours, they were smashed at the front *and* the rear. An Austin Allegro was the third car behind ours and had suffered the most damage. Either it had been travelling at a really excessive speed and been unable to stop in time with the car behind ploughing into it, or the only other option was that an Austin Allegro was made from recycled baked bean cans. I looked at the occupant of the car and he looked fine, a little shaken but certainly not stirred.

In a short time a motorway police officer had opened the drivers' door and asked us to grab something warm and stand on the embankment at the side of the hard shoulder. An officer would take a quick statement from the driver and we would be on our way, providing the car was serviceable. I remember thinking as I was climbing out of the car, that I hoped the boot would open when I went to grab my coat or I would be freezing. I walked to the rear of the car, grabbed the handle of the boot, pushed the button and hey presto, it opened. Thank fuck for that, I thought. Taff and I stood on the bank while everyone worked frantically to push cars to the hard shoulder and clear up the debris. We offered our services, but were told to stay where we were, it was fair enough. The people involved looked like they knew what they were doing. Some cars drove, others were pushed by police and vehicle rescue people. The B.S.M drove the Capri onto the hard shoulder very gingerly and received a nod of approval from the police officer. The bobby jumped back into the Capri and after a short time he climbed back out. He walked over to the Volkswagen Passat ,which was the car that had hit our rear end, the lady had recorded some details on a small slip of paper, she handed it to the officer who in turn walked back and passed it to the B.S.M. He looked at the officer, said something and then the police officer left him and walked towards the next car. The B.S.M opened the passenger window and shouted towards us. We couldn't understand a word he said because of the wind, we just walked towards him anyway. I opened the car door and bent over to listen to what he had said.

"Come on, let's go," he said.

"Have they re-opened the motorway sir?" I asked.

"I hope so because he has just told me to pull off carefully and that I was free to go," he answered. Taff and I jumped back into the car and the B.S.M started to pull out. We were on our way again. The B.S.M did nothing but stare in his rear view mirror for the next mile or so to see if there had been some kind of mistake and the officer shouldn't have let him go. We were the first car to be released and there wasn't another vehicle in front of us. We had the motorway to ourselves, well up until the next junction. They had closed the M6 right from the site of our accident to the next junction. The B.S.M increased his speed until he was up to about seventy miles per hour. He sat in the centre lane and proceeded with caution. The last thing we needed now was for the car to go into a skid and crash into the central reservation. That would have done it for me; I would have walked the rest of the way home up the hard shoulder.

The last words I heard the B.S.M mutter before we came out of the sleet and snowdrift was, "Fucking Eggs." I thought to myself, fucking eggs! Never mind the fucking eggs, what about us three? At least we all escaped without injury, and were now like the Lone Ranger speeding up the M6 on our own, undamaged. Leaving the whiplash claims behind. 'High ho silver away'. Happy days!

I got home to my mothers house at two pm and after a quick hello to everyone, decided to ring my mate Tommy McCann for a few pints.

Before I knew it, Sunday lunchtime had passed and we were being picked up in Formby by the B.S.M. We made our way to the motorway and headed south, I felt a little more relaxed on this journey as not only was the weather bright sunshine but the roads were dry and clear. If all went well we would be back in Colchester before it was too dark. The B.S.M was in a good mood and made the journey with no stops on the way. He didn't even ask us if we needed the toilet, but we were used to that, after all if you couldn't cross your legs for a few hours, then you were no good to the British Army. I'd heard many stories about the SAS in various fighting theatres around the world carrying out their number ones and number twos into plastic bags and passing them back to their mates to bury while they were carrying out tactical observations for weeks on end whilst sat in a trench. Mind you, this practise may have raised an eyebrow had I done this in the B.S.M's Ford Capri. I don't think Taff would have been too obliging either had I passed him a plastic bag full of shit back and said 'ere Taff, bury that'. We arrived at the barracks in Colly at teatime, the B.S.M parked up in his GOD spot, Taff and I thanked him and paid our fivers. As we started to walk away from his car, I turned to remind myself of the damage that the car had sustained.

The B.S.M looked over at us both with his bag slung over his shoulder and shouted, "Don't be late for parade in the morning."

"No sir, we will be there," I shouted back. Like, we would be late for the B.S.M's parade, not a chance. We entered the accommodation block to the smell of cooking. "Mmmmm," I said to Taff. "The slop jockeys have outdone themselves I think". Taff looked at me and nodded a 'yes'.

"I'll see you in there in five minutes," he replied.

I dropped my bag into my room and went straight to the cookhouse while Taff dumped his bag in his room; his was a little further away from the cookhouse. I could smell Bratty (Bratwurst) and Jockeys (Jockeys Whips – Cockney Rhyming slang for chips) I loved the Bratwurst, but the problem was that the British Army had taken it upon themselves to disregard hundreds of years of German culinary intellect and instead of grilling the Brattys like the Germans do, the Aldershot Concrete Company or the Army Catering Corps decided to boil them. Let me put that into context for you, that would be like us grilling garden peas, you just don't do it. Gordon Ramsey would do his nut. Where the hell we got the notion to boil them in the first place is anyone's guess, but it was wrong. However out of bad things always came good and this was no exception because as a result of the 'slop jockeys' boiling the Brattys, hardly any of the troops would eat them. We had all been stationed in Germany where they were grilled to perfection by the Germans so why would we settle for boiled Bratty? I on the other hand had developed the BRP (Bratty Rescue Plan). I would grab about ten of them at a time and take them over to the large commercial grill where the troops used to make their own toast in the mornings, heat the grill to as hot as it would go and then place all ten on the grill and leave them for a short while. The Brattys would come out charred beyond belief, just the way I liked them. They were that burnt that I would often pick them up off the grill pan and they would snap in my hand. I would then go and pinch half a jar of mayo and sneak them back to my room to trough over the next couple of days. This was on top of the five I would polish off during tea. I always kept a few cold Brattys in my fridge, it was good that I liked them as burnt as I did because it meant that no one would nick them from my fridge during the week.

Taff and I had a good chinwag. We were joined by Rocky Rowland from 'K Sub' who asked us if we had a good weekend. Taff and I looked at each other and began to tell Rocky what had happened on the way up to Liverpool on Friday morning. He just shook his head when I was explaining about the B.S.M's actions when the woman piled her car into the back of his. He as well as everyone else within the battery knew what the B.S.M was like. All who knew this man, knew a lot about what he had done in the past, but no one knew exactly what he was capable of and there would be no time in the future that we would have the opportunity to find out.

Chapter Four

Tea For Two

At 03.45hrs on Monday 15th March, I reported to the B.S.M that my gun crew were present and correct. It was a freezing cold March morning and we had it all to do. I had lined up my One Tonne Land Rover and Light Gun with My F.H70 Gun and Foden Wagon Behind that. This was going to be a nightmare of an exercise. We had never taken two guns on an exercise before and it was all because some Rodney wanted to see the F.H70 firing. If he were that keen to see it firing, he could have pitched up a couple of days previous and watched thousands of pieces of glass breaking as well! I had reservations about my gun crew holding it together. It wasn't difficult to know your gun drill and apply it to when you were firing an artillery gun, but when it was two guns which were completely different it was more difficult. After all we were only 'Gun Bunnies', so we weren't the brightest when it came to retention of information. What pushed it over the edge for me though was the weather. Sennybridge was a fiercely bleak and cold place to be at any time of the year, so with this and the fact that they had to apply two entirely different gun drills to perfection was of great concern to me. Should you slip up when you are firing a 'high explosive artillery shell' miles and miles away, the consequences could be catastrophic. I had been to Sennybridge many times and on each occasion it had rained or snowed every day. What a hole. On the plus side though and deep down, I knew if anyone could do it, my crew could. They were very bright and experienced and could all carry out each other's roles. Added to that fact we had just won the coveted 'best gun competition', this made me feel a little easier. I had convinced myself that all was going to be fine on this exercise.

I decided to make my way over to the gun cages in the garages as a way of a final check to make sure that we hadn't left anything behind. Once we were back in Sennybridge, there was no way we could go to our troop sergeant major (T.S.M) or B.S.M to tell him we had left an important piece of equipment behind in Colly. As I approached the garages, I noticed our troop commander Lt Dave Joplin frantically jumping around, screaming at all his crew and the crew from the B.Q.M.S (battery quarter master's stores). He was shouting at the driver of a four tonne HGV wagon, Bombardier Don Robinson.

"I don't care, just get the fucking thing started," he screamed. "I have to report in to say we are ready to move, now get it started," he added. I knew exactly what had happened, the batteries on the wagon had become flat over the weekend. We could jump start the wagon in seconds, all we needed was some jump leads and another wagon, then as long as Robbo didn't stall the wagon for the next few miles, the problem would be solved. Someone had forgotten to switch the battery master switch off on Thursday prior to us 'knocking off' and the remaining power in the batteries had drained away leaving not enough power to fire up the engine.

"Bombardier Connolly, get in that Land Rover and 'Tow Start' the wagon," I heard coming from the officer. I smiled back at him in disbelief; he was asking me to tow start a heavy goods vehicle with a Land Rover. I had recently completed a 'Driver Maintenance Instructor's Course (DMIs), where you learn all about military vehicles and instructing people how to drive and maintain them. Now it is common knowledge to every military driver at this time (or so I thought) that the brakes on a land rover work by your foot compressing fluid, where as the brakes on a wagon work by your foot compressing air which is drawn from your air tanks. When you have no air in the tanks, you have no brakes and that becomes a problem because you can't stop. However Mr Joplin was now ordering me into the Land Rover.

"I want you Connolly, to jump in the Land Rover, we will tie this ten foot lifting strap to the front of the wagon and over the tow hook of the land rover, then you will drive forward. Bombardier Robinson will take his handbrake off in the wagon, put it into second gear and when you are going fast enough, he will take his foot off the clutch and it will 'bump start'. All we have to do then is keep the engine running while we take the lifting strap off," he said.

Fuck me, I thought to myself, I did know how to bump start a vehicle. I was doing it when I was twelve years old when I worked on the farm.

"No sir! Please let me explain," I answered desperately. I looked around and I could see that everyone had noticed what was about to happen and 'done a runner' leaving the crew and myself to deal with this idiot! "When Bombardier Robinson bump starts the wagon, he won't be able to stop. The wagon will have no brakes because there is no air built up in the tanks, so it is likely to hit the Land Rover. Then you have the added problem, Sir, of possibly causing extensive damage to the clutch on the Land Rover as the four tonner is far too heavy for the land rover to pull. It will rip the back out of it."

"I am ordering you and Bombardier Robinson to get in those fucking vehicles now and do as I say," he answered irately

"Ok, Sir, but I am making it clear to you, that should this go 'tits up' and the battery commander investigates, I will be telling him two things," I replied. "Firstly, I carried out this order under duress and secondly, I strongly advised you not to do this."

At that point, he screamed, "Just drive the fucking Land Rover Bombardier."

I looked at Robbo who was sitting in the driver's seat of the wagon. He shrugged his shoulders as if to say 'I know this is going to be a disaster'. I climbed into the driver's seat of the Land Rover and waited for the Rodney to give me the 'all clear'. This was my signal to say that the tow strap was on and I was to start. I was going to drive as slow as possible with just enough speed for Robbo to start the wagon and then I was going to kiss my arse goodbye and any further chance of promotion in the British Army when he piled into the back of me. I was getting a little sick of vehicles hitting me up the rear. Lt Joplin gave me the all clear and I proceeded, very slowly at first and reached a speed that I was sure he would be in second gear. Suddenly, I felt a little jerk as he lifted his clutch foot and within two seconds of that I felt the back of the Land Rover crunch as Robbo piled into the back of it. I put the handbrake on and got out of the Land Rover, the four tonner had cut out again, as Robbo had not managed to keep it going once he had impacted the Land Rover. The damage was unbelievable, it had pushed the rear end of the Land Rover up to a point where it was impossible to open the tailgate, and all the lights and light holders had been damaged beyond repair.

"What the fuck did you let it cut out for?" shouted the troop commander, towards Robbo.

"Sir," I said. "Never mind the four tonner. Look!" I pointed to the damage at the rear of the Land Rover.

Joplin turned back towards Robbo, "Look what you have done you lump headed fuck wit." Robbo was in shock and couldn't reply.

"Hang on a minute, Sir," I shouted.

"Keep your fucking nose out Bombardier," he shouted back at me. As he stormed towards the four tonners driver's door. By this time the B.S.M was stomping over to the garages, having heard the collision. I can imagine what his immediate thoughts were, 'two Bombardiers trying to tow start a wagon, the process turning pear shaped and the Warrant Officer catching them in the act of damaging a land rover and a four tonner. Oh look, and one of them is Bombardier Connolly, he must be a bit partial to being shunted up the rear by now'.

"Bombardier Connolly, on me now." I sprinted over to the B.S.M and came to attention. He stared down at me. "Truth," he said.

"Yes, Sir," I replied. He knew I would tell him the truth and that he would receive it right down to the finest detail. I explained how I had practically begged Lt Joplin not to do this. Mr Joplin had acted against my professional advice and that I could have sorted it the correct way for him and in a shorter time with no damage to either vehicle, using jump leads. The B.S.M told me that I may have to repeat all of this to the battery commander, as this would be investigated further. Now, in the British Army an officer like Mr Joplin is a few ranks above the B.S.M, but even this lieutenant troop commander was shit scared of our B.S.M. This was clarified at the point were Joplin came from the driver's side of the four tonner and saw the B.S.M talking to me. Mr Joplin was reduced to the authority equivalent of a 'one star' army cadet, as the B.S.M screamed at the top of his voice.

"Mr Joplin, Battery Commander's office now."

"Yes B.S.M," came the reply.

The B.S.M asked me to accompany him to the vehicle, when we arrived there he ordered Robbo out of the wagon it was only then that either of us noticed how the incident had affected him.

66

The B.S.M then spoke in an 'un B.S.M' like way, "You ok Robbo?" I had never heard the B.S.M call anyone by a nickname or first name before then.

"Er, yes sir," Robbo replied.

He was now stood at attention facing the B.S.M. "Stand easy lad." Robbo relaxed a little and dropped his shoulders. The B.S.M turned to the rear of the Land Rover and then back towards Robbo, "What happened Bomb?" Robbo gave it to him chapter and verse, exactly how I had told it. I knew that the B.S.M believed us, he had shook his head and muttered something along the lines of 'Fucking Rodney's, they're about as much use as an ashtray on a motorbike'. There was a long pause before he said, "Right then, Bomb Connolly back you go to whatever it was you were supposed to be doing. That will teach you to stick your fucking nose in, wont it?" and at that he turned to me, gave me a little smile and a wink and left.

I knew he was only joking though because I had worked with him for years, and he knew that it wasn't in my nature to stick my nose into something where it wasn't needed. He also knew that I had vast experience and it was part of an N.C.O's job to take time to help someone if they were stuck. The problem was, would everyone else? There was a big ugly sergeant who worked in the REME workshops who was certainly going to be pissed off when he saw the damage on this Land Rover before we had even got out the camp gates. This was to say nothing of what the battery commander was going to say.

We learned later on in the week that the Land Rover was a 'write off'. The chassis was twisted beyond repair. Ooooops! I thought. Mr J is in the shit but it served him right. It was common for young, recently commissioned officers to issue orders to long experienced N.C.O's to do something in a way that was either wrong or unsafe.

Before we knew it we were on the road to Sennybridge and I had just watched Sergeant Major Mick Mayers (Chindit) running over something on the main square. Big Ged Snailes from the rear echelon had come running out of the cookhouse with one of those new unbreakable flasks, challenging anyone to break it. Big mistake. Chindit had witnessed this and taken up the challenge. He placed the flask under the tracks of an AFV (Armoured Fighting Vehicle) 432 (a tank to the layman), and ordered the driver to drive forward. When the flask came out the other end it was as flat as a pancake, obviously obliterated. The scalding tea which was in it had exploded everywhere; I remember seeing the ground steaming hot where it lay. Chindit had shouted over to Ged that they hadn't perfected this 'unbreakable flask thingy' yet and that he was certainly not going to buy one. Ged looked absolutely devastated; everyone was laughing their heads off. (I think he had paid thirty quid for it, which was a lot of money then). A bit of humour had been just what the doctor ordered while we were freezing cold and about to deploy to Sennybridge.

I was riding up front in the Foden Wagon pulling the F.H70. My driver was Kev Diamond. Kev was a gunner in the Royal Artillery who had done driving since he joined the battery five and a half years ago. He was a good driver, kept his head down, looked after his kit and his wagon but never received any credit. He was one of the only drivers to master and beat the Foden Gun Tractor, which was a complete bastard to drive. The cab on this wagon was so high off the ground it was unbelievable, it had a sixteen speed gearbox and would have no problem doing ninety miles an hour down the A12 with a gun on the back. If you missed a gear on the way up the gearbox you had to stop and start again, so it was important to get it mastered. Each driver carried his own twelve mil spanner in his top pocket because the REME declared that a top speed of ninety miles an hour was too fast for a large wagon towing a gun, so they came up with this bright idea of putting a bolt under the accelerator pedal to stop you putting your foot flat down to the floor. It was a pretty prehistoric modification though and we had it beaten within a few days. Before we went out on a drive we used to take the bolt out or wind it right down so it didn't restrict the vehicle. On our return to camp we would simply refit the bolt or wind it back out again.

There were a couple of naughty tricks that we used to play with the Foden wagon though, the first being the exhaust pipe which came out just underneath the driver's door and was at the same height of a car passenger window. When we stopped at the traffic lights or in a traffic jam, whilst in neutral, we would leave our foot off the accelerator for a minute and then drop it flat to the floor back on the throttle. This would give a massive cloud of thick black smoke which was great if you had a car in the lane next to you with the passenger window open. As soon as the lights changed to amber, you would drop your foot on the accelerator and watch the car next to you fill up with smoke. It was worse when you pulled away from the lights and when you looked in your mirror you saw a motorcyclist lying on the floor with his motorbike wrapped around his head because we had just filled his helmet with carbon monoxide. The second trick was that all the best drivers knew how to make the exhaust backfire, making it sound like a bomb exploding. Again, this proved quite funny, but came with consequences, whereby if you did it too often it would eventually blow a large rip in the side of the exhaust back box.

There was a 'Wendy House' on the back of the Foden wagon; this was like a small porta cabin which measured approximately eight by five feet. It had windows all round and a door at each end. Inside, there were soft bench seats, which would seat approximately six crew members comfortably whilst travelling. Then when we were on gun positions the Hiab jib would lift it off if necessary. It meant that when you came into a gun position you had somewhere sheltered to sit should you be deployed and remain in the same position for days, it would also keep some of your personal kit dry. You could lift the shutters on the windows and turn the lights on and no one could see them on the outside if you were on night exercise. The crew would often make a brew on the move and pass it through the window of the 'Wendy house' through the back window of the driver's cab for the gun crew commander and the driver. It was very handy as it also meant that the gun crew commander could pass messages back by shouting through the two windows.

The journey to Sennybridge was a bastard of a ride; it took five or six hours of driving in convoy, at times having to negotiate routes yourself. We should have been arriving in Sennybridge for around ten a.m. which would then have left the rest of the day to get everything sorted and our billets in order before Monday evening .Two hundred and sixty miles and no M25 at this time, which meant we were driving right through the centre of London. Deep joy. It was only in 1986 that Maggie Thatcher opened the M25. I remember a couple of years before, that all six guns had lost each other driving into London and by sheer fate, we had all come out at the other end and met at the same point. It was like a scene from a film where all six vehicles and guns came onto this huge roundabout from six different points at the same time. It certainly wasn't down to good map reading, we were squaddies and none of us could read a map well! We wanted to be through London before the capital had a chance to say 'who the hell was that lot trundling through here like they own the place'. I didn't know it at the time and I should have guessed by the reaction of Kev, that we were entering the outskirts of London.

"Next lights and I'm in the back, right."

Kev looked at me, confused at first but he got it after a moment.

"Brew and I am not having one of those maniacs doing it, they'll set the Wendy House on fire." I had my pint mug with me and it was empty. I had smoked four cigarettes and I had a throat like a 'Swiss angler's maggot box'. This was the plan. I had passed a message back to the 'Wendy House' for Paul O'Neil to race to the cab when I gave him the shout. He was going to ride 'shotgun' in the cab with Kev until I had made a brew in the back and drank it. I would make one for Kev, which would be passed through the windows. When we had all finished our brew we would wait for another set of lights or a traffic jam, and both doors would be flung open and we would switch over again putting me back into the Foden cab. I had executed this plan in my head many times, but it was a new one to my crew. They had seen me do some strange things, but this was a new one for the book.

Up ahead, I could see a set of traffic lights which went into three lanes.

"Right Kev, try and time it so that we are going to hit a red," I said.

"No worries," he replied. I looked into the 'Wendy House' and could see that Paul was ready to go. Kev stopped the wagon. I nodded to Paul through the windows and as I opened the big Foden door I heard the door of the 'Wendy House' fly open and hit the sidewall. I moved as fast as I could and Paul did the same. We crossed each other climbed up into our new places. Kev had been watching through his passenger mirror and he was satisfied that we were both safe, and then we were rolling again.

"Right lads, this is what we are going to do," I said. I explained to them because I was gagging for a brew we were going to make one now, on our two ring camping gas cooker. They all looked at each other puzzled. "Joe, pass me the kettle," I went on. Joe passed the big ten-man kettle back. I pointed to all the equipment in the corner of the 'Wendy House' and said to Rab, "Rab, get the cooker and a jerry can of water." Rab piled into the corner, pulled out a twenty-litre jerry can and passed it back to Mickey, who passed it over to me. I opened it and then called over to Rab. "I want water Rab."

"Oh fuck," he said. "I'm going to mark these jerry cans up later if it's the last thing I do," He added. We all knew where he was coming from. When we were preparing the equipment for exercise we always made a point of chipping in a few quid each. This was not only for our brew kit and the cleaning gear we needed, but also a few bottles of 'darkies bum' (Rum) to fill two out of our three jerry cans with rum and coke. It was great when you needed a snifter on exercise when you were freezing cold. We could hardly write on the top of the Jerry Can, 'Rum and Coke' but it was a good place to keep it. We had to be very careful because alcohol and 'Live Firing' were not to be mixed. It was a bit like drinking and driving, if you got caught you would be right in the sit. Rab passed another jerry can, this time it was water.

"Joe, fill the kettle," I said. Joe filled the kettle which he placed on the floor of the 'Wendy House'. I hadn't realised that we were coming into a built up area until I saw that Joe was spilling quite a bit on the floor in the 'Wendy House'. Oh well such is life. I am getting this brew if it's the last thing I do, I thought.

"Right lads, listen in," I said. "Joe, Mickey, you two are responsible for holding the cooker while its on and Rab, you will have to hold the kettle for the whole time it's boiling, okay?" everyone nodded. Our cooker was really fierce, even though this was a ten man kettle; it would take no time at all to boil. "Rab, open a couple of windows first," I said. Rab opened the side window and the one leading to the back of the driver's cab. It was already hot in there and we hadn't lit the cooker yet. Mickey placed his foot on the left hand bracket as I lit the cooker; the downward pressure of his foot clamped the cooker to the floor of the 'Wendy House'. We had a box where we kept all the brew kit together so it made things easy for the person on brew duty. Mickey passed me the box and I got everything ready for when the kettle boiled. We had loads of 'ten man' tea bags from previous exercises that we had not used, they were just like any ordinary tea bag in the way that they worked, but not in their size, they were massive. Probably about twelve times the size of a normal tea bag. It was no easy task, boiling a big kettle and making a brew in a moving vehicle, but we had a plan:

1. When kettle nearly at boiling point, Rab to lift lid off.
2. Sean throw teabag in
3. Rab quickly replace lid
4. Wait for water to boil fully.
5. Switch off gas, Rab to remove lid
6. Sean to stir and then leave to brew for a couple of minutes before removing the tea bag.

Hey Presto, enough brew for the whole crew and one for the Queen as we passed 'Buck Palace' if she wanted one. The plan appeared to be flawless, except that we were fast approaching the centre of London and the Foden was being thrown all over the place.

I said to Rab, "Okay mate, lid off," and with that he lifted the lid off with one hand while holding the kettle tightly with his other hand which had a glove on to protect him from the rising steam. I dipped the large spoon into the kettle and at the same time told Mickey to turn the cooker off. I collected the huge bag onto the spoon on the first attempt, which was not too difficult as it was so large. I removed it from the kettle and Rab replaced the lid. I turned towards the side window and let rip with the spoon, catapulting the bag from the 'Wendy House'. I looked up and thought oh fuck, I wanted everything on the planet to be frozen except for me. I had visually followed the trajectory path of the tea bag and quickly realised that its resting place was going to be on the right hand side of a female police constable's face. The teabag was not only massive, but it was scalding hot too. Unfortunately for me though, the world didn't stop in order for me to retrieve the teabag before it landed in my estimated place of explosion. I remember seeing it hit the W.P.C on her right cheek and her reacting as if she had been shot in the face. I ducked down into the cab and told my crew to get down. Slowly I raised my head again and I could see the W.P.C's colleague all over her, wiping her face frantically. I think they had realised that she hadn't been shot, but were frantically searching all over the road as to where this thing had come from. We were now too far gone for them to put two and two together and they certainly didn't see me throw it.

I prayed for months after that no one had witnessed my police assault and taken the vehicle registration. Oh my God, I thought, what have I done? My crew were wetting themselves with laughter, but for once I wasn't. I gathered my thoughts, poured Kev a brew and got one of the lads to pass it through the window. The lads helped themselves and Rab poured one for me. I sat and drank a pint of scalding hot tea and had another cigarette. All I could think of was 'what if'? We reached Sennybridge within a couple of hours and I managed to get the lads out of the cab and motivate them enough to fall in, in front of me. They stood to attention, but I could see they were all concerned with the weather that was pouring down on us all. It was a hard driving rain, but I knew in my heart that at this time of year we were in for some sleet or heavy snow. Either way, it was freezing cold right them.

We had all purchased these long sleeved, all in one waterproofs which were D.P.M,(disruptive pattern material). They just looked like a combat trouser suit that the army *should* issue, but unfortunately they weren't issued by the army and we had to buy them ourselves. This pissed us off, but there were two issues here. If you wanted to keep warm and dry-ish on exercise then you had to have them and the second issue was that the British Army didn't have such a thing as a fully waterproof garment. In all fairness though, the 'all in one' tank suits we were buying didn't keep us one hundred percent dry. We were even spraying them with tent waterproofing, but even that didn't keep you fully dry. Had the waterproof issue been today, I am sure we would have purchased Gortex. Twenty-five quid for these suits in the early eighties was a lot of money, but what could we do? When I look back, most of the equipment the British Army issued you then was really poor and definitely not up to the climates and conditions they threw us into.

As I was about to fall my gun crew out to get the two artillery guns parked away in the garages, the B.S.M's driver ran towards me.

"Bomb Connolly the B.S.M wants everyone to fall in over by the wash down now," he said breathlessly.

"Cheers pal, no problem." It was easy as I had my lads at attention already. "Move to the left, left turn," I screamed. "By the front, quick march, left, right, left, right, left." We marched about one hundred metres before I shouted. "Detachment halt, right turn, stand at ease. Stand easy." We were the first ones there and I could see everyone scurrying around trying to get all the troops together. Troops started to fall in next to my crew and I could hear various officers and senior ranks shouting at junior ranks to shift their 'sorry arses' as the B.S.M was waiting.

"Yes, Sir," came the replies with a lot of the troops running around like headless chickens.

Eventually we were all 'on parade' for the B.S.M, who marched in front of the battery and screamed at the top of his voice. "Battery shun." We all sprang to attention and froze on the spot. Out of the corner of my eye I could see the battery commander marching into sight. I had noticed the B.S.M and the B.C. talking to each other as we drove into the garage areas where we were about to park up. At this point I shit myself as I was now sure that WPC had worked out who had launched the 'teabag missile' that had given her a right cheek that resembled a melted wellie. In my opinion, this still wasn't funny. The B.C. halted in front of the B.S.M and they both saluted at the same time.

"Carry on Sergeant Major," the B.C. said.

"Yes, Sir," he replied. He saluted the B.C. again and turned about, marched to the side of the battery and fell in right next to me. I remember thinking that I must keep still or the B.S.M will be all over me like a rash.

"Right you lot," the B.C. started. "There is good news and bad news. The bad news is that we start the exercise at five in the morning."

Well that's not too bad, I thought. After all, we weren't in this shit hole for a holiday, that's for sure.

"The good news is," he went on, "providing you can prove to me that you can use this 'Light Gun' and we can complete the live firing which is on Friday with the F.H70, then we will not be continuing the exercise for the last week we will be heading back to Colchester."

Wow, what fantastic news. If that wasn't a morale booster then I don't know what was. Someone had seen sense here and it meant that if we put a lot of effort into this week, we only had four days in this hell hole. It was obvious that Lt Joplin had fuck all to do with this decision as we would have been there for a month! This was no doubt a decision made by the B.C. and the B.S.M along with other more senior officers. We later discovered that they had all agreed that the priority was to confirm the training on the Light Gun, complete the F.H70 live firing and then get back. This was great as it gave us a week in Colly to get cleaned up, have a good de-brief, then get ourselves sorted before deploying to Belize. Bargain.

The troops were buzzing when we fell out. The B.S.M called the gun number ones (the crew commanders) and the second in commands over to him. I marched over with some of the other senior ranks.

"Stand easy lads," the B.S.M said. "OK, let's have this right lads," he went on, "no fuck-ups. Tell your troops from me, anyone fucks up and they will have a one to one with me."

Now call me stupid, but I think all the senior ranks would have agreed with me, when I say that the 'not fucking up' option suddenly became an instant priority in our lives. He went on further to say that he, above anyone, did not want to spend another minute in this bleak crack of the world than he had to, so it was in our interests to get him home quickly. This mission was getting more and more attractive by the minute, but saying that, I wouldn't want to be the individual who cocked up that bad that we had to stay in Sennybridge for an extra week.

After speaking to the B.S.M we parked both guns under the frontless garage without any problem and then reversed the Limber vehicles next to them. I made a final check to ensure that all vehicle isolator switches were switched off. The last thing we wanted to do in the morning was to be running around jump-starting all the vehicles because we couldn't be bothered switching the master switches off. All we had to do now was hand our personal weapons in to the armoury. The armoury was on the way to the accommodation.

The accommodation was grubby, very basic and stank of dead tramps. I opened the main door to the Nissan hut (accommodation) and balked, I thought it was impossible for a smell to get any worse than it was. Did no one ever clean this accommodation after the troops had gone? The huts had a big stove type heater in the middle of the room which we could light as soon as we got in and I made the decision that we weren't going to allow it to go out until we left. They would take a while to heat the accommodation block as they had forty odd single beds in this room. We would send one of my lads out on the rob for fuel for our fire. Your wood or coal wasn't supplied by the army. That would be seen as kind and soft. The fire would be great for heat but it was also needed to take the dampness out of your clothes. When you came to get dressed in the morning with your clothes still wet, you felt like crying, it was the pits. The billet I was sleeping in would have the stove roaring hot.

"Rab, go and get some wood," I ordered.

"Yes Bomb," he replied. Rab knew the score; he took his Gollock (machete) out of his webbing and disappeared out of the door. He was without doubt, my favoured wood thief. There was none of this 'I couldn't find any Bombardier' with Rab. He always returned with the goods. I grabbed the bed closest to the fire stove to make sure that when we left in the morning I had a head start. The longer you can keep dry in this shit hole the better. As soon as you were wet through, your morale started to flag. It was my job to make sure my crew was happy, not pissed off because they were soaked through to the skin and freezing cold. I placed my webbing under my bed and unrolled my washing and shaving kit. I had only brought one clean pair of Bill grundies (undies) and almond rocks (socks), my washing and shaving kit from the gun lockers and. We were only sleeping here for one night and after we had left in the morning we would be sleeping rough out in the field. If we were to cram two weeks' exercise into one then we weren't going to be getting a lot of sleep.

Rab appeared about half an hour later.

"Fuck me Rab, where the fuck have you been?" I asked.

"Sorry Bomb, got delayed," he answered. He looked over at one of the other lads in the billet, "Give us a hand Dave," he said. Dave walked outside the billet and between them they lifted a wheelbarrow into the billet.

"Where the hell did you get that from?" I asked. "No don't answer that," I quickly added. I noticed that the wheelbarrow was full of logs all cut to size and shape ready for the fire. It was clear to see that these had been cut by a saw and not his Gollock. I was a little concerned as it meant that someone was not only missing a lot of wood, but also a brand new wheelbarrow. They unloaded the barrow by the fire and before I turned around again Rab had disappeared with it while Dave set about getting the fire going. What a bloke, I thought to myself. It was the overwhelming need to get warm which stopped me pursuing this any further. Sennybridge camp was well lit at all times of the day and night. The last thing the MOD wanted was a serious accident within the confines of the camp when there were miles of exercise area outside the camp gates where we could kill each other. The Refuelling area was on the opposite side of the road in a massive lay-by. It is commonly known throughout military circles as the P.O.L point (Petrol, Oils and

Lubricants) It was brand new then and the first time we had used the facility..

It was really weird that whenever we stopped at a P.O.L point anywhere outside Colly, I thought of the Lance Jack (Lance Bombardier) who got a one year sentence in Colchester jail (Military Corrective Training Centre) for theft of petrol. Apparently he had been approached by a taxi driver while he was downtown in Colchester one night after he had just put away a few pints. He was offered a few quid for every twenty-litre Jerry Can of army petrol or diesel he could nick. He was told that there was always taxi drivers interested in some 'cheap juice'. One night when the Lance Jack was on duty P.O.L he decided to take them up on their offer. It was very late in the night when he filled about eight jerry cans with army petrol and drove them down town. The second time he filled fifteen and the third time, he stole thirty cans of army petrol and took them down town in a four-tonner wagon in the early hours of a Saturday morning and got caught. The M.Ps had watched him committing the crime after their suspicions had been aroused when he couldn't account for two hundred odd litres of fuel in the account book the previous time. He was set up with the assistance of the R.S.M who put him on duty again a few weeks later. The M.Ps and the SIB (Special Investigation Bureau) followed and filmed him from start to finish. There was no getting away with this one and off he went to Colly Nick.

Once we filled the one tonne Land Rover up we were to go fully tactical. That meant no noise, no lights and as little movement as possible. It was the last part of a training period which confirmed to our head honchos that we were able to use the Light Gun proficiently and professionally enough prior to deploying on an operational tour. Let's face it though, after the F.H70, this was a piece of cake, it was tiny compared to our guns. Our only problem today was that it was well below freezing and the sleet was falling very heavily. The drivers had to be careful as they were filling up the one tonne Land Rover as this was petrol, where as when we fill up the Foden wagon on Friday it will be diesel.

"Remember lads, no fuck ups," I shouted to everyone. We all made sure we were wrapped up as best we could and then zipped up our DPM tank suits. I knew that these wouldn't last long in this weather. I don't think any of us cared that much; we only had four days on exercise if everything went well. Four short days and we could be on our way back to Colly. Happy Days. We were driving out of the refuelling area when I looked over to my left, I couldn't believe that some Tosser had vandalised the new fence, nicked all the fence posts for about two hundred metres, but were kind enough to leave the new wheelbarrow. Rab, you Tosser, I thought. I wouldn't have minded but he must have carried out an SAS raid, as it was virtually opposite the guardroom which was occupied twenty four hours a day! I just wasn't going to mention this to anyone. The battery was now ready to deploy as we would for war, this was serious shit.

"Right lads get the B.V on," I shouted. The B.V was the 'boiling vessel', another name for a kettle. We drove out of the camp and headed for the Beacons, this was going to be a long slow drag, so plenty of time for a brew and anyway, we couldn't go to war without that and a fag. We had rigged our B.V to work in the back of the One Tonner so we had a brew on all the time. The B.V was approximately twelve by twelve inches square; it had a lid on it that could be removed so you could fill the vessel and inside it had a square container which was used as a pan. This was removed if you were only making a brew, you would fill the B.V. drive down the road for fifteen minutes and the B.V would be scalding hot, in order to release the water you pressed a little plunger type tap on the side. Sure enough, when the convoy stopped, I looked out of the passenger window and Rab was standing there with a scalding hot brew for me. Superb', I thought a pint of hot tea. At that moment I didn't care how wet I was going to be, or so I thought.

After half an hour or so, we could see the vehicles up ahead slowing down. They were turning left off the main road and into a farmer's field on the edge of Brecon. As soon as we turned off the main road, we had to turn off our main lights and switch on our convoy light. The convoy light was a tiny dimly lit light which was normally at the rear underside of the wagon above the differential. The idea was that the enemy wouldn't be able to see you, but the guy driving in the vehicle behind would. This would avoid any chance of him piling into the back of your vehicle, when the first vehicle had stopped. We had to take a minute while our eyes adjusted to working with no lights. The idea was to work slowly, quietly, and with the minimum of fuss. Vehicle revs had to be kept low and no talking, remembering that noise travels a greater distance at night. The plan was for each gun to deploy in different areas of this massive field and then bring the gun into action so that we were ready to fire. We had to camouflage the gun with a large camouflage net which went over the gun, unload the one tonne Land Rover and all the ammunition very quietly. Once the gun was set up, the one tonne Land Rover would drive over to an area where all the vehicles were hiding called the 'Echelon area'. The driver would have to switch off the engine and camouflage the vehicle on his own. I was more than happy with the way the crew went about their business, they all knew what, how and when to do it. They were brilliant. By the time we had set up, it was just starting to get light; it was also still freezing cold and raining heavily. I looked over at a building that was very close to us, I was unable to see what it was, but there was definitely the silhouette of a building in the background.

After another hour had passed I could see someone walking towards our gun, I halted him in his tracks and waited until he identified himself. He was the farmer who owned the field and was well up for helping us out with anything we needed, I invited him to come under our camouflage net, his name was Davies. (Well it would be, wouldn't it?). The reason why these farmers were so kind to us was simply this. The MOD would pay them an absolute fortune if we wrecked their fields while we were on exercise. All well and good but if we caused any damage to any part of their farm or belongings, it was like Christmas. These farmers did well out of the MOD they would obviously be informed well in advance that the army were coming on a certain day to carryout manoeuvres on their farms, so everything and anything that was broken on the farm would be saved until that day. Even dead sheep!

"Run over that for me boyo," was the common request from the farmers.

"Yes no problem Taff, as long as you look after us," would be the reply. It was a case of 'you scratch my back and I will scratch yours' and it worked. I know for a fact that one gun number one had a fully stocked fridge brought out to his camouflage net and my God was it stocked well by the farmer. It was amazing to see a one hundred metre extension lead trailing from one of his barns all the way to the rear of an artillery gun. The smell of fresh bacon and sausage coming from this gun for seven mornings on the trot was unbearable to say the least. On another occasion, a Sergeant was asked to drive a seventeen tonne tracked vehicle through the back of a barn and right through the rear supporting wall so the farmer could claim for a new building. The deed was done and the gun crew got free showers and breakfast for a week at this location in the farmer's house, a small price to pay for a barn!

"What you need boys?" he asked.

"Any breakfast kit available?" I asked him. "We are here for at least 24 hours," I said. We wouldn't normally know that, but the B.S.M tipped me off as we came through the gate. Top man.

"No problem man, give me an hour, I'll get fresh," he replied. Oh I couldn't wait. If the rain went off for a couple of hours now, I would be in heaven. Taffy was just about to turn away when I stopped him. "Do you have one of them electric cattle fences Taff?" I enquired.

"Fuckin right I do son, Why?" He asked.

"What's the chance of you putting it up like a ring of steel around this cam net tonight when it goes dark? We are supposed to be getting attacked by the enemy later in the night. I can get one of my lads to help you if it's a problem," I replied.

"It's a doddle son, leave it to me," He said. I smiled to myself, however he did warn me that should anyone touch it they would be a little more than surprised. I was already aware of this due to my brother making me touch one when I was little and I think I filled my pants as a result. Oh come on, I was only four and it did hurt.

By the time ten a.m. came and went my gun crew (me included) were all wobbling about under the cam net like fat bloaters. I had eaten four fried eggs, six sausages, four thick rashers of the nicest welsh bacon you could ever taste and a full tin of baked beans. If I didn't eat for the remaining time on exercise, I wouldn't starve. Farmer Davies did us proud and we had loads left over for tomorrow. The smell on the 'gun position' was not dissimilar to the outside of a trucker's café. Before we knew it we heard the radio communications spring into life.

"Fire. Mission. Battery!" With that we raced to our positions behind the light gun, the crew were confident with their roles and that in turn filled me with confidence. We went through all the drills and eventually fired off our first Light Gun round down the ranges. Calculations told me that we were only firing about seven miles away and before long we had punched thirty shells of high explosive down the range. The 'Live Firing' went well.

"Any problems, Bombardier Connolly?" My heart sank, I knew that voice. It was Lieutenant Joplin. That's all I needed. I wanted to reply with 'There is now you've arrived Sir', but I didn't.

"Everything's spot on here, Sir," was my answer. I knew what this Rodney was up to, his big conk had homed in on the beautiful morning breakfast smell that was still hanging over the 'gun position' and he was looking for a spare sausage. He had two hopes, Bob Hope and no fucking hope. Not only was I not prepared to feed him, but my crew would have hung me by the neck had I done so.

"Right, okay Bomber, I will leave you to it then," he replied with a wanting voice.

"No problem, Sir, I will give you a shout when we need you," I replied sarcastically. Not a fucking chance. I wouldn't call for help off this man if hell froze over. He would be the last person I would call. By the end of the day we were soaked through to the skin, the rain would not stop. We had no shelter and no way of drying ourselves. What made it worse was the drop in temperature, it was so cold, even our warm clothing had no effect. On a positive note though, we had a fantastic day of firing the Light Gun. This is when a Gunner is in his element, firing shell after shell down the range. It had been a top day. I don't know how much it would cost for a 35lb High Explosive (H.E) shell for a light gun, but I knew an F.H70 shell was four hundred quid, so if this was a hundred pounds, I had just sent four grand down the ranges. Remember there are six guns in this field, so that's some serious money if they all fired the same as me. Mind you, we did cheat a bit, if we were told to fire three rounds 'fire for effect', we would load and fire as quick as possible and fire off an extra one. No one was any the wiser and it was good practise for my crew. As long as we knew how many we had fired, we were all right. My crew had only carried out one day 'Live Firing and they were super quick already.

When we finished firing an hour before last light, Taff the farmer came over and asked us if we wanted a little shelter. Fucking hell we said not half, with a little smile, he disappeared and returned several minutes later with a tarpaulin cover in a plastic frame. What a shelter we now had under our net, it was brilliant. The next best thing about it was that it was dark green in colour which was great for camouflage. We got Joe Smiley to start a small fire, and I got each one of my crew in there for approximately quarter of an hour to warm up and dry out a little. Not only was the fire a bonus, but it meant that I got a brew out of it too. Taff the farmer came back and climbed under the cam net.

"You boys fancy fish and chips then?"

And a little Scottish voice coming from my loader shouted, "Is the Pope Catholic? Does a bear shit in the woods?"

I couldn't believe what I was hearing.

"I could bring it over as soon as it goes dark if you like," he added.

"Not half mate, can you make it six portions?" I asked him.

"No problem," he said and then he was gone. I couldn't believe it, we were getting fish and chips while we were out on exercise. We had been issued our food compo rations and the only thing we had touched was a can of baked beans and a ten-man tea bag. I just couldn't believe this and thought to myself, what's the pay back then?

The rain had eased a lot and we were all sat around at the rear of the gun. Mickey was in the tent making my next brew, it was very dark now and we were exchanging stories about our junior leader training with each other when Paul O'Neil piped up, "Smell that". No sooner had he said it we all snapped our heads over towards the North West. There was a very strong smell of chips and vinegar; next we heard a rustle from the cam net at the rear of the gun.

"There you go lads, get that down you," Taff said. Joe had taken them off Taff the farmer and passed us all a portion and again before we knew it, Taffy was gone. Mickey heard him say something about an electric fence; I didn't care at this point as I was in the process of tipping tomato ketchup on my chips. We tucked into our 'jockeys' whips' and couldn't believe how fresh the fish tasted. I think we all went through at least five 'mmmmms' each before we finished. With my brew and a sly cigarette afterwards, I was in seventh heaven. If I died in a war, with my belly as full of food as it was now, it would be a good time to go.

At about nine p.m., we heard a voice from the other side of the cam net.

"Are you there boys?" the voice whispered. We climbed under the other side of the cam net for the first time that day and there stood Taff the Farmer. He was covering up a gigantic wagon battery which was lying in the long grass at the side of the field.

"Will that do you?" I squatted down and looked up towards the sky, where I could just see the outline of a wire fence running around the gun. I brushed my hand across it as fast I could. Ow, it got me, but I couldn't shout. I had to hold the pain and just frantically shake my hand.

"That's brilliant Taff,". I said. "Great."

"If you need me now just come and bang on my door. If not I will see you in the morning with some fresh eggs," he added.

"Goodnight and thanks mate," I said as I watched him walk away in the direction of his house. I made the lads pack everything away that we didn't need, if we had to 'Bog out' in a hurry, I didn't want to have to leave anything at all behind. I was now hoping that we would be there until just after brekky, so we could repeat the experience that we had been fortunate to participate in yesterday. I instructed Mickey Hall to make a 'stag list'. A 'stag list' is just a list of who is guarding us while the crew sleeps and at what time they are on stag and when your stag time finishes. It also tells the person on stag who to wake up next. With that all sorted, I climbed into the tent with the rest of my crew and held my rifle to my chest and felt myself drifting off to sleep in the silence of the night.

At three thirty in the morning, I heard an almighty scream. "AAAAAHHHHHHHH my fucking arm!" it said. Never mind about waking the dead, this would have woken the whole of Wales.

Inside, we were shouting. "Shut the fuck up."

The cam net lifted and we were all out with our rifles and SMGs (Sub Machine Guns) pointing in the direction of the noise. Our first thought was that it was the enemy attack we had been waiting for, but it wasn't, it was Chindit and he wasn't best pleased.

"Bombardier Connolly, get here you Wanker," he whispered aggressively.

"Yes, Sir," I replied.

"What the fuck have you done and what the fuck is that?" he asked.

"It's an electric fence, Sir," I explained.

"I know that you dipstick. I have just put my S.M.G on it to hold it down while I climbed over it," he added. For those who have never seen the nine-millimetre Sterling Sub machine gun, I can tell you that it is

83

mainly made of steel, so by the time you have placed it over an electric fence and the shock reaches your fingers it will have increased ten fold.

"Are you mad? You could kill someone with that you dick," he explained. "I didn't think you would grab it, Sir, I was waiting for the enemy," I replied.

"Enemy or no enemy, it's got to go," he finished.

"Okay, Sir, consider it done," I answered. I ordered Rab to disconnect the battery while Chindit sat down to share a cig with me, he was still shaking like a leaf. I could see Paul O'Neil out of the corner of my eye, laughing his head off. I told Chindit where it had come from and he knew the score; it wasn't that many years before that he would have tried something similar. Remember he had attempted the SAS twice, so he would have learnt tricks a lot more sadistic than mine. He liked my initiative, but not my will to kill a pretend enemy. I liked both! I got one of the lads to make him a brew and we whispered for a short time. I was made up because he tipped me off that the immanent attack was due to happen soon after breakfast time, I didn't think we would get attacked during the hours of darkness. This attacking during hours of darkness business was being reduced more and more during the hours of darkness. Too many troops were getting injured.

The last time that an attack had occurred during 'dark' o'clock, I was on exercise as an umpire for the infantry, my role was to act as a neutral, which was to score and act as a referee on a tactical exercise. There were two sergeants, an officer and myself, observing two infantry platoons coming towards each other in the dead of the night, we were lucky as we had the infrared night sights, so for us it was just like looking into daylight. One of the platoons was playing the enemy and they were attacking another platoon from the same regiment who were well 'dug in' and camouflaged up in these little woods. Next thing all hell broke loose and they all jumped up from their individual hiding places and charged at each other firing blank ammunition from their rifles. When they met each other on the outer edge of the wood, they started punching each other and smashing each other in the face with rifle butts. The umpire officer who was with us saw this and couldn't believe it.

"What the fuck," I heard him say; he jumped up and started to blow his whistle loudly. That was to indicate 'DANGER' and on hearing this whistle everyone and anyone was supposed to freeze where they stood.

As a result, the exercise would be temporally suspended pending the results of a quick investigation.

Not a chance, these two platoons were killing each other. It was like a scene from 'Desperado' with screams of pain coming from most of the beaten troops, had this been a real enemy watching something like this, they would have turned and ran. We all sprinted the two hundred metres and had to start breaking them up, they were literally killing each other. We had to be really careful that infantry adrenaline didn't kick in and kick us! It turned out that these two platoons were rivals and this happened every time they came together. Not only were they in the same regiment, but they were both in the British Army. How bizarre I thought.

Chindit said that after our attack we were going to meet the Royal Engineers. We were going to be shown how to apply and detonate plastic explosive (P.E.). The idea being that we were going to be digging the guns in, in layman's terms that means we were to dig a chuffing big hole and put the Light Gun into it, in order to fire from the pit in the ground. If you can imagine burying a Volvo Estate Car, then you would be pretty close to it. The ground, which was full of slate and flint, was really hard to dig. This small P.E. explosion would loosen the ground to give us a good start. That made my day. I loved explosives although I had limited experience of using them, and if I got to blow this shit hole up it was a double bargain. Chindit left our gun platform a reasonably happy chappy and I walked away from the whole ordeal with my head still on my shoulders.

Chindit had also told me that he was disappearing back to Colchester after lunch because he and twenty-five other troops were deploying for Belize the next day as part of the advance party. I didn't give that much thought as an 'Advance Party' ideally should have left a couple of weeks ago in order to get everything taken over from the outgoing battery and set up for when we all arrived. Chindit wouldn't mind though, he was always well organised and could deploy anywhere at very short notice. Half the lump heads I knew would still be scratching around for their bum powder and nail varnish in the U.K while Chindit was applying the finishing touches to his Basha (make shift shelter) in the jungle.

Daylight arrived along with 'Chucky Egg Taff, who had brought with him, two dozen of the finest eggs I had seen for a long time.

"Right lads lets get trough on quick," I ordered. "Taff, have you got a minute?" I asked him. With that I took him to the rear of the cam net and asked him outright what I could do for him. We would be gone soon and we had been treated like royalty.

He didn't want anything at all doing as between all six guns we had destroyed his field and some of the surrounding fence. "Oh I tell you what mind," he said in his broadest welsh accent. "Look at my gate and gate post."

"Say no more. Leave it to me," I answered. I knew exactly what he could do with, which was a new gate and two posts. Not a problem. I walked under the cam net to my breakfast being handed to me by Mickey Hill. I sat on a Jerry can full of rum and coke and troughed it like an animal. It was as good as it was the day before. What a taste, I thought.

I was under the impression that the attack would come while we were eating our breakfast, but it didn't arrive for another good hour after that, by which time were all cleaned up and packed away. Suddenly we heard the sound of blank ammunition being fired and a bunch of lunatics screaming and pretending to be the enemy.

"Bog out lads," I shouted, and that was it. Two of my crew fired back at the idiots while the rest of us brought the Light Gun out of action. We hooked it up to the Land Rover and jumped aboard, we were now ready to roll so the enemy had gone to attack one of the other guns. The exercise finished and before we knew it there was a steady steam of vehicles waiting to exit onto the road through the farmer's gate.

Taff the farmer was standing by his farmhouse and Joe and I gave him a final wave. He waved back at us like Zebedee from the Magic Roundabout. As we drove closer to the gate, I told Pat to stop the one tonne Land Rover. He turned to me looking puzzled.

"Let everyone go before us, I want to be last one out," I said. "Trust me," I added.

He pulled up on the right hand side of the field and waited, then as the last vehicle left the gate, I took hold of my radio mic. "Hello alpha one zero, this is three zero bravo, close the gate over."

Bombardier Bert Bradley who was stood by the gate swung round and looked straight at my wagon. "Say again over," came his reply.

"Close the gate. Out," I ordered. The penny had dropped with him, but not yet for my crew. He jumped on the army motorbike and sped off. "Drive to the gate Pat, when you getting close, slowly nose right up to it so you are touching it, then push it over."

He turned to me and smiled, clink another penny had just dropped. Pat did as I had asked him to do. He had come to read me well over the years. He had pushed the gate to the point that he was now driving over it, as the gate came down, the two posts followed. I stuck my head out of my window and saw the gate and the two posts flat on the ground. Job done, I thought, well worth the royalty treatment we had just received.

We arrived ten clicks up the road at the next gun position, parked up and went over to meet the Royal Engineers Sergeant.

"This is Sergeant Hornby from the R.Es," Joplin said. "Now listen in! He is going to show you how to apply and detonate P.E," he added. I looked over at Pat my driver and knew exactly what he was thinking. I have seen this on telly so it will be a piece of piss. We shall see. The sergeant pulled a tiny piece of plastic explosive from the ball, about the size of a marble. Well he isn't going to do much with that, I thought to myself. What about the ball in his right hand? He placed the tennis ball sized piece into a plastic bag, sealed it and placed it into a webbing bag. Then, he passed it to his corporal who walked over to the rear of their land rover, opened the lid of a box and dropped the webbing bag into it, he then shut the box and walked back to where his colleague was carrying out the demo. I noticed that Rab had watched every move the corporal had made. I hope he was thinking the same as me, I wanted more. I had missed most of the waffle from the R.E sergeant, but I got the idea of it anyway. God he was boring. There is something in the army called R.S.V.P (Rhythm Speed Volume Pitch). These are the qualities that every good instructor must have in order to get his point over to a bunch of squaddies whose heads are either in a brothel and thinking of nothing else other than sex, or the local town bar. However, this guy was monotone and sounded like a tortoise walking through the grass. There was more life in a tramp's vest.

We were all ordered to retire approximately one hundred metres away, where there was no possibility of anyone being hurt when the explosion went off. I wouldn't have bothered because by the time he had counted down from five to one, which was an achievement in itself, we realised that this was about as explosive as someone setting fire to a box of matches. This gave me the confirmation I needed; I was having the big ball of P.E. I looked over at Rab, who was already looking in my direction, I gave him the nod and he slid into the crowd of people who were about to walk back to the explosion site.

"Do not return to the explosion site until all the debris has fallen," the sergeant ordered. I thought, what debris? There is more fall out when I make my bed back at the barracks in Colly. When we had been given the all clear, we walked back to the explosion site and leaned over the point of detonation. There was a hole the size of a baked bean can.

"There you go lads," said the sergeant in a proud voice. Is that it? I thought. We were expecting total devastation and someone mentioning The Richter Scale at least, but nothing. It was pathetic. Tommy looked over at me and started to giggle. It was embarrassing.

"Corporal, have you got the crews explosive and dets?" the sergeant enquired. Corporal Kermit then stepped forward and passed each gun number one a tiny piece of plastic explosive, a detonator and huge piece of wire. "Right! If you all fall out and report to Lt Joplin, he will issue you with a grid reference," said the sergeant. "You will all be deployed at separate locations but within a one kilometre square, where you will all carryout your controlled explosion." He added, "We will come round and check to see how you are doing when you start to dig your holes. Are there any questions?"

I could think of one, but I would have been in a lot of trouble if I'd have asked it. With no takers we all started to walk away slowly.

I turned to Tommy and whispered under my breath, "Tommy should I ever meet up with this guy later on in life remind me not to take him on at scrabble." Tommy laughed and said he would never forget this demonstration. It was crap.

Armed with my grid reference, I headed over to my crew, "Mount up men," I said. The rain had gone off, so I was in a happy mood. "We are off to see the wonderful wizard of Sennybridge," I joked. I was about to lay my map on the engine cover where I was going to plot it, when I noticed something in the floor well of our vehicle. What the hell is it? I thought. On further investigation, I discovered a grey coloured ball rolling around the cab. Rab had been shopping and relocated Corporal

Muppet's ball of P.E into our one tonne Land Rover. Oh yes. Now we are talking, I thought.

"Pat, get the hell out of here," I snapped to my driver. He didn't reply, he just drove out of the field and onto the main road. Rab had done it! He had nicked the big ball of P.E from the back of the Royal Engineer's Land Rover. By the time we reached our new location the rain had started again and it was clear that the temperature was plummeting once more. There was ice on the ground as it had been raining here for days. We all jumped out of the wagon and quickly found a good part of Wales to blow up. Mind you, we would have said any part of Wales was good to blow up in those days.

We set the P.E up as we had been shown by 'Sergeant Monotone' and retired a good couple of hundred metres away, we weren't daft. This wasn't your average marble, pea sized bit of pop fizz; this was going to be the grand daddy of all explosions. I gave the honours to Joe as I did the countdown.

"5-4-3-2-1 FIRE." What followed next could only be described as a repeat of Hiroshima. It felt like the world had come to an end. Debris rained from the sky for what seemed like ages, rubble, soil, trees, fences, sheep, and cows. No, there weren't really any cows or sheep, but there was a considerable amount of debris and the tail end echo from the explosion went on for an age. The ground shook to the point that we nearly fell over. Once it had all died down I looked towards the one tonne Land Rover where I could see Mickey standing, then I spotted Rab, he was holding onto the passenger mirror for his dear life and looked as if he was about to be shot by firing squad.

"Oh my God! What the fuck was that?" I said not expecting an answer. I walked over to the explosion site and saw that what was once a lovely green and snow covered meadow, was now black and depressing, soil and flint covering, what one minute ago was the backdrop for a Rembrandt painting. Even a massive old oak tree had been reduced to something you would find in a 'Swan Vesta Box'. What had I done? I looked down into the deep hole which was still smouldering. I wouldn't be surprised if RAF Valley, which was a few miles down the road, hadn't scrambled the Tornado fighter jets in fear of an attack from the Russians. I had destroyed Wales! This had to be the worse thing I had ever done either in or out of the army.

The idea was for the plastic explosive to loosen the flint and soil a little so we could dig a hole big enough to put the Light Gun into it. I had just removed part of the Brecon Beacons, to the degree of being able to put a Radisson Hotel in it. In the words of our forefathers, I was in deep shit. My gun crew started to scurry round looking for spades and such like to fill in some of the hole but I told them to leave it. There was no way of hiding this enormous fuck up, it was done, and all I could do now was to wait for the fall out. I knew Sergeant Boring was going to be here any minute now and there would be no bluffing him. The idea of telling him that it was the small piece of P.E he had issued us, that had caused this mess wasn't an option. He hadn't reached the dizzy heights of a Sergeant in the Royal Engineers on the pretext of being a nugget. Not only would Wales have heard this explosion, but so would Cornwall, Devon, London, Liverpool and the M6 Corridor.

I lit a cigarette, it felt like the old cowboy films, "Any last requests before you die Gringo?" Ah stuff it, I thought. I would just have to take what comes; I had been in worse scrapes than this. Actually, I haven't, I thought. Not anything as monumental as this, Oooops! I looked over to my right hand side and towards the track that we had driven down fifteen minutes ago, I could see them, Dick and Dorf hurtling towards us in a long wheel based Land Rover. I walked towards them in the hope that the crew couldn't hear me having another arse hole ripped into me by Sergeant Hornby.

He jumped out of the passenger side of the vehicle and walked towards me, whilst surveying the aftermath of Armageddon. "Tell me the truth Bombardier," he said. He was now looking directly into my eyes. Even if I hadn't spoken, the fact that his tennis ball sized chunk of P.E was now deficient from the back of his vehicle, would have made this a difficult stunt to deny.

"I took it Sarge," I admitted.

"I know you fucking took it, look at the state of Wales," he said. "You stupid bastard, you could have killed yourself and all your crew, not to mention a herd of Bison and Rhino at the same time. That's a massive amount of P.E to be fucking around with," he finished.

"I realise that now Sarge, and I am so sorry," I replied.

"Right, is everyone OK?" he asked.

"Yes Sarge," I answered. "Everyone is fine."

He then started to tell me a story about a Royal Engineer, who eighteen years earlier had done something almost identical to this, not long after signing up. He and two of his mates had stolen a ball of plastic explosive, and at seventeen years old and thinking they knew what they were doing, they ran off onto the firing ranges to try it out later that day. They found an old tank which had previously been used for direct fire target practise and blew it up. The tank had been obliterated in the massive explosion but that wasn't the issue. The UK was on a heightened state of security and everyone in a military uniform was very touchy at that time. The point of the story is that it was Sergeant Hornby who had carried out this act and he was helped out of trouble by his Troop Commander who could see a bright future in him. It was now his opportunity to help someone whose turn it was to be in the same sinking boat. That someone was me.

"Listen to me and listen good," he started. "Shout your crew over here".

"L Sub, get over here now," I screamed towards my crew. As they were jogging over towards us, he said that he was going to give me the same chance that he had been given, if I promised right now not to do anything as stupid as this again. I gave him my word there and then, amazed at the possibility he was going to save my skin. My crew arrived at the top of the raised mound that the Sergeant and I were standing on and at the same time I could hear the roar of a tracked vehicle and the sound of numerous Land Rovers. I could see Joplin racing towards us in the first vehicle, which he drove right up to us before carrying out an emergency skid in the mud that I had created. I could now see Joplin was about to climb out of the Land Rover

"So there you go gentlemen. That's the end of the demonstration," said Sergeant Hornby. "Any questions?"

My gun crew and I were all in shock and staring frantically at each other. "No Sarge," I replied. He turned to Joplin and explained to him that my crew had used our piece of P.E when he turned up at the gun position but one of the gunners was dying to see what a bigger piece of P.E could do, so he gave us a demo with the remaining P.E. that he had left over. After all, he didn't want to travel back to Wisbeach with it. Lt Joplin looked at me, and then towards the sergeant. I could see that he had swallowed the story hook, line and sinker. Why wouldn't he? The only worry was that Corporal Muppet, the sergeant's driver was now getting out of his cab. He was the only other person who knew the true account of what had happened.

"Stay in the cab, I am coming now Corp," the sergeant shouted. The corporal climbed back in the Land Rover and awaited the arrival of his sergeant.

Mr Joplin looked at the sergeant, "Everything OK then, Sergeant?" he enquired.

"Yes, Sir, I am going back to H.Q location now to send a tracked digger to this gun position to fill in what the crew doesn't need, then the jobs a good en, Sir," he informed him.

"Very good and thank you for everything today, Sergeant. Fall Out," Joplin replied.

I couldn't resist turning to the sergeant and calling after him "Thanks for all your help Sarge."

He turned around and looked at me with half a smile before he climbed into the Land Rover. I had just escaped with my Army career intact but only by the skin of my teeth. This was a stupid act which I couldn't repeat. As we finally got the Light Gun into the pit, the digger turned up and filled in what we didn't need.

CHAPTER FIVE

HOW MUCH IS THAT DOGGIE IN THE BARREL

Our fire missions were very slow throughout the day which meant we were stood 'in action' at the Light Gun, ready to fire, but were constantly kept waiting due to poor visibility at the 'Observation Post' (O.P) end. We were firing about four miles away and it would prove pointless if the troops whose job it was to spot the shells landing couldn't see them as a result of the mist and rain, a complete waste of ammo. I think we only fired fifteen shells all day and we were soaked through yet again and so cold. However, we would rather this than dropping a high explosive shell through the roof of Mr and Mrs Blodwynn's farm cottage while they were trying to settle down for daytime TV, just because our O.P's couldn't wait for a bit of mist to lift.

"Joe, go and get a brew on," I said to my ammunition's man.

It was then that I heard a deep voice, "And don't forget mine Bomb Connolly, one sugar." It was the B.S.M, he was standing at the top of my gun pit and he was holding what looked like a yellow canvas tarpaulin, which looked really heavy. I instructed two of my crew to go and help, but he said he could manage. He asked if we had finished the last fire mission to which I replied that we had. This meant that it was clear for him to proceed under the net. Once, we conned a certain Chindit into walking in front of our gun barrel and as he did we fired a H.E shell twenty odd miles down the range, the force of the blast was so strong that it picked him up and dumped him on his back like a judo throw. As he got up smacking both ears with his hands, I fired again. He was not best pleased, but there was nothing he could do. I was being told when to fire through my headset and couldn't hang on while Chindit was rolling around like one of the Teletubbies. The B.S.M had heard about this story and he was taking no chances.

"Good," he said, "I will have that brew with you then." He smiled over at me and made his way into our reasonably sized hole. "I heard Hornby gave you an extra demo with the P.E?" he enquired.

"Yes, Sir, spot on," I replied. If the B.S.M found out what had gone on here today, he would have beaten me the full length and breadth of Wales.

"Good, he was all right for an Engineer I suppose," he added.

"Yes, Sir, a good bloke, in fact a really good bloke." I finished the conversation.

"Anyway, try them on," the B.S.M said and threw the yellow canvas on the floor; they were waterproof jackets and trousers. The kind that fishermen wore.

"I don't understand, Sir," I said.

"Just try them on, come on," he snapped.

My gun crew all tucked in to the waterproofs and were soon dressed and looking rather dapper in them. All right, they looked like the picture of the front of a packet of 'Fisherman's Friends' but who cared. I picked the remaining set up off the floor and started to put them on. Now when I said there wasn't such a thing as 'one hundred percent waterproofs', I lied.

"Where did you get these from sir?" I asked him. "The local fire bobbies lent them to me. Eighteen sets," he said quite proudly.

"That's fuckin ace sir, but we can't bend our fucking arms or legs," I replied smiling. It was like being in a set of armour.

"Ah don't worry about that, at least you will be warm and dry that's the main thing. Fuck the R.E.M.Fs; they aren't out in the wet enough," he said. Paul passed the B.S.M's brew over to him. "Thanks lad," the B.S.M said.

"What about the colour sir? We are under a camouflage net to hide from enemy aircraft and blend in with the landscape, but bright yellow doesn't help us to do that," I said slightly sarcastically.

" Needs must Bomb," he said, "I'm sure if you had to fight a war pissed wet through and without bright yellow waterproofs, you could, but to be wet with no point to it, then that's a different matter."

Fair point, I thought to myself. I was now going to get stripped off, throw my nice clean, dry and warm gear on and then put my new 'penguin suit' back on.

On my R.M.A (Regimental Medical Assistance) course down in Aldershot, we had spent three weeks studying for all the theory exams and so we had just been let loose on the practical side of the course for the remaining three weeks. We had to learn a number of medical procedures that we could be called upon to carryout in a field hospital. This could be anything from giving soldiers morphine to carrying out a Naso-Gastric where we would have to draw fluid from the casualty's stomach. On this particular day we were practicing 'quick drying plaster casts', we left this lad from the Pay Corps immobilised on the operating table with a full body cast on, and then did a runner to the cookhouse leaving him to struggle on his own. When we returned after lunch he had fallen off the medical couch and was begging for us to cut him free. Wearing these waterproofs probably felt the same.

We spent the rest of the night in the 'gun pit' and R.V'd (Rendezvoused) at an old disused farmyard in the morning at 09.00hrs. We were so on it, we had just had a good brekky from the rest of our extra rations and best of all, we were bone dry. Okay we couldn't walk or bend our arms, but we were toasty warm and dry. I wondered how these firemen ever tackled a fire wearing this lot, I couldn't even write on a notepad without dislocating my shoulder and straining my elbow. It could have been this reason that they were kept as spares in the local fire station. Anyway, we didn't care, we were more than grateful. I know there were a lot of other people within the battery at that moment in time that were running around the exercise pissed wet through. I felt really sorry for them. *NOT!* It was a case of I'm all right Jack and so is my crew. We only had two days of this exercise left, after that, we were home and dry.

We pulled around to the front of this old barn and I noticed that the rest of the battery had already arrived. I could see Tommy with a big smile on his face, I think he had a slight inclination as to why the whole of Wales had shook at early o'clock the day before. If not, at least he knew I had something to do with it; I winked in his general direction as if to say, 'I will tell you later'. I climbed out of the one tonne Land Rover and marched over to where all the gun commanders had gathered. It was good to see that I wasn't the only idiot dressed like something out of 'War of the Worlds'. All the gun number ones had the same outfit on. I must admit though it was funny watching everyone trying to retrieve notebooks and pens from their inside pockets. I had saved myself the embarrassment by having mine ready before I got there. The B.C appeared from the back of our little group, as soon as we noticed him we all came to attention. He stood us at ease and told us to relax.

"Right gents," he said. "Today is the final day with the Light Gun and then Friday you've got live firing with the F.H70. It's the 'Direct Firing' phase at lunchtime, so get your barrels cleaned and then report back here at 13.00hrs. I will issue you with five grid references, you will have to plot your way around the five check points and the first one to finish on the top of Merton Hill will get to level the village with direct fire."

This had now become exciting; to me this is what being an artilleryman was all about. We would receive the five grid references from the B.C., then, spend some quality time plotting our maps with great accuracy. After this we would drive with our gun and crew and get our map stamped at each of our five checkpoints. The first group to visit all five, would then stop on top of Merton Hill.

The Royal Engineers had spent two weeks building a small town made purely of Plywood. I had done this once before in Canada and if it was on the same level, it would look very real. They even painted the buildings to look like houses and shops. The winners would then be able to bring their gun into action and the gun crew would then proceed to blow the small town to pieces using 'direct fire'. In simple terms, 'direct fire' is me looking through a pair of binoculars and directing the live, high explosive ammunition onto the village. The gun commander with the best map-reading skills and the best gun crew would get to flatten this village before the other guns got there. It was now 09.30 hrs and we had plenty of time to get a brew on, clean up the kit and pull the gun through. It was a joy to clean the Light Gun barrel as it was only a few feet long, but it was much harder on the F.H70.

"Rab, I have just heard over the radio, the 'Battery Bar' is open, get a list together and go and get some clatty bars."

"Yes Bomb, no problem," he answered. T

he Battery Bar is best described as a 'Tuck Shop'. It was looked after by the battery captain (B.K.), and he was responsible for the stocking and selling of; crisps, chocolate bars (clatty bars), cans of pop and cigarettes to the troops. It would normally be the B.K's driver who did the selling though. Oh incidentally, we were aware that Captain didn't start with a 'K', but we already had a B.C. (Battery Commander), hence, B.K.

My crew carried on with the maintenance on the gun and then started a bit of 'personal admin'. This was the term used by the army for when the troops were looking after and maintaining their own personal kit. I looked over at the barn where the B.K's and the B.C's wagons were hiding, tucked under cover. I noticed Rab jogging back towards the gun, and looking back towards the officers vehicles.

"Hey Rab, what's up mate"? I asked.

"Quick Sean, in the back," he whispered. What the hell is going on? I thought to myself. By which time he had literally dived over the rear tailgate of the wagon without touching it and was scurrying about in the back.

He was frantically searching his pockets. "Fuck me Bomb," he said with a very shaky voice.

"Christ mate, what's up? Are you okay?" I was getting a little concerned; I really thought he was falling ill.

"I am better than okay," he replied. He was now flicking through the pages of his little military notebook. "Look at that," he said pushing this book into my face. I knew immediately what I was looking at.

"Tell me it's not," I said.

"It fucking is," he replied.

"How did you get these?" I asked.

He went on to show me 'K sub' on one page and 'L sub' on the other. 'L Sub' was my gun. Underneath each gun were five grid references. It turned out that the B.C had left his notebook on the passenger seat of the B.K's wagon and while Rab was in the queue waiting to be served, he had seen the B.C's notebook through the window. He could see 'J sub' and five numbers under it. He put two and two together and guessed that this was the grid references for this afternoon's competition and then he put another two and two together and came up trumps again to see also that when he turned the page, ours would be next. He slid the passenger window open and had a peep. He had hit the number 4 on both points. He put the book back down on our page, quickly took out his own book and recorded our five grid references and 'K sub'. I wasn't bothered about 'K' sub, but I was excited to see ours. He had replaced the B.C's book as he had found it and ran back.

"Fantastic mate! Okay, jump out and give the lads a hand," I said. With that, he was gone. I climbed into the passenger seat of the one tonne and started to plot the grid references. Once I had plotted all five, I checked them and then double checked them. I spent a good half hour plotting the map and when I had finished, I decided to study the map further to see if I could recognise anywhere. I knew this area quite well, as I had been to Sennybridge many times before both as an army cadet and an adult soldier. I looked at each grid reference and then closed my eyes, by the time I had finished, I was confident of reaching each checkpoint and felt I could do it even without a map. All I had to do was check that the numbers the B.C issued at 13.00hrs were definitely the same. It was the plotting of your map that took the time; I couldn't believe what Rab had done. The B.C stood in front of us and he started to read all the grid references, gun by gun.

Before I knew it he called, "L sub'. First one," he started, "163233." I wrote the number on the blank page in my notebook.

"Yes, Sir," I replied.

"175327."

"Thanks, Sir," I answered again and so he continued until I had all five numbers. It was the last number which confirmed it to me 749666. It was the treble six at the end of the last grid reference that told me that we had the right numbers.

"Thank you, Sir," I said at the end.

He continued reading all the numbers for the remaining guns before he looked up. "Is everybody happy? Go, Go, Go," he shouted. I sprinted back to our gun and jumped into the one tonne. Everybody had their engines running and was waiting for the number ones to plot the maps, I had to spend one minute to make it look as if I was plotting the first route. As soon as we left, the map was getting binned; I definitely knew where we were going and how to get there. I even knew a couple of short cuts to the checkpoints.

Wait, Wait, Wait, I thought to myself and then, "Go Pat, Go," I screamed at the top of my voice. Now either two of the other guns had done the same, or they had just plotted the first of their grid references and none of the others. I hit the road first and Pat was really giving it some welly, he was really going for it. "Left at the 'T' Junction mate," I screamed and with that he knocked it down to second gear and hammered it round the corner. "Up here about half a mile and you will see a track on the right leading up a hill, go up there," I added. Before we knew it we were heading up this really steep hill, the ground was really wet and muddy and Pat was doing a good job of controlling our vehicle. We could now see the brow of the hill and a body standing on the edge of the wooded area, it was Bombardier Bert Bradley. Pat had spotted him and headed straight towards him he slammed on the brakes about five metres away from him and locked the wheels. I was out of the cab well before the vehicle had stopped and nearly ended up face down in the mud for my eagerness. The one tonne and then the gun slid past me and left me standing looking directly at Bert. I waded through the mud to him.

"Clip that Bert," pushing my map at him.

As he was clipping my map, he looked up at me and said, "Go for it mate, good luck."

I didn't even answer him I just snatched my map from him and ran back to the vehicle. "Go Pat," and with that we were hammering down the other side of this really steep hill.

We battered our way around the course and every one of the remaining checkpoints was exactly where I thought it would be. Each checkpoint had an N.C.O.. from our battery stood by a small orange flag. I had learned through experience that the last checkpoint usually ended up with a surprise attached to it.

This one was no different; we were only one more checkpoint away from the finish line so I looked over at Pat and said, "Don't look for the body, look for the orange flag."

I was spot on. We drove around a disused barn and spotted an old well in the middle of a farmyard. There was something dangling on a piece of string hanging from what was left of the little roof. That was our final punch to stamp our map.

"There Pat," I pointed. He spotted it and accelerated towards the well. I dived out of the one tonne for the last time and sprinted to the well. I took hold of the punch and clicked it onto the map. I squeezed it as hard as I could. It left twelve little holes punched through on my map. I ran back towards the vehicle to the cheers of the crew in the back.

Oh shit, I thought, I had forgotten about the crew in the back of the wagon until now, they must be black and blue. We had hit some severely deep holes and battered the vehicle on all types of terrain; I hoped they were okay, because it was the 'Direct Fire' stage where I really needed them.

"You lot okay?" I shouted as I was running past the back of the vehicle, to my door.

I heard Joe shout back at me, "Just go Bomber."

Pat drove out of the rear end of the disused farm and I spotted Merton Hill directly ahead of us, less than two hundred metres away. The crew in the back of the vehicle were screaming for Pat to put his foot down, but the vehicle wouldn't go any faster up the steep hill.

"Faster you Tosser," someone shouted from the back.

"Fuck off, it won't go any faster," Pat shouted back. At the top of Merton Hill we could also see about ten people looking towards us. I looked all around and scoured the countryside for any of the other guns. I could see another Land Rover to my right approaching at speed. He was too far away from us to make any impression though, but the one I had now spotted on my left was closing in fast. His approaching hill wasn't as steep as mine.

"Pat, look," I screamed. I sat back in my seat so he could see the fast approaching vehicle.

"No fucking chance," he shouted back. With that he dropped it down to second gear and screamed the revs to maximum. I was sure we had them, it was going to be close, but even with our steeper climb we were only yards away. When we hit the tape, the other gun was only about ten metres behind us. We had done it. We had beaten the other guns.

"Well done mate, that was shit hot," I said to Pat. It was obvious by the way he had taken the hill that he knew exactly what he was doing.

"Cheers, Bomb."

"Not calling him a Tosser now are you?" I shouted into the back. Funny old thing, there was no reply.

We sat across the line after everyone had congratulated us and pondered on how the hell everyone else could have got here so close to us. We must have had fifteen minutes on everyone, surely. The B.C's team took all the maps away to confirm our win. When he returned, he told us all to 'fall in', all six guns had now made it across the finish line and we were stood waiting for the B.C to address us. I still couldn't believe that the other five guns had got here so quickly. We were like shit off a shovel and we had plotted all the references earlier in the day. I didn't care though as it was going to be us who flattened the village.

"Well done everyone," the B.C said, looking over to the B.S.M. "That was brilliant and good initiative from most of you," he went on. "There was only one gun who didn't take us up on our offer," and that was 'J sub'." What was he saying? We didn't understand. He went on to tell us that he had planted his book on the passenger seat of the B.K's Land Rover and then sent a radio message around the battery to say that the battery bar was open. When the first troops got to the bar, they had made a point of making them wait because the B.K's driver was still to be in the process of setting the bar up. This would naturally make the troops form a queue. The B.C, B.K and the B.S.M had watched the performance of the queuing gunners from inside an enclosed part of the bar and they had witnessed all but one gun crew leave with the information from the notebook. What a plant, we had all been taken for a ride (pardon the pun). However, the exercise was about initiative and we had taken the initiative. Okay we thought we were being smart by stealing the information and putting it to good use, but so did all the other guns, except for one. More fool them. The B.C was laughing his head off looking at the B.S.M. I thought to myself, fancy us thinking he would leave crucial information like that lying around. No wonder the other guns were so close to us at the finish. For a moment there, I was beginning to think I was losing my touch.

It wasn't many months before that we had won the 'Best Gun Competition' where initiative had played a big part in our victory. The best gun competition had comprised of all eighteen gun crews within the regiment driving around ten different locations. At each location there was somebody waiting to test us on various subjects such as first aid, field craft, gunnery, vehicle recognition and physical fitness to name a few. It was on the physical fitness stand that my crew and I had come into our own. We'd had to run fifty metres to a stationary Bedford wagon where there was a pallet of fifty F.H70 shells weighing in at 103lb each. The wagon had the side canvasses rolled up, so everyone could see the waiting pallet of shells. We had to get across to the Bedford wagon taking the shells off the pallet and then run another fifty metres to stack them behind another line. That wasn't the brief from the officer who was in charge of this stand though, I listened very carefully to what he was saying and what he said was that the gun crew must run from the first white line to the back of the Bedford. That bit was no problem, we would run the fifty metres and then climb over the back of the Bedford and get off the other side. I was going to leave one man on the rear of the Bedford to off-load the shells. The officer had then made a point of saying that 'we had to get the shells from the back of the Bedford to a pallet, behind the line'. Why didn't he say we had to *carry* the shells to the other side of the line? I thought. The reason had become clear to me because at the side of the little court they had set up for this race, there was an eager beaver (forklift truck) parked up. I could see quite clearly from where I was standing that there was a set of keys in the ignition. That was the give-away; you never ever leave a set of keys in the ignition of any vehicle in the army. I was sure it had been left this way for us all to see.

"What's the best time so far sir?" I'd shouted.

"Six minutes thirty two seconds," came the reply.

"Okay, Sir, we are ready," I'd called towards him. My crew had lined up like five sprinters behind the white line.

"On your marks, get set, go," he had screamed as loudly as he could. My crew had shot off like rabbits being chased by a greyhound.

"Stop," I had shouted at them. They immediately froze and turned around and were now looking at me very puzzled. "Pat, go and jump over the back of the Bedford then come back round here and get that Eager Beaver."

"What?" he had replied

"Just do it, and you lot carry on over the Bedford."

I looked over at 'The Rodney'. I was just waiting for him to stop me and tell me that I couldn't do that, but he didn't, he just smiled as if to say, 'yes, you've got it smart arse.' I was chuffed to N.A.A.F.I breaks as we bumbled up to the wagon and climbed over it very slowly. Within twenty seconds Pat had returned with the stacker truck and Rab was guiding the forks under the pallet of ammunition. Within the blink of an eye it was raised up off the wagon and Pat was reversing nice and easy over the rough ground until he was well over the line. He had lowered the pallet, removed the forks and parked the truck about five metres away. By this time we had all walked across the finish line.

I looked over at the officer and shouted, "L sub complete, finished, Sir."

"Two minutes eighteen seconds," he had called. "You are the sixteenth gun today and no one has even got close to your time, that's because no one has completed the task in the same way as you have. Well done lads. Fall out"

Joe had come over to me and said, "You clever Bastard."

"Nothing clever about that mate, sometimes you just have to listen," I had replied.

There was something in the army that you were always told countless times by instructors when you attended a course. R.T.F.Q. (Read The Fucking Question). It was meant for when you were taking exam papers at the end of the course, if you read a question carefully and then again, it would actually sink in as to what it was saying, and not what you wanted it to say. We also applied this way of thinking to a number of other scenarios and this had been a perfect example. Sometimes listening to the exact words that you are being told can save you a lot of hassle later on. Joe smiled at me as he walked away. I must admit though, I couldn't wait to tell the other gun crews once the competition was completed.

We only had one more stand to go and that was First Aid and we only needed a very small score from this to win the whole competition. I was getting very excited as I was a trained medic too, so there was little chance of us getting this wrong. Not only did we guess the physical fitness right, but we also guessed the First Aid stand right. It was a big casualty simulation scene where an Improvised Explosive Device (I.E.D) had been detonated and there were casualties all over the place with some pretty impressive and horrific injuries. I went to take charge of the scene as I would do under normal circumstances, when this officer stepped in and screamed to my crew that I had been shot dead and someone else would now have to take control of the situation. We were ready for this and Joe jumped in as we had rehearsed and did brilliantly. We got it right and yomped away with another high score, securing the win and the title of 'Best Gun' in the regiment. I was so proud of my lads; they had put a lot of effort in well before the competition and it had all paid off.

"FIRE MISSION ONE GUN, Direct Fire," screamed Lieutenant Joplin giving us the okay to flatten the village. I passed the orders over to my crew to prepare the Light Gun for firing. I looked along the level of the barrel and checked that it was aiming in the direction of the make shift post office. I looked again through my bino's to see the picture of a woman standing in the window of the post office waving. I looked closer and it became clear that the engineers had been playing. If there was one good bit of kit the army supplied the chosen few with, then that was the binoculars. They were really powerful and very robust. We found this out on more than one occasion when we struck our troops over the back of the head with them. Just as I was about to give the order to 'Fire', I did my final check and I couldn't believe what I saw, The Royal Engineers must have been bored when they were building this village because they had painted the woman, stood at the window with two fingers sticking up. It made me chuckle though.

"Number three, FIRE," I screamed. I watched the shell leave the barrel and followed the arse end of it until it piled into the base of the post office. As a result of this direct hit, we traversed the barrel and adjusted the elevation as we zeroed into all the buildings in the village. On some occasions we fired two or three shells. My crew were in their element and they were doing what they did best, making a mess.

"Bollocks to three shells in one minute," I hear Tam shout. "Come on lads, faster," he screamed. I would have been well upset if I were one of the ten men stood over on a small hill to the right. These were the engineers who had spent all that time building the target village. All that time and in all that rain and cold too, they had put all that effort into it and we pitch up and level it within ten minutes. We fired forty-five rounds into the village and it was totalled.

I didn't realise at the time, but as soon as I shouted, "End of Mission," there was a loud cheer behind us; it was the rest of the battery who had been watching us throughout the 'Direct Firing'. I think they enjoyed it as much as we did. I had managed to pass Paul O'Neil a big lump of tin foil just before he loaded the last shell. I didn't have to say anything to him as he knew what the tin foil did. It was a well known fact within the artillery that if you threw a load of tin foil up the barrel before the last round, it would make a reasonable attempt of cleaning your barrel. All you would have to do when you were finished was to give the barrel a quick pull through and it would be spotless. It was four o'clock on the Thursday and we were made up, we had finished the live firing phase with the Light Gun and were about to take it back to Sennybridge camp. The plan was to clean the gun and the one tonne, make sure our personal weapons were cleaned and then knock it on the head for the remainder of the day. As soon as we stopped at the garages, I detailed the crew to carryout various jobs on the gun, but there was one thing I wanted to do personally and that was to take the gun crew to the rear of the gun and give them all a bloody big pat on the back as they had all worked exceptionally well during this last phase. They were chuffed to N.A.A.F.I breaks and appreciated the 'Well done' from their crew commander. I got Joe Smiley to collect all our small arms and go away to the sleeping accommodation. He was to hand them into the armoury when he had finished and then come back up to the garages to help us if we weren't back in the billet by the time he finished.

We went through the wash down with both guns and one tonne, and when we drove out at the other end things didn't seem as bad as what I had first thought. One of the lads stripped down the breach and Mickey Hill took care of the muzzle break, which is at the other end of the barrel. The rest of the crew pulled the barrel through, which didn't take long as we had thrown the lump of tin foil up before we finished firing. Within an hour we had finished, I was impressed. The Light Gun was a lot quicker to clean than the F.H70 that was for sure. It may be the fact that the F.H70 was four times bigger than the light Gun. Joe Smiley had done well too, he had cleaned six small arms and handed them into the armoury. He was jogging back over to us when I shouted to him to give the F.H70 and Foden a quick once over so they were ready for the morning, it wouldn't be too bad though as we were having a late start.

The range wardens were behaving like little children at that time and working to rule, that meant that they wouldn't open the ranges until 09.00hrs. They were pissed off because the army had stolen two hours a day pay from them, apparently. I found out this info while I was having a pint in the N.A.A.F.I bar. I did only have one pint as well, this Welsh beer tasted like 'Wombat Bile'. I think they must have squeezed the water from the sodden peat outside the N.A.A.F.I door, dropped it into my glass, added a little gravy browning and served it to me at an extortionate price. It may have been funny to them, but I certainly wasn't laughing. If they wanted comedy, they had Max Fucking Boyce down the road; they didn't have to laugh at my expense. Wait until you come to Colly, I thought to myself. There were only about four lads from our battery in the bar, they were knocking the white ball about on the pool table, not because they didn't have the money for a game of pool, but because someone had broken into the N.A.A.F.I the night before and stolen all the money from the fruit machine, the pool table and the charity box. As an N.C.O they'd nicked the balls from the pool table. I sat at the bar thinking to myself, how low can the despicable man sink to? I mean steal everything else in the bar yes, but not the pool balls. That's lower than a snake's belly.

By the time I made my way back to the billet, it was clear that almost everyone was asleep. If we had to sleep and still hide from the enemy, we would be in serious trouble. The snoring sounded like a bunch of drunken tramps falling down the stairs in a library. It was horrendous and thank God, I had brought my earplugs. There was wet kit dangling all over the place and the fire in the middle of the room was blazing. It was so hot, that most of the troops had fallen asleep on top of their green maggots, even before they had made it to the shower. Sorry, the green maggot is what we used to call an army sleeping bag. Due to the fact that it looked like a green maggot! I wasn't going to fall in the same trap so I decided not to sit on my bed before I had taken my shower. I looked at my Maggie Thatcher (that was the name we gave our bed. Maggie Thatcher, *Scratcher*. Cockney rhyming slang. It was called a scratcher as that's what the troops used to do when they were laying on their bed... scratch... say no more!). No surprises in the showers then. The water was absolutely freezing. I wasn't asking for hot, just warm, it is really hard trying to scrape dried camouflage cream off your face when you have no hot water. It meant that you had to get your face in front of a mirror and scrub and scrub until it was all gone. You were left with a face like a slapped arse, beaming red. We had detailed four gunners to come and clean these ablutions in the morning, they were disgusting, it didn't take much to wash a shower after you had used it and place all your crap in the bin provided, but oh no, not this lot. There was empty soap wrappers, toothpaste tubes, shower cream and deodorant cans all over the place. I wouldn't have minded if the bin was full, but it was empty, the animals. I dried myself off, wrapped my towel around me and headed back towards the billets. It was only about twenty metres away but it was icy cold. Oh, it was heaven when I stepped back in the hut, lovely and warm I thought to myself. I then committed the ultimate sin, I sat on my bed. Next thing I remember is waking at quarter past three and climbing into the green maggot and then straight off to sleep again.

I woke up and looked over at my little alarm clock on the bedside table, it was only five a.m. I was so pissed off. I turned over and tried to get back to sleep, but my head was spinning. I was going over and over the gun drills for the F.H70 later on that day. We were all going to have to concentrate when we were live firing later, not only because we hadn't fired it on the ranges with live ammunition for a while, but also because we were at a critical stage of the exercise and so close to deploying for Belize and I didn't want any of my crew to be injured in any way. We were working fantastically well as a team now and I didn't want anything to spoil it. I looked beyond my clock and noticed a body leaning over a bed. He was dressed in his P.E kit and looked as if he was going to do a bit. It was Lance Bombardier Bob Baker.

"Where you going Bob?" I whispered as quiet as I could.

"Five miler," he replied. "Black Post Hill and back," he added. Black Post Hill was as it said, a black post on the top of a steep hill, two and a half miles from the camp. It was a good run and not too rough on the old feet. "You coming Sean?" he asked. And in the blink of an eye, I was out of the green maggot and tying the laces of my trainers.

"One minute," I said. I put a T-shirt and a sweat shirt on and my lightweight trousers. Before I could wipe my eyes, I was jogging down the road. What the hell are you doing? I asked myself. I had just joined Bob on a run, and neither of us had to do it. Truth be known, I enjoyed running and I was reasonable at it too. Bob also liked running and was very good at it, there weren't many in our regiment who could keep up with him, this being the reason, for me threatening to break his legs if he ran off too fast and left me. Bob came from Yorkshire and I think all those years of running from the law, when he was nearly caught nicking lead or coal had paid dividends. We made it back to camp in time to get a shower and grab some breakfast in the cookhouse.

"What the fuck is that?" I heard Tommy shout at the chef.

"Scrambled egg Bombardier," the chef replied.

"Scrambled egg, are you having a laugh?" he snapped. I was laughing at Tommy until I looked at the hotplate. Tommy had a point, I couldn't compare it to anything I had seen before; it was that bad it had what looked like a layer of dirty dish water over the top of it. "If you bunch of tossers fed me before I went to war, the enemy wouldn't need to pay their troops they could just pay you lot to cook for us. They wouldn't need fucking weapons,". Tommy said and with that he walked straight past the scrambled egg and onto what looked like a rubber fried egg, which was full of grease lying under the hot plate lights.

Tommy was proper on one, he liked his food, but he didn't like what was being served this morning. I sat down with him and he was still bumping his gums off.

"Don't worry mate, when you get on your gun, you can get one of your crew to knock you up a butty," I said.

"Ah, good call mate," he answered. He seemed to relax a bit once he was aware that there was a bacon butty in the offering later. "No wonder they call them 'slop jockeys' eh?" he started again.

"Just think of the butty mate," I answered.

When we got back to the billet, the N.C.O's split up and went to check that all the facilities we had used while we were there were now ship shape and Bristol fashion. I drew the short straw and went to check the bogs and showers, I walked in and I couldn't believe what I was seeing. They were still in shit order, it was only twenty minutes to the B.S.M's inspection and those bogs and showers were minging. I hurried back to the accommodation block and told the other N.C.O..s about the state of the toilets and showers.

"Right, you, you, you and you, in the bog block now."

All the other N.C.O's did the same and by the time we'd made it back to the toilets, there were fifteen to twenty lads scrubbing away, in the toilets, on the floors and in the showers.

"Come on move it you lazy bastards," I screamed.

"If we get it off the B.S.M, then you lot will get it back ten fold, and that's a promise," Bombardier Mark Wilkinson shouted.

Fifteen minutes later the toilets were clean and presentable. The B.S.M had done his rounds and bar a couple of points, all was well. Phew, that was a close call, I thought. I briefed my gun crew and specifically told them that I wanted more haste, less speed when we were bringing the F.H70 into action, I didn't want any injuries. They all nodded as if it really didn't matter to them. The F.H70 was capable of causing some serious injuries if you weren't careful. You didn't receive minor injuries from this piece of equipment, it was renowned for dishing out the bigger stuff like the odd broken foot, dislocated shoulder, burnt face, finger and/or thumb amputation and so on and so forth. The other concern was that there could be no mistake in laying this gun. The 'laying' of the gun was the process of making sure all the correct data was applied to the sights to ensure that the barrel was pointing in the right direction. If we aimed wrong the consequences could be catastrophic. One tiny bit out on the sites could be a long way out when that shell landed on the ground twenty miles away.

We were probably the last crew to finish setting up but we were all safe and well at the end of it. We still had the oil skin water proofs on that the B.S.M had scrounged for us. It was an ordeal trying to climb all over this gun with those on and I for one was sweating like a stuffed pig. I didn't care though, I was dry. I looked over at Paul and he gave me a big smile as he pointed at the kettle.

"Oh yes, nice one Paul, get the brew on mate," I said. He was already on to it, he must have read my mind, but I did like a cuppa though. If any of my team was in the shit with me and they approached with a brew in their hand, they knew they were in for an easier punishment, if they approached without then it was always going to be a bit of a disaster. This was an un-written law.

With the gun set up for the last day of 'Live Firing', Mickey Hill and Joe Smiley set about unwrapping the ammo. I looked at the first of the High explosive (H.E) shells to come out of its tube and be placed into the ammo shelter out of the wet. Shit, I thought. How big does that look compared to the Light Gun? We all got stuck into the job and unboxed the remaining shells. All except for Paul, his mission was a number one priority, the troops brew. We placed the last of the shells in the ammo tent and pulled the flap over them. Wet ammo was a big NO, NO in the artillery. It would cause you all kinds of problems when 'Live Firing', so it was in the gun crews interest to look after it. I looked up from the ammo shelter and Paul was shoving the hot brew in my hand.

"Oh cheers mate, you're a star," I said.

"No worries," he replied. I looked around at the other guns and they were still unpacking their ammo, we had caught up and with some good teamwork we had overtaken them. The exercise was no longer tactical so we retired to the back of the gun position and had a smoke. We were now waiting for the words 'FIRE MISSION BATTERY'. I had just put my cigarette out when I looked to the rear of the gun position, I noticed Lt Joplin leaving the command post vehicle and he was heading straight over to us. Oh no, not Joplin today, I prayed to myself. My prayers went unanswered as he began to speak.

"Listen in L Sub. You may know some of what I am about to tell you, but you will not be aware of the rest of it." It was clear to see that I wasn't the only one who was puzzled as I looked around at my crew. "We have got a number of young officers watching you perform today and as a special surprise we are privileged to receive another visit from the GRA."

Fucking privileged, I thought. Now, this was a pain in the arse, because when the General came to visit you in the field, he brought with him that yappy little dog he owned. 'Rufus' a small terrier thing which was an out and out bastard. He would let it roam around the gun position, shitting and pissing all over the troops while they were stood to attention. It had bitten eight of us on the ankles and feet last time he came to our gun position, and one N.C.O had to have a tetanus jab after the exercise because it bit him and broke the skin while he was feeding it some spam. The ungrateful little shit. I loved animals, but this one was an exception to the rule. Oh yes, there was another turd in the drainpipe regarding this animal.

When the General came to visit us on exercise he always flew in a Gazelle helicopter. His fucking mutt however, was driven in the C.O's car all the way from headquarters to whichever gun position he was visiting. That could possibly be a journey of over two hundred miles, in the C.O's car. The Commanding Officer's wife would have been made up the next night when she was picked up to be taken to the 'Summer Ball' and jumped in the recently polished car only to land on top of a dog turd. That would have looked smashing in the officer's mess that night showing off her one thousand pound designer dress with the newly acquired terrier turd as the 'not yet released' designer label on the back. Would you believe it? It was a bitter pill to swallow

110

and it got worse; if the General arrived and his dog wasn't at the location, there was hell to pay, Geordie Mee; the driver had to be on the ball. How ridiculous was that?

Oh, it got worse still for Geordie, because the G.R.A instructed him not to play music on the cassette player while the mutt was in the car as it would get distressed. That would have done it for me. Geordie told me once that he had actually put this to the test on the M11 one day and wacked on 'Paradise by the Dashboard Light' by Meatloaf. The dog turned into Devil mode and went ballistic; he had to turn it off, when the mutt started diving head first at the closed windows in an attempt to get out of the car. I think after this, I would have been tempted to leave the back windows open on the M11 and try out my new Madness tape on full blast. So, what had started out as a reasonable day had just turned to rat shit. I remember thinking, I didn't have a clue what this bog eyed general was called but I knew his bastard dog though. I think we nicknamed him General Isaiah due to the fact that he had one eye higher than the other. I had just finished a nice cup of tea and a cigarette, the rain had stopped during the exercise, my belly still felt full of food, I was warm, fit and healthy, until 'Lieutenant Happy' drops that bombshell on us. Marvellous, I thought.

"Oh, I look forward to seeing him again soon, Sir. We didn't get to meet him last week when the windows fell out back at camp," I said sarcastically.

"Don't be a smart arse Bombardier," he replied.

"Sorry, Sir," I answered. I looked over his shoulders and right on cue, the C.O's car appeared into view.

Oh look, I thought, not only has the poor Geordie had to deliver the mutt, but he has spent all that time cleaning it for the bloody dog! What the fuck is going on in the world? I could just imagine what was going thought the B.S.M's mind now. The car pulled up behind the command post vehicle but it stayed on the solid track so it didn't get bogged in, this was a disaster because it meant the driver was going to have to carry the dog. I was worried, thinking it might bite Geordie's face; he opened the rear door of the Ford Granada and out jumped the little dog. Thankfully, and for now at least, it was on the lead and poor Geordie didn't have to man handle it. The driver was under strict instructions not to let it off the lead until the helicopter had been and gone, we all had visions of it slipping its lead and being sucked up into the rotors of the chopper one day. How funny would that be?

'FIRE MISSION BATTERY,' someone screamed and we all sprinted back to our guns.

At the same time, I could hear that distinctive sound of a Gazelle helicopter flying towards us. The Gazelle is like the sports car in helicopters, and it landed with a ferocious speed. Sure enough, it was the G.R.A, he had landed on the gun position and before you knew it he was climbing gingerly out of the chopper. He was fair getting on a bit this chap; however, I wouldn't have liked to have guessed his age. The Gazelle took off again as soon as he had moved a clear distance away from it. The C.O's driver took his cue and let the 'Beast from Hell' go, it ran as fast as its tiny legs would carry it to the General then it was licking him and squealing all around him. When it had finished greeting its owner, the little dog took great delight in running around the position barking and biting everything it could. I could hear the troops all over the field shouting at it or whinging because it had attacked them. Numerous shouts of 'get the fuck out of here' and 'piss off' were ringing all around the gun position. The General would walk behind the six F.H70's and as he arrived at each gun, the crew would stop firing and 'fall in' at the rear of the gun. The gun number one would salute the General and introduce him to each member of their team while the other guns continued firing.

When the GRA had finished with one gun crew, they would start firing again and he would proceed to the next gun. The firing had commenced just as he started walking over to the guns. The young officers, who had arrived in a Bedford wagon, were placed to the side under a tree but in a good position to see what was happening. As soon as the G.R.A disappeared, they would join our gun crews and receive some serious training.

I heard Sergeant Taff Terry scream above the noise of the Artillery firing, "Detachment Rear." When his crew heard the order they all jumped off the gun and 'fell in' at the rear. We all carried on firing, it seemed like an age, before I spotted Taff's men jumping back into action on the gun and the G.R.A made his way to the next crew which was Sergeant Martin Tolly.

"Detachment Rear," I heard him shout. It was our turn next. I didn't look over, but I knew who was the last gunner on Martin's gun and as soon as I heard the general talking to him between bangs, I called my gun crew to the rear.

"Good Morning, Sir," I said as I saluted him. This guy was 'God' in the Royal Artillery world and with all joking aside he deserved a lot of respect. The gun crews all knew this and certainly gave it to him. I fell back in and remained at attention while he moved along the line talking to the remainder of my crew. It was hard at times to hear what he was saying as I was facing my front and the continuous bangs made it more and more difficult. There was a lot of high explosives being fired fifteen miles down the range by our boys.

Now, if I were to forget everything that ever happened in my army career, there is one event that will remain with me until my dying day. My head was facing straight forward, but my eyes were looking over at Taff's gun crew. There appeared to be a lot of activity going on around his gun. It was at this point I had to do a double take, I was sure I saw Ronnie Rowland pass the General's dog to Johnny Ashton and I was positive Jonny Ashton had just fed it into the barrel of their gun. No, surely not? Taff was staring at the General as if he was keeping watch. The charge was placed into the barrel after the dog and I then heard a distinctive loud clunk of the breach block dropping, sealing it closed. I was absolutely sure I could hear the echo of a small dog whimpering inside Taff's gun barrel. Oh my God, I thought to myself. They were going to fire the General's dog down the fucking range. Please Taff, don't do this please don't do it! I silently prayed.

The order came from the command post (C.P), "Number Two down Safety, Number Two FIRE."

I watched in what seemed like slow motion Ken Browning pressing the 'Firing Tit'. There was an almighty bang from Taff's gun, normally if you stand behind an artillery gun, you will see the shell flying from the barrel and you should see it for miles until it leaves sight. I did see the shell go, but I also witnessed bits of light material fling off to the right, left and centre and then float on down to the ground. I had never seen this before. I was in shock as the GRA threw up another salute in my direction. I hadn't realised it, but I had saluted him back and he was now making his way towards the next crew. I jumped back onto my gun and looked over at Taff; his gun crew were falling about laughing. Taff didn't even look phased, but he wasn't laughing like the rest of his crew. The dog had gone, it was no more. FUCKING HELL. I was trembling as the GRA finished meeting all the 'Gun Bunnies' and had started to make his way over to our command post, I could see him looking around for the dog. We had finished the display for the officers and expended ammo, there was nothing left to fire. I raced over to Taff.

"Taff, what the fuck, have you done?" I asked him.

"Did you not hear me shout?" he answered.

"No, what happened?"

"The bastard bit right through my boot and into my ankle and drew blood. I just saw red and thought it's your fucking turn son. How about you see red when you're flying down the barrel of a gun?"

He had instructed his crew to throw the bastard up the barrel as it had just bought a one way ticket to oblivion. That was it 'END OF MISSION', arrows in the head, brown bread, dead. The young officers didn't get to have a go on the guns as we had used all the ammo while meeting the G.R.A, but they didn't mind. They were young lads and would have ample time in their careers to fire big bangs. They had enjoyed the guns and commented on how professional we were. Fucking hell, if they had been at the other end of the line watching Taff make 'hotdogs', I wonder if they would have offered the same nice compliments? I was still trembling, because I knew what was coming next. I also knew how much this man loved his dog and what would happen to Taff if he found out where the dog was now. I couldn't believe that Taff had done this right under the G.R.A's nose. Fucking Hell, I always knew him to be mad, but not this mad.

"Fall in at the rear of the position," the B.S.M screamed. This was echoed by a number of sergeants shouting the same. It was like a mad hurry to get everyone together to speak to us all. You didn't have to be the brains of Britain to work out why. Oh shit, this is going to end in tears, I thought. Within a short time, we were all 'fell in'. We were stood 'at ease', waiting for someone to come out to the front and talk to us.

"Battery Shun," the B.C shouted. Everyone slammed in their left foot and came up to attention. "The G.R.A's dog has wandered off somewhere and we can't find it. Has anyone seen Rufus?" he asked.

Oh fucking yes Sir, Rufus is now a test pilot for 'The God Squad' and you won't be seeing him, I was thinking to myself.

"No, Sir," everyone shouted. He must have thought it strange that nearly seventy men and no one had seen the mutt for the last twenty minutes. I certainly would have.

"Right, I want you all to 'fall out' and the B.S.M will coordinate a search." We all turned to the right, and 'fell out'. It was pretty obvious that the B.S.M was going to have the 'Gun Bunnies' searching the area around the guns and likewise, all the echelon staff who were responsible for the second line services were going to look around a large area at the rear of the gun position where most of the vehicles were parked up. The last remaining area was around the command post and associated officer's vehicles. This was covered by the young officers and the remainder of our own troops. We all dispersed to head towards our areas of search. There were approximately fifty of us that made our way over to the guns, under the supervision of Lt Joplin. That's all we fucking need, Lt Lump head at the helm. If this guy found any traces of a terrier dog, then Taff would be right in the shit. We all walked over to the rear of the right hand gun, this was Taff's gun. If my heart sank, I can't imagine what Taff was thinking, he would be for Court Martial for sure had this 'murder' been discovered.

We all spread out in a long line covering fifty metres in front of the gun and fifty metres behind the gun. Lt Joplin set us off on a slow march scouring the ground and the undergrowth in front of us. We all sounded like a bunch of pansies wondering through the live firing ranges shouting 'Rufus' at the tops of our voices. Taff and I made sure we walked in front of the barrel of his F.H70 and made sure we had the rest of his guilty crew close by. We had only gone twenty metres when I looked on the ground at a point level with his gun barrel when I noticed clumps of what looked like rabbit fur in an area of about three metre square. Taff looked over at me and we both looked over at Joplin. Thankfully, he was on the opposite side of the line and he was talking to Bombardier Arnie Arnold. Taff, his crew and I quickly scurried around and started stamping on bits of fluff in the hope of concealing them in the mud. We were in luck, the rain had fallen for days and the ground was very wet and mushy underfoot. I was shitting myself, if we were caught now, it would be game over.

"Come on, keep up at the end," Joplin screamed.

"Yes sir," Taff shouted back.

That was it, we had our window of opportunity and now it was gone. It was time for us to catch up with the rest of the troops. I looked back and from what I could see, I was sure we had covered Taff's crime. It was now quarter past six in the evening and we had been looking for the deceased mutt for three hours and ten minutes, it had been dark for hours. We had every portable and vehicle light in use, lighting the area up like Wembley Stadium. The outcome was obvious for some of us, the GRA would order our B.S.M to leave a team to search for the dog throughout the night. We were right, and Taff got to brief them before we came away. It was reported the next day as predicted that the team had no luck in finding the dog! From what I heard, the G.R.A was gutted that his dog had done a runner and rumour had it, he made several visits to drive through the ranges of Sennybridge looking for this dog for months afterwards.

Chapter Six

GET ON PARADE

We finally got back to Colchester very late that night after enduring the heavy weekend traffic through London. When we returned to the barracks we were ordered to hand our personal weapons into the armoury and leave the guns until Monday morning. P.U.F.O. we called it. 'Pack up and Fuck Off' (leave all the mess and cleaning up for Monday morning). This wouldn't have been possible had we had to stay on exercise for another week because we would have been winging our way to sunny Belize on the Monday. The reality sank in as I walked over to the accommodation for a shower and a cold beer, one more week and we were off. God I could murder a beer, I thought as I opened my fridge door, there was one can of McEwen's Export. Fantastic, I thought as I pulled the ring pull and knocked back the first half in one gulp. I went from having a throat like a 'Swiss angler's maggot box' to feeling all revitalised in that one swig. After a long hot shower I polished off the rest of the can in one more swig. That was me done and ready for my Maggie Thatcher (scratcher). I lay on my bed with my television on, I turned the volume down, so I could just hear it and pondered over the previous week's events. I thought to myself how things would have to change, I had nearly scarred a W.P.C for life on the way to Sennybridge, my crew and I were responsible for changing the geological profile of Wales with the biggest chunk of plastic explosive known to man, and my act of 'I will always know better' and lastly, I had been witness to Taff destroying the G.R.A's dog. It dawned on me before I fell asleep that my life was NOT normal and something had to give.

The weekend went with a blur, we all spent most of it washing our personal kit, eating, drinking, sleeping and then getting our kit up to scratch for the Monday morning battery parade. I had a notion that because the last few battery parades had gone without a hitch, then this was the one. The B.C. and the B.S.M. were both pissed off on Friday night, so I thought that someone would be on the receiving end of a bit of brutality on Monday. My kit was going to be immaculate as I didn't want that someone to be me. I let Tommy know my thoughts in the cookhouse on Saturday lunchtime and he agreed. His theory was the same as mine, after some thought, and he too was going to be putting a bit of effort into it. We were to repeat our normal practise of me bulling his boots and him ironing my kit. He sent my trousers and pullover back to me on Saturday night. I couldn't believe how good he had ironed them. He could have marched them down the corridor on their own they were that starched. I was determined to do a job on his best boots for this. I spent an hour on mine while watching the TV on Saturday night and then I got stuck into Tommy's boots. They weren't that bad when I started, but when I had finished, they were super immaculate. I had even given them the finishing touch by water bulling them under a slow running cold tap in one of the large sinks in the toilets. This gave them an ultra deep glass like shine. By midnight that night, I was well impressed with them. It was too late to go and disturb Tommy, so I covered them over with a large yellow duster. I would pass them over to him on Sunday. My bulling finger was knackered and laying limp on the arm of my chair; it was now having a breather!

In addition to my thoughts of the B.S.M. and the B.C. tearing us to pieces on Monday morning on battery parade, I, along with the rest of the N.C.O's in the accommodation decided to hold a cleaning parade at seven o'clock on Sunday night. The troops had all cleaned their muddy kit in the toilets over the weekend and left them 'minging'. Our battery offices were above the accommodation, so it was obvious that the B.S.M. and B.C. would see the state of them on Monday. I didn't mind if the other accommodation block wasn't up to much, as long as we weren't 'picked up'. I walked to the cookhouse a number of times during the weekend and it was clear to see that the other troops living in this accommodation had made no effort to clean their side of the block; this could come back and bite them on the arse on Monday.

We all 'fell in' outside the battery accommodation on Monday morning ready for a ten mile run. Seventy men on parade, all whinging about the cold weather. It really was freezing cold and we were all wearing lightweight trousers, boots and a red T-shirt. I was feeling well rested, surprisingly fit and up for a bit of banter with the other lads. This was a bit naughty and always got a few peoples' back up, but it passed the time away and made the run a lot easier for some of the less fit troops. These runs had gathered a lot of pace now and we were fair shifting. Thankfully there were no Rodneys in attendance, so Chindit was taking the run. Unfortunately though, Paul O'Neil got the job of front marker and I dipped and got the job as the rear marker. I hated this as you were stuck fifty yards behind the squad to warn vehicles coming up behind you, of your presence. I was gutted and all thoughts of having a laugh with my crew were now well gone from my mind. If any of the squad were struggling with the pace and started falling back, my secondary role involved kicking their arses in order for them to catch up with the squad. Sometimes this meant physically dragging them along by the jacket. This was really hard work and gave me another reason to hate 'rear marker'. Mind you, I would rather be rear marker than front marker. Front marker was the guy who would be the first to be run over on a bad bend by the pissed up 'Raver' driving home in his car early in the morning. There were many near misses we could have recorded, where the vehicles had come way over onto our side of the road on a blind bend and nearly wiped out the front marker. You really did have to have your wits about you running or speed marching along the road. Remember we are talking 1982 here. These were the days well before High Visibility clothing. The nearest to high Vis clothing would be us tying a piece of white tape around our arm.

It was clear that Chindit was on one and before the run that morning he had taken his running pills and Lucozade. He was off like a rocket, I could hear all the fatties in the squad whinging about how fast the pace was, but it was in their interest to keep up. If you upset him and didn't at least make every effort to keep up, you could end up on remedial P.T. and believe me you didn't want remedial P.T. Not only was remedial P.T taken at night, every night for a week in the garrison gym, but it was taken by the 'Chinese torture squad'. It wasn't really, it was taken by our P.T.Is (Physical training Instructors) and there was only one word to describe these guys and that word was 'animal'. After a night of physical hammering by these animals there were three possible ways of leaving that gym; by stretcher (and not knowing what day it was), being

violently sick or in a wooden box. We were in the gym one night playing
Volleyball and watching the sick, lame and lazy receiving a pasting from
the P.T.I's and I have to say, I could have cried for them. It was nothing
short of brutal.

We had only gone about three miles when the slower members of
the squad started suffering. They were dropping like flies and falling
out left, right and centre. Chindit didn't have a care; he just ploughed
on at the same old pace. We all thought that somewhere along the line
he would slow the pace down to let them catch up. We must have
reached the five mile point and it was the B.S.M. who took the initiative.

"Chindit, slow it down, we have lost fifty men," he shouted between
breaths.

"No worries," he replied as if nothing had happened. The B.S.M.
was very fit, but I had a sneaky suspicion that even he was suffering a
little. I was lucky because I had been ordered by Chindit at the
beginning of the run to leave the stragglers and keep up with the squad.
It was a good job, with only twenty men left; it meant that I would have
had a job on my hands trying to retrieve fifty men. Chindit was a very
fit man. I am not saying I found it hard, but it certainly wasn't an easy
run and I was a lot younger than him. What a Monday morning wake
up call. It was normally the B.S.M. who instructs the senior that is in
charge of the run to give us a hard time. It was not normally the person
taking the run.

We arrived back at the barracks with only a few of the troops
remaining. I didn't know how many at first until I caught the squad up
once they had stopped outside the accommodation again. When I
stopped sprinting, I looked up and counted the remaining heads. There
were only eight of us left, one of them was the B.S.M, but I am guessing
by the look of him, he only just made it. I am sure that Chindit kept the
same pace, even after the B.S.M. had ordered him to slow down. There
would be something said about that later. We had lost all of the senior
ranks too, which wasn't good, three sergeants had fallen by the wayside.
Not that I am blaming them because it was such a fast pace. Looking
back now, I wish I had timed the run.

"Right, fall out and I will see you all at nine o'clock."

"Bombardier Connolly, you wait here until they all finish and make
sure they know to be on battery parade at nine," he said calmly.

"Yes, Sir, no problem."

With that every one disappeared, well, all accept Mark Hadfield who had positioned himself leaning over the gutter. He began to fill it with the sweet corn, peas, carrots and the customary yellow bile you get after mixing it with sixteen pints of Tenants lager and a ten mile run. Squaddies had no problem in being sick and reciting any sentence thereafter that started with 'God, Oh God, and God I am dying'. Mark wasn't the first soldier I knew who had thrown that much beer down his neck the night before a run. It was unfortunate for him that he drew the short straw with this one. Chindit had pushed it a little more than normal, so this had a major effect on his Sunday session. I had lost count how many times this had happened to me. To do this run at a normal pace with a shed load of beer was no problem, but Chindit had thrown a turd into the drainpipe today. After a steaming hot shower and a run at that pace, the cold light of nine o'clock, didn't seem too cold. Saying that though, I had to wait forty-five minutes for the last of the shirkers to arrive, before I could get near my shower. By the time the last man came in, I was freezing.

The B.S.M. saluted as the B.C halted in front of him. "Ready for inspection, Sir," the B.S.M. shouted.

"Thank you B.S.M. would you like to follow me round?" he asked.

"Yes, Sir," the B.S.M. screamed. He turned to the left and followed the B.C. with his pace stick under his left arm. "Bombardier Connolly, How are you?" he asked very quietly.

"Very good, Sir," I replied.

"Good boots and very good pullover Bomb. How long did your pullover take you?"

"Forty five minutes sir" I replied with a confident voice. Tommy must have nearly fainted when he heard me say that to the B.C. with him being the one who had starched my pullover to that standard. I felt a little guilty to say the least, what made it worse was the fact that Tommy was standing right next to me. The B.C. walked up to Tommy and stood in front of him. He looked him up and down a number of times. I thought to myself, if he finds anything wrong with Tommy's 'turn out' I would be very surprised.

"Good Exercise Bombardier Bamber?"

"Very good, Sir, although the rain got a bit boring near the end."

The B.S.M. gave Tommy the 'don't be a smart arse; I crack the jokes' smile before the B.C. spoke. "Very good Bomb. How long to do your boots?"

"One hour fifteen minutes sir for each boot," Tommy shouted as if he believed it himself. You lying bastard, I thought. Tommy must have been laughing his head off. The one thing Tommy would have agreed with though was the fact that we had got through the inspection without getting picked up. The inspection wasn't going as bad as I had expected with a few moans and groans until the B.C. and B.S.M. stopped at Gunner Mick Mcginty who was stood behind me. They commenced ripping him to pieces starting with his beret and working down. I made sure that my gun crew were in good order before they went on parade; thankfully this gunner was nothing to do with me. They tore him apart criticising every bit of his uniform until they got down to his boots. The B.C. looked at the B.S.M. who in turn looked back at him. The B.C. was pointing down at the welts on the gunner's left boot.

"B.S.M. look."

The B.S.M. looked at the boot and then looked at the soldier. "Mcginty look down at your fucking boots," he screamed in his face. I obviously couldn't see what he was pointing at, but I guessed he wasn't offering compliments to the lad. He must have spotted some dirt on the lad's boot as his next words were "Where does dirt belong? I will tell you where dirt belongs, in the fucking garden. Now get those boots off," he added. There was a short pause while I could sense that he was now removing his boots. I then heard a loud 'whoosh' at the right hand side of my head. One boot and then the second came whizzing past my head. The B.S.M. had thrown them about fifty metres away and they landed in the gardens outside the accommodation.

"Right, get yourself to the guardroom and lock yourself up for two weeks, tell the Provo sergeant, I will be ringing him shortly. Now fuck off out of my sight and don't you ever stand in front of the B.C. looking like that again."

"Yes, Sir," the lad screamed back. With that I heard him sprinting off in the direction of the guard room. My gut instinct was right and I knew this was coming. I thanked my lucky stars it wasn't me or anyone on my crew. The B.S.M. and the B.C tore through the ranks and all but jailed another soldier. This was getting bad now as it was an N.C.O.

That's all we needed, an N.C.O. in the nick. It would mean instant demotion for him on his return to the battery after him serving his time. It took an age for them to complete the inspection and there were berets, boots and pullovers all over the parade ground. The B.C. dismissed and marched off the square. The B.S.M. stood in front of us all and ripped us another arse. He went mental and said that this was one of the worst turn outs he had seen in a number of years and the next time he inspected the battery and we were found to be at this standard then he would jail the lot of us. He wasn't happy with the junior and senior N.C.O.'s. His last instruction to us all was that on Wednesday morning at 09.00hrs he wanted the whole battery to go to athletic trials. This is where the regiment fills a full day picking the teams that would go forward representing the regiment. I hated athletics, they was boring. Enough to make a glass eye weep, I thought to myself.

The B.S.M. wasn't stupid and he had Tommy and I well sussed. He had known us for a long time. He also knew what our individual strengths were. As we 'fell out' he shouted us over.

"You two, over here now."

"Yes, Sir," we replied together. We sprinted over to him and came to attention. I was puzzled as to what he wanted us for.

"The truth you two. Who did the boots and who did the pullovers?"

I got in as quick as I could before Tommy started to tell him a lie. "I did the boots sir," I said. Tommy stammered and then thankfully kept his mouth shut. It didn't take the brains of Britain to know who did the pullovers then.

"I am glad you told me the truth even though I knew the answer," he said. I have seen Chindit's best shoes and he told me Connolly had bulled them, so I knew who was best at bulling boots. I would like you to bull my parade shoes Bomb," he said. "I will slip you a few quid, don't worry," he added.

"No problem, Sir," I answered. I was just relieved that we weren't in any shit. He knew the score and he would be the first to tell a troop of soldiers that you work together as a team. You find out who is best at something and you swap tasks within the group to get the best results. There was one thing for sure; I wouldn't be bulling his best shoes until at least October. There was no need for best shoes where we were going that's for sure.

For the remainder of that morning we were issued the rest of our kit for Belize and then we spent a hard couple of days getting stuck into the cleaning of all the guns and vehicles. I wished we had started them late on the Friday night, as they were minging. Even if we had cleaned the barrel of the gun and all the working parts, it would have given us a good start that day. On Thursday we were to send the Light Guns back to Larkhill with the one tonne Land Rovers. The interruption in the middle of all this of course was the bloody athletics day!

We battered on through the Monday and Tuesday and had completed most of the work on the Light Gun and one tonne. One hour on the Thursday morning would do it and they would be ready to go back. That gave us the Friday to clean the F.H70 and the Foden and lightly grease them up for six months as we were flying out on the Monday morning. When you leave an artillery gun for that period of time, you have to put it into what they called 'Light Care and Preservation'. A very technical term for slapping grease over any part of the gun you possibly could so that it didn't rust. We would all set about the gun with a gallon tin of XG279 grease each and we wouldn't stop until our tins were empty. It was a bastard to remove six months later, but it was better than removing rust. Only an artilleryman would understand how proud he was of his gun. Your gun is the 'Queen's Colours', so with that in mind, you really looked after it. I used to go mad when we had visiting artillerymen from other countries, who would come onto my gun position and start slouching and sitting all over my gun. They often found themselves running around the gun position with a 103lb artillery shell above their head as a result.

CHAPTER SEVEN

THE LAST HURDLE

On the Wednesday morning as instructed, the battery paraded at the Garrison running track and athletics stadium down by the old medical centre. The sport's arena was a large area and well used by all the regiments within the Colchester garrison. It had a fantastically maintained running track which had all been white lined for the occasion and an open fronted seated stadium looking down onto the last one hundred metres of the track. How boring this day was going to be, I thought. Every man and his dog were there to watch you make a fool of yourselves. With the other batteries of the regiment present, there must have been over three hundred officers and men. It was a good job we weren't in uniform as we would have spent the day saluting the Rodneys. It was days like those that you get all the 'pomp and ceremony'. The officers spent their time boasting to each other and the sergeant-majors spent theirs telling each other whose lives they had just ruined. There were a lot of the officers and B.S.M's who were in uniform and some of them had brought their dogs along. Why can't this lot get roped into trying out for some of the athletic events, I thought to myself. What a blow, I suppose this is one of those times where rank has its privileges.

We were all dressed in our P.T. kits and we had to sit around in the outdoor stadium in the freezing cold until the B.S.M. picked us to join in a race or throw a shot, javelin or some other stupid drab athletic sport. I had done my exercises for the day. We'd had a nice run (without Chindit) that morning and anyway, before all this fitness stuff, I used to jump out of bed and say to myself, 'Up One Two' and then the other sock! That was about it for us lazy slobs. What a waste of a day when we could be getting on with cleaning the guns. We had little time left before the weekend and then the move to the Caribbean. I hoped the 'Advance Party' had got me a nice bed in Belize. I had two mates who had gone early so I was expecting something good. At least a bed near the bar.

One of the headquarters' officers had been given the job of looking after the shot putt with one of the PTIs. They had chosen three men from each battery to go through the trial. We all watched from the stadium as that and the triple jump got us underway.

"Hang on," I said to Taff. "Look over at the shot putt they have put Ron Harrison in it."

"You cannot be serious." Gunner Harrison had the coordination of a wooden leg and I just knew right from the word go that this was going to end in tears. Taff replied with a short, "Oh Fuck." Ron Harrison threw last and it was confirmed immediately that we were right. The shot landed with a thud with the long wire and the handle making a slapping noise on the ground. This would have all been fine and not a bad throw if truth be known, except it landed in exactly the opposite direction and landed only four feet away from the P.T.I. Bombardier who was running the triple jump. He claims that while he was spinning round with this thing, he lost his coordination before he let go of the shot. We would argue that he never had any coordination in the first place. I think everyone who spoke to him had the same answer and that was 'why didn't he just stop when he felt he was losing it'? Not Ron, it just didn't enter his head. We thought it would end in tears and it did. The Bombardier was a lot fitter and a lot faster than Harrison was and, having now caught up with him, beat him about the head with his right fist in front of the whole regiment. I was just glad that he didn't abuse him with the offending shot.

Lunchtime came and a number of people went to their own homes if they lived nearby. Some of the troops had robbed the cookhouse that morning so had brought their own sandwiches. Some of the troops stayed in the stadium and approximately twenty of us piled into the 'Bay and Say' pub on Layer Road for a quick pint. We were told by the R.S.M. to parade back at the stadium after lunch at 14.00hrs. Our B.S.M. repeated this, but added the bit which referred to broken skulls should we choose to be late. For Tommy and I, this wasn't even an option. I thought we were pretty quick getting to the pub, but I was wrong. By the time we arrived, there were already ten of our lads in the corner fighting over the pool table.

"Behave, you shower," Tommy shouted over to them.

When they heard his voice, they all calmed down a little and sorted themselves out. We ordered a pint and a bag of cheese and onion crisps each and went over to join them. I could see the relieved look on the barmaid's face before we turned away and headed in their direction. She was happy now that there was someone in her pub that could get a grip of this rowdy bunch of squaddies, should the need arise. Saying that though, these lads were all bark and no bite. They were just like babies having their teddies taken away from them. It turned out that they all wanted to play pool at the same time and it took Tommy to explain to them that ten people playing pool at one time wouldn't make for an exciting game. Most of the babies sat down leaving the two alpha males holding the cues. Paul O'Neil, from my gun and Pat Walters from Tommy's started to play the game and we threw back our beer and decided to have another pint.

We didn't worry too much as it was hardly likely that we would be picked for any athletics now. Most of the events had been covered that morning. Tommy went to the bar and ordered another round. Pat Walter spotted this and immediately jumped on the bandwagon, when he realised that it was his boss in the seat. It was really amusing though because Tommy hated spongers and Pat was as porous as they came. Not only that, but Tommy always told it as it was.

"Get your own you scrounging little fucker," he shouted across the pub.

"Ah come on Bomb," Pat replied.

"Fuck off," he snapped and that was his last word. The best Pat was going to get from Tommy was that he would put the order in at the bar, but Pat would have to pay for it himself. Paul won the game, so Pat downed his second pint and commiserated with another one. He had to get the round in anyway for losing the game, so it was a done deal that he was going to have another one. By the time we all left the pub, we'd all had more than two pints, I was half cut and was sure that the others must be the same. Shit, I thought. I hope I can hide in the seated stands out of the way for the rest of the afternoon as I would definitely struggle throwing the javelin or trying the high jump, that's for sure.

When we returned we did exactly as discussed. We all climbed right to the top of the seated area and got down as low as we could. 14.00hrs came and went and I had done a physical head count of my crew, all present and correct. That was it, I was going to relax with the lads for the rest of the afternoon. We just wanted all the keen athletes to volunteer for the remaining events and that would be it. It couldn't go on for much longer than an hour because of the early dark nights.

The B.S.M. stood at the bottom of the seated area and shouted up to all the battery. "Right heat one for the 400metre high hurdles, will be you lot," and with that he pointed to a right group of non-athletes from our battery. He couldn't pick a worse eight guys if he tried. I thought this was good; perhaps we had got away with it. Then, it dawned on me, 'Heat One', it was then I realised that there was going to be another eight people picked for 'Heat Two'. Shit. This was not good. He looked at the top corner where we all sat.

"Heat Two, Bombardier Connolly and your band of cowboys," he ordered.

"Yes, Sir. No problem sir," I lied. It showed how much I knew, he could pick a worse group than the first lot and that was this shower of shit. I couldn't believe it. He then picked 'Heat Three' and finished with 'Heat Four'. Even if we had missed 'Heat Two', we would have been captured one way or another. The top two in each race were going to have it out in a final race at the end. All the other lads in the battery, who knew we had been on the swill at lunchtime and who hadn't been picked for one of the heats, were now laughing like a bunch of school children after putting chewing gum on the teachers chair.

"Shut up dick heads," I said as I was walking down towards the track.

"Look at the fucking height of them," said Tommy pointing at the hurdles.

"I know, I'm not blind, it isn't called the high hurdles for nothing," I replied.

"Bombardier Connolly," came a call from behind me. It was Pat Walter.

"What's up Pat?"

"What's up?" he asked. "I'm as pissed as a fart. There is no way I can do that."

"Look, just run through them," I said. "You are allowed, I have seen it done," I added. "You don't even have to attempt them."

He looked relieved upon hearing this bit of news. What a bunch of piss heads, I thought. There was one consolation though and that was, I wasn't the slowest out of the eight runners, nor was I the one with the most beer inside me. I was sure that this would be a regimental disaster. As the yanks would put it, a 'Cluster Fuck' of the highest order. The starter pistol sounded for the first heat and the eight lads sprinted off. Well when I say sprinted, if you can call a resemblance to a wind up toy soldier a sprint then yes they sprinted off! It would be the second heat that would prove to be the laughing stock, not only for our battery, but the whole Regiment. This was going to look like something from a 'Laurel and Hardy' film. True to form, by the time the troops from the second heat got to the third high hurdle they were physically wrecked. It was fine for me and my bunch of pissed up Olympians to be laughing like fools, but it was our turn next. The first group were now running down the back straight and just entering the final bend. When I looked back at the hurdles that they had just jumped, or not jumped whatever the case may be, there was nothing but devastation. Hurdles were lying all over the track and some of them even away from the track. I would estimate that at least four out of the eight were limping before they even finished the race. The roar of laughter from the stand was huge. It was like a footballer taking a penalty for the opposing team and completely mis-kicking the ball in a cup final. The race ended with one of the best of the idiots not making too bad a show of himself. The rest limped home in dribs and drabs.

"Come on 'Heat Two', get your arses on the start line," the P.T.I. shouted.

You are having a laugh mate, I thought to myself. You will have to send out to the hurdle factory and arrange another delivery of hurdles; the last group have destroyed the first lot. The staff were frantically putting the track back together and lining all the hurdles up again. It was Tommy in lane one, Paul in lane two and then me in lane three. Pat was in lane four on my right and then the rest of the 'piss heads' on the right of him. We all shot off at the sound of the gun, I had told them all to pace themselves. Tommy not only had a gut on him, but he was only three foot six, he couldn't put a fag out. There was no way he could jump a high hurdle, so he just sprinted though them as if they weren't there. He obliterated the first hurdle which had a big affect on me. Firstly, with the beer inside me and then that I couldn't breathe, I was in bulk laughing. I could hear the carnage behind and at the side of me. I managed to make my way to the front but immediately thought about the consequences of the first two winners having to do it all again in the final race. I slowed down until three of the runners passed me in succession. This proved hard, because I was very fit and my height was six foot two inches, so jumping the hurdles was a doddle. If I didn't want to make the first two however, I needed to make them into a problem. Although it wasn't pretty, I could see and hear the first three lads starting to struggle in front of me and they weren't that far ahead. I could hear Tommy running through the hurdles with a loud slapping noise as he rammed them into the ground. I could also hear Pat on my right shoulder doing the same, but with not as much force as Tommy. Tommy may have been short and had a bit of a gut on him, but he was a very powerful man. Pat was a little taller, but a lot thinner and weaker than Tommy was.

We came into the final straight and I was dead on my feet. How the other three managed to stay in front of me was anybody's guess. I had two more hurdles to go and there was no way I was going to make a fool of myself in front of the whole regiment. I could see all the troops on my right hand side, up in the seated stadium. As each one of us jumped our remaining hurdles the crowd gave a loud cheer. I took an extra hard run up to my penultimate hurdle and cleared it easily. I was chuffed to pieces. I heard the loud cheer as Tommy slammed through his and then Pat through his. The last two lads were well back at this stage and a thought was just passing though my head that they had stopped for a 'puke break' at the side of the track when I heard the hurdles falling way behind us. Tommy, Pat and I now only had one left to clear. Me first, and again an extra special effort, and then a sprint to the line. Yes, I thought, as I was landing on the other side. As soon as I landed I heard Tommy's cheer and then slap as his last hurdle hit the ground. Just as I was crossing the line, I heard a crash and an almighty scream; it was one of the most sickening and most painful screams I had ever heard in my life.

I fell over on the finish line, I was attempting to turn around to see what had happened. I looked to my left and Tommy was just about to cross the line, he pulled up and we both turned together. I will never forget the image of Pat screaming on the ground. His upper body was riveted to the ground, but he was screaming in agony. I had heard a loud impact a split second before the scream and as I pulled myself from the ground and ran back towards him I noticed that the crowd was silent. I stood over him and looked at his right leg. I had years of medical training and had just completed a six week medical course prior to us deploying for Belize, however I think Stevie Wonder would have been able to see the injury that Pat had sustained. It was clearly, a broken femur which had turned the top of his leg to a right angle and the bottom part pointing downwards. It was a clean fracture, but very nasty. Pat lay there screaming and looking up at me with 'please, please help me' eyes. I screamed for Tosh Bagley to get a blanket from the ambulance. I needed to stop Pat seeing the extent of his injury and I knew that if he saw it, we would have no chance of calming him down. The first aid treatment for this type of fracture would have been to splint the leg and immobilise as soon as possible but there was no chance of splinting this leg due to the position it was in, and Pat was now thrashing out at anyone who went near him. He was in agony.

"Right get out of my way, I will sort him out," the B.S.M. of 48 Battery said. I looked up at what he was doing. He was disconnecting the lead from his dog's collar. For a minute, I didn't understand what he was attempting to do. I was about to tell him not to try and splint the leg, when he piped up again. "Right, we will tie his hands with this lead so that he can't hit anyone." This was a big mistake because as he said it he was starting to move down towards Pat on the ground. Pat was screaming before seeing the B.S.M. coming near him, but when the B.S.M. knelt in front of him attempting to catch one of his thrashing hands, Pats right fist came from underneath his body and sent a 'hay maker' to the top jaw of the B.S.M. Putting two and two together and witnessing the blow as well as hearing the crack, I was certain that the B.S.M. from 48 Battery was now sporting a broken bottom jaw for his troubles. What a stupid stunt to pull, where the fuck did he get this brainwave from, I thought. The B.S.M. went mental at Pat shouting how he was going to Court Martial him, but Pat was screaming back at him.

"Get away from me you fucking freak," he shouted. "I will fucking kill you and I don't give a shit who you are." I don't think anyone had heard any other soldier talk to a B.S.M. like this. It was understandable though, Pat was in agony. I looked over at our B.S.M. and I didn't have to say a word. He knew exactly what I was thinking. He stepped in and confronted the other B.S.M. His excuse for stepping in was to get him away from the scene, but also to get him medical attention as soon as possible. I just wanted him as far away from Pat as possible. He was a flapper and he had just made a bad situation worse.

It took me ten minutes to calm Pat enough to stop him shouting. I had ordered some of the crowd away as this was also affecting him. We had covered his injury and this in itself had helped the situation. My mind started racing and I was thinking about some pain relief, then I reminded myself that he had a belly full of ale, so unless we lied, he certainly wasn't in for any morphine. I looked up and looked over to my left.

"Thank god for that," I said under my breath. I could see the army ambulance pulling up on the running track. All the hurdles had now been removed to allow easy access. The two medics rushed over to see Pat lying on the ground. I raised the blanket from his leg. As soon as the corporal saw the leg, he asked me if I had administered pain relief. To which I replied, "No."

They never asked me or Pat if he had been drinking, and before I knew it the medic was drawing a capital 'M' on his forehead and writing the time he had administered it. I hadn't been away from Pat, but I never saw a needle or a syrette, anywhere. It was clear however some minutes later, that Pat had received some morphine. He now had a pair of pinpointed pupils and a lot of the pain had eased off. Later that night I learned that Pat had been turning to the crowd 'showing off' as he approached his last hurdle. He went to make a proper attempt to jump it to earn his big cheer from the crowd, but the alcohol and the exhaustion of nearing the end of this race had got the better of him and it all ended in tears. Most of us had witnessed some horrific injuries during our time in the British Army, and a considerable amount of us had seen death more than once, but the noise of that large bone snapping and the cries of pain that subsequently followed, I will never forget. To someone who was a trained medic then, and a trained EMT paramedic now, and who doesn't mind a bit of blood and snot, it has to be said that this was a sickening injury to treat.

The two medics returned to where Pat was laying on the running track and we agreed a plan on how we were going to lift him onto the stretcher. Military ambulance stretchers had a lot to be desired. Had there been such a thing as a 'scoop board' and inflatable splinting in 1982, the moving of casualties would have been much easier. With ten men and even more screaming from Pat we managed to get him onto the stretcher. Extra care was needed because although he was lying on his back, the fracture site was overhanging the edge of the stretcher. We lifted the stretcher together, on the medics command and the count of three we walked towards the ambulance.

"Bagley, get the door," I shouted. The two doors at the rear of a Land Rover army ambulance are on big return springs, so it's important that one man holds the door open so that it doesn't close on the medics while they are lifting the stretcher into the back of the ambulance. Between the ten of us we carefully passed the two handles on the foot end of the stretcher into the ambulance where two lads were now waiting. We continued feeding the stretcher in very slowly and very carefully. As I was on the opposite side of the open door and we had fed approximately half of the stretcher into the ambulance, I heard what I thought was a small bang and then instantly an almighty scream. I was confused.

"Bagley, I am going to fucking kill you," Pat screamed at the top of his voice. It was only then that I realised that Bagley had accidently lost his grip on the door and let it go. He was now scrambling and fumbling to retrieve it. We had all stopped in our tracks at the sound of the screams and when I looked up the ambulance door was resting up against Pat's broken femur.

"Get it you fucking idiot," I shouted at Bagley. He quickly regained his grip on the door and pulled it away from his leg. I spent a few seconds calming Pat down before we managed to get him into the back of the ambulance. The doors closed and one of the medics jumped in the driver's seat while the other stayed in the back with Pat. The 'blues and twos' were on and away he went.

"You fucking idiot Bagley, can't you do anything right?" I shouted at him.

"Sorry Bombardier," he replied.

"Fuck off out of my sight now," I said calmly. I had had enough and felt exhausted.

When I got back to our barracks it was time for some trough. I was starving and the shock of seeing Pat like that must have added to the hunger. There are times in life that you wish it could have been you, this was not one of them. I know he screamed a lot, but he was a braver man than me. There is no way I could have done that.

As soon as I opened the door to the cookhouse, Tommy appeared behind me. As we walked in, everyone was laughing and whistling the 'Jake the Peg' song. You bunch of bastards, I thought to myself, but I knew that this was their way of dealing with the trauma of what they had witnessed. It was a known fact that the SAS upon returning to Hereford after an operation would sell all their comrade's kit if he had been killed in action. This was a similar thing; it was their way of dealing with it. I also heard that the money raised by the S.A.S. Troopers at the auction was always passed over to the family of the deceased. All squaddies acted as if they didn't care, but they did, and jeering in Pat's general direction was the way this bunch of morons covered it up. However, they were all keen to know what would now happen to Pat. There was one thing for sure, he wasn't going to Belize. He would be sorely missed because he was one of the characters, always central to the joke. His sort was needed on a tour like this. I was waiting for my crew to appear and join in the banter; I knew my crew were real sickos when it came to things like this. I scoured the cookhouse but couldn't see any of my team and just as I had relaxed my guard, Rab jumped out from behind a six foot partition holding a chicken drumstick.

"Oh my leg," he shouted in a girly voice. "I think I have fallen over and bruised my knee," he added. At the same time he held the chicken bone up level with his face and proceeded to snap it. As soon as it cracked, the whole of the cookhouse were in raptures of laughter and applause and Rab started to mimic a cry like a little baby. Paul was standing behind him copying the same cry. We had to pass these two idiots before we got to the plates and chose our meal. As I walked past them both with Tommy in tow, I looked over at them.

"You pair of knobs," I said.

This was supported by Tommy who dealt them his favourite one worder. "Twats," he said.

134

It was funny though and we did say it with a smile on our faces. As I said, it was the troop's way of dealing with it. If Pat had two really 'good mates' in the regiment, well these two soldiers here were them two 'good mates'. They weren't hiding it from anyone, they were really concerned for Pat's well being. Tommy was even more gutted, he and Pat had served together for a long time and could practically read each other's minds when they were on the gun. Tommy never had to shout orders to Pat as it would be done before Tommy could draw breath. Apparently, Pat was brilliant at his job. I thought he had an 'all right' reputation regarding his work, but I didn't know he was that good. We endured the remaining 'dinner jokes' pertaining to chicken legs, spare ribs, frogs' legs etc whilst eating our meal. Then we had twenty minutes finishing our brew before we collected our plates and placed them on the 'plate wash' hatch. By the time we left the cookhouse, there were only three or four people remaining. The chefs had come from the rear of the kitchens and were just about to sit down for a cigarette to celebrate a job 'well done'.

It was 18.30hrs and I lay on my bed. I had every intention of turning my TV on, but instead I just let my mind rewind to the days events. I was an N.C.O, why the hell did I let a mate, get pissed knowing full well that he could be picked by the B.S.M. for something as stupid as high hurdles and get injured? It wasn't good. I closed my eyes and pictured him screaming on the running track in front of me. His leg bent at a ninety degree angle, I couldn't even imagine the pain he must have been going through. A long time ago, when I had first joined the army, I had been serving my basic training in Junior Leaders in Nuneaton. I remembered something that happened to me which made me think that I had broken my femur. I hadn't, but remembered distinctly that the pain was unbelievable. There were a number of sergeants riding around Bramcote Barracks on little mopeds. The sergeants rarely wore a helmet and the motorbikes weren't M.O.T'd or taxed as they were never taken off the camp. Once we had finished our first six weeks basic training, things on the camp got a little easier and we weren't beasted as much. I thought that if *they* could ride around the camp then there was no reason why *I* couldn't, so I went home on my first leave and bought a monster of a trail bike. I bought a Suzuki TS 185 cc. Any motorcycle under 250cc could still be ridden in those days under a provisional license.

With my provisional all in order I hit the road, I only had two days with my new purchase and had to be back at the barracks in Nuneaton. I put my motorbike on the train for the journey back to Nuneaton, I was still only a kid and there was no way I was riding down the motorway. I couldn't spell M6 let alone ride down it! It was an easy choice, the guards made sure they looked after my bike on the train and secured it well at Liverpool, Lime Street. When I took it off at the other end, I sent my suitcase to the barracks in a taxi and followed it on my bike. It didn't take long to ride to the barracks as it was only a few miles out of the town. I paid the driver of the taxi and then registered my bike, before I went to the guardroom for my case I took the bike to the accommodation block. My suitcase was full of food parcels and fags. The difference this time though was that I would get to eat the entire food parcel and not the dregs of them. In the first six weeks basic training, the sergeants used to open all your food parcels and steal all the chocolate, sweets and fags that your parents had sent you. They were complete bastards and bang out of order. Our parents had to fork out a lot of money to fill these parcels and send them to us, it was not good that these greedy bastards stole ninety percent of each one, handing over the only ten percent to the rightful owner. Had I been sent to Bramcote Barracks to train the new young soldiers later on in my career, I would have had more than something to say about the robbing from food parcels and certainly would not have been part of it. I thought at the time that it was disgraceful, and I still think it's disgraceful.

I went inside the accommodation block to put my 'skid lid' in my locker and on my way back out I was joined by five of my mates who wanted to ogle over my bike. After a few minutes, I left them to it and walked off towards the guardroom. That suitcase weighed a tonne; I felt every food parcel on the way back up to my accommodation. I couldn't wait to unpack it all and secure my goodies in my locker. Not that the lads would have touched it, we had got rid of the thieves in our troop, so it wasn't an issue leaving stuff around anymore. Once I had finished unpacking my 'tuck shop,' I noticed it was time for tea, I was starving and couldn't wait for something to eat. I went to grab my crash helmet, but then realised I didn't need it while I was on the camp. I put my gloves on and started my bike. When I arrived at the cookhouse all the lads were queued up waiting for the doors to open. I sat on my bike with the engine switched off and had a cigarette. As the doors opened and the lads began to file in, I finished my ciggie and joined the back end of the queue. There were a number of bikes on the camp now, but what was about to happen was going to piss me off no end. We had finished our work on the Thursday and I was going to take my bike up to the area where we used to carry out our P.T training and cross-country running. When I jumped on my bike, there was no one around. Once I started up, I made my way two hundred metres to the 'T' junction up by the sergeants' mess. I turned left and was immediately halted by the troop sergeant who had just come out of the mess. He jumped straight in front of my bike and it took all my efforts to stop me from hitting him. Had it not been a new bike and the brakes not as sharp as they were, then I am sure I would have hit him.

"Where the fuck is your helmet?" he shouted at me.

"I don't need one sergeant, I'm on the camp."

"What do you mean, you don't need one?" he snarled. I explained to him that no one wore a helmet whist riding around camp.

He went ballistic. "Who the fuck do you think you are?" he said. He wasn't impressed when I answered with my number rank and name. In fact he went stupid on me. "Get that fucking bike up to the garages and park it up. Bring the keys to me and then report to your B.S.M. in the morning," he screamed. "And walk the bike."

I was gutted, but had no choice but to obey him. I climbed off my bike and pushed it the quarter of a mile up to the garages. There were approximately thirty empty garages, so I walked it into the first garage. I put my bike on its stand I used my ignition key to lock the steering lock and then made my way back to the sergeant. He was standing at the side of the road where I had nearly run him over and he was quick to snatch the keys from me. Before he turned and walked away he reminded me to report to my B.S.M. the next morning. I was gutted. What about every other soldier who rode around the camp with no lid. Did it mean that if you were a sergeant then your head was harder than a junior soldier's head? What a Tosser, I thought.

At 08.00hrs the next morning I reported to the B.S.M's office. Sergeant Jones from my troop had marched me round to his office at a really fast pace. I slammed my foot in and stood to attention in his office. He made no secret that he had spoken to the Porteous troop sergeant and agreed fully with what he had said to me. The B.S.M. dangled my bike key in front of me. I was gutted and felt that I was already hung drawn and quartered. When I voiced my objections with respect, he went mad.

"Who the fuck do you think you are?" he screamed. "You are a little boy of seventeen, now fuck off and you can have the bike back when you leave Nuneaton. Dismissed."

No ifs or buts, that was it, no objection overruled. Shit. I was done. My sergeant marched me out of there quicker than I had entered. I was marching back to the block thinking that it was a new motorbike with seventy miles on the clock. It was going to be nearly a year before I got it back, that it was a travesty of justice. What made it a lot worse was the fact that all the sergeants continued to ride their bikes around the camp with no crash helmets. The other couple of junior soldiers who were riding around as I was were now wearing their lids. Good on them, but too late for me. Every month I was permitted to start the bike for a short period but not ride it. I had to march around to the B.S.M, collect the key from him, start the bike and run it for ten minutes before returning to the B.S.M. with the key. I would wash the bike every week on a Sunday morning and then polish it before locking it up once more. It upset me every Sunday and every time I heard a moped or motorbike come past me or even if I heard one in the distance. I would go into Nuneaton on Saturday afternoons, with a couple of my mates, and I was guaranteed to see at least one Suzuki TS 185. Most of them were the same colour as mine too, I think someone up there was rubbing it in.

As the time went by, I was getting more and more frustrated with the fact that I was the only one punished for this offence and everyone else got away with it, and still continued to get away with it. I hated that B.S.M. for this and it got to a point that I hated being in his company. Whenever I had a choice to be in his presence, I was gone. He was a complete knob and I hated him. He was spineless and I should have had the balls to either tell the sergeant to 'fuck off' and leave me alone, or at least to approach the Regimental Sergeant Major (R.S.M.) and attempt to stop the rest of the sergeants from riding around the camp with no helmets.

In September of the following year, it was time for us to leave Junior Leaders, we had been told what regiment we were going to and we had been issued our train and air tickets to send us on our way. I was off to meet my regiment in Gutersloh, West Germany. With my case packed and the taxi ordered, the time had come for me to face the B.S.M. one final time. I took great pleasure in asking him for my motorbike key for the very last time. The bastard could have let me have it a week or two before we left, but no chance of that. He really was the full package.

"Where have you been, I have been waiting to go to the mess?"

"Sorry, Sir."

He pushed the key along the table and I stopped it falling on the floor. The bastard never even said goodbye, he just pushed past me and stood holding the door handle. He waited for me to walk out of the room. I marched out and heard him lock the door. Like him, I was going to make no attempt to say anything further, I didn't like him and there was nothing nice to say to him. All he was interested in was getting pissed in the sergeants' mess. I sat on my bike and waited for the engine to warm up fully, knocked the choke off and then clicked it into first gear. I thought about locking the garage after me, but that's as far as it got. I couldn't be bothered with it as I wasn't ever going back there so why should I care. I was still fuming with the B.S.M. and I couldn't get the details of the final meeting with him out of my head. The heartless bastard, I thought. It was no good, I just couldn't leave. I arrived at the junction where I should have turned left to head down to the guardroom and the main gate. I looked directly in front of me and I could see the B.S.M's office where I had marched every week. I knew he wasn't in his office, so maybe one last visit I thought. The lawn outside his office was immaculate and there was something that pulled me towards it.

I proceeded with caution in case anyone was watching me. I stopped outside his office. I looked around for a minute, but couldn't see anyone around. It was late Friday afternoon and everyone had knocked off. I turned my bike onto his lawn and leaned it right over to the left, keeping my left foot on the ground; I revved the bike and let the clutch out. The bike spun round in 'doughnuts' up to the point when I was starting to feel dizzy, like spinning around in the playground when I was little. I grabbed the clutch and stood the bike back up, the bike stopped and I looked down at the mess, it was a lot worse than I thought it would be. It was at this point that I shit myself, I panicked and hammered the bike off the lawn. I rode as fast as I could towards the guardroom and headed for the main gate. If someone had witnessed me causing this vandalism, they would have had to make their way to a building and then to a telephone where they would have to ring the guardroom and tell them to stop me.

I stopped outside the accommodation and said a silent prayer to myself. I was hoping the car outside the block was the taxi that was taking my case to the train station. It was, and I practically threw my case into the Cortina. I overtook the car before he even pulled away from the building and I screwed it through the gears, the bloody bike wasn't even 'run in' yet and I was riding it as if my life depended on it. It did! If I had been stopped I would have been in a lot of trouble. It was a stupid thing to do anyway, as I may still not have got away with it. I had the main gate in sight; it had an electric barrier operated by the staff in the guardroom. I slowed the bike right down and tried to keep it as quiet as possible, I was getting too close to the guardroom now, but before I had decided to pull over and try to hide, I noticed a car pulling up at the barrier. As soon as it had been cleared to enter the camp and the barrier started to rise, I was going to go for it. Within a few seconds it happened. The barrier stuttered and then started to rise, I seized the day and hammered the bike through every gear until I was at a point when there was no way they could stop me leaving without shooting me.

I was so relieved as I turned out onto the country road and in the direction of Nuneaton train station. Before I could say 'get a new lawn sir', I had arrived at the station. I parked right outside the main doors of the station and waited for the taxi to arrive with my suitcase. I stopped one of the station staff and asked him about the train to Liverpool. The train was on time and with no problems. He was looking after this particular train anyway. It was only after he had gone that I thought, I should have asked him which platform I needed to go to with my bike. As I was finishing my cigarette, the taxi pulled up. I asked the driver if he would hang on for one minute while I put my bike on the train. He nodded his assent. I told him that I would make it worth his while. I started my bike up and rode into the main part of the station when suddenly; I spotted the chap who had originally helped me. I stopped at the side of him and raised the black visor on my full faced helmet.

"Which train mate?" I asked him.

"There mate." He was pointing to a train sitting at the very first platform. "I have put a ramp for you to push your bike up when you get to the guard's van," he added.

"Thanks mate, you are a star."

By this time, I looked down the platform and had noticed four gorgeous girls standing by the ramp outside the guard's Van'. Push my bike up the ramp my arse, I thought. Not bloody likely, with my black full faced helmet, black leather jacket, black chord trousers and cowboy boots, I accelerated my bike down the platform towards them. I was going to show these girls just what I could do. The bike must have reached thirty miles per hour down the platform when I decided it was time to slam on the anchors, I hit the brakes and skidded until I was about six feet away from the girls. I could see them all nudging each other and I was sure that they were well impressed. They hadn't seen anything yet, I ripped the accelerator as I let the clutch out leaning the bike to the right. I was now dead in line with the ramp. I kept looking at the girls, I stopped and lifted the visor on my helmet. They were all staring at me and smiling in my direction, I dropped the visor once more, engaged first gear and pulled off with a cracking wheelie. The bike shot up the ramp and onto the train, as I dropped the front wheel, I turned my head to the front.

It was at this point that I noticed the other side of the carriage was open and it was impossible to stop my bike. It flew off the other side of the carriage with me sitting on it and I crashed to the ground. The pain in the top of my leg was so intense I was nearly crying. It must be broken, I remember thinking. I couldn't shout though as I remembered the girls, I could hear shuffling around on the train behind me and I just knew it was the four girls. I could hear them laughing at me and I am sure I heard one of them say 'what a Tosser'. I was so ashamed and embarrassed and could do nothing until help arrived. It did, and it was the guard who had pointed me to the train.

"I told you to walk the bike on, not ride it."

"Sorry mate." After the initial pain had subsided a little and the girls had disappeared, the guard and his mates helped me and the bike up. We managed to get the motorbike back on the train just as my suitcase turned up for the journey. It turned out that it wasn't only my pride that was hurt and of course the front forks on my bike which cost me a fortune to replace. I hid on the train all the way to Liverpool, I really didn't fancy bumping into any of the four girls, they must have thought I was a complete idiot. I just felt lucky that I hadn't broken my leg. This was what is now known as a 'near miss'.

As I lay on my bed now, I thought back to the incident with Pat and the hurdles. I couldn't even begin to understand the level of pain Pat must have felt while he was laying on the running track with a snapped femur. I felt sorry for him again.

Two months later while we were in Belize, we heard that Pat had been taken to Woolwich Military Hospital where they had to do a special job on his leg. The army was poor at keeping you informed about the welfare of a sick mate. Apparently, it was a bad break and it called for some specialist treatment. Woolwich hospital had some of the best military medical staff in the world. Pat hadn't received the nice clean break that I thought he had. When we returned from Belize and saw his scar, I couldn't believe it. It went from just under his stomach to the top of his knee cap. Apparently he had a tungsten frame wrapped around his leg for six weeks. What followed after that six week period we all thought was very funny and could only happen to Pat. The day they removed this cage from around his leg was the day Pat decided that he would escape from the hospital and go to the pub, anyone else would have waited until they had been discharged from the hospital, but oh no, not Pat. He is the only soldier that I have ever heard of that had been charged for misconduct while they were in hospital.

Pat decided that he would somehow get himself to the pub closest to the hospital. It had to be one that was within hobbling distance and then he could throw a couple of beers down his neck. Remember the bit where Pat drank too much one lunchtime and it ended in tears on the running track, well he hadn't heeded the warning and he had just done it all again. Although he didn't mean to, he got wrecked and tried to get back into the hospital late at night without anyone seeing him. He had made it to the lift and when he got in it he slid down the wall and fell asleep. He was found upside down by one of the nurses who must have shit herself at the sight of Pat out cold on the floor. She surely must have thought he was dead. I believe 'Harry the Bastard' (our R.S.M.) drove down from Colchester to Woolwich to charge him. This was another stain on his career that he could well do without. He was a funny guy Pat, but he knew how to drop himself in the shit without too much effort.

On the Thursday morning, the day after Pat's misfortune, I bumped into Gunner Mick Mcginty in the Cookhouse.

"Hey Mick, what the fuck are you doing out?" I asked.

Mick was the gunner standing behind me on battery parade on Monday and had been told to lock himself up for two weeks and he was now in the cookhouse on his own. When you get thrown in the nick, you aren't permitted to go anywhere without two of the regimental policemen escorting you. He had no one with him so I had guessed he was a free man.

The B.S.M. had had to release him because we were going to Belize on Monday. Now there was me thinking that the B.S.M. was the same as me, and that he too had a heart pumping the blood around his body. Silly me. I thought it was too good to be true. The B.S.M. had told him that he could continue his sentence when we get back from Belize. I was laughing my head off.

"Just think Mick, it could be worse, it could be me," I said sarcastically."

"Bomb, with all due respect, fuck off," he replied. I left the cookhouse with a big smile on my face.

As I was walking over to the garages after breakfast, I could see everyone beavering away on the guns. The lads had finished the Light Guns and they were busy working on the F.H70. The Foden was already cleaned and was parked up on the regimental square. It had been finished and wiped with the oil and it looked immaculate. I was just about to shout over Joe Smiley when I heard a voice behind me.

"Bombardier Connolly," it called. I turned round and it was Sergeant Bernie Diamond.

"Hello Sarge," I said. "What can I do for you?"

"No, it's what I can do for you he replied." Bernie was a really good sergeant, one of the best and a nicer man you couldn't meet. He was often criticised by his peers for being too friendly with everyone, but he was one of these N.C.O's that didn't need to shout at a soldier to get him to do something. He would get better results from his team by instructing them when it was needed. I had a lot of time for him.

"The B.C. is going to inspect the guns at lunchtime tomorrow and if they are up to spec, he is going to knock everyone off for a long weekend," he started. I looked at him. This was good news, but I felt he wanted to tell me more. "I can't go anywhere as I am orderly sergeant, unless of course I am out on a test."

Orderly sergeant was a bastard of a duty for a senior rank. It tied them to the camp for twenty-four hours at a time. There were however, ways of escaping if you knew how and Bernie knew how, the penny finally dropped. Bernie was a Qualified Testing Officer (Q.T.O.), a driving test officer, for all classes of licence. I had previously taken five H.G.V. lessons and had to put further lessons on hold because of Belize.

"Do you want to take your test tomorrow on the Foden?" he asked me.

"Too right Sarge," I answered.

"It beats sitting around in camp for the day and it's the only way I can get out," he explained.

"No problem Sarge," I said.

"One o'clock at the training wing. I will bring the wagon over, and don't be late," he finished.

"No Sarge, not a chance and thanks, I'll be there."

I wasn't ready for my test, I was sure of that, but my driving instructor must have told Bernie that I was or he wouldn't have asked me. Shit, I thought, I had better get back in the cab of the Foden and try and remember everything I had been taught. If the B.C. had given a hint to us knocking off early tomorrow then it was a dead cert that I was going to be taking my test in just over twenty-four hours. I climbed up into the Foden cab and sat in the driver's seat. It was only a matter of minutes before I remembered all I would need to start and drive the thing. The Foden was a huge wagon and it was important that you quickly appreciated this as it would be too late when you were parked on the top of a Ford Fiesta. They were very fast too. The thirty miles an hour speed limit was very difficult to keep to. You would often look down at the Speedo and see that you were doing fifty through the town centre.

I climbed down from the Foden to the sight of the Light Guns disappearing through the rear gates, knowing the next time I saw a Light Gun I would be in Belize. Those six that were now being returned, they'd done us proud over the last few weeks and I was beginning to enjoy working on this artillery piece. My next stop was the garages and kicking the lads' arses so that the F.H70s were finished by Friday lunchtime. I wasn't just chasing my lads up, but all six crews. Everyone was working hard and fast and I was pretty confident looking around the garages that we would be knocking off at lunch time. This was good for me, because it meant I may be the holder of a H.G.V. licence before I flew out to Belize.

There was one small issue though and that was that I had to pass my test. Bernie, the testing officer was a fair man and we got on well, so I was hoping that he would go easy on me. All of the Foden were now on the main square and were clean. This was good as it meant that all of the crews were mucking in on the guns. On Friday morning there was no early morning run to put up with. All the efforts were put into getting everything cleaned up from the exercise and parked up in the garages. The B.S.M. had sent a message round to all the senior ranks within the battery to tell them to have all the equipment, gun and Foden ready for inspection at eleven o'clock. The B.C. was going to inspect the equipment and address the Battery before we deployed for Belize on Monday. This would be the chat that reminded us all that if we didn't turn up on Monday then we were in severely deep shit, for which he would control the boot on our heads that pushed us deeper and deeper. This would be the one where the R.S.M. and the guardroom staff would take you to a new level of pain should you decide to turn up late and miss the flight. It's a conversation that I would be repeating with my gun crew after the B.S.M. and the B.C. had finished. We had rehearsed and practised hard with the Light Gun and I didn't want to get to Belize with one or two men short. I have to admit though, I was pretty confident about my crew turning up on Monday as they all really wanted to go to Belize. If they went out and got wasted on the Friday and Saturday nights, it wouldn't do them any harm to not drink on the Sunday night but I needed to reiterate this to them.

At ten o'clock, the last gun was brought onto the square and received the final wiping down ready for the inspection, we had plenty of time to sort any last problems out should there be any. One word about knocking off to the troops and they would pull out all the stops. We waited for the arrival of the B.S.M. and then the B.C. The B.S.M. carried out a smart salute to the B.C. and then he fell in to the side of guns. The B.C informed us that he was going to inspect the guns and Foden and if they were up to scratch he would knock us all off until 04.00hrs Monday morning. The B.S.M. joined the B.C. once more and they walked around the equipment, from what I could see everything had gone to plan and there were no real problems with anything. The B.C. marched to the front and told us all to move in closer to him and stand at ease.

"As you all know on Monday 5 April the battery will be deploying to Belize with one hundred and three men for an operational tour of duty," the B.C. said. "Remember that figure, because when the B.S.M. counts you all on Monday morning, that's the number, I want him to report to me. Not one hundred and two, but one hundred and three. Does everyone understand me?" he added.

"Yes, Sir," we all shouted.

"Should you be the individual who decides to fuck my maths up, then don't bother coming back," he added. "Now the good news is you may all knock off and have a long weekend." He turned to the B.S.M. and said, "B.S.M. take over please," and with that the B.S.M. brought us all up to attention. He and the B.C then swapped salutes.

The B.S.M. waited until the B.C. was out of earshot and he looked at the rear of the squad to make sure there were no other Rodneys present. "Let me echo what the B.C. has just told you. Anyone late on Monday will have me to deal with, is that clear?"

"Yes sir," we shouted. That pretty much did it for us all really, the thought of the B.C. hunting you down for the rest of your life, or the vision of the R.S.M. and his Provo staff punishing you until you were fit to cry, and then the picture of the B.S.M. breaking your sternum with the hardest punch you were ever likely to receive, just about sold it for me. It would take a coronary thrombosis, a coma, or an incident, where I was sat upstairs on a double decker bus which had just driven under a low bridge, to stop me turning up on Monday, there was no way I was going to miss that parade.

The troops all raced to put the guns away after the inspection. I was one of the N.C.O's who had been detailed by our troop sergeant major (T.S.M.) to stop them behaving like naughty schoolboys and crashing into each other while they were in the process of doing so. They could be a little heavy handed and a little hard on the accelerator when they were excited. One hundred and three men running around like the first year primary school going to the swimming baths for the first time. I looked over to the far side of the square and I saw Bernie driving one of the Fodens towards the training wing. My heart skipped a beat but I don't know if it was from the excitement and anticipation of me taking my test or because I thought I wasn't ready for it.

He returned a short time later and walked over to me. "See you at one Bomber," he said in passing and he threw the vehicle keys at me.

"Okay Sarge, I'll be there," I replied. He carried on walking in the direction of the cookhouse. The order sergeant duties must have been a pain in the arse at meal times. As well as reporting to the cookhouse and watching us eat our lunch, they had to deal with, and often carry whichever officer was on orderly officer duty because nine times out of ten, the Rodney didn't have a clue what to do. The sergeant and the officer had to walk around the cookhouse asking all the soldiers what the food was like. If a junior soldier complained about a particular food or meal then the sergeant or officer would taste it. If, it was then confirmed that it was below standard the sergeant or orderly officer would go and have it out with the 'slop jockeys'. This was a very dodgy process though because the 'slop jockeys' would always be watching, and the squaddie that made the complaint would normally be wondering why their next meal in the cookhouse, tasted of human sick.

By the time lunch had arrived, I had studied, another good half hour of the 'Highway Code' book which made me feel a little more confident. Tommy and I met as we were walking into the cookhouse as we went through the door we could hear that Bernie was already having a dig at one of the cooks, but we couldn't see what it was all about, we were too far down the queue. It had to be something serious to get Bernie in a state. It was only when I was half way through my lunch that I thought to myself, Well done 'slop jockey'. Piss my sergeant off why don't you? That's gonna go down well on my driving test in an hour's time. Well, thanks for fuck all, oh and by the way, your food is shit.

"Are you two coming for a pint in the N.A.A.F.I. after lunch"? Mick Hall shouted over.

Tommy replied, "Yeah count me in, I could murder a pint."

"What time you going?" I asked.

"Two o'clock," Mick answered.

I was confident that the driving test wouldn't be much more than an hour and I could kill a pint as well, so they counted me in. Tommy wanted to come down to my room and go over to the N.A.A.F.I. together, but I said that I would meet him over there. I hadn't told anyone that it was my H.G.V. test and I had sworn my driving instructor, Sergeant Shaky Moor to secrecy.

"What the fuck are you up to?" Tommy asked.

"Nothing, I have just got something to do and then I'll be over. I'll tell you after". He looked at me as if I was about to drop myself in some kind of trouble again. "It's all right, it's nothing bad," I said.

"I hate it when you go all 'cloak and dagger' on me," he finished, as he was standing up to dispose of his plate.

"See you in there," I said as I left the cookhouse. I went into my room, picked up the keys for the vehicle, my licence and my 'Highway Code' book then headed over to the training wing. I arrived at the vehicle fifteen minutes early and checked the Foden over. Tyres were a big thing on this particular vehicle as they were known for losing big solid chunks of tyre tread at both low and high speed. There wasn't much we could whinge about with this wagon, but this was definitely one of the negatives. Having started the engine up, I checked my lights and indicators. All was well, the vehicle 'Work Ticket' was on the passenger seat so I filled my details in on the new page. My number, rank, name, destination and that I was taking my driving test. When I lifted my head up and started to set the position of the seat, I could see Bernie in the distance walking towards me. When he arrived at the Foden, he walked around to the passenger seat and climbed into the wagon.

"How's it going Bomb?" he asked.

"Good Sarge, just carried out first parade," I replied. First parade was a name that had been adopted by the army for checking the vehicle over before you drive it. The first driver of the day would have carried this out well before me taking my test this morning, but I thought it would always stack up in the old 'Brownie Points' locker, if I had checked the wagon over prior to the test. The old saying went, 'if you can't dazzle 'em with brilliance, baffle 'em with bullshit', it's a saying I still abide by.

"Okay, let's go," he said as he started to fill out the test sheet. Brilliant, I was off, by the time I got to the 'T' Junction, he hadn't told me which direction to take. It had to be left or right, but he was still engrossed in filling in his paperwork.

"Which way, Sarge?" I asked him.

"Oh er er just go right and then stop at the newsagents," he replied.

No problem; I thought. There was a little newsagent which was part of Colchester Town Football Club, it was very popular. I pulled up as close to the shop as I could. Handbrake on, out of gear, hands back on the steering wheel, text book, all good, I thought.

"Right, hang on here," he snapped and he was gone. It was only when I waited a second that I saw the top of his head, it was clear that he was going into the newsagents. He returned with a newspaper and two bags of crisps. "Right carry on," he ordered, and with that he opened the 'Daily Mirror'.

I couldn't believe it, he never muttered a word. I drove right down Layer road and headed to the town, but came to a point that I thought he didn't know where we were up to or even possibly that he had forgotten that he was taking me on a driving test.

"Where do you want me to go Sarge?" I had to ask. He looked up from his paper for the very first time.

"Oh just go along the High Street and then through the town centre and then go the back way into camp," he replied. He started to open a bag of cheese and onion crisps. "I saw you in the queue, did you eat that lunch?" he asked. I couldn't believe it, I was on my test and he didn't have a care in the world. His newspaper was still on his lap and he was now tucking into a bag of crisps. He had given me the worst directions I had received during my army career and all he wanted to talk about was the cookhouse. Fine by me, I thought.

"Yes why Sarge? I saw you talking to the chef," I said.

"Talking to him," he snapped. "I found a fucking mouse tail in the bratwurst; believe me I was doing more than talking to him." He finished talking and sunk his head back into the paper. "I wasn't eating that shit," he muttered.

It turned out to be the best drive I had ever had in the Foden and I was a little pissed off that he was missing it. I felt very relaxed and had no drama to contend with throughout the test. Had it been two or three hours later however when Colly was gridlocked in the rush hour, then it may have been a different story, fortunately for me it was only a little after one o'clock so the town hadn't yet spilled over. I did as Bernie instructed and took the semi rural road back to camp. It was a great drive and another plus for this vehicle, was that it was so high off the ground, you could see above most other vehicles and any other obstructions, which helped when it came to reading the road ahead. I was bombing down these country roads and looking over the high hedges to see what was coming around the bend from the opposite direction. I was having myself a little competition at this stage. I was seeing how far I could get through my test without Bernie looking up from the newspaper and I was doing well. He hadn't even moved except to turn the page. It was really funny at times as I looked over and could see that he was so far into a particular story that I could have piled the wagon into a concrete bridge or been pulled up by Colchester Police and he wouldn't have even known anything about it. I had a little laugh to myself as I left the country roads and re-entered the built up area to the rear of the married quarters. God forbid if I had got lost, he wouldn't have even known where we were to pick up the directions. I didn't care, his newspaper was taking all the attention away from me, and I was having a ball throwing this wagon all over the place. My only concern was that if I missed a gear, I would have had to stop the vehicle to start my gear changes again. Surely he would have spotted that, wouldn't he?

I entered the final straight from one of the only tight junctions on the route it was a T-junction on a sharp bend. I needed to work out which one of these options would turn out to be the lesser of two evils. Do I risk pulling right across the other side of the road and an oncoming car piling into the front of the wagon, or take the turn without swinging out too much and mount the kerb. I took the first option and swung right over to the other side of the road to save from mounting the pavement. With me being on my test, there was no way I was mounting a kerb at anyone's expense. I was lucky as I certainly didn't hear the bang of a car piling into me. I had never seen a car come into contact with the front of a Foden but it would easily disappear under the height of this vehicle.

I braked gently and parked in exactly the same spot as I had started from, I put the handbrake on, took the vehicle out of gear and put my hands on the steering wheel. I looked over at Bernie who lifted his head from the paper.

"Oh," he whispered. He closed his newspaper, picked up his half-filled check sheet and opened the passenger door. He climbed down from the wagon and started to walk over towards our battery garages. I was sitting in the driver's seat in shock, he hadn't *said anything* to me, let alone asked me any Highway Code questions and he was now walking away from me. When he crossed the front of the wagon I opened the window of my door as he was getting away.

"Sarge," I called after him. "Have I passed?"

"Oh yeah, no problem Bomb. I'll send your pass certificate over, park the wagon over in the garages and I'll see you on Monday," he finished. I couldn't believe it, no thanks, kiss my arse or nothing. I had never seen anything like this, I don't even think he was aware that he had been in the same wagon as me. I was chuffed to pieces and couldn't believe I had passed my heavy goods licence and passed it so easily. Had I known that it would have been so simple, I wouldn't have worried so much. When I told Tommy and the others, they couldn't believe it either and even less that I passed in the manner which I had.

A few years previous, I had taken my Land Rover test in Germany and had gone though hell. My Land Rover license got me my normal UK driving licence so I put a lot into it. Some German sprog in a little cobbled town called Luneburg had thrown a large toy into the road in the path of my vehicle causing an unscheduled emergency stop. I was reported by the testing officer as the only British soldier to request an immediate change of underpants during a driving test. However, the irresponsible act by the German child did play a major part in my being awarded a 'pass' on the day.

CHAPTER EIGHT

WHITE KNUCKLE AIRWAYS

At 03.55hrs, Monday morning 5 April 1982, we were stood on parade freezing cold and suffering from A.H (accumulative hangover). We had spent from Friday afternoon, after I had passed my H.G.V. test, until five o'clock Sunday morning on the razz and I was now feeling the effects of every single pint that I had drunk. It was a good job that we were deploying to Belize for the following reasons: firstly, the flight time would mean I couldn't have a drink, so there was a period of at least twenty-four hours without beer and secondly, I was skint. I had drunk all that I had saved from last month's wages. That included the hundred quid I had returned to me from my mate at home. The new car I had been saving for was even less of a reality now my funds were that low, I probably couldn't afford a glove box for a Fiat Panda. I tried to stay optimistic, we were going to the Caribbean where the sun was shining and we would be leaving this drab, cold and wet climate for six months. We were going to be receiving an extra two pounds and eighty-seven pence overseas allowance (L.O.A), for every day we are out there. That can't be bad; I would be able to buy a nearly new car just on the L.O.A (nearly seven hundred quid). This was a lot of money in 1982. What made it even more inviting was that we had been told that there was cheap beer and cigarettes out there. Well that was it, I was more than happy, but then the thoughts started going down hill again.

We were taking over a hundred lunatics to someone else's country. Belize could only be found on a few maps at the time, but believe me when our lot had finished, it would be on a damn site more, probably for the wrong reasons though. I pitied the Belizeans in advance as I could picture carnage wherever we deployed. We tended to adopt this subconscious attitude that if we caused carnage in another country, it wasn't our country so it didn't matter.

As we stood on parade I could see a number of stragglers still turning up. I initially thought they were late, but it turned out that a couple of them had been running messages to the guardroom for the B.C and one of the T.S.M's. I prayed for the sake of any potential offenders who may turn up late, but as I was doing so I noticed that the B.S.M. was absent. I for one wasn't going to question where the B.S.M. was, but this did seem a little strange. He was the man that was always there kicking arses before most parades. It was W.O.2 Andy Tyrer who finally took the parade and marched over to the B.C. There was the customary salute and then a long drawn out chat between them. I was always the right marker, so therefore was always the closest to them when they were talking, but I couldn't hear a word that was being exchanged. I didn't give it any further thought at the time. The B.S.M. would have phoned the regiment if he was going to be late, he would have got a message to the B.C. one way or another.

"All present and correct, Sir," the T.S.M. said to the B.C.

"Very good sergeant major, fall the men out and get them onto the coaches," he ordered.

"Yes, Sir," Andy replied. The sergeant major marched to the centre and front of the battery and screamed at us. "Officers on parade fall out." With that we all turned to the right and saluted. The B.C. who was standing slightly to the right saluted back then turned about and marched off. I looked over to my right and couldn't believe what had just turned up. The bloody army coaches, there was me thinking we were going to be starting this journey in style and travelling on civvy coaches but no such luck.

Let me tell you about the great British Army coach, had these coaches been on the road today, the M.O.D would have been answerable and held accountable to the police, The Highways Agency, Customs and Excise, the Department of Transport, the Health and Safety Executive (H.S.E), the R.S.P.C.C, the Disability Discrimination Agency, oh and not to forget the Immigration Agency due to the drivers' nationalities. They were the worst excuse of a vehicle you could imagine and I can't even begin to think what type of licence you would need to drive one of these things, I think a dog licence would have sufficed. We called them 'A Mess Tin on Wheels' because they were literally like a box on wheels, they were always painted, either green olive or white. Inside wasn't much better; the seats were like the packing cases from the Pickford's advert, there was no heating, nowhere to store luggage, and the top speed was seven miles an hour. All the drivers had dyslexia, one eye, a hair lip, a cleft pallet and couldn't speak a word of English, which didn't matter much as verbal communications were impossible anyway because of the one hundred and forty decibel noise coming from the coach engine. This is the equivalent noise rating of an F-16 fighter jet when in take off. It would take four and a half hours to get to Brize Norton, which would normally take two hours. Had the M.O.D. forked out for decent coaches, we would have been there in a flash.

True to form, we arrived at Brize Norton at 09.20hrs. My back was in pieces and my right cheek had the imprint of my suitcase label where I had been trying to sleep. I thought of how we would have a whip round for the driver on a normal coach, but the only tip he was getting from me was 'don't eat yellow snow' and even that was generous, it mattered not to these drivers though as they couldn't understand us anyway. We were ushered through document control like sheep going for a haircut and then on into the departure lounge. Once we were all in and the doors were bolted behind us Flight Sergeant Brylcreem appeared with one of his trolley dollies to give us a strict briefing on the don'ts and don'ts while travelling on the aircraft. No Do's, just Don'ts.

In the army in 1982, homosexuality was still a bit of a taboo subject so unfortunately the flight sergeant's mucker received a lot of cheap jibes from the troops. So much so, that the N.C.O..s had cause to intervene and stop all the insulting comments. I did feel sorry for the lad though, as he stood and took some pretty low shots about his sexuality from our rabble. What made me laugh, about these type of briefings from persons outside our battery, was that as soon as you told our troops not to do something they went ahead and did it. The perfect example was the 'no smoking on the aircraft' thing, as soon as we climbed onto the aircraft the bogs were full of smoke. Why bother? If the R.A.F. boys had used their heads and got one of our sergeant majors to pass this message to the troops, then it would be obeyed. The flight sergeant disappeared and then returned fifteen minutes later, he walked over to W.O.2 Andy Tyrer and spoke with him for a moment.

"Right you lot, dig in, we are here for the day," Andy called to us. It turned out that our aircraft had developed a fault with the engine and they were working to fix it but it wasn't a fault that would only take minutes to rectify. Brilliant and I was going to be flying on this shed.

However at five o'clock that afternoon we left the terminal. As we walked out onto the pan I was the very last person to walk through the door, there was Brylcreem Boy and the R.A.F. corporal who was standing with a clicker counter.

He turned to the flight sergeant and said, "One hundred and two Sarge."

"Correct," the flight sergeant replied as he checked his counter. Hang on a minute I thought, there should be one hundred and three. Crap, the B.S.M. was still missing, I didn't see him in the terminal so where is he? We were about to take off for Belize and he was nowhere to be seen. I looked up and saw this large aircraft.

"Tommy what the fuck is that aircraft?" I shouted ahead.

Tommy looked back and snapped at me. "Don't fuckin start, what with that and the buses, it's all we fucking need."

I left him alone after that. I was going to ask him about the B.S.M. but I thought it may not be a good idea. I wasn't ready for the 'How the fuck should I know' reply from him at that time of day so I decided to let it go. I looked again at the aircraft now in front of me and wondered to myself if Arthur Negus from the 'Antiques Road Show' had seen this as he would have been in his element. I had no doubt that he would have offered twelve quid for it, it was a relic. I didn't dare ask myself if this journey could get any worse. I knew it was our plane as I could see troops starting to board. What was it? I had never travelled on an aircraft like that before. When I climbed the steps I was greeted by another male trolley dolly (cabin crew) I bet he took some stick as one hundred army blokes had just passed him on the steps. When I entered the aircraft, I was shocked to see that the seats were facing the wrong way; I didn't understand this and had never come across it before. I took my seat and was starting to worry about the amount of space we had. With me being six foot two, I was more than concerned that I was going to sit here for twelve hours with my knees pushed into my chin holding a rifle in front of me, I couldn't move. We were refuelling in Dulles Washington on the way and then dropping down and landing in Belize City Airport a few hours later. A total of twelve hours flying time and it had become obvious that I wasn't going to be getting much sleep at this stage. A member of the cabin crew approached me so I took the opportunity to ask him what aircraft I was sitting on and why were the seats the wrong way round.

"It's a VC-10 C1," he said. "The seats are this way round because you are better seated rearward in the event of a crash. You have a better chance of survival."

"Are you having a laugh mate? If we fall thirty three thousand feet at a gazillion miles an hour, you've got fuck all chance of survival in a crash and if you are kissing your fat arse goodbye, it won't matter which way you are facing."

What intelligent being decided that it's better to face backwards in case we crash? I couldn't believe it and all the troops that had heard this conversation tore the poor guy to pieces. They were still laughing at his reasons for the reverse seating hours later. My journey consisted of sitting down, standing up, sitting down again, going to the toilet, eating my food, sitting down and standing up again, it really was a trauma. Some of the troops were really good at switching off to it and getting stuck into a good book. I couldn't, I was a bad traveller. A considerable number of the troops went to sleep. Occupying the seat next to me and closest to the window was Gunner Mark Hadfield, he was only five foot four inches, so he had no problem curling up and going to sleep. I hated him for this, the bloody 'Short Wheeled Base Tree Rat'. I was so jealous.

By the time we landed at Dulles Airport, I had lost the will to live and wished they had issued us live ammunition for this M15 Armalite weapon that I was attached to. My back felt as if it had been punched for an hour by the B.S.M., I was in agony. I may have been the last one to climb onto the aircraft, but I going to make sure I was the first one off it. It was dark in Washington, but I didn't care, I just wanted to get away from this aircraft and enjoy the relief I was now feeling. We could get into the air terminal and have a smoke. The aircraft had parked on the military area of the airport and it was lit up like Wembley Stadium as you would expect. I remember thinking how big it was and noticing all the different types of military aircraft belonging to forces from all over the world, many that I hadn't seen before. I grabbed some coffee from a brew trolley that had been set up for our arrival, we appreciated this as we were gagging for a drink and other than a small kiosk there were not that many facilities here. I walked over to the 'smokers section' of the lounge, lit up a cig and had a look out of the window; I could see an R.A.F. A.W.A.C.S (Airborne Warning and Control System) stood on the pan, what a machine! This was a sneaky beaky machine, an 'all hush hush' aircraft with a large surveillance dish plonked on the top of it, I had to have a photo. I finished my cigarette, took my camera out of my top pocket and started to make my way over to a single door which led out onto a small balcony. Once on the balcony I was in a perfect position and pointing my camera at the aircraft.

I had taken one photo and was about to take another, when I heard an American voice, "Sir, I must ask you for your camera."

"What?" I replied.

"Your camera, Sir, I have to confiscate it."

"How about fuck off, you aren't getting it" I said.

I heard the click of a popper unfastening then he produced a colt hand gun that Dirty Harry would have been proud of, "Your camera, Sir," he repeated, then suddenly another four American military policemen came to help him restrain me. I was then thrown against the railings of the balcony whilst they searched me. They ripped my camera out of my hand and proceeded to issue me a bollocking for being in a restricted area and taking a photo of a 'highly secret' military aircraft.

"Hang on mate, I am in the fucking military," I said. "It's not like I am a civvy, now give me the fucking camera," I shouted.

"I am sorry, Sir, you are in a restricted area and you should not be taking photographs of this aircraft," he barked.

"Well take the fucking film, you don't need the camera," I screamed.

"I am sorry sir, we cannot do that." By this time, W.O.2 Andy Tyrer had come out onto the balcony where I was being held.

"Bombardier Connolly, what the fuck is going on?" he asked. I told him what had happened and the fact that Sergeant Gung Ho from the American Military Police had confiscated my camera and would not settle for just removing the film. "You are a dick and you should know better. Stay here," he said. With that he turned to the yanks. "Who is the senior soldier here?" he asked the two sergeants.

"I am, Sir," one of them replied. "Can I have a word?" he said to him. They walked over to the corner of the balcony where after a short conversation; I watched the yank remove the film from my camera and then passed the camera only back to W.O.2 Andy Tyrer who had then secured it in his pocket.

"Bombardier Connolly, over here," he said sternly at me. I walked over to him and the American sergeant. "Apologise to the sergeant for telling him to fuck off," he ordered me.

"I am sorry sergeant," I said under duress.

"See me when we get to Belize and you can have your camera back," he said.

"Thank you, Sir," I answered.

"Now fuck off back inside the terminal," he finished. I looked at the yank and scurried inside the building. Tommy was laughing his head off as I walked back in.

"Why didn't you chin the fucker?" he asked.

"Oh yeah, very good Tom, did you see the size of his fucking gun?" I replied. Tommy kept quiet and wiped the smile off his face because W.O.2 Andy Tyrer had just walked back into the terminal.

"Bombardier Connolly, you keep out of trouble for ten minutes and by the way, why didn't you smack the fucker?" I immediately looked over at Tommy who was now sporting the 'see I told you so smile'.

"Fucking hell, Sir, he had a handgun with an eighteen inch barrel. I would be 'Dead on Arrival' (D.O.A.) to Belize if it had gone on much longer." At least I knew my camera was safe until I got to Belize.

I went and helped myself to another brew and then sat down to have another smoke, I was well pissed off with the antics of 'Hank the Yank' and started dreaming of when he came to visit my country and how I would be waiting for him. As I was finishing my cig, I looked up and just happened to see the corporal who had tried to remove my camera. He had a small pistol strapped to his right hand side and was now sitting at a desk close to where the brew kit trolley was situated. I thought, I could easily sneak over to where he was sitting and remove his small arm without him even knowing, then I landed back on planet Earth and thought, hang on a minute, I have nearly been arrested for my silly antics once today, and suddenly it wasn't such an attractive idea after all.

The aircraft had been refuelled and the crew had been given enough time to decipher the next part of the Bible in order for them to drive the crate the rest of the way to Belize. We left the terminal and made our way back across the pan and onto the V.C-10 for the rest of our journey. I still wasn't too happy flying with 'White Knuckle Airways', but what could I do? The captain of the flight kicked into life again over the speakers. Smart Arse, either he was pissed or he was happy that he only had another couple of hours in control of this aircraft, and now realised that there may be a small possibility that we could make it in this plane.

"Good evening Gentlemen and Gentlemen," he started, before reeling off a batch of light-hearted Air Force jokes that only managed to raise one laugh throughout the whole of the aircraft. 'Please remove all sharp objects from your pockets such as hot engine fragments' seemed to be his favourite, he had cracked it once already when we first got on the plane. Brilliant! a pilot with Dementia. That's all we needed, I just hoped he wouldn't forget when one of his crew shouted, 'lower the wheels'. Before we knew it we were climbing to thirty thousand feet again and every time the captain told the troops not to smoke in the toilets, they would make a point of going into them and filling them with smoke. I think that was one that they were always going to lose.

My focus for the last leg of the flight was to concentrate on what I was going to do with a couple of hours. I did pretty much the same as I did on the first leg. Again it was imperative that I sat down for the least amount of time, I wanted to get off this aircraft under my own steam and not on a stretcher. I even borrowed Tommy's playing cards in a last ditch attempt to pass the time away, I didn't have a clue what I was going to do with them, but if I could eat the clock away then all the better. Before long we were being thrown back in our seats and told to fasten our seat belts, my plan with the cards had worked. The captain informed us that it would be ten thirty a.m. Belize time, when we exited the aircraft. The toilet close to me was absolutely full of cigarette smoke and the cabin crew were doing their nut. They weren't happy that the majority of the troops had disregarded the instructions given to them, nothing new there then. I watched over the tops of the seats as the RAF boys scurried around the aircraft for a final time to make sure we were all at least, abiding to the 'Fasten Seat Belts' rule, then they had just enough time to sit down and fasten their own. We could hear the wheels being lowered, or at least that's what I prayed it was. We were dropping out of the sky in what felt like chunks of fifty feet at a time. Someone should have gone and told the pilot that the army would have liked to introduce the word 'gradual' into the RAF book of flying words. It felt like the aircraft was gliding for another twenty minutes or so. I was thinking, it was either that or Hank the Yank had short changed us on our fuel rations back in Washington and we had run out two hundred miles away. That wouldn't have surprised me after they had thrown their teddies out, because I had tried to take a photo of their precious plane.

Suddenly, I felt a surge of relief run through my body. You know, that feeling you get when you realise everything is going to be all right and you aren't going to die at the hand of an avionic madman who thought he was a proper pilot. The wheels touched the ground, well one did anyway. Ground on a runway would suggest flat, black, tarmac surface which was level-ish and at least in a condition that an aircraft may land on, So why was the aircraft bouncing up and down like we were riding a horse on the beach? We ground to a halt and released our belts; I raced off the aircraft like my life depended on it. When I stepped out of the plane onto the steps, I remember thinking that the engines of the aircraft were absolutely roasting. I climbed down the steps of the aircraft and it was still as hot.

"You cannot be serious Rab," I said. He picked up on it right away and said. "Tell me this is freak sunshine won't you?" At this time of the morning it was one of the hottest temperatures my body had been in by far. We were dressed in 'jungle combat clothing' which is very thin cotton jungle wear and they were soaked with sweat already. This was opposite to what was normal. I looked around and saw where we had just landed, had I known that we were landing on this surface I would have been frightened to an extent that they would have found me shaking uncontrollably and crying like a baby in the toilet. The runway reminded me of a scene from the film 'The Battle of the Somme'. My eyes scoured the immediate area for the terminal building, but I couldn't see it. Where the hell were we going now we had got off the aircraft?

All of a sudden a loud speaker came to life, "Welcome to Belize International Airport, de heart of de Caribbean Basin man. Please make ya way ova to de terminal building."

I looked again, what terminal building? I thought. Tell me that shed over there is not the terminal building for Belize International Airport.

It was and it looked as if there was someone outside it waving us over. It was clear by the time we had marched the four hundred metres we were nearly dead, every one of us was now soaked through with sweat, and more than half the troops were grabbing at their water bottles. This heat was beyond a joke, it was fierce and relentless. It became obvious on entering the building, that it was also unbearable inside a building if you didn't have ceiling fans. Most of the troops were now sitting on their suitcases; some could only make it down onto one knee with their heads bowed in their hands. These Belizeans would have seen it all before and were probably not bothered. It took the staff there an hour to stamp our passports, when they were completed we jumped on the six Bedford wagons which had arrived outside the terminal.

If I thought it was hot in this shed, the back of the wagon was even hotter, all we could do was sit on the back of the wagons and ooze sweat from our brows. D Troop and all the supporting staff jumped on Bedford's one, two and three and C Troop jumped on Bedford's four, five and six, these were my lot. The other troop had a twenty minute drive before they arrived at their camp in the North of Belize (Holdfast Camp) but we had just been informed that we had another twelve hours to go before we reached Rideau camp in the south of the country. We had to sit on an open R.P.L. (Ramped Powered Lighter) boat, this was a large steel boat that had a large ramp that dropped down onto the beach in order for the infantry to drive their vehicles on. It looked just like a square open top container bobbing in the water and manned by the Royal Corps of Transport and must have been brought in from World War One. If we were to drive the journey to the south of Belize in the back of Bedford wagons, it was two hundred miles and on these roads it would take a lot longer than twelve hours. They really were in an appalling state.

We pulled up at this jetty and I could see the R.P.L. as soon as I got down from the Bedford. There were two urns of ice-cold water waiting for us to collect before we got on the boat. The crew were just securing a short wheel based Land Rover to the hull, before we piled on. In the meantime, I tasted what I thought was the water, I nearly choked. One of the urns was full of this cold juice that tasted a little like orange juice and the other of lemon juice. It tasted like someone had mixed Blackpool beach with each of the juices before they had sent them out to us, it was disgusting and I certainly wasn't going to drink any more of it. The urns were placed in a shaded part of the boat in an attempt to keep them cool but it wasn't long before they were going to be as hot as us. We climbed aboard and quickly realised that the midday to three p.m. sun was going to ruin our day even if we hid in the shelter. Our battery was adamant that no one would suffer from the effects of the sun, so we either had to be hidden from the sun or only be exposed to it for a matter of minutes because it could burn you in no time. This would obviously be compounded when we were outside in the midday sun, bobbing up and down on the Caribbean Sea at two p.m. The crew of this boat had only been here for six weeks and looked like the 'Chogies', this was the name that was given to the Belizeans. It wasn't meant disrespectfully, we inherited it from the last regiment and this was better than most of the other names that I will not mention, as I feel them far to close to the bone.

We set sail for Punta Gorda which was the town closest to our camp at Rideau. It was hard to believe that we now had to endure twelve hours in this heat with nowhere to go for shade. Once we reached Punta Gorda, the camp was an additional twenty-minute drive away from the RPL landing site, on a road called Southern Highway. We had only been on this boat for one hour and we had hit the open waters, it was really rough and not what I would have expected. There was no way of seeing out of the boat and it felt like we were in a deep hole being tossed all around the place causing that horrible sick feeling. The troops were frantically drinking as much of this orange and lemon as they could. I found out from one of the boat crew that it was a high protein, high salt and sugar drink which was made from a powder, they called it jungle juice. It may have tasted vile, but it could contribute to keeping you alive in these searing temperatures. Another important thing the N.C.O's had to keep telling the junior ranks was to cover all of their skin up. These conditions were like none other I had, or have to this day, been in.

After we had been bobbing up and down on the high waves for approximately three hours, I was at a stage where I needed to find some shade, I couldn't bear the direct sun for much longer, the intensity of the heat was driving me mad. I looked at the Land Rover which was chained to the deck of the RPL and on the crest of a wave made a dash towards it. As I knelt at the side of the vehicle I bent over and looked underneath it, I made a snap decision that I would be able to crawl underneath and be sheltered. Once under the vehicle I turned over so that I was lying on my back, it was still very hot, but nowhere near as bad as what I had just escaped. I took deep breaths and chilled out until I felt somewhere near normal again and I was throwing water down me like there was no tomorrow, I had drunk my two water bottles and had re filled them with the jungle juice I know I said that I didn't like it but I was throwing it down my neck. Needs must! Another hour passed and I could see it was starting to get dark, I was so grateful just for the fact that the sun was disappearing. The heat was still an issue, but I could live with that and after a short time I felt I could come out from underneath the vehicle. The waves were settling and there was one of the boat crew walking amongst the troops dishing ration packs out, the ration packs were normally a little white box with a sandwich, an orange, a biscuit and a carton drink in it. I devoured mine in seconds, then took the Twix from the back of my webbing and poured the chocolate out of the wrapper into my mouth.

At a few minutes before midnight we hit the R.P.L. ramp and I mean that literally, I don't think there was a soldier left on that boat still standing.

I burst out laughing as I heard Tolly shout, "Can someone tell Captain Magoo we have arrived."

His timing was perfect, equally as perfect was the captain of the boat shouting back, "Fuck off and drown."

We were absolutely knackered now and all we wanted to do was sleep, just a short twenty-minute Bedford wagon ride ahead of us and that was it, bed. It was a little after midnight and we were all still sweating like pigs; it had obviously cooled down, but not much. How could it possibly be this hot at this time of night? Surely, this wasn't right. We rolled into camp at one o'clock, dead on our feet. Thankfully a hell of a lot of hard work had been done by the advance party.

Chindit's face was a welcome sight, "Bombardier Connolly, how the devil are you lad?" he asked.

"Fucked, Sir, where's my pit?" I replied.

"You won't be wanting a brew then?" he asked knowingly.

"Come on, Sir. Is the Pope Catholic? I've got a throat like Ghandi's flip-flop," I finished. It was rare that I turned down a good brew and this wasn't going to be one of those rare occasions. It was heaven, a pint of really strong hot tea. Marvellous, I thought.

When I had finished my tea, we were being sent in the direction of some accommodation Nissan huts. Nissan huts were huts in the shape of half circle with corrugated sheet walls and roof. They made very good accommodation for jungle locations but I would have preferred to have stayed near this ten gallon tea urn and polished off the delightful serving of Rosie Lea. We walked the last couple of hundred yards of our epic journey. It wouldn't have been as bad on the return journey as we knew we would be going home then. It really was a killer of a trip and one we wouldn't be repeating again. I was shown into my accommodation by Bombardier Bert Bradley; Bert was a PTI by trade, but also a good driver. I could see even by the dim lights in the accommodation that he had already been soaking up the rays and was very brown, he looked more like one of the locals than the locals did.

"There you go Sean, you're in there mate," he said while he was pointing at the bottom bunk near the entrance door. The bottom bunk was great because the mosquito net was tied from the underneath of the top bunk which was very relevant as Bert told me to stay wrapped in the net at night at all costs and no matter how hot it got, stay inside it. I didn't know how the guy on the top bunk gets on, but for that night it was a case of, 'I'm alright Jack'. At the other end of the billet was another open door which you would think assisted the three big ceiling fans in making a nice through draft, but not a chance. It was so hot and sticky.

"See you in the morning mate, I can see you're knackered," Bert said.

"Cheers mate," I replied and I just had enough energy to strip off and pile into bed. I wrapped the mossy net around me as advised by Bert and within twenty seconds I was out.

At 04.30 hrs I was woken by the most ridiculous noise I had ever heard. It felt like someone was riding a motorbike with a dodgy exhaust through our accommodation and out the other end. I looked up and saw a soldier, who I recognised from the engineers, he was carrying a machine over his shoulder. It looked like a garden vacuum and was making this horrible droning noise, it was sending out this really thick smog that was so thick you couldn't see your hand in front of your face, and the smell was evil.

"Shut the fuck up and get the fuck out," I screamed. It was no use anyway, he couldn't hear me. Not only was the noise of the engine too loud, but he was also wearing a pair of big yellow ear defenders. When he left the building the smog seemed to take ages to clear.

"That's better," someone said down the other end of the block.

"What the fuck was that?" I asked.

"That's Swingfog. It's designed to kill all the beasties in the room," he answered.

"Bollocks to the beasties, it nearly killed me," I said.

"It's done twice a day, once in the morning at first light and then in the evening at last light," he finished. So that was the first thing I hadn't been told anything about when we were back in Colchester. It was an amazing machine this Swingfog, it ran on Diesel and some other chemical. It was very effective, when they left the room after one application there were thousands of beasties dead on the floor. I would be definitely having a mess around with that.

At 05,00hrs the N.C.O's who had been on the 'Advance Party' came screaming into the room, "Come on, up you get you lot. Get your hands off your cocks and onto your socks. Time for a run."

"Don't talk stupid," I answered. "We only arrived a few hours ago and we won't be running anywhere for two weeks until we have acclimatised. That's what we were told back at Colly and that's what Chindit will tell you, now fuck off and let us sleep."

"Sean, it's Chindit who sent us to get you all up for a run," Bert replied.

We quickly climbed out of our beds and had to rummage though our cases to find our P.T kits. I put my trainers on and jumped into my new shorts; I then grabbed my red army T-shirt and walked outside. The scenery around the camp was stunning, it had a large hill or mountain behind the camp and what looked like a swamp to the front right of us. That's where the mosquitoes would come from, I thought. It looked like every soldier in the camp was sorting themselves out and going for a run.

I spotted a good mate of mine down the bottom of the camp; it was the Sergeant Medic Dave Dawkins. Dave was a really funny guy and completely off his head, he also had a reputation of being able to drink with the best of them. He was unlike all the other medics I knew in that he looked after himself, medics didn't do that. He did a lot of running and worked out in the gym quite a bit, from what I had heard he was a handy lad to have on your side in a pub brawl. I watched him for a little time in the hope that he would look over at me and see I had arrived, but he didn't.

Chindit stood in front of us and looked surprised. "Right you lazy bunch of bastards," he shouted. Hang on, I thought, where did that came from? There was one thing that we were not, and that was lazy. "Firstly go and get your water bottles and then get back out here," he snapped. We all shuffled through the door to the accommodation, took our water bottles out of our webbing and followed the crowd of soldiers to the cold water machine outside the building. We waited in the queue in order to fill them with freezing cold water and then 'fell in' once more in front of Chindit. This felt very awkward as we had to carry our water bottle in our hands, we were dressed in civvy P.T kit so we didn't have our webbing on for us to carry it in. "

We're going on an eight miler, anybody not up for it?" he snapped. He knew as well as the rest of us that there wasn't a man present that would dare stick his hand up. There were two reasons for this, firstly he would be ripped by the rest of the troops on parade (the word 'Wanker' springs to mind), secondly and more importantly the person taking the run would stick you on remedial P.T for a week. He knew full well that no one was going to admit to not being able to make any run.

I raised my hand. "Bombardier, what's up?" he said calmly.

"Sir, with all respect the B.C. said we wouldn't run for two weeks and that we would be granted the time to acclimatise," I said bravely.

"The B.C. is up north, I am in charge here, that's why I am only giving you eight miles and not more," he finished. Well at least he hadn't ripped my head off. Everyone was looking at each other, we had only arrived four hours ago and he was going to push us eight miles in this heat, it was suicidal. Even the sergeants were clearly shocked at what we were about to do. Chindit had been very clever in not waking the officers up this particular morning as they may have had something to say about this crazy act that he was about to put us through. I felt at my peak, but I worried about my own stamina let alone the lads within the troop who were not great runners. I had to remind myself what we were setting out to do; we were going to attempt to run eight miles with a maniac who was already acclimatised, in this raging heat. It was five thirty in the morning and the lads were dripping wet with sweat and we were just standing on the road outside the accommodation. This had disaster written all over it.

"Bombardier Connolly, bring up the rear in front of the ambulance," he shouted.

"Yes, Sir," I answered.

I was the one that would be running approximately fifty yards behind the squad kicking the arses of the 'sick, lame and lazy'. The ambulance which was a Landover with nothing in it but a 'Jerry Can' of water, it was being driven by Lance Bombardier Bob Baker, this was great except he wasn't a medic or even a first aider. I somehow had the feeling that I was going to be very busy during this run and it was going to be very strenuous to say the least. We turned to the right and set off down a slight decline towards the guardroom and main gate. We hadn't even made the couple of hundred yards when I could see the troops, one after another, frantically sucking on their water bottles. It was getting closer to six o'clock now and it was bloody hot, there was no wind and it remained very clammy.

Chindit set off at a ridiculously fast pace, it would have been difficult to stay with him under normal conditions, but he was acclimatised now, so this gave him the upper hand. We pulled out of the camp and onto the main road, it wasn't the type of road surface that we know; it was full of rocks and large stones, dirt and dust and had the most ridiculous cambers on both sides where they had sunk during the monsoon season. It was the most awkward running surface I had ever had to negotiate, it felt like we were running through a quarry. I later found out that this was 'Southern Highway' and it was the best kept road in the Toledo District of Belize. I wouldn't like to have run on the worst one. All I could do right then was listen to Chindit screaming at the lads to keep up, every two hundred yards. Although I was only an N.C.O. at this stage of my career I could see that this was going to turn bad really quickly, we should never have been made to attempt this run having just arrived in Belize but a distance like this on this surface was ludicrous but Chindit was 'on one' and that was that. We hadn't even run half a mile when Mark Wilkinson pulled out of the squad, he had done exactly what I suspected someone would do but a lot quicker than I imagined.

"My foot Sean, I have broken my foot," he said as I caught him up. He was walking on it and it wasn't broken but it was surely sprained.

"Get in the wagon you soft twat, you have sprained it." The Land Rover stopped and Mark climbed in the passenger side.

Chindit shouted to me from the front. "What's up Bomber?"

"Damaged ankle, Sir," I shouted back. He never muttered another word, just turned round and carried on running.

Within another three hundred yards, John Ashton pulled over to the side. He was shaking violently and collapsed at the roadside, he was soaked with sweat and in 'dehydrated mode'. I stopped to attend to him but when I pushed his head back I realised he was in a more serious condition than I first thought. I waved the Land Rover over and quickly realised that not only did I need to start pouring water down his neck but I needed to get him out of the sun, on this vehicle and back to camp as soon as possible. I got Mark to jump in the back with him and start pouring water into him. I had to pick up the pace and catch the squad up, as soon as I left the back of the Land Rover I looked up the road. I could see one of our lads in the gutter on the left, another one on the right and Andy Berry running slowly behind the squad wobbling all over the place as if he had just consumed twenty pints of strong lager.

"Oh shit," I said out loud. I looked at the driver and pointed, he knew exactly what I meant. By the time the Land Rover got to the casualty on the left, I had caught him up; it was exactly the same symptoms as Lance Bombardier Ashton. We managed to get all three casualties in the Land Rover. I shouted to Bob Baker, "Get this Rover back to camp and get a Bedford Wagon out here now. Make sure the Duty medic Sergeant sorts this lot out."

I didn't have to tell him twice, he turned around in the middle of the road and headed back to camp. I sprinted up the road, I was alone but I had to catch up with the squad. I could just about to see them a couple of hundred yards away. I sped up and after a while I had caught them. I nearly passed out myself. There were lads suffering badly with the heat all over the squad, four or five of them were balking and puking while they were still running. I shouted to Chindit.

"Sir, they are dropping like flies, can we stop? We need to take water on board. I have sent the Amby back to camp it was full, he is coming back out." I thought he wasn't even listening to me. It looked by the way the troops were carrying their water bottles that they were all empty.

"Fucking wimps," he shouted. "Four mile point is just around this corner, there are two 'Jerry Cans' of water in the shade, we will stop for a replen for two minutes," He finished. We made it around the corner and even before we had halted there were five or six more of the troops doing the same. Two of them were completely out of the game and I had no medical wagon, I was fuming. What the fuck was this man trying to prove? None of the senior ranks would approach him to tell him how stupid this was.

I walked over to Chindit. "Sir, can I have a word please?" I asked.

He took his water bottle away from his mouth. "What's up Bomb?" I couldn't believe what he had just said. Fucking hell, Ray Charles could have seen what was 'up'.

"Sir, we have lost fifteen odd men, four of which I think are in a serious condition. Look at them, Sir," I added. I pointed to the lads who were now flaked out at the side of the road. It was worse than I could ever have imagined.

"Fucking lazy Bomb, that's what it is," he snapped.

I couldn't believe that he couldn't see that some of the lads that had fallen were amongst the fittest in the regiment, let alone in the battery. I pointed this and begged him to at least let me wait until the Bedford arrived. The remaining troops replenished their water bottles from the 'Jerry Cans'. The water which he said that he had hidden at the side of the road had been left in the sun, so it was like turning a hot tap on and then drinking the water from it. This situation was deteriorating further, now one of the sergeants Don Nelson had a foot sprain and it was his turn to throw the towel in. Chindit gave him the daggers as if to call him a wimp, senior ranks were not permitted to drop out of a run. I looked at the rest of the troop sat out in the open, the temperature was rising fast and the sun was beating down on their heads. We didn't even have hats on and I knew that the 'return to camp' part of this run was going to be a lot worse than the outward journey. If we had lost this many already, how many would we lose on the way back. I heard Chindit ordering the lads to their feet. I looked to the left and noticed the Bedford speeding towards us.

"Sir, I need a man," I shouted.

"Take Benson," he said reluctantly.

"Benson here and quick," I shouted. Gunner Dave Benson was a very fit guy and he was one of the only remaining troops to be unaffected. Mind you, it didn't matter how fit you were when dehydration struck; it had already hit some of the fittest troops I knew. "Get these lads on the wagon Benson," I said.

"Right Bomb," he replied. With that I dropped the tailgate at the rear of the wagon while Bob and Dave loaded the sick into the back.

"Benson, on the back and don't let anyone fall off," I said to Dave Benson.

"Roger Bomb," he answered.

"By the front, double march," I heard Chindit say and they were off. "Bring up the rear Bomb Connolly," Chindit shouted.

"Yes, Sir," I said. The pace was ridiculous; within five hundred yards two more lads hit the deck. I stopped the wagon and we threw them on the back. I caught up with the squad and another one of the gunners went down. We stopped the wagon again bundled the casualty aboard and then off again. By the time I caught up again there were three more down and the wagon was filling up fast. I did the arithmetic in my head and realised that if this was to continue at this rate then the wagon would not be able to hold all of the casualties. I was exhausted by the time, we turned the last corner. In the distance I could see the camp. Thank God for that, I thought to myself.

I counted the remaining troops, we had ten people left, too late Sam Morrison hit the deck like a sack of spuds closely followed by Tommy Johnson. "Make that eight," I said to myself as I finally got to them. The wagon arrived with me and we got them on the back. There was literally one hundred yards to go and they couldn't make the last bit, the wagon was stuffed with all of our sick troops.

"Troop Halt," Chindit shouted. What fucking troop? I thought. I was seething with anger.

"Get that wagon to the medical centre Baker," I screamed. I shouted so not only Bob heard me but also in an attempt to make Chindit realise what he had done and in the hope that he would get the message. No such luck, it looked to me like he didn't give a shit. We had started the run with forty-six men and we were finishing it with eight. Chindit had cracked up, he knew full well that we shouldn't have been attempting this run at this time. Even when we were ready for this run we should not have been wearing trainers, we should have been wearing boots for the support on our ankles, and webbing so we could carry four full water bottles. Lastly, we should have been better prepared medically. The whole event was a 'cluster fuck' and I was sure someone in authority would be speaking with Chindit. I found out later that I was right.

"Fall out. See you on parade at nine," he said as calm as you like. He turned to his left and started walking off down the hill to what looked like the sergeants' mess.

I dropped to one knee, took my water bottle in my left hand, unscrewed the cap and poured the contents onto the back of my bowed head. I looked out of the corner of my eye and saw two of the remaining sergeants scurrying away, I would be seeing them later and having an 'off the record' talk' with them. I wanted answers as to why they hadn't even challenged Chindit regarding this fiasco. Chindit had just filled the medical centre because of his neglectful actions, then told the troops to parade at nine o'clock. Who the fuck did he think was going to be on parade? The Third Foot and Mouth Brigade! There was hardly anyone left to attend the parade. Two of the eight wouldn't be there anyway as one would be working in the office and the other one in the stores and they were exempt from attending parade. There were only two of us left from our room, the queue that was at the drinking water machine before our run, was now nothing more than a pair of thirsty squaddies taking it in turns at sucking on the squirty spout on the top of the machine.

Big Ged Snailes turned to me and said, "Sean, what the fuck was all that about?"

I looked at him, realised that I wasn't dead and thought 'perhaps I can now answer him'. "I don't know mate, Chindit has lost it," I answered. With that we both entered the accommodation block and walked towards our beds while chunering under our breath. I couldn't believe I had managed to finish the run, but I had. I felt sorry for my mates as some of them were in poor shape. I would have guessed that four or five of them would have to stay in the med centre. I didn't know at this time, but the medical centre had no facilities to bed casualties for overnight periods. If you were that bad a helicopter would have been sent for to fly you to the military hospital in Belize.

I collected my washing and shaving kit and followed the crowds of squaddies in the hope that there would be a cold shower at the end of this pilgrimage. It wasn't long until we turned into this open fronted building, as I entered I noticed thirty odd sinks to the left, they were very old, but at least they were clean. When I was inside the building, I continued to follow the rabble and sure enough, it stopped at the showers. It was an open room with approximately ten showers, it was a lot bigger than I had imagined too.

"Don't expect hot water," someone shouted.

"I won't and I don't want hot," I replied. True enough it was freezing.

"Colder than a witch's tit," Ged shouted.

"Trust you", I answered. It took me a few minutes to get into the shower, but once I was in it I felt so much better. My plan was to have a good shower, a good brekky and then have a quick look around the camp before parade. I was approaching my room after my shower and I could see a Chogie sitting on the little wall outside our accommodation. What the hell is he doing? I thought. When I was just about to go under the shelter outside our room, it became obvious. This was the boot boy; at his feet were approximately thirty pairs of jungle boots. He would clean your boots each day for twenty-five cents and for fifty cents, you would get twice a day. I don't know how much exactly fifty cents was but it was small change, this was fantastic. I also noticed a short but really large Chogie woman taking clothing out of a bin outside the room, I put two and two together for this one and I was right, it was the 'dobie wolla'. I can't remember the price for washing our combat gear, but it really was a pittance. We were issued four sets of combats each which I thought was really generous for the army, but it turned out to be premature credit as you could go through four sets in one day if it was really hot or wet. This woman was on call all day with her mate in reserve and would easily take your stuff in the morning and have it back to you by late afternoon; it was clean, dry and smelt of shit. Just the job, none of your 'Robin' spray starch here you know. I kept having visions of this woman sitting with her mate on a big rock watching this big black pipe coming out of the back of the toilet block, with my combat trousers in her hand. She would be clutching the last dregs of a bar of Camay soap that one of the troops had left in the washroom that morning, which she had now liberated and put to good use.

"Here it comes flo. I think he's flushing now, get scrubbing you bitch, ya only have twenty seconds of water you know," she would say to her mate. Oh dear how I hoped I was wrong.

As I was getting changed for breakfast, I gave the room a once over. To call this accommodation shit would be an insult to the word shit, it was way below standard. It consisted of a concrete floor with nothing on it, just bare concrete. There were three massive fans running down the middle of the hut, which were about as much use as tits on a bull, absolutely useless, it was stifling in this room. Each bed space was split into bunk beds and between two soldiers you were given the luxury of three foot. You were issued a small steel locker each which was way too small to unpack your kit into, but that's all you had. I could see that the best plan of action would be to leave what I didn't need in my case and throw it on the top of the locker. The windows were glass slats running across little openings which were covered from the inside with mosquito netting. It was obvious to see that the doors at each end of the block were rarely closed. It was wise to put an old towel on the floor and stand on it while you covered your feet in Mycota Powder then apparently you had to give your boots a good shake out before you put them on, many of the troops have been stung by scorpions for not bothering. I threw my Paludrine tablet down my neck and then I was off for some brekky.

I noticed that whenever anyone left their buildings they immediately headed for this small concrete path running down the back of the camp. "What's all that about Ged?" I asked.

"It's called the M1 and it's the only decent surface to walk on. Saves getting your boots shitted up again". He answered. I liked that, they had knick named it after the M1 motorway. This path was only about three foot wide, but it was a deep concrete path that ran from one end of the camp right down to the main gate after bending at the bottom by the cookhouse. It was true what Ged had said, the ground was a bitch to walk on and you thought your ankles were about to snap at any time when you were walking across the small rocks and stones. I looked down the M1 and there was Tommy disappearing into the cookhouse, there was no beating this man to his food and he was even quicker if it was free, which it was. I wondered how he managed the run that morning; he had a lot of guts in more ways than one. It was part of the reason why he was a good soldier, he was hard and he never gave in to anything. I sneaked up behind him in the queue when he was just about to fill his mess tin.

"Save some for me fatty."

"Fuck off, you come back at lunch," was his reply. I might have known from Tommy. When I said fill his mess tin, I meant fill his mess tin. I think he would have struggled putting anything else on the top of it other than a flagpole. I wasn't going to comment as I may have found myself getting changed into my next set of combats of the day. I sat down with Ged and Tommy. It was Tommy who started the ball rolling.

"What a shit hole," he said.

"I did try to tell you a couple of weeks ago, but you and Taff weren't having it," I answered. "You are here now, try and enjoy it eh?"

"Don't have much choice do we?" he said like a five year old child. It was a done deal that when you were on a long drag like this then you would have a good gripe about your new residence and then that was it. You would normally get on with it.

"What do you reckon to Chindit Tommy?" I asked.

"He's fucked in the head, isn't he?"

"Yes and I can't see him lasting long," I said.

It was Ged who next spoke, "Yes but it's the 'not lasting long' to killing one of us that worries me."

"We will be fine, trust me," I said with my fingers crossed! I walked over to the tea urn which clearly had freezing cold liquid in it. There was so much condensation on the outside of it. I could have just spent the day licking the outside of the urn and I would have been as happy as Larry. I knocked the juice back, oh dear it was that fucking jungle juice again, vile but it would do us a world of good, especially after that morning run. We all needed to put the salt back into our bodies. When I say all, there were only three of us at breakfast who had managed to finish the run. I started to walk back over to the table and had not heard the cookhouse door open and close.

Tommy screamed like he had been shot and pinned himself against the cookhouse wall. "Wow mate, what the hells wrong with you?"

He couldn't speak. He was badly traumatised to a point that I thought he had swallowed some food and it was now choking him. I looked at Ged with a confused face and he beckoned me with a nod of his head to look over at the hotplate. I spun my head round to the three slop jockeys (chefs) standing on the other side of the hotplate.

"Arrgghhhh," I shouted. "What in God's name?" I screamed.

There was a chef stood talking to his two mates with all these black blobs walking all over his shoulders, face and his head. Ged told me that this chap had been here four months and he loved tarantulas that much he had decided to fill his room with them, he had clearly lost the plot. There must have been thirty to forty spiders crawling all over him, some of them were huge, at least three were easily the size of my beret. Ged reckoned that he had two hundred plus in his room, say no more. What a nugget. He was proving the theory that the tarantula won't bite a human being unless it is pushed or backed into a corner and I am glad it was he and not me who had volunteered to prove this theory. I was convinced that that lad wasn't going to make it home at the six month point. There was of course another theory that I had read and I wasn't prepared to challenge that either, that was that tarantulas can jump six feet from a standing jump, I wasn't prepared to get within six foot one inch of this guy. It was ridiculous; I had never seen anything like it. I was surprised that his boss was allowing this, he was putting his life at risk and more importantly there was a risk that the troops may not get fed should he die within the next few months. Very inconsiderate, I thought.

We made our way back to the accommodation, when we were about thirty yards away, I could see a sign outside a building to my right. The building was called an atap, which was built from natural jungle wood and finished with palm tree leaves on the roof, very waterproof and very strong when constructed properly. The only problem being that the roof had to be replaced every few years. Most of the 'none army' buildings on camp were built by the Ghurkhas, and they were the masters at building ataps. The sign read 'The Bellwood' I knew it wouldn't take long. Ged said that this atap was our battery bar, I didn't go in but it looked all right from a distance. There was one thing I could see and that was a massive old rusty fridge, I would have to be giving this a once over later. There was only one problem with this battery bar and that it was a bit close to my bed. That meant when the bar was in full swing and the battery barman was blasting 'Bat out of Hell' from the speakers, I wasn't going to get any sleep until 7.am at the weekends. So as the saying goes 'if you can't beat them, join them', and that is what I did.

I walked into the accommodation and realised I only had five minutes before we were to be on parade. After the display from Chindit this morning there was no way I was going to be late, my walk around the camp would have to wait. As I entered the accommodation, I noticed three of the lads who had been shipped to the medical centre this morning, were now lying on their beds. All three of them still looked as white as sheep.

"How did you get on lads?" I asked.

Gunner Sean Morrison sparked into life, he was closest to me. "Fucking hell Bomb, I thought I was going to die," he said with a shaky voice.

"Don't talk wet, you daft bastard. Do you think I would let you die you soft shite?" I replied.

"Yes," he said.

"Fair comment," I answered him as I was walking out of the door. As I was walking from the building onto the road where all our troops were forming, I noticed how hot it was for that time of the morning, it was scorching. Thankfully I was wearing my beret, so I was thinking that would keep the direct sun off my crown. Then I realised that my beret was nearly black, so that wasn't going to work. It may keep the direct sun off me, but it would also attract the heat.

There were six of 'C' troop stood on parade that particular morning, Chindit was marching up the road towards us and he was accompanied by Lt Joplin. I thought to myself, Where the fuck, were you this morning while Chindit was killing the troop sir? I let it go until Rodney arrived at the troop.

"Where is the rest of the troop Sergeant Major?" he enquired.

"Erm we all went for a jog this morning, Sir, and they couldn't hack it."

"Why didn't any one wake me?" he asked. Before he let Chindit answer him, he beckoned him over to the accommodation block. They disappeared out of sight for two minutes and then they reappeared. I hadn't seen Joplin as angry as this before. I knew this was going to come back and bite Chindit on the arse and it was. Sergeant Shaky Moor was taking the parade and then handing over to Chindit. I could see, and so could everyone else that Chindit's feathers had been well and truly ruffled. Joplin was going to report this further up the line to the B.C.

"Right you lot," he started. "This is your official welcome to Belize. All that training you have been carrying out will now be put into practice. Sergeant Moor will be giving you the guided tour of the camp this morning and then you've got the 'monkey talk' straight after lunch."

The 'monkey talk' was the speech that the Royal Military Police (R.M.P) gave you when you landed in a new location for an operational tour. It was normally a 'don't do this' or 'don't go there' or 'if you are caught fighting down town' etc etc. Pretty boring shite really, but it justified their existence and made them feel good so why not? Anyway, it was a good opportunity to take the piss out of the military police while they stood in front of you in starched shorts and shiny boots, if they only knew how bad they looked. Chindit went on about all the rules and regulations regarding the camp. He mentioned 'Swingfog', which we had already experienced the delights of earlier that day. Then there was his warning about the importance of taking our Paludrine tablets, and the consequences if we stopped. Never mind the malaria it was what he would do if he caught you not taking them, that worried most of us. He emphasised the point of booking in and out of camp, we knew that anyone who didn't think they were going to adhere to this rule would end up in jail. He was quite jovial about the fact of booking in and out of camp, he was saying that if the Guats (Guatemalans) had caught or killed one of us then he needed to know at the earliest opportunity, that we hadn't returned, so he didn't neglect his duties by not informing the family back home. Brilliant, I thought. As long as you carryout your duty while I am upside down in the jungle with a spear parked up my arse hole, that's all that matters is it? That Chindit manages to ring my mum up to give her the bad news before he fucks off to the mess that night!

We were beginning to bake in the sun by now and Chindit could see this, he wasn't too bothered but he saw Joplin giving him the evil eye, so he cut his speech short and handed us over to Shaky Moor. I saw little point of the tour around the camp at this stage as there were so few of us. Poor Shaky would be carrying out the tour a few more times yet. On the other hand though, it would be some time before all the troops were released from being on 'the sick' and strong enough to attend Shaky's tour. I didn't want to wait for ever for mine. Shaky started the tour at the guardroom and we walked around the camp in an anticlockwise direction. He actually took us into the guardroom and it was so hot inside, I had literally come out as soon as I had seen inside one of the cells. I think in the short time I was in the guardroom, I had noticed at least one person sucking hard on their water bottle. My thoughts drifted to when I would have to carry out my own duties of Guard Commander and be stuck in this hole for twenty-four hours, Oh dear, I thought. We left the area of the guardroom and main gate and walked in the middle of the main road, it was dusty and very bumpy, but it was at least bearable. I found it hard to believe that vehicles actually drove on this surface. We looked over to our right as Shaky was pointing out numerous buildings, he showed us the M.R.S. (Medical Reception Station) where my mucker Dave Dawkins was probably now beavering away fixing up the troops that Chindit had nearly killed that morning. I was going to remember that building as that's where I was heading as soon as we got knocked off for lunch. We were then able to jump onto the M1 and start to enjoy the walk on solid ground as we passed the sergeants' mess accommodation block. We fully understood that there was such a thing as 'privilege of rank' but the comparison of their accommodation to ours was the 'Dorchester Hotel' in London to a room at the 'Travelodge' without a TV, bed or a bog, sprang to mind. Talk about getting the 'shitty end of the stick'. We reached the sergeants' mess building, where we noticed a number of Anglian Regiment sergeants sitting laughing and joking on a decked area. There was a beautifully coloured parrot sat on a perch just behind them. I soon realised what they were laughing at, the parrot spoke better English than any of us and it was swearing like a trooper.

"Fuck off, Fuck off," it kept saying. I must say though, it did tickle me. I found it hard to believe at first, but quickly grasped an understanding of the situation. The sergeants would have devoted years of their time over many operational tours to teach this bird to swear. Then we continued past the sergeants' mess and up the M1 to the cookhouse. Shaky asked us if we had been in the cookhouse yet, I looked at him and nodded, 'yes'. We walked up the M1, past our accommodation block and he pointed to a mountain at the back of the camp, it was called 'Saddleback Hill'.

"Fucking hill, Sarge?" I shouted to him.

He laughed and said, "Yes, I think Roy Orbison must have named it, he obviously didn't climb the bastard though, if he had, he wouldn't have called it a fucking hill."

It was huge this mountain and I was later to find out that we had troops at the top of this 'hill' laying in an O.P (Observation Post) twenty-four hours a day, everyday. It was their job to make sure that they detected the Guatemalans should they decide to be stupid enough to attack us in the camp. Our lads stayed at the top of this hill for one week at a time, it must have made them stir crazy. The Puma Helicopter would do a change over on a Friday morning and not only swap the troops, but carry out a re supply of any stores and water that was needed. We walked past the 'Bellwood Bar' sign, and again I thought about how quick the troops were to start making reference to Colchester. It wouldn't take long before there were bits of Colly all over the camp, they never missed a trick. The N.A.A.F.I was across the road from our accommodation, and as we walked towards it I noticed at the rear of the main building there was a large compound with very thick green netting around it, that was obviously put in place to prevent anyone seeing inside, I thought it was to keep all the stores for the N.A.A.F.I. It would have been important to look after stores out here as they would make good money on the 'Black Market'. Shaky smiled as he was pointing to this and told me to have a look through a tiny hole in the netting.

"Look at the plants on the side wall in pots," he instructed me. I peeped through the hole and couldn't believe my eyes.

"Tell me it's not," I said.

"Oh yes," he replied. There were twenty odd large marijuana plants in full bloom staring right at me.

"Shit! You can't do that," I said

"Bobby, who runs the N.A.A.F.I. can," he concluded.

It turned out that even the R.M.P. who were coming to do our pep talk later knew full well about this little 'personal use' stash. I was in shock, it was ludicrous. The thought of the British Army having Bobby the Babbling Barman running our N.A.A.F.I. was unbelievable. As we proceeded towards the P.O.L. point (petrol's, oils and lubricants) I couldn't help but think of the situation we found ourselves in, regarding the drugs on our camp. The P.O.L. worried me a little as there was a pump for the issue of Diesel and another for petrol. There was a large brick building with a steel netting front, this held a large number of petrol jerry cans. I wasn't sure if they were full or not, but the heat in this camp was tremendous, so I had serious concerns. I wouldn't like to be anywhere near when the fire started here. We walked back down the main drag towards the guardroom with Shaky pointing out the stores, the office block and the gun garages. We could see in the distance the atap where we would be working on the guns when we were in camp. At least it looked as if it wasn't going to be too hot to work on them down there. As he finished, he pointed down this long straight dusty track to a compound, I looked the two hundred yards and saw two large steel gates, securing what was the ammunition compound. The camp turned out to be a little bigger than I first thought and considering it was holding less than fifty of our troops and one hundred and fifty infantry there appeared to be more than enough space for everyone.

When we returned to the accommodation I asked Shaky if I could go back to the M.R.S. to check how our guys were getting on with their recuperation after the run this morning. This was half true, I also wanted to see my mate, Dave Dawkins. I had my 'joker' tucked in my wallet and I was in a mood to catch him out. A few years ago during a good session in the bar, Dave and I decided to rip a joker playing card in half, he took one half and I took the other. The idea was that if Dave was to sneak up on me and show me his joker I would have to produce my half, there and then. If I couldn't then I would have to pay for the beer all night and that could be very costly. If I pulled mine out and he couldn't find his then he would have to pay for the wets all night. It was just a bit of fun really and we were currently sitting at one each, I saw him out running early one morning in Colly once and I knew he wouldn't have his wallet with him and I knew he kept his joker in his wallet at all times. I drove past him in the Land Rover and pulled up at a bus stop a few hundred yards ahead. I chose my moment to get out of the cab and making sure he didn't see me I jumped from the vehicle and hid behind a large bus shelter. I was watching him through a tiny gap in the bus shelter, he was getting closer and closer, I picked my moment to just hold my arm out from the bus stop and slap my joker right in his mush. Within one second I heard his words.

"You bastard," he puffed. "Fair cop," he added. I sniggered quite loudly.

"N.A.A.F.I. 7 p.m. please," I answered. "

"Fine no problem." He laughed. Fair to say, I was pretty pissed that night and it didn't cost me a bean.

His revenge was sweet however, when a few years later I was hammering across the Prairie in Canada in a tracked vehicle. We had been out in the field on exercise for seventeen days and my driver was driving like a man possessed trying to get us back to the camp before the 'Gag and Puke' closed. The Gag and Puke was just like a MacDonald's takeaway, you can probably imagine the attraction after so long without takeaway food. I was sitting with my head out of the turret of the gun, a scarf wrapped around my face trying my hardest to keep some of the dust from entering my lungs. The dust was almost unbearable, but it was either that or slow right down to the point where we wouldn't make the Gag and Puke and that wasn't an option, speed was of the essence here. When we had been travelling for approximately twenty minutes a vehicle came up along the right hand side of us, I caught sight of it out of the corner of my eye. The side window opened and an arm appeared out of the window, waving in a manner that made me shout down the microphone for Rab to stop our vehicle, which he did immediately. I was clawing frantically at all the dust that had collected in my eyes, then, as I removed my hands my eyes were met with half a joker playing card. Dave had got me; my joker was in my locker back at camp. He was on the ball that particular day and I wasn't, none of my crew even knew he was in Canada. I had to buy him tons of beer that night and it cost me an arm and a leg, thankfully because we were in Canada, the beer was a reasonable price.

I stopped outside the medical centre and prepared my joker ready for the sting, I turned the doorknob really slowly in order not to alert him; I wanted to use the element of surprise as much as I possibly could. Suddenly, I heard his voice, he had his back to me and he was attending to one of the 'sick, lame and lazy' brigade. I couldn't see who it was he was attending to and I didn't care, this was clearly more important. The possibility of having my first 'piss up' in Belize on Dave was so exciting I found it difficult to contain myself. As I tapped him on the shoulder, he turned quickly in a tense fashion. The second he realised he was looking down the barrel of my joker, his shoulders dropped to a slouch and I could see he was not impressed.

"You utter bastard. I don't believe you," he said in a totally dejected tone.

"Oh shall we say the Gag and Puke first and then straight to the bar after a good trough?" I said in a chirpy voice.

"I hate you," he said as he shook my hand really pleased to see me. There weren't many people who would mix with the medics, so it could have been a lonely tour for him, but now I was here things would be a little more fun for him.

The medics were fine, even better than fine when you were a gibbering wreck because you had injured yourself out in the jungle; it was always a mystery to me why the troops never got on with them. He discharged Johnny Ashton from the medical centre and then proceeded to show me around. Dave Dawkins was off his head, he really was a crazy guy. He was telling me that the fridge in the medical centre was supplied in order to keep the snake anti venoms at the right temperature and ready to use, he opened the fridge door.

"Look," he said very proudly pointing inside. It was full to the top with bottles of 'Belikin Beer'.

"Where are the anti-venoms?" I asked him.

"Over there," he said and at that pointed to a kitchen worktop on the other side of the treatment room.

"Dave, what the fuck are you doing?" I said.

"Ah they will be okay," he replied.

"Won't they go off?" I asked.

"Probably in this heat," he replied, "but my beer won't."

He wasn't right in the head he had binned the anti-venoms for the sake of his beer. This meant that the chances of the anti-venom being any use in the event that someone had been bitten were pretty slim.

We had been warned about the 'Beasties of Belize' before we left Colly; two of the snakes stand out in my mind to this very day, the Fer-de-Lance and the Central American Coral Snake. Neither of which I wished to get friendly with during this tour. The Fer-de-Lance was the one that delivered one hundred milligrams of venom; it only took fifty to serve as a fatal dose. Fantastic ,I thought, but what concerned me even more was the fact that it was a pretty unpredictable snake and although most snakes would rather turn and run, this one may stop and have a scrap with you just because it was a hard bastard and it knew it had a bite that would make you fill your pants at the thought of its teeth sinking into your thigh. The problem was though that it wouldn't be much of a scrap, the bite was normally above the knee, which of course is where the old crown jewels are situated, I didn't wish to be bitten at all but the thought of receiving a bite on my nuts was enough to make a glass eye weep. The second thing was that this was one of the most popular snakes in Belize, if you were going to get zapped by a snake, then this was probably going to be it.

The coral snake was another one to be feared along with the other dozen you wouldn't want to step on. The coral snake had a black and red body with yellow hoops around its body and would cause you respiratory distress not long after being bitten, this was another snake I didn't want to meet and I would be twice as worried if I did, having just witnessed that all the anti-venoms were now turning sour in front of my very eyes. Marvellous, I thought. It was at this point of the tour that I was wishing I could be bitten by a tarantula or stung by a scorpion as opposed to any snake. There was a demijohn sitting on the top of the fridge, which was full of small snakes soaking in formaldehyde. Dave's beret was sitting on top of the jar with the Royal Army Medical Corp cap badge facing forward. I initially thought that the collection was something to do with Dave, but it had been left by the last battle group and it was here to stay. It was weird knowing that Dave Dawkins was off his head like that, but I can say that we were in very good hands if we needed him, there was no better man that I could think of that could equal his field medical knowledge or experience. On top of that he was also a qualified pharmacist.

CHAPTER NINE

GREEN STRIPE GRIEF

As I stood on parade in the afternoon sun, I was thinking of the lunch I had just eaten. I couldn't understand how the 'slop jockeys' could fuck up something as simple as watermelon. It was as dry as a squaddies throat before a good beer session. If there's one thing that must be on the ball in a shit hole like this then it's the food. It was far from being right and more like a disaster, to make things worse, we were about to embark on six months of this excuse for cuisine, I couldn't wait.

Lt Joplin brought the troop up to attention and handed us over to the R.M.P. (Royal Military Police). There were two coppers, Sergeant Coleman and his corporal sidekick. It looked something like the 'Laurel and Hardy' show, but more like the 'Twit and Twat' show. I looked along the ranks and could see that we had a troop present for them to talk to now. Everyone, who had flaked out earlier were now back on their feet and fighting fit. 'J' Sub would be the first gun detachment to spend two months down south in another little camp called Salamanca. This camp was a tiny purpose built facility big enough to house a gun detachment, a few infantry bods and the associated supporting staff. It made sense for this camp to be a third of the size of Rideau Camp. Once 'The Monkeys' had delivered the briefing 'J' Sub would be gone and the next time we would see them would be at the two month change over point.

Sergeant Coleman stood right in front of the troop. "Stand at ease, stand easy and pin your ears back you lot," he growled. He looked like an old American gunnery sergeant with the square head and the stuck out chest. One of those who looked as if he had thirty years' service under his belt and the minute he left the army he'd die because he wouldn't know what to do when he became a civvy.

"I want you all to listen to what I am going to tell you. Once I have told you, I want you all to digest it and not let it just waft over the top of your heads," he said. He started with the usual rubbish about how great the Royal Military Police were, then he burbled on about how we were guests in 'their' country so we weren't to upset the locals or piss them off. We weren't to steal anything off them, kill their animals, upset their wives, disrespect their property and that included nicking their cars when we got pissed down town. It turned out that we couldn't do fuck all the way he was carrying on. After he had completed his long list of 'don'ts', he gave us his three favourites which he had kept in reserve.

"Right." He started again. "You have been posted to the Caribbean for six months and I know, that you know, this place is flooded with marijuana." The thoughts of the rear yard in the N.A.A.F.I. came flooding back into my mind. "The two main places you will come across it are Belize City when you fly or sail up North, or when you are down town Punta Gorda." Punta Gorda was only a short drive from Rideau Camp and it was where the troops went for their weekend recreation and 'piss ups'. I was now thinking that 'The Monkeys' would be very busy when the troops were letting their hair down at the weekend. "If you are caught smoking weed or having it in your possession, it's back to Blighty and straight to Colly nick and that's a promise," he shouted. "Is that clear?" he added.

"Yes, Sarge," we all shouted back. He then started to tell us about a whorehouse in Belize City called 'The Rose in the Garden'. The second he mentioned the word 'whorehouse' the troops' heads sprang up like a gopher peeking out of his den. He said that if any of us were to visit this establishment, not only would we be in the shit as it had been classified as 'out of bounds' by the military police, but we were sure to catch a dose of the 'Surrey Docks' from the women who worked there. If we didn't catch any sexually transmitted disease then he would guarantee that he would chop it off if he caught us. They weren't sure if there was a brothel in Punta Gorda (P.G) but they were going to find out, he didn't want us bringing anything back from Belize that you couldn't put on the mantle piece!

"The last thing I need to warn you about is 'Green Stripe'," he said. We all looked at each other with blank expressions. "Do not, at any cost drink Green Stripe," he added.

We learned that Green Stripe was a local spirit which tasted like a peppermint version or Pernod. It was full of many different types of chemical poisons and although you could be enjoying the tastes of it at the time of drinking it, you would turn blind shortly afterwards and remain blind until lunchtime the next day. I couldn't believe this, I had tasted local drinks from all over the world and I had never heard of such a thing. The Belizean bars had another drink called 'Stick Rum' which was as it says. It was a demijohn sat on the bar with clear liquid in it and stuffed with twigs. The clear liquid was nearly neat alcohol, which produced eleven poisons, this was also discouraged. He didn't say forbidden, only discouraged. We were advised to stick to the 'Belikin Beer', which is the locally produced beer. When I say this, I use the term loosely as the words 'locally produced' and 'beer' didn't mean quite the same as it would in the UK. If you can call dipping a rusty tin can into the Caribbean to wash it thoroughly and then filling it with the contents of a Saturday night Belizean disco urinal then 'locally produced' and 'beer' will do for me.

The military police had no understanding of the run of the mill British squaddie, it was a known thing that whatever 'The Monkeys' told you not to do, you could guarantee that the good old British squaddie would go and do it at the first opportunity. It was about time someone had the balls to explain this to the R.M.P. The whore house sounded a little scary as we neither wanted the non surgical removing of our private parts by 'The Monkeys' nor did we wish to receive a touch of the Caribbean that we couldn't tell our mums about. You could rest assured though, that come Saturday night there would be more troops bombed off their heads on 'Green Stripe' and spliffs walking round P.G. with a pint glass of 'Stick Rum' in their hands looking for some of the local Chogies to upset. In fact bollocks to Saturday night, I could guarantee most of them would be at it that night. I wouldn't be drinking to this excess until the weekend. The thought of the ten miler with Chindit in the morning was already enough to make me feel sick.

'The Monkeys' finished their sermon and I watched them jump into one of our Land Rovers as they were being driven round to the helipad where a Puma helicopter would take them up North, back to Belize City. Although the Puma was coming to Rideau to pick up the military police, it would almost certainly be bringing other stores or the camp mail in the process. The second they jumped into the Land Rover the comments of 'they can get to fuck' and 'not a fucking chance mate' started. They were quickly followed up by 'away and shite' and finally 'see you down town tonight'. I really wished they had given the pep talk a miss. The same thing had happened in Canada and within six hours, we had one bloke caught doing one hundred and forty miles an hour in a Ford Mustang down the main freeway. He had just rented it from 'Rent a Wreck', and within seven minutes of driving, he was pulled by the Canadian police. Then we had six of our lads who were banged up for fighting in the 'Sin Bin' in down town Medicine Hat. The Sin Bin was the nick name given to the Sineboi Hotel.

A group of enormous Indians had walked into the bar, we called them FBIs. (Fuckin Big Indians) and one of our lads had stood on a stool and shouted, "You fat Bastard." That was it, the fight had begun. We then had one N.C.O who was admitted to hospital for injuries sustained as a result of him throwing himself off the N.A.A.F.I roof after twenty seven bottles of Bud. Ra Ra and well done the Royal Military Police, had they not said anything, I am sure none of this would have occurred on the first night!

They disappeared out of sight and to be honest I had a sudden feeling of relief when I knew they were gone. It wasn't like we were up to anything bad, but you never wanted 'The Monkeys' around.

When the military police had departed Lt Joplin stepped in and informed us that we were deep into 'siesta time'. We should get our heads down until three o'clock. Siesta time in Belize was from twelve o'clock until three o'clock every afternoon when it was so hot, that it would be suicide to work or play during these times. At three o'clock you would then normally go onto work until five or six in the evening or we were to play sports most afternoons. We had a volleyball and basketball court only fifty yards away from our accommodation, that afternoon we were playing volleyball.

I remember stripping off and placing my head on my pillow. We were going on the rifle ranges in the morning to zero our rifles in and get used to this M15 Armalite. The Armalite was an American rifle that was very light and was able to operate well in these temperatures. It was so hot at that minute in time that it was nearly unbearable. Brilliant, try and have a kip in the afternoon when it was so hot, not the best idea I had ever heard. There were a number of the lads that just couldn't stand the heat and therefore couldn't fall asleep during siesta. I wasn't one of them my mind went all fuzzy then within a minute I would have dropped off.

At three o'clock I found myself staggering through the accommodation door like a drunk leaving his drying out clinic. I don't know how it happened but I was dressed in my volleyball kit and trainers. Taff Terry picked five teams and we created a mini league and sorted the order that the teams would be playing. There was one stage of the games that each team would have to stay on for three straight games which was a bit of a worry in that temperature, it was still roasting hot. My team was playing second and I was looking forward to it. Volleyball was one of my sports as I was six foot two and not a bad player. We sat at the side of the court and watched the first two teams. It was a good game as they both had star players in their teams. The only worry about the court was that it was made of concrete and you just knew that there was going to be some cracking injuries from it. The first game however was a close game and it passed without incident or injury.

Our team was on next and we were to stay on for the run of three games right from the word go. The opposing side had a strong team with four out of the six players known as very competent players. Our store's Staff Sergeant Des Sumner was on the opposite side, he was a big guy and some inches taller than I was. If he spiked the ball when he was standing at the net, you certainly knew about it if you were unlucky enough to be in the line of fire. That's just what happened to me, it was our third game and I was getting ready for a well earned break when I had made my serve. I quickly took up my position behind the three lads at the net, I was still moving forward when Big Dave, unbeknown to me, had met my serve on the full volley and smashed it back like a torpedo over the top of the net. While I was still running forward the ball contacted me square in the face, it was like I had been hit by a train. I suddenly went blind as I was being lifted off the ground. My head shot back and before I knew it there was someone pouring water onto the front, top and back of my head, I knew then that my head was the first thing that had come into contact with the ground. It must have knocked me out for a short time. What a shot, it was so hard. I can't ever remember being punched that hard before, let alone hit in the face by a volleyball. What also hurt was my pride. He had won this point when the ball was clearly going out had I left it. There wasn't much chance of me leaving it as it came over like a bullet from a gun.

When I had regained consciousness fully, one of the reserves had taken my place and joined the game. I don't know if he would have thanked me though after seeing what Dave had just done to me. Tommy had come over to join me which gave me concern. His way of showing he cared was to laugh, ridicule and take the piss out of you while you were in this condition. I didn't mind it from him at least I didn't wake up to Dave Dawkins flashing a 'joker' in front of my face.

We finished the volleyball, or should I say, *they* finished the volleyball and we all headed back to the room. Shaky reminded us not to be late for the run in the morning. He also informed us, but in a much quieter voice, that the distance would be nowhere near what it was this morning and the pace would be half. We were to wear our shorts with boots to protect our ankles. Thank God, I thought I don't think any of us could do that morning's run again. Dave Dawkins would be speaking to Chindit later in a quiet spot to reiterate the message Joplin had given him about how detrimental his act had been to the wellbeing of the troops. Chindit knew he had gotten away with it so I would be surprised if he tried it again; I felt relieved when I knew Lt Joplin was coming on the run too. With that in mind, I was determined to have a go at this 'Belikin Beer' in the N.A.A.F.I later. For now though, I didn't need any shitty beer, I was already feeling pretty dizzy without it.

Ged and I walked towards the accommodation when I noticed a Chogie squatting down amongst some short grass. He caught my eye for two reasons; firstly he had a machete that he was using to cut the grass, but it was no ordinary machete, it was approximately twelve inches longer than ours and the second thing about this chap was that he looked one hundred years old if a day.

"What's the crack with him then Ged?" I said.

"He's harmless," he replied. "He's employed by the M.O.D. to cut the grass here and that's all he does. He works twelve hours a day on his haunches like that. Twelve hours a day, seven days a week. He comes into camp at six every morning and works until six in the evening. He squats down throughout the day and doesn't even stop for the siesta period," he said. "Do you know how much we pay him?" he asked me.

"Go on," I asked.

"Fifteen pounds a month," he finished. We worked this poor chap eighty-four hours a week in this scorching sun without a day off for fifteen quid a month. Would you believe it? I was shocked.

"Don't knock it," he started again. "This guy is minted for a Belizean. He is well respected in society because he earns so much money," Ged added. I found it difficult to believe what I was hearing; this man was looked upon as being rich here in Belize as the British government paid him fifteen quid a month. It was the Belizean economy that dictated what he should be paid and it was clear to see that he truly earned his money. At the end of his working day, he was permitted to report to the cookhouse when the troops had finished eating and take his old empty catering can. He would fill it with waste food from the slops' bucket in the cookhouse; he wasn't allowed to take any food that hadn't been thrown away by the squaddies. This was the food he supplied to his family on a daily basis. For the second time I couldn't believe what I was hearing; this man took food from the slop bucket in our cookhouse to provide for his family.

I waited for Ged and Tommy to be ready before I left the accommodation to go for my evening meal.

"Ged, what's the scran like in the N.A.A.F.I. if the food in the cookhouse is shite?" I asked.

"Equally, as shite," he replied.

That wasn't what I wanted to hear. Normally when you were away on tour or on exercise, if the 'slop jockeys" food was crap, you could depend on at least somewhere else to get some decent trough. It always cost you dearly but you got some good food inside you.

"Brilliant," I finished. We walked into the cookhouse and I could see Tommy scouring the area behind the hotplate. He was looking for the chef with the tarantulas. I tried to tell him he wasn't there, but he was having none of it. We picked up our plates and I looked at the food for the first time. It looked fairly good, I thought. We all filled our plates and I made a point of grabbing two of the biggest lamb chops in Belize. Pudding could wait until we finished our tea. That's if there was any room left for one. We tucked into our main meal and after only a few bites, I realised Ged was right. Either the chefs were taking the piss or the chefs had mislaid their copy of 'the good food guide'. All the vegetables were raw and I could have sworn I saw one of the 'slop jockeys' shaving my lamb chops with a Gillette Two razor, it was disgusting and I wasn't prepared to wait for the orderly sergeant to make a complaint. I was furious; had I been neglectful in my job and my artillery shell landed after seven miles in flight instead of eight, imagine the potential consequences. Even in peace time someone could die. When you are burning up calories at this rate of knots it is important to make every attempt to put them back. If we carried on the way it was now, I would be leaving Belize weighing in at three stone.

I walked over to the hotplate and asked the corporal to walk over to the side. I introduced myself because I was now dressed in civvy clothing after my shower and I had planned on what I was going to say to him. This however depended on how he reacted and what his reply to me was to be.

"Corp. Sorry to bother you, but have you tasted this?" I said while I was pointing to my plate.

"No mate, I have just got in, why what's up?" he replied. So far, so good I thought to myself.

"There is nothing on my plate that is cooked, in fact, I don't think anyone has even lit the oven to be honest," I told him as I was pushing my plate at him. He grabbed a piece of carrot and one of my lamb chops and bit each one in turn and on both occasions he spat the food back into his hand. He grabbed the plate and turned to me.

"Sorry Bomb, come back in twenty minutes and I will make it right," he promised.

As I walked back to my seat, I saw him walk behind the wall at the back of the hotplate. It was then the smashing of a plate I heard followed by him screaming at one of the chefs. Within ten seconds, two chefs appeared and stopped the queue of troops from helping themselves. They took the trays of food from the hotplate and into the back of the cookhouse. This left the hotplates completely bare. The same corporal I had spoken to returned to our side of the hotplate and addressed the waiting squaddies.

"Gents, I am sorry for the standard of the food. This will not happen again on your tour," he added. "Food will be served in fifteen minutes," he finished as he turned and walked back to his kitchen. Everyone in the cookhouse cheered and whistled.

One of the troops shouted, "Way to go Sloppy," as he was walking away.

Within fifteen minutes the hotplates were re-stocked and we tried again. This time the food was 'Heaven'. Everything was cooked to perfection and my chops were just the way I liked them. This was to be the best meal I had in Belize and although I was made up with the actions of that chef, he was actually coming to the end of his tour and we ended up with two lads who had worked in nothing more glamorous than a fast food restaurant and decided to call themselves 'chef' because they wore the same hats. That was about as near to being a chef as they must have got.

Later that night I sat down in the N.A.A.F.I for my first taste of 'Belikin Beer'. The word 'Belikin' was Mayan and it translated to 'Road to the East'. Yeah I thought. East from where I was sitting was the bog, so they got that bit right. Tommy brought me a couple over. It came in a tall brown bottle with a green label and was like a malty version of Budweiser but nowhere near as good. Its 4.5% proof impressed me as I was expecting a lot lower than that. Even so, for the first four bottles it was like sucking on a wet pair of swimming trunks. I could see some of the troops were also tucking into cans of Schlitz. This was a small red and white can and after tasting it once I decided the taste would only be deemed as good if you had throat cancer or suffering from tonsillitis. I could see no other use for this drink than to remove weeds from your garden path or as a de-scaler for your kettle. It really was the Schlitz! This abruptly ended my relationship with this drink. It was either 'Belikin' or shorts, there would be no shorts tonight though as we had our run in the morning. The heavy session would be saved for the weekend.

The early morning run passed without event and it looked like the 'Green Stripe' dragon was staying in until the weekend, other than Steve Humphries puking the full distance of the run there were no other alcohol induced victims. Chindit had slowed it down and taken us even less than the four miles we thought we were going on. With my lightweight consumption of 'Belikin Beer' the night before, I was feeling surprisingly fit. I looked at the faces before we started and it was clear to see that the lads who had fallen the day before were looking really worried. There was no need to be though and it turned out a doddle.

What was also of benefit was that we all managed to take our own water supply. I had four large water bottles stashed in my webbing and they were freezing cold from the water fountain outside our accommodation block. It turned out to be a bit of a waste though, I only managed to get through one bottle and that was with taking my daily dose of Paludrine too. The troops were chuffed to N.A.A.F.I breaks to make it back to camp, but Chindit ordered us to 'fall out' and then he carried on with the rest of the run. I would guess that he was going to complete his ten miles. He would often tag along with the infantry company as they were into this 'running business'.

After my shower, I got dressed into my jungle combats. It was range day, we were going to take our farty little American machine guns and 'zero' them in on the nearby ranges until we could shoot the bull's eye out of the centre of the target. There were two ways to 'zero' this weapon and they were to either do it manually by using an adjusting tool and turning all sorts of grub screws or just plain and simple 'aiming off', which was my preferred method. If I was firing off to the left, I would just simply aim one inch to the right. If I was firing high, then I would just aim one inch lower. It worked for me and it meant that if anyone else fired my rifle there would be a possibility that it would fit them without adjustment or they could just aim off as I did. Don't for one minute think that as an Artilleryman I was a good shot. You couldn't be further from the truth, I was crap. If I was standing six feet in front of a life-sized target, I would miss with all twenty rounds. Every soldier had to complete an annual personal weapons test (A.P.W.T). During the test we would take it in turns to be positioned in the butts underneath the target, in order to change it between shooters. On your turn it was the done thing, to help out your mates and shove a pencil through the target several times near to the bull's eye which would bluff the senior ranks into thinking you were a crack shot. Bargain! On the downside you could have thirty perfect holes in your target and only have fired ten... OOOOps!

I placed my left foot into my new jungle boots. Now normally, if we were back at Colly, we would take them outside and piss on them to make the leather supple or leave them in a full bath of water with a brick on them for three weeks, but we couldn't really do this with the jungle boot as it was mainly canvas. I had only worn them once so the ranges would be a good time to start wearing them in. I bent over to tie the lace and at this point I thought to myself, you fool you didn't check your boot. We were told well before we got to Belize that you should NEVER put on an item of clothing, or footwear without checking them for tarantulas or scorpions. Shit, I had just got dressed into my combat gear and I was now wearing my left boot and I hadn't checked. Bit late now, I thought. I picked up my right boot and shook it upside down towards the ground, at first nothing appeared and then as I was about to stop shaking something dropped to the floor. I looked down and there was a dark red, nearly brown scorpion looking up at me, I broke out into an immediate sweat and shouted Ged to come and have a look. Ged turned up with his machete and without saying a word made a swipe at the beast and missed.

"Oh yeah Ged, why don't you piss it off even more," I screamed.

"Stop being so soft you big girl," he replied and with his next blow he chopped it clean in half. It had scared me half to death and it was only when we were walking down to the armoury to collect our rifles that I thought back. What if I had put my other boot on first and stood on it, oh dear! This turned out to be a quick lesson and would never be repeated.

We marched from the armoury around to the range which was only approximately four hundred yards. Even that short distance rendered us all soaking wet through with sweat, and not fit to open a sweet wrapper let alone fight a battle. We didn't mind though as our episode of zeroing the weapons in was going to be more fun than I had first thought. We had been issued hundreds of Armalite rounds to blast down the range. This was unusual for small arms ranges as you were normally there for a purpose and that was to either zero your weapon or carryout your annual test. Either way, I knew we were in for some fun. We had two good sergeants with us in Dave Norman and Nick Coulter. I was pretty sure we would be getting the zeroing out of the way and then settling down to a fun shooting competition. I was also sure that there would be a prize of a few beers riding on the outcome of it too.

The range was a hole in the side of Saddleback Hill, it looked just like a JCB digger had charged into the base and removed enough soil, rocks and debris to make a large 'dug out'. This wasn't done for our benefit, it was clear that it had been here some time. The sides of the ranges were piled high with the soil taken from the hole, this formed a barrier between the unsuspecting Belizean who could have been walking into camp on his way into work, and some mental case squaddie having a bet with his mucker, that he could shoot the spliff from his lips as he passed the range. There was a new, shiny bright corrugated building situated at the bottom of the range that was clearly supplied by the British Army to serve as a 'range warden' shed. It stood to the left of the targets as we were looking at it from the firing point. This shed is where all the targets and the glue were kept locked away when the range wasn't being used. The range warden was a huge Belizean bloke who would dress in shorts and flip flops and no shirt. He was carrying the figure eleven targets and standing them up in the readymade holes for us to destroy. A figure eleven target stood about three foot tall and was supposed to represent a picture of an enemy soldier charging at you with a rifle but looked about as real as E.T. The three colours on the target were a dark red, black and white. We had buckets of what looked like flour and water paste, a brush and the same coloured patches to patch up the target once the bullet had gone through it.

On the firing point there was only room for six squaddies to shoot at any one time, normally a firing point would hold at least double that figure. This meant that if you were firing with a large troop, it would take a considerable amount of time for them all to complete the shoot; our numbers were good as we had twenty-five men. I grabbed four of the troops and spruced the firing point up a bit. The old sandbags that had obviously been there for many years needed fluffing up if we were going to use them to rest our elbows on, so the lads set about making them right. I was a little worried in case any beasties came pouring out of the sandbags, fortunately there were none. We found a couple of old nine millimetre brass cartridge cases, which told me that the last regiment hadn't put any effort into cleaning the range up. This was a blow, any regiment worth its salt paid particular attention to clearing the range after firing.

The range warden came over to speak to our two sergeants, what a blow. It turned out that we only had approximately two hours live firing as the American detachment were coming on to use the range. They had booked it six weeks ago and were due on here at midday. I was seriously pissed off as this was our time and now 'Hank the Yank' had put paid to that. It meant we would have to act with a bit more haste now in order to get the zeroing out of the way. This should leave a good hour for play.

Dave Norman split us up into four groups of six. I was in the first group and as soon as I had finished firing I was going to help the senior ranks to organise the rest of this rabble. The area beyond the firing point was cleared and every person was accounted for before we started firing. Ron the Rock Rowlands was on the opposite end of the line to me and shouted over.

"Bomb Connolly, watch this space and I will show you how to do it."

Every person on the range started laughing uncontrollably, including the two sergeants who should have been in 'serious mode' at this time. Gunner Rowlands always had this thing about competing with me. No matter what it was he had to try and beat me on the ranges, it did my ego a world of good because he couldn't do anything right and it was always easy to beat him. Three months ago on the ranges near Colchester he said something similar and after he had fired eighty-six rounds of 7.62mm, he had managed to get one round in the target, scoring a massive two out of a possible one hundred and ninety-two points. We pissed ourselves then and we were pissing ourselves now, he did entertain us.

"Fuck off, you couldn't score in a brothel with a fiver stuck out your ear," I shouted back. I was a bad shot, but at least I faced the target! He was terrible and I had to give myself 'some' credit. If he was a good shot then I was waiting for the chief of the M.O.D to come and take me away for special operations sniper duties. We took up prone position on the firing point, and I reached down to my webbing to remove my water bottle which I placed out to my front. Sergeant Coulter let us take our time, this was evident by the way he was shouting the orders to us. It was actually a relief to hold the Armalite as it was very light, with a full magazine it only came to just over seven pounds.

"In your own time, at the target in front carry on," Nick shouted and with that all hell broke loose. The noise was quite deafening on such a weird little range. I hadn't heard anything like that before and didn't expect the intensity. It was no problem and after a few rounds down the range, I had got used to the strange noises.

I concentrated my rounds to what I thought was the centre of the target and remembered my 'Marksmanship Principles'. That wasn't me being a good shot it's what is taught to every squaddie before they fire on the ranges. The marksmanship principles are four points that help you improve your set up when firing your rifle, if you can apply these four points, you will soon see that they do actually work and your shooting will be improved. When we had expended ammunition we were called forward to the targets by the two sergeants. For obvious reasons, everything on the ranges is controlled by a senior person and safety is of the utmost importance at all times.

When we reached the targets, I was impressed with my grouping. Not only did I not need to 'aim off' but the elevation was spot on too. There was a tight three inch group in the centre of my target with the odd stray round where I had snatched the weapon on firing.

"Well done Bomber. Paste up," Nick said.

"Yes Sarge," I replied. No sooner had I grabbed the tin of glue and the patches when I heard Dave Norman roaring with laughter.

He called me over. "Look at that Bomb Connolly," he said between laughs. There wasn't one hole in Ron's target.

"Fucking hell Ron," I started. "I think the best thing you can do is Da Doo Ron Ron Ron Da Doo Ron Ron back to camp with your head held low." I laughed.

Nick was funny too, to add insult to injury, knowing there was not one hole in his target, he turned to him and said, "Oh and don't forget to 'paste up'. Well that was it, every person on the ranges was in raptures. I laughed so much I nearly paid my TV licence. Ron couldn't lift his head with the embarrassment.

I joined the two sergeants and assisted in the running of the range while the next three groups went through and zeroed their weapons. There were some really good shots being fired by everyone, so much so we came fourth out of four groups. Mind you when you have got 'Smoking Ron the Rock Rowlands' on your team, you have got absolutely no chance of winning. We knew this at the start of the competition and we knew it even more so at the end. This was going to cost us dearly in the N.A.A.F.I. that night. One of the groups finished with four times as many points as us, I rest my case.

The live firing passed without incident, then I noticed the two yanks walking towards the range. One was a 'master sergeant at arms'. He had more stripes than a herd of zebras and the other one who was only a corporal had the same rank banding as us which was two stripes. I had to be impressed by those guys because not only were they bang on time, but the sergeant was carrying something that I had to get my hands on. This weapon slung over his shoulder looked similar to a sawn off shotgun however this one had a barrel that had a two inch diameter.

"What the fuck do you put in that?" Nick said.

"Well, the weapon is an American M.79 grenade launcher, Sir," he replied to Nick.

"It's okay Sarge, I'm the same rank as you, you don't have to call me Sir," Nick answered. "I say again, what the fuck goes in it?"

The American pulled out of his webbing pouch what I could only say looked like a six inch vibrator, it wasn't a vibrator though it was the grenade projectile that you slotted into the broken weapon before firing, again just like a shotgun. The sergeant agreed to give us a demonstration of what this thing could do, I was so excited at this new toy as I had never seen anything like this in all my service and I thought two things. Firstly, why haven't the brits got anything like this? Secondly, and more importantly, when can I have a go?

"Have you got any more rounds with you?" I asked.

"Twenty, Sir," the corporal replied, they didn't drop this 'Sir' shite, so I wasn't going to correct them anymore. The corporal pointed to a large square ammo box with the remaining twenty rounds in it.

"Has one of those rounds got a British name on it like Sean Connolly?" I enquired. The sergeant turned to me and smiled, he immediately knew what I was after. He glanced over to his corporal who was smiling gingerly before turning back to me.

"I am sure I saw that name on one of the rounds earlier, Sir," he answered. Good man, I thought.

I turned the 'switch a la sensible' in my head and flicked it to the 'on' position. I watched the demo very carefully, Nick and Dave were happy for me to have a cabby, but no fucking about. I had been warned.

The sergeant stood on the firing point while the corporal barked the orders at him. This is easy, I thought. The Americans were using the same firing orders as the British Army would receive. He simply broke the weapon at the breach and loaded the six inch black dildo into it before snapping it closed again. No problem, I thought again. Just like a shotgun, I had fired a shotgun when I was twelve years old on the farm so I was confident with this bit.

"Aim high by one inch for every fifty yards," the American sergeant shouted to me.

"Roger," I answered. I knew that he would understand that.

The corporal screamed to the sergeant, "In your own time, go on."

I watched the Sergeant as he aimed well above the figure eleven targets. There was a huge rock embedded in the side of the mountain. It must have weighed four or five tonne easily. There was a pause while the sergeant clenched the cheeks of his buttocks and said his last goodbyes before he squeezed the trigger.

It sounded like a full battery of artillery guns going off., the noise was deafening. It was amazing how you could watch the projectile flying through the air whilst standing behind the sergeant, I watched the yank first as he was thrown back with the recoil of this monster. Shit what a punch in the shoulder, a lot worse than a shotgun that was for sure. The grenade passed over the top of the targets and hit an area three feet away to the right of the rock. The force of the explosion was only a little less than when I blew Wales up a few weeks before, it picked the rock up and threw it to the front of the targets as if it was a stone and had cleared the targets by about eight foot. This grenade launcher was something else.

The sergeant called me forward and as he passed me my projectile, he said, "This has got Mr Connolly written all over it, Sir."

I smiled. Now I knew for sure that no one was going to take this moment away from me, it was all mine. I could see all the troops sitting on the ground behind me, time to put on a show, I thought. I was never going to fire this grenade at the target, but I didn't have a clue at this time where it *was* going to land. In the blink of an eye, I looked at the warden's shed at the side of the range. Yes, no, yes, I am thinking. Surely, I couldn't blow the range warden's shed up? Too right I could, it may get me in a little spot of bother, but would it be worth all the shit? Yes, of course it would.

"In your own time, carry on," the corporal shouted. I snapped the weapon open and fed the large black projectile into the barrel, then snapped it closed and raised it up to my shoulder. I faced my front, but glanced out of the corner of my eye at the shed. I kept my feet grounded and just swivelled my hips to the left, I had judged the distance to be one hundred yards so I aimed two inches higher than the roof of the shed, before anyone could challenge my antics, I let rip, I squeezed the trigger and braced myself for this massive kick in my right shoulder, when it came it was as fierce as I had imagined. I watched the grenade travel through the air as if it was moving in slow motion, as it came to land and connected with the roof of the shed, then there was a huge explosion and the shed was flying through the air. It must have lifted twenty feet off the ground as a whole piece, but as it was landing it disintegrated before our eyes. I could see two six foot pieces of 'wriggly tin' (Corrugated Iron) and nothing else.

"Oh my fucking God," Nick said. "Sean, what the fuck have you done?"

"Just relocated the shed, Sarge, that's all," I replied.

"Relocated it, you have obliterated it you tit."

I handed the weapon back to the two yanks who were still in deep shock and looking down the range in the direction of where the hut used to be.

The only words I heard from them before they scurried off the range were, "Thank you, Sir," as I passed the weapon back to him. The rest of our lads were laughing their heads off, but the range warden was none too happy, Dave was trying to comfort him and was promising him frantically, that we would sort another one out for him very quickly.

Dave and Nick took me down to the targets and proceeded to beat me senseless with a severe tongue lashing. As long as they didn't tell Chindit, I would be okay. I knew the bollocking was coming from Dave and Nick, but I also knew that I got on that well with them and they would keep it quiet. Mind you, I had major favours to pay back now and I didn't have a clue where the fuck a shed was going to appear from but Dave had made the promise, so it was important that it was carried out. If he didn't get his new shed, I was sure that he would put the bubble in. I thought, did I enjoy it? Yes. Did it do the job, I thought it would? Yes. Would I do it all again? Fucking right I would!

Chapter Ten

Glass Back

I walked into the medical centre to tell Dave Dawkins about what had happened on the range when I heard a voice I knew.

"And if that hurts, you are fucking dead," the voice belonged to Lance Bombardier Don Brown. They called him 'One Punch Brownie', as he would only hit you once and it was rare that you got up from it. He was huge and had hands like JCB shovels. When we were stationed in B.A.O.R. (British Army on The Rhine) he would often be found beating the Germans up, he was an animal. He would strut about as if he had two tennis balls under his armpits and his chest was pushed out that much that it would arrive three minutes before the rest of him. It was a rarity to see him walking without his tongue stuck out the side of his mouth too. He worked in the stores and was a bit of a R.E.M.F, but there weren't too many people who would have the balls to call him a R.E.M.F. to his face.

Before we came to Belize, I'd had a good chin wag with Brownie, it was touch and go that he would make it to Belize because he had damaged his spine playing rugby and as a result was subject to regular lumbar injections. Dave was the medic and there would be no problem with him injecting Brownie.

"Come in Sean," Dave shouted.

"You don't mind Sean coming in do you Brownie?" Dave asked him

"No, he's our medic so I aint got a problem with it," Brownie replied.

I walked into the treatment room, where my eyes were met by Dave priming this huge needle, I had attended a six week field medical course the year before and dealt with other medical supplies, but I had never seen a needle like this one. It resembled a javelin, it was huge. Brownie spotted the needle, but it wasn't as much a shock to him as it was to me as he had seen this size needle a few times now.

"Did you hear me? If this hurts, you will fucking hurt," he said again.

Dave Dawkins never batted an eyelid. "Lean over the medical couch and pull the top of your shorts down," he said as he was looking at the needle.

As I have previously said Dave Dawkins was a fit man and very hard, Brownie had more than met his match here. Brownie was now leant over the couch with the top of his shorts pulled down. He had a 'builder's crease' like the Rhonda Valley, had I brought my bike with me I would have had somewhere to park it.

Dave Looked over at me with those 'Watch this' eyes, he was grinning like a Cheshire cat, then just like a joiner striking a six inch nail, he brought the needle down and speared it into Brownie. Brownie screamed like a baby and was trying to stop himself from turning round to attach his monstrous fist to the side of Dave's face. Dave changed his hand position and put one hand on top of the plunger and the other holding the body of the syringe he then pushed the plunger down as hard and fast as he could and Brownie let out another whimper. Dave sped up his actions, no sooner had he finished squirting the liquid into Brownie's back he ripped the needle out, by that time Brownie was getting up very quickly and turning at the same time. Dave dropped the syringe on the floor and let loose a big 'right hand hay maker'. He punched Brownie so hard that I thought he had caused him permanent damage. I heard the crack and truly believed that it had shattered his jaw. Brownie slid down the couch and landed on the floor in the 'sitting up' position, he was dazed, but not so much that his tongue couldn't stick out of the side of his mouth again.

"Don't you ever come into my fucking medical centre and threaten me you piece of shit, now fuck off," Dave ordered.

I was in shock as Brownie took a minute to gather his thoughts. Dave was a mental case, but for him to smack someone in his medical centre when they were in his care, was even a surprise to me. It was a peach of a punch and caught him a corker but Dave was supposed to be fixing up the troops not breaking them. There must have been some facial damage surely, but I had watched Dave looking at Brownie and he was a first class medic, so if he said there was nothing wrong with him, then there was nothing wrong with him. Brownie wobbled out of the medical centre and must have forgotten about the pain in his back because the way he was holding his jaw it was clear that he was more worried about that.

After Siesta we were playing basketball which was a favourite sport of mine, my height came in very handy too. There were a few of us in our troop that were tall, so it made for some interesting games. The shorter, slower players just fouled you every time they got near you, because they felt disadvantaged. A right elbow or forehead was usually their favoured method of attack. It wasn't funny, the 'short wheeled base tree rats' were out to get us tallies! The sides were picked as they were the day before, six men on each team. Gunner Mick McCarthy was on Tommy's team and I could see the look of disapproval on his face, not only was McCarthy crap at all sports, but he also had the co-ordination of a split lip. He was useless and he didn't hide the fact, his preferred sports were bed bouncing, dreaming about athletics and sunbathing.

Tommy shouted over to Mick and instructed him to stand in the centre circle, "When the ref throws the ball in the air, all you have to do is catch it, and throw it to one of us."

"Leave it to me Bomb," Mick replied. The referee blew his whistle whilst throwing the ball up in the air and into the middle of the court. Gunner McCarthy and Lance Bombardier Andy Berry jumped for the ball, I was impressed, Mick out jumped Andy and caught it cleanly, landing with both feet on the court it really was a good catch. I looked around at Tommy's team and saw that two of them were wide open to receive the pass from Mick, both of the team members were now standing on the wings. Tommy was heavily guarded and there was no way he could have received the ball and as Mick landed back on the ground after this magnificent catch he must have had a rush of brilliance. He made a dash towards the basket, leaving everyone confused and looking at each other. He was one of these non proficient players who could only bounce the ball while he was looking at it, but the minute he tried to look up he would lose it.

He went round one player and then another, there were three of his team now screaming at him for the ball. "Pass the ball you fucking blimp," Shaky shouted from the side line.

Not a chance. Mick wasn't having any of it and like a man possessed he continued sprinting towards the ring. Everyone on the court had stopped in their tracks as he leapt into the air, a good distance from the basket and still travelling forward, with both hands he lifted the ball and then semi dunked it into the basket. What a shot, I thought, it would have been even better had it been in the right net! He had just fired the ball into his own net scoring one of the best own baskets I had ever seen.

Unbelievable! Tommy was going daft, he ran towards him screaming.

"You fucking imbecile, what the fuck are you doing?" he asked.

Everybody was laughing but Mick still hadn't got it. He was waiting for the applause from his team, but instead had received the wrath of Tommy. "You prick, that's your fucking basket," he was pointing down the court to the ring at the other end. "All you had to do was pass it to another member of our team, and you couldn't even do that."

"Oooops, sorry Bomb," Mick replied sheepishly.

"Fucking hell, if we give you a rifle you wouldn't shoot your own men would you?" What worried me was the fact that Mick had to think about his answer. Suddenly I hoped that when the 'fire fight' started Mick McCarthy was nowhere near me, I think I would have to shoot him before I shot the enemy, he was too much of a liability.

This game was going to be a blast if it were to carry on like this. Dave Sumner who was trying to referee the game was laughing so much, he had to sit down but after a short time he managed to regain some composure and stamped his authority on the game once more. I sat back down on the side line and as we were on next, I wanted to make sure I got enough water down my neck before I went on the court. I sat on one of the old plastic chairs which were at the side of the court obviously these old chairs lived outside. They had faded beyond recognition and the legs were in a poor state.

I remember looking down at the front legs of this chair as it didn't feel safe. As I looked up again, I noticed a Rodney from the Anglian regiment walking up to the 'fuel dump'. I recognised his face as I had worked with him on a field ambulance training exercise. He was a decent bloke for a young Rodney, during the time I worked with him I'd quickly realised that he was a good young officer. He was about twenty yards from me and I was in two minds as to whether or not I should shout him. He wouldn't have known I was in Belize, and I certainly didn't know he was going to be. It was a pleasant surprise and I would try my best to have a beer with him somewhere along the line. As he drew level with me, I thought he had seen me but I must have been mistaken, because he carried on walking.

It was unusual that he had come from the direction of the medical centre and he was carrying his T-shirt, it was also unusual that everyone in range of him was laughing in his direction, including all the troops on and off the basketball court. Once he had walked past me I discovered the reason why the troops were laughing so loudly at him. There was some text written on his back in purple writing, it read 'I am a Twat, please kick me' I was taking a swig from my water bottle at this time and nearly swallowed it. He had obviously come from the Med. Centre and had received treatment for some kind of skin disorder, there would only be one person in the medical centre at this time of day and that was Dave Dawkins. I couldn't believe what he had done, if I was correct in my thoughts Dave was in the shit.

Before we deployed to Belize we were shown some photographs of troops who had previously carried out the six month stint. The Medical Corp had come up to Colchester and given us a really interesting talk on various tropical diseases and ailments that we may encounter, there was a condition where your skin goes through a minor rotting process whereby you end up with large scabs, appearing mainly on your back, it was crucial that those scabs didn't become open sores and get infected. There was a purple dye that they nick named 'Purple Haze Wet' that the medics would paint over the scabs; this placed a clean seal over the site of the sore, thus keeping it very clean. It was fantastic stuff, but it had one drawback. It was on your back for about two months before it started to disappear, similar to having a semi-permanent tattoo on your back. Dave Dawkins had decided that it would be a good 'morale booster' to paint it on with a message for the troops. It would only be a short time before Dave was being dragged up on orders for the stunt; it was going to cost him dearly. I had to get my game of basketball out of the way and go and see him, I had to stop him doing anymore before it got out of hand. One officer would be hard to pacify, but more than one would be near impossible. Dave was off the scale, he was scared of no man, so this didn't bother him in the slightest. We had only been in the camp for a couple of days and he had caused so much trouble already, it would only be a matter of time before he got drummed out of Belize.

My game passed without event and we got beat by a bunch of morons, they left the court cheering and we just managed to crawl to the edge of the court for an urgent re-supply of water. It was murder playing sport in this weather. I asked Dave Sumner if I could nip and see Dave Dawkins in the medical centre. At first he thought that there was something wrong with me, but I reassured him that I was fine and he sent me on my way. There was no way my team would be playing again and that was a fact, we were shit at basketball. Anyway, I didn't care about basketball at this moment in time as I needed to get to the medical centre before Picasso painted anyone else. Who knows, it may be worse next time and I wouldn't put it past him to start painting male genitalia on a Rodney's back. I was walking in the direction of the medical centre wondering what the hell he would get up to next. As I arrived I could hear 'Meat Loaf, Bat out of Hell' blasting from inside the building, I walked into the main treatment area and there was Dave, sitting on a chair at the side of the treatment couch with his feet on the bed and pushing himself back on the two rear legs of the chair. He wouldn't have done that on the chair I had been sitting on that afternoon, that's for sure, it would have collapsed leaving the medic needing a medic!

"What the fuck have you done with that dye?" I asked.

"Good isn't it?" he replied.

"You are not right, what happens when Rodney's mate sees his back?"

"Fuck 'em," he said. "Want a beer?" he asked me.

We had nothing else on that day, so I took one. "Fuck it, yeah, go on." He opened the 'snake anti-venom fridge' and grabbed a couple of 'Belikins' out of it. I smiled knowing that we were all going to die if we get bit by a snake, the anti-venoms which were on the worktop had now disappeared, Dave had binned them for sure. He put the bottle top in his mouth and pulled down then wiped the top and handed it to me, the bottle top was gone and was now falling from his mouth onto the floor, he then repeated the actions with his own bottle, glanced at the Mayan Temple on the label and tipped it back into his throat. He downed half a bottle in one gulp and I did the same, it went down really well in those hot, sticky temperatures.

206

"Listen mate," I started, "you need to take it easy, these Rodneys will have you if you raise your head above the firing line. Try and keep a low profile, I don't want to see you getting sent back to Colly and losing your stripes when they bust you down."

"Ah," he said in his cocky manner, "I didn't know you cared."

"Fuck off, I don't," I answered. "If you go back, I won't be able to get a cold beer in the daytime." I smiled. He knew where I was coming from. Infantry soldiers saw the Medical Corps as R.E.M.Fs and I am not saying all, but some of the officers would take great pleasure in getting a soldier in the Medical Corp busted. The fact that these medics could be called upon to work their magic and keep you alive, in the battlefield had nothing to do with it. Dave and I talked idle chit-chat for about an hour, he was going to struggle out in Belize as he was based in the camp for most of his tour, he didn't like the camp life and I always knew he had joined the wrong regiment. Dave was fit and strong, so should have picked something a little more adventurous, it would be near on impossible for him to get out of the camp gates and deploy on an exercise. He felt that his skills were wasted in camp and would be better served out in the jungle on patrol or exercise. What he meant to say was that he wanted to get into the heart of the jungle and bomb the shit out of the place. I would be in the medical centre as much as possible to see him and see if I could pick up some free tips. The only time I wouldn't see him would be when it was our turn to spend two months down South in Salamanca camp.

I left the medical centre and agreed to meet Dave in the N.A.A.F.I. later. I had a feeling that if we were in the N.A.A.F.I. we would be reasonably safe from Dave's antics, surely there wasn't much in there he could get up to. Then I remembered all the marijuana that was so conveniently growing in the yard at the rear of the N.A.A.F.I. and unless we wanted Dave Dawkins bombed off his head waltzing around to the tune of 'We All Live in a Yellow Submarine' it was in all of our interests not to remind him. He could drink like a fish as it was, so throwing drugs into the mix as well would not be a good idea. I remember paying for all his beer one night in Canada where the beer was mega cheap, it cost me a fortune.

When I got back to the accommodation block, I could see 'Big Ged' lying on his pit (bed). "Who's your mate Ged?" I said to him. He looked confused until I nodded my head pointing at a four foot long iguana sitting on the floor looking up at him. It was a beautiful creature and the colours of its rough skin were amazing, I took my 'Jack Knife' out of my top right hand pocket and began to undo the lanyard that was holding it fastened to my button hole. It was clear that Ged was more than startled at the presence of this magnificent reptile. Ged screamed at me to get my machete.

"No," I whispered. "Let me sort it," I said. With that, I made a noose in my Para chord and lowered it down right in front of its face. It never moved a muscle and I thought it would run off at any time but it didn't and I managed to lower the rope over its head and down onto its neck, I had expected it to jump and thrash around until I let go of the lanyard and then disappear into the undergrowth outside our buildings.

"Come on Iggy," I said to the iguana, leading it away from Ged's bed space and over to mine. It was amazing, it walked like a little dog, when I arrived at my bed I walked it over to a part of the floor where I wanted it to wait until I got myself ready for my shower. I tied the Para cord around my locker handle and told Ged that Iggy was coming to the showers with me.

"You're not right in the fuckin head you," he grunted. I smiled at him, he was only right.

I walked Iggy from the block to the showers and the troops were diving all over the place when they saw me walking towards the shower block with this beast. There was an expectation that it may try and pull away or bolt, but it did neither, it was as if he was looking forward to his shower. Iggy sat down in the corner of the shower looking up at me. The plan was for him to get some water on his back and then run off before any of these cruel bastards got their mitts on him but he wasn't going anywhere and clearly loved every minute of being in the shower. At the end of the shower I turned the showers off and walked him back towards the block. He walked with his chest stuck out and a cheeky spring in his step. I heard the groans from the troops as I returned to the accommodation with Iggy, even the ones who liked animals thought I was a little simple.

Once I was changed and ready for my evening meal, I waited outside for Tommy. "What the fuck are you going to do with that?" Tommy said.

"I'll walk it down the M1 and let it go by the cookhouse," I answered. With that we set off for the cookhouse. I pulled my lead very gently and Iggy followed, it amazed me how tame he was, however Tommy had warned me to be careful, iguanas had a knack of thrashing their tails and causing some serious injuries. When we were about fifty yards from the cookhouse, I turned round to look at Iggy, his lead was very loose. He had started to shed his skin which was so fascinating having never seen this before.

He paused for a moment and looked up at me, there was a large iguana skin sat on the M1 and Iggy was now turning away. He stopped once more for a second and then scurried off into the monsoon ditch at the rear of the accommodation blocks. I bent down and removed my lanyard from around the neck of the shredded skin and put it into my pocket. It was good to know that none of our hooligans would be able to get anywhere near it.

The 'slop Jockeys' only had three standards of cooking and it was good to see that they hadn't changed the habit of a lifetime. The food was at the highest standard expected and that was 'shit'. They had broken a record tonight for me, the worst food I had encountered whilst on operations. I still couldn't understand how they managed to destroy something as simple as baked beans or custard, but they did. It must have been at an all time bad as there were no Chogies filling their big catering cans from the slops when we had finished eating our meals. We walked back to the block after eating our evening meal wishing that Wolfgang was there at that moment in time.

Wolfgang was a fast food seller in Gutersloh, West Germany. He had a huge white Mercedes Van and used to drive onto our camp most nights when we were stationed in Germany (B.A.O.R.) to sell his hot food. He cooked the best takeaway food I had come across anywhere. The troops would trough bratwurst, chicken, schnitzels currywurst, bockwurst and chips nearly every night. We often said that he should have joined the British Army as his map reading skills were second to none, he would often drive out to the firing ranges and find us when we were out on exercise some nights. It was brilliant because he had this big hand bell that he would ring loudly with one hand out the window of his vehicle while he was driving across the ranges to let us know he had arrived on site. What a welcome sight this was. Not only

209

was his food good, but he also sold the 'Yellow Suit Case', this was the cardboard box that wrapped around the ten stumpy bottles of Herforder Pils that we used to drink on a regular basis. What we would give right now for a 'Yellow Suit Case'.

After another cigarette, I looked at my watch. It was seven-thirty and before I had a chance to say anything, I heard Taff shouting from the bottom of the block.

"Bar's open pussies."

"See you in there Taff. Won't be long," I replied. I loaded a few Belizean dollars into my pocket and left the rest in my lockable drawer in my locker. There was about two hundred dollars in there which I had concerns about. I wasn't bothered about our own troops but I didn't trust the Chogies as I didn't know them. It was only later into the tour that these fears were found to be unjust as it was said that the Chogies wouldn't touch a nickel either inside or out of your locker. It was a fact that they wouldn't risk losing their jobs for the sake of nicking money from the troops.

Tommy and I nearly clashed as we walked out of the accommodation door. "Why don't we have a couple in the N.A.A.F.I and then one in the battery bar," Tommy said.

"Good idea," I replied. "I don't want to kick the arse out of it though Tom because of the run in the morning."

"No worries mate, I understand," he finished. There was a little wooden bridge which went over the top of the monsoon ditch. It was just wide enough for one person to walk over at any one time, I went first in the dark of night with Tommy close behind me. No sooner had we got over the bridge and started to cross over the main road that ran through the camp, I thought that someone had thrown a stone and it had struck me on my right temple. I dropped to the floor like a jock catching fifty pence and I found myself kneeling on my left knee, I couldn't understand what had hit me so hard.

Tommy came over to me pretty quick. "What the fuck was that Sean?" He asked

"I don't know mate, but it fucking hurt." I replied.

"I heard it strike your head whatever it was," he added. He started to look around on the ground to see if he could find some evidence. I was still on one knee, but couldn't help but join him from where I was.

"What the fuck?" I heard him shout, he was some ten feet away from where I was now getting back to my feet. I looked down to where he was pointing and there was a large creature, lying lifeless. It measured about four inches in length and looked like something out of a horror film, a cross between a locus and a grasshopper. It must have been flying past minding its own business when my rather large head crossed its flight path. It hurt so much that I thought that there had to be blood, there wasn't but it did leave a large purple mark on my temple which was very sore. I would be watching out for these low flying beasts from now on.

I plonked into the chair in the N.A.A.F.I. while Tommy went to the bar to get the wets. Why did everything in this shit hole have to be fifty times the size it was back in Blighty? I thought. Bloody spiders the size of my beret and scorpions the size of pencils and now this thing. Had this beastie hit an aircraft, the pilot may have had good reason to presume that he had just sustained a 'Bird Strike'. When Tommy told Dave Dawkins what had just happened to my head, he didn't ask how I felt, but commented that had I not been here, he would have had to get his own beer from the bar.

"Thanks for fuck all Dave," I said.

"Don't mention it," he answered.

The N.A.A.F.I. was filling up pretty quickly and there were a number of the Anglian Regiment pissed up in one corner shouting abuse at everything that moved. I distinctly remember this as the TV was in their area and it was showing something from about six weeks ago. I knew the British Forces Broadcasting Service (B.F.B.S.) was slow, but not that slow, I think B.F.B.S. ran on an annual budget of eight pounds a year, it was the pits. I don't know where it was broadcasted from, but I had a feeling that the producers and editors must have been bombed out of their heads all day everyday. There were no other channels on the B.F.B.S. so it was either B.F.B.S. or a video and there was no up to date TV channel anywhere in Belize. I was on my second beer and still rubbing my head from time to time when Joe Smiley placed another bottle of 'Belikin' on the table. I wasn't going to have more than two bottles as I didn't want to miss the run in the morning. Tommy and I were going to go over for a pint in the battery bar but it looked as if I had drunk my quota here in the N.A.A.F.I. so I would leave the battery bar. I thought that if I got that down my neck now, I would be able to slide off and get my early night, but no such luck. The next bottle arrived on the table from another member of my crew then Mickey Hill dropped another on the table.

"Cheers mate," I said to him.

"No worries mate."

This was getting serious, if I were to finish all these bottles that were suddenly appearing from every crevice of the N.A.A.F.I. then I would be in deep shit. It got to about nine o'clock and I was naturally looking at the N.A.A.F.I. door. Steve Bradley walked in, carrying a bottle of something in his right hand and he was arseholed. He bounced off the tables to the left and then the tables to the right. How he stayed on his feet was anybody's guess. He wobbled over to our table and plonked the bottle right in front of Tommy. As soon as his hand left the bottle, I knew what it was; Tommy took the lid off and offered me a sniff.

"Green Stripe," I said to Tommy.

"No way," Tommy replied. Steve Humphries finished his double Bacardi and Coke, and Tommy nicked his plastic cup then poured what looked like a single shot of Green Stripe into the cup.

"Tommy, what about the run?" I said to him.

"It's only one. It won't do any harm," he continued. He put the cup to his mouth and tilted his head back quickly, swallowed the contents and sat looking at the empty cup in front of him. I could smell Peppermint and Pernod. "Fuck me that's nice," Tommy said. "I will be doing a bottle of that at the weekend."

He poured another shot and passed it to Joe Smiley who went through the same routine. "Wow," Joe said. "Beautiful." That was him sold too.

Tommy took the cup and filled it a further four times. The lads threw it down their neck like it was going out of fashion. He slid the cup to me, I looked at it, what the heck was I going to do? I was half pissed, so what was this going to do to me? There was no choice everyone at the table was looking at me. There was no pause or further sniffing of the drink, I just picked it up and threw it back. I had to admit it was really nice and I could quite easily drink the remainder of the bottle, but the thought of the run stopped me in the nick of time. Joe Smiley was sitting there still enjoying the aftertaste of his Green Stripe.

"Blind my arse, typical fuckin monkeys, they are just trying to keep it to themselves. There's nothing wrong with it," he slurred. I certainly didn't feel the effects of this Green Stripe and it certainly hadn't made me blind. We all shook our heads and couldn't understand where the monkeys were coming from.

Steve Humphries finished his last bottle and stood up. "Time for my pit," he said and raised his right hand. "See you all at run o'clock' lads," he finished and with that he was gone, fair play to him. That's exactly what I was going to do when I got to the end of my bottle, I swigged my last quarter of the bottle and stood up, two other lads joined me and we headed back to the accommodation. I was checking for low flying beasties on the return to the block.

The next morning it wasn't the 'Swingfog' or the sound of one of the gunners who was on guard the night previous that woke our room up, it was the Guard Commander. Bombardier Don Robinson, screaming at us to get out of our beds. What the hell had happened? To sleep through the 'Swingfog' was one thing, but to miss the noise of a gunner with a big gob screaming down your lug hole was another?

"Robbo, what time is it?"

"Never mind that Sean, get the fuck up," he answered. "You have got five minutes and Chindit will be outside to take the run," Robbo said.

"Oh fuck," I shouted. Everyone dived out of bed at the same time. It was then that the trouble started. I was blinking my eyes really hard. I couldn't see properly. It was like the latter stages of a migraine coming on, but I didn't have the headache. I could see daylight and shapes but everything else was blurred and hazy. This was it, this was the blindness that we had been told about. It was awful. I tried in vain to see in front of me, but the more I tried, the harder it got.

"Tommy, how are your eyes?" I shouted down the room.

"I am fucked, I can't see anything," he replied.

"Joe what about you?" I shouted again.

"Same," he answered.

Shit, we were going to be in a lot of trouble when Chindit saw this. All the rest of the troops who had drank Green Stripe were experiencing something similar but at different levels. I didn't know what to do, I had done it again and this time Chindit was sure to pop.

It took me all my time to find my clothes and put my boots on. We fell in outside the block and waited for Chindit, I could hear all the troops within the squad throwing water down their necks as if it was going out of fashion. I was extra thirsty too and doing the same.

Shaky brought us to attention, "Right you, shower. It's a good job that W.O 2 Mick Mayers can't make it this morning, isn't it Bomb Connolly?"

"Yes Sarge," I shouted. Thank God for that, I thought. Shaky knew what had happened last night and he was partial to a few good wets.

"I will be taking the run," he finished. We ran out of camp with all the troops who were blind holding onto the T-Shirts of the lads who could see. It was ridiculous as I couldn't even see the rocks under my feet, it was a sure fire way of twisting our ankles and it was difficult to get a good drink of water as it meant letting go of the person in front of you. I could hear the odd person falling over on the road and this was always followed by some serious cursing by the injured parties. I think we all agreed on something and that was; this Green stripe was never going to be consumed again by the troops who had a run the next morning.

Shaky took pity on us on this occasion and cut the run short, I would guess that we only did about five miles, if that. He obviously remembered the times in his army career when he'd fucked up and needed the break. I remembered quickly my first tour of Canada when Shaky briefed us all on 'Rest and Recuperation'. We'd had four days to go and got drunk after a long exercise on the prairie, there was about eight of us who piled into this mini-bus taxi and ended up in a town called Brookes. Shaky was the only one who'd done Canada before, so he gave us a 'Safety Briefing'. One of his 'Golden rules' were to stick together.

"Never, ever go off on your own," he told us. "You will end up getting rolled." So, we got bladdered that night and all stuck together, well all except Shaky, who forgot to practise what he preached. We all waited in the reception of the hotel at ten o'clock the next morning and lo and behold shaky appeared walking across the car park. He was wearing nothing but a pair of 'Y'fronts and it turned out he had gone out on his own the night before and got rolled, they had taken his wallet, his money and all his clothes. When we saw him and realised what had happened, we pissed ourselves laughing. We'd given him a break then and we needed this break now.

CHAPTER ELEVEN

MESSAGE IN A BOTTLE

We ran back into the camp and entered through one of the main gates, my sight was beginning to return and I could see a shape in the way of another body standing to attention, it was still a bit of a blur, but I could at least make out that he had a beret on. A number of people told me that my sight would only be fully restored by lunchtime the next day after drinking that shit. There was one problem with that, I needed my wits about me as I was signing for the gun later on that morning. That meant the Light Gun, the One tonne and all the ancillary equipment, I had to make sure it was all present and serviceable, then lock it away in a secure place. There was always a problem in that once you had signed for all the kit on your gun you gave everyone a licence to come and nick it all off you. There was no serious thieving between the troops in the army, but silly little things which you knew you had on your gun, would go missing from time to time.

Another one of my dad's 'advice sessions' that I had forgotten about until that point went something like this, 'do unto them as they would do unto you' and he was right, this thieving went on everywhere and you had to be a bit smarter than the rest on three accounts. Firstly, never lose the bit of kit in the first place, secondly try and keep more than one and third, if you have one nicked, nick it back.

I remembered back in Colly about a year before, the P.T.I's were late to the gym, for our beasting session and one of my mates who used to work in the Regimental Quarter Masters' Stores (R.Q.M.S) in the clothing exchanges had been brought in to the stores. He had to bag all the clothes up, throw them in this big wooden barrow and push it down behind the gymnasium to the incinerator. His task was to burn all the worn, exchanged, confiscated or buckshee (spare) clothing. That particular morning, I decided to find out where all the smoke was coming from behind the gym, I never imagined that there could be an incinerator here but my mate had made a mountain out of clothing, boots, sleeping bags etc.

"What's happening with that lot Kev?" I said to him.

"It's getting burnt mate. It's a waste isn't it?" he replied.

"Waste my arse," I answered while I was pushing a cigarette into his face. All he was doing was standing by this large incinerator and occasionally feeding it with the large stack of clothes which were on the ground. He looked confused, so I instructed him to go over by a huge tree which was about ten yards away and turn his back while he smoked the cigarette; finally he twigged and had only walked about four paces when he must have heard the rustling of the empty bin bags being filled with clothing. I filled four bags and then leapt out of the bushes and rammed them into the boot of my car. I spent the next year, reporting to the 'Q' stores exchanging tons of clothing and equipment for the shit that I had 'nicked' from behind the incinerator. You should have seen the looks he gave me as I handed this kit over to him every week in exchange for brand new. Within a year, I had three times the amount of clothing and equipment that I should have had, I made a few quid along the way too.

I flopped onto my bed and I had a feeling that there were little flies buzzing around in front of my eyes, but I had no means of squatting them! I thought that if I splashed my eyes with water from the shower it would help it to clear. This wasn't the case, but I did sit down on the plastic chair for what seemed like ages, with the cold water falling onto the back of my neck. There was no way that I was going to drink Green Stripe ever again. There was one thing that I was looking forward to though and that was the pleasure of watching the rest of the troops performing with Green Stripe this weekend down Punta Gorda. They may enjoy the sweet taste of this drink during Saturday night, but it would all come to an end when they had to cope on Sunday morning whilst tapping their white sticks on the outer edge of the M1 still suffering from the blinding after effects. I had only drunk one tot of this stuff and felt like my world was going to end and I was on a mission, to stop my mates going through the same.

By the time we had made our way to the 'Gun Shed' my sight had returned to a reasonable level, the time in the shower had certainly done the trick but I did not prepare myself for what happened next; the gun and all its associated equipment was in a right state, it had been classed as 'Serviceable' by the R.E.M.E (Royal Electrical Mechanical Engineers) but surely, as a result of them receiving a massive bribe from the 'Out Going' artillery battery. It may have looked a lot of things to us, but it definitely was not serviceable. When we thought of the Light Guns that we had handed back a short time ago in the U.K, I was certain that these R.E.M.E lads had been drinking Green Stripe before they'd signed the kit off. It was obvious that the guns would be in a lot worse state here than in the U.K because of the miles of tracks that the Belizeans had the cheek to call roads. There was dust at a level I hadn't seen before and the heat didn't help as it rotted everything. My intention initially was to swap my Light Gun with the spare one, but it looked in a worse condition than ours. The one tonne wasn't much better; it would never have passed an M.O.T or made it on a British road. The 'Gun Shed' was a big old atap building with no sides, the problem with these buildings was that there tended to be more beasties living in them which could drop down and land on your head. Not what I wanted to experience! As well as the guns there were a number of the troop Land Rovers and ancillary vehicles in there. Each gun detachment had four steel lockers to lock all their kit away, but it was nowhere near enough space. In Colly we had big secure cages that gave us more than enough room but these steel lockers would have to do us as we certainly wouldn't be receiving anything better.

Lunchtime came and we thrilled ourselves on the usual trough that the Aldershot Concrete Company (A.C.C: Army Catering Corp) had the cheek to call lunch. Had this food been served today, I would imagine Trading Standards would have been all over them like a rash. Their food was about as far away as night and day, bless 'em, They did try. Try to piss us all off that is and they did a good job too. It was unusual for them to put mashed potatoes on at lunch and it was equally so for the mashed potato to pour like water from a soup ladle. Just when you thought it couldn't get any worse, the jungle juice, was in the exact same place it was that morning and hadn't even been changed. It was warm and upsetting all the troops who had queued up for a cold drink.

"Where the fuck, are the slop jockeys?" Ged had called in the hope

217

that one of them would show their ugly heads. Funnily enough, there wasn't one of them brave enough to come out from the kitchens and take the abuse due to them.

"Get one of them out Bomb," Rab shouted.

Ged took up this challenge and disappeared behind the hotplate and then the kitchen wall, then re-appeared seconds later. He had kidnapped a chef who must have been cowering down behind the kitchen door. As soon as the troops saw the colour of this white apron and chef's hat, it all turned pear shaped. Within the blink of an eye there was pandemonium, there wasn't a single man in the cookhouse who didn't take something off their plates and throw it at the 'slop jockey'. The familiar Glaswegian quotes such as 'away and shite', 'you try and eat this pesh' and 'ye call thes food you barmpot' echoed through the Cookhouse as a barrage of food that would have impressed 'meals on wheels' landed in his general direction. The chef went from being nice and clean to covered in food within two seconds, a couple of the lads even threw pints of the warm jungle juice at him. We had unsuccessfully tried to bring this slop to the attention of the ACC on many occasions but as our requests for reasonable food had fallen on deaf ears, we had decided, it was time to take matters into our own hands. There is no way we could do a six month tour living on this cack.

I had a good siesta but woke with a throat like a Swiss Angler's Maggot Box. Tommy was shaking my arm, "Come on mate, football" he said.

I sucked the guts out of my cold water bottle before re-filling it on the cold water machine. Some bright bastard had organised a game of football with the Chogies, very clever. The Chogies were between sixteen and twenty and apparently as fit as a fiddle, we on the other hand *thought* we were fit as fiddles and were going to play, in the baking sun, on a dried mud equivalent to a local recreation ground. They played in bare feet and shared a Man United top between the whole team, I didn't know how that was going to work, but I thought that even one of them wearing it for a limited time was a crime against humanity. The rest of us were all looking forward to it as we just had to sit on the side line throwing stones at our shit players, so I was thankful this was one sport I couldn't play. Once the football match was over that was us finished work until Monday morning. The B.C had sent a message from up north that we were to have a long weekend and that he wanted every man who wasn't on essential duty to benefit from the time off. This would have pissed Chindit off as he wanted nothing more than to beast us at every opportunity. We, on the other hand, were chuffed to N.A.A.F.I. breaks as we would have a few days on the piss. We would start with the N.A.A.F.I. and battery bar that night and hit Punta Gorda the following night. The infantry had a 'duty driver' and were putting on a Bedford Wagon to take us all down town, Punta Gorda would be under siege, they just didn't know what was coming their way.

Our team turned up in the battery football kit and I must admit, they looked as smart as a carrot. Sure enough, the Chogies appeared from the tree line and walked in a straight line across the pitch. They looked like 'The Magnificent Seven' in slow motion except, there were about thirty of them. They quickly picked their first eleven who stayed on the pitch, whilst the remainder sat on the side line away from our troops. I was hoping that we could all mix and get to know each other, but it wasn't to be. Getting to know them could have come in handy that weekend, who knew what would occur down town that could perhaps do with a friendly face. There was also the possibility of that same friendly face pointing you in the direction of the camp when you were bladdered, or even tying you to the back of a moped and delivering you to the camp gate. Whatever happened, I wanted those kids on my side while I was in their country. The match kicked off and I was quietly confident in our team as I knew we had some extraordinary talent. I was sure that some of our lads could have turned professional, there must have been a number of times in their lives that they would have looked back and thought the same too.

'Team Punta Gorda' kicked off and put together about ten passes of extremely high standard. One of the boys was running around as if the ground was burning the soles of his feet. These lads were well acclimatised as they lived here and, more importantly, they were very good footballers. Our lads didn't know if they were being kicked or punched. The frightening speed of these lads was more than enough to cope with, but coupled together with the pinpoint accuracy and determination of a dying soldier, they were amazing. There couldn't have been more than three minutes on the clock when they scored a fantastic goal against us, I could have cried for the lad who hit it with his right foot on the full, with no boots on but he never batted an eyelid. I heard the slap of the contact between his foot and the ball, it sounded as though someone had dropped a baking tray in a supermarket. Five minutes later we had given away another goal, this time it was a soft header they scored, because our goalie caught it and then dropped it over the line. The plus side of this was that we managed to throw our stones at him as a result.

"Wanker," Shaky shouted.

To which, Brownie stuck two fingers up. He was normally a good goalkeeper, so this error was out of character for him. Within twenty five minutes it was three- nil, we were getting battered by a bunch of kids and they had not even broken into a sweat. Unlike them, we were playing crap and sweating like there was no tomorrow. These little Chogies had got the better of us, every time the game paused for a minute our team was over the line and taking on loads of water. We had warned the A.C.C, that if they brought the jungle juice at the same temperature it had been earlier the chef was going to be hanged. We had managed to hold them to three goals at half time but we hadn't scored. Our 'slop jockeys' brought the tea urn up to the football pitch and I walked over to feel the side of it to make sure it was cold. After confirming that it was, our lads started to throw it down their throats like it was going out of fashion. The battery team was exhausted but still had forty five minutes to play. We all questioned in turn where they were going to draw the energy from for this next forty-five minutes. The honest answer was that they didn't know, we were getting taken apart, and the word 'cheat' was mentioned on more than one occasion but we couldn't do it in the end. We were very jealous of these kids though.

They kicked off for the second half and it seemed as though they had swapped the entire team, but they hadn't. Why should they? They were pasting us, and within forty five seconds they had scored again. Their supporters were giggling at how crap we were, I was hoping that our lads didn't see them as this would have caused some violence which was the last thing I wanted when I was trying to get some Chogie mates. It wouldn't look good if our lads were seen filling the Chogies in, before we had even got to know them. I could just see it in the local Chogie newspaper, the front page headline 'New soldiers beat the shite out of P.G. football club'. Although it had a certain ring to it, it may not have gone down too well with the local public relation's board. With ten minutes left to full time, we were swapping players at about one every two minutes. Our lads were suffering in the heat of the day and even though they had kept their heads covered, most had gone past the stage of sweating and were becoming dehydrated, so were taking on massive amounts of fluids The Chogies were still running around like they were ballet dancers and I think they must have shared the total of half a bottle of water between them. The fulltime whistle blew to the relief of our team, then with the customary shaking of hands out of the way, we retreated sharply with our seven – nil thrashing. We truly had been given a lesson in how to play football it hadn't all been down to conditions but down to the football skills of the Chogies.

By the time we got back to the accommodation, we were all gagging for a cold drink, never mind the lads who had just played ninety minutes of football in the baking sun, what about poor old me who had just walked the half mile back to camp. Barry Brunn who lived in our block came over to my bed.

"Bomb Connolly, do you want me to open the bar for some stims?" Barry was the battery barman and he had the keys to the fridges, one was full of beer and the other full of stims. Stims were small cold bottled drinks like coke, Fanta and cherryade. One bottle of stims cost us one Belizean Dollar which in 1982 was approximately fifty pence. Had Barry not volunteered to open the bar then there would be nowhere else to buy drink from at that time of the day. I walked into the battery bar with a few of the footballers and ordered two bottles of Fanta from Barry. I looked around the bar and although it was pretty basic it looked quite good. It was another large atap building which I could tell had been there for many years as the leaves on the roof were dark brown with age. It would only be another year or two before it would have to be re-roofed. There were two lads in our block who collected empty stims bottles apparently there was good money in it if you collected enough. I personally couldn't be bothered having thousands of bottles under and around my bed space. It was a small space as it was, so I didn't want to fill it with bloody bottles.

My first bottle of Fanta never touched the sides, even the fizz didn't make me stop swigging the bottle down in one go but I took my time with the second bottle. When we got back to the accommodation block the troops were getting sorted and cleaned up for tea. I wondered what delights the 'slop jockeys' were going to offer up tonight, whatever it was I wanted to get my timing right that particular night, as I had been listening to a number of the troops going on about how the day turns into night. Apparently, it was a bit of a phenomenon, it was said that the daylight disappears in the blink of an eye and turns into darkness, this was something I was keen to see and that night was as good a night as any.

After a quick shower, I took my writing kit out under the atap veranda which was attached to our accommodation. Some of the married soldiers had beaten me to it and were writing home again. This was to be the first of my letters home to my mum. It was only a few lines to let her know I wasn't dead and then that was it for another month. I did feel for the lads who were in serious relationships as six months away from home was a long stint. I filled my water bottle with cold water and started to write my letter whilst keeping one eye on the sun. I didn't want to miss this so called event even though there would be ample opportunity to see it again and again if necessary. The wait wasn't long, just as the sun had dropped behind Saddle Back Hill, it was as if someone had turned the light switch off, it was true. It went from bright to dark in the blink of an eye. I have been lucky enough to have done a lot of travelling since 1982 but I still haven't witnessed anything similar. After watching the phenomenon I made my way to the cookhouse. The M1 was lit up well and it was really weird watching all the night beasties flying all over the place. This part of Belize was famous for its bats and I was getting used to them flying all around my head as I was walking to my meal. These didn't bother me, but the scorpions, snakes and tarantulas did. Even with Dave Dawkins' medical skills just around the corner, I would prefer not to put them to the test.

My evening meal went down well, the food wasn't bad that night so I had loads and felt really full walking back up the M1. This wasn't big and it wasn't clever, I was going on a bender and I didn't want a belly full of food. This food was taking up valuable beer space!

As I reached my block I heard Dave Dawkins, "You ready for a bevy mate?"

"Is the pope catholic?" I replied

"Come on then, let's go and get shit faced," he finished. I had a quick army shower (a squirt of deodorant) and before I knew it we were walking over to the N.A.A.F.I. My eyes were everywhere as I climbed over the small wooden bridge, I didn't want to be dive bombed by another night beast while walking over to the N.A.A.F.I. I could still feel the after effects of the last beastie attack.

"We will be having some of these tarantulas this weekend," Dave said.

"Sorry?" I answered.

"I'll explain when we get in the bar mate don't worry," he explained.

When we got to the N.A.A.F.I, Dave walked straight to the bar and I grabbed the last two seats in the place. One of the infantry lads had brought a Wog Box (portable Hi-Fi system) and was playing 'Paradise by the dashboard light' by Meatloaf. It was being played very loud, but it wasn't causing anyone any problems so no one bothered the lad. He was already lagged up and would be lucky to see eight o'clock let alone the end of the night.

"Let's start as we mean to go on," Dave said and at that he plonked twelve bottles of 'Belikin' on the table.

"You daft bastard, they'll be warm in ten minutes sat in the heat," I laughed whilst grabbing my first bottle.

"Well I suggest you get them down your neck then," he said as he was started to neck his first bottle, it became apparent that we were going to be very drunk and very soon.

"What's this tarantula thing you mentioned over the monsoon ditch?" I asked

"Oh yeah," he said.

What he wanted me to do was help him lift the paving flags up in the monsoon ditch that weekend and catch some of the larger tarantulas.

"Are you fucking mad?" I asked. We were apparently going to keep them in a box until we were ready to work on them, then we would use an old pair of washing machine tongues to hold them over a one inch thick piece of polystyrene. Dave would then inject the spider with some formaldehyde and then pin all its legs out. The formaldehyde made sure they set fast and ensured that they lasted years. We were going to see one of the Chogies and ask then to knock up some small glass fronted wooden cases and then sell the tarantulas to the troops so they could take them home when they had finished their tour. He was completely off his head, but his idea was good. I didn't particularly like the idea of messing about with bloody big spiders that could not only give you a nasty bite, but could jump either away from you or at you in the blink of an eye, this was a big worry.

"We can make twenty dollars each one," he said.

"I'm in then," I replied. That did it for me, there was good wedge to be made here and looking on the bright side, I would make sure that I wasn't in a position for the spider to have me. We could make a small fortune, no one else could do this as they couldn't get the equipment like Dave. It turned out that most of the troops were doing something to make a few extra quid in Belize. We had two of our lads who cut hair and were making a very tidy sum of cash. Of course everyone wanted a 'crew cut' and often blade one or two in these temperatures. Ten bucks each was a good crack and there were a lot of people in our camp let alone when the troops get to see it from Salamanca in the south and Airport Camp in the north. They would all want one once they heard of them. We finished twelve beers within half an hour it was after my first six that I had that good old feeling that it was going to be messy. 'Meatloaf boy' was still dancing round to his 'Bat out of Hell' tape and he had already turned it over. All of the infantry lads were clearly enjoying the music as they were banging on the tables and stamping their feet.

"Shall we have one more here, before we go over to the battery bar?" Dave asked.

"Yeah, go on," I said as I set off to the bar. I bought a 'repeat prescription' of six beers each and dropped them on the table. Again we set about them and I noticed that this 'Belikin' was sliding down my throat with great ease, so much so, that by the time we had reached the battery bar, I was feeling tipsy. Dave looked as if he had just come out and he was as fresh as a daisy, I knew he could drink though as I had seen it many times before. When we entered the battery bar it was full of our troops, anyone was allowed in our bar, but with it being our battery bar, it was normally just our lads who drank here.

At the present moment all our troops were in there and singing very loudly, "We call on Big Ged to sing us a song, we call on Big Ged to sing us a song, we call on big Ged to sing us a song, so sing, sing or show us your ring. Sing ya bastard, sing."

Then immediately after that, Ged burst into the first verse of 'A Yellow Bird'. This 'Sing Sing or show us your ring' song was what the troops sang to an individual in order to get them to sing an army song. If they wouldn't sing they then had to turn around and drop their trousers, as in 'showing your ring', as you can imagine it was in your interest to sing something even if it was bad. It was much better than showing your arse in public.

"Dave, what shorts have they got behind the bar?" I shouted.

He looked over at the bar and shouted to me all the normal grog as he was reading them off. "Bacardi and coke please mate," I shouted again through all the singing, my earlier evening meal was still sitting on my stomach so I wasn't going to last much longer on the beer. It was time to go on the shorts; he came back with a full half pint of Bacardi and coke with a few lumps of ice in it. We grabbed a seat with Tommy and Andy Berry.

"You hitting P.G. tomorrow Sean?" Andy asked. There was a load of our gang going downtown Punta Gorda and I wasn't missing it for the world. I hadn't seen this town properly yet and had only travelled through it when we arrived. I was dying to see what it looked like at sensible o'clock.

"Yeah too right," I answered. Even though the food was okay in the cookhouse that particular day, I was still looking forward to going to buy some decent food. If it meant that I had to pay for good grub then that's what I was going to do.

I lay in my pit the next morning with the mother of all hangovers; honestly I had a head like a robber's dog. I couldn't lift it off the pillow it was that bad. When I finally got up, I looked around the billet, there were five other lads in their beds asleep, everyone else had disappeared and looking at the time I guessed that everyone else was probably at breakfast. I couldn't face food with my hangover so decided to go and have a cold shower instead. The temperature even at that time of the morning was unbearably hot and I was going to sit on the plastic chair for half an hour in the cold shower. I walked across to the shower block and noticed all the Chogies running around the camp like little ants going about their work. The little old man was there as usual, cutting the grass on his haunches with his extra long machete, I felt sorry for him. I walked into the shower block and couldn't believe what I saw, there were eight of the lads from the infantry having a shower party. They were all wearing what looked like Roman Togas (White bed sheets) wrapped around them and all of them were drenched wet through. They all had plastic chairs in the showers and all the shower heads were set so they were pointing to the ground and onto the troops while they were sat on their chairs. They were bladdered and occasionally getting up off their chairs and dancing to the Wog Box which they had trussed up in a black plastic bin bag so it didn't get wet from the water splashing from the shower.

"Don't mind me lads will you?" I said.

"No worries mate, crack on," one of them answered. I carried on with my shower but there was no way I was going to spend half an hour in the cold shower on my own. These lads must have been on the ale all night judging by the state of them. On most occasions when they stood up, they fell over making it obvious to me that this had been an all night session. It only took one of these mentalists to shout 'Shower Party' and they would all be up for it, some of these infantry lads were as bad as our lot.

There were three, four tonne Bedford wagons being put on for the troops to go down town, the first one was just after lunch. This was the one I wanted to be on so I could see some of the town in the daylight, before I got pissed. There must have been twenty five of us waiting to get on the four tonne which was too many, the infantry had quickly realised this and arranged for a second drop. The wagon driver was none too impressed but he was a driver supplied by the infantry and not one of ours so he was told in no uncertain terms that it would take as many trips to get us all down town as it would take. Even though there were to be other vehicles it looked like this lad was going to be ferrying troops down to P.G. all afternoon. As I watched all the lads scurrying onto the back of the wagon, I walked over to the driver and asked him who was 'riding shotgun' (Passenger).

"No one mate," the driver answered.

"May I?" I asked.

"Yeah of course," he finished as he lifted and secured the tailgate. I don't know how many lads were on the back of the wagon, but it was well overloaded.

"Dave, jump in the front with me," I shouted into the back of the

226

wagon at Dave Dawkins. He leapt over the tailgate and made his way to the passenger side of the cab where he climbed in first and then I followed. It was a double seat in the front passenger side of the wagon so we were hoping for a comfortable ride down to Punta Gorda.

The driver pulled out of the camp onto 'Southern Highway' and turned left heading towards the town. The roads were very unsafe and had more potholes than I had seen on any road. The camber on the road meant that the wagon practically drove on its side all the way to P.G. and we felt the size of every rock we drove over. The speed mustn't have reached above twenty miles per hour at its fastest point. It was so terrible, I was thinking that I would have to get seriously drunk for the return journey as there was no way I could put myself through this again. What about the guys in the back, I thought. As we entered the town the camber in the roads levelled out and it was only two minutes before we pulled up in the town centre and I began to feel safe again. What a journey, and it appeared that the lads in the back of the wagon had it worse than Dave and I. As they all jumped off the back of the Bedford I noticed that each one of them was covered in a thick layer of dust. Mick McCarthy was still choking on all the dust he had swallowed and dived into the nearest building. He re-appeared a minute later with a big bottle of water and he was swigging it frantically. I quickly learned that the building he had just run into was a shop, it had looked more like a shed with no front door to me.

The driver shouted at the top of his voice, "I will be making return trips every hour from five o'clock from here, the last one being midnight tonight," and with that he locked the tailgate of the wagon, jumped into the cab and drove off. I looked around and noticed that there was a large clock tower behind me that looked as if the local hooligans had painted it in sky blue with a bog brush.

"What the fuck have we let ourselves in for?" Mickey Hill said.

What a dump, I thought. P.G. was the most southern town in Belize and belonged to the Toledo District. No wonder they stuck it this far south, they didn't want anyone to see it. I would have given it to the Guatemalans if it was my choice, what a hell hole. I could see a school with a big yellow school bus parked outside, but it was the thirty foot sign on top of the building which said 'School' and the fact that there were loads of little Chogie kids playing in the playground that gave it away. We were only one hundred yards from the Caribbean Sea but there was no beach, the water looked filthy and not what I would have expected from these waters. As we were about to follow some of the infantry lads who obviously knew where they were going, I noticed some Chogie kids running towards us, they were really poorly dressed and looked like they hadn't been fed in ages. I couldn't understand why they weren't in the school with the other children, it turned out that these kids were vagrant and just roamed around the town scrounging anything they could from the military, our lads immediately started handing dollars to the children and it was clear to see that they were very happy with this.

I had spoken to the infantry troops and asked where the best place to get food was and I could tell by the smirk on their faces that good eating houses were going to be limited here.

"Follow us mate, we'll take you to Bobby's," one of them said. I didn't have a clue what Bobby's was, but they knew I wanted food so I was hoping that it was some kind of eatery anyway. We walked for about four hundred yards and by the time we had reached this large shed with a signpost outside saying 'Bobby's Bar' our troops had spread out over two hundred yards. It was a very hot day and I was starting to get desperate for both food and drink, the infantry troops got to the door first and pointed to another door to the left of the one they were entering.

"That's the restaurant in there mate," they told me

"Thanks lads," I replied. I stepped up onto this decking and walked towards the doorway, there was no door on the entrance but then again there was no door on any building I could see. Finally, I could smell food, chicken? Yes definitely chicken. Dave, Tommy and I entered this shed that was known as the infamous 'Bobby's Restaurant', I nearly died when I saw what met my eyes it was an old shed, with no flooring. If you think of an old chicken coup then you are right on the money. There was seating and tables for twelve people with one table occupied by four Chogies playing cards. I had seen some shit holes in my time but this took the biscuit, I was beginning to think it was a bad dream and that I would wake up anytime soon to find myself in the Adelphi Hotel in Liverpool. I wouldn't have believed that it was an eating establishment, except for the fact that I had seen one of the locals serve a plate full of food to one of the Chogies playing cards. I think to call this gaff a restaurant would be an insult, to call it a café would be a breach of trading standards and to call it anything remotely connected with food, would be as equally wrong. I sat down with Ged, Tommy and Andy. I can remember the manner in which I sat down, it was like being told by the doctor that a close relative had died, I was in total shock. I didn't think a place like this could exist anywhere.

"Hello gentlemen," I heard a voice say. "My name is Bobby and I will take good care of you." I spotted a pair of brilliant white teeth gliding through the air towards us. I rubbed my eyes and looked again, through the darkness and the dusty air I could make out a very black body connected to this pair of teeth, this was Bobby. He was the local entrepreneur, apparently not only did he have the restaurant and bar next door, but he also owned a shop and two houses. Well, when I say two houses, I mean, mud huts. He was the guy that all the troops had been talking about at camp and it was he who arranged the boat trips to the Cayes (pronounced Keys) small Caribbean islands.

"Ya'll having some food and drink man?" he enquired. "

Yes please mate," I answered. He shouted something in deep Creole to someone in the back and this little boy appeared in an instant, he must have been no more than ten years of age and he was wearing nothing but a pair of old red shorts. In his right hand he was carrying a number of A4 cards which looked as if he had just picked them up off the floor. They were either very old or he had just knocked them up from the flaps of an old cardboard box when he saw us walking into the place. He dropped four of them on to our table and smiled then it clicked these were the menus. I picked up all four of them and as I handed them to my mates, I turned them over and instantly smiled to myself. The only text on the menu was; Menu. 'Chicken and chips in a basket 2 dollar' and that was it. I turned the card over again in the hope that I had missed something on the other side. I traced the young boy's steps back to the counter in the hope that he had dropped the rest of the menu on the floor. Bobby was walking towards the front door.

"Bobby," I called.

"Yes, Sir," he answered.

I told him that there appeared to be some mistake the rest of the menu was missing. He walked over to us confused. When he reached our table he smiled. "No, Sir, that's it, chicken, Sir." And that really was it, he turned and carried on about his business.

We couldn't understand why the Caribbean Sea was two hundred yards away and the place wasn't busting with fish of every kind! I looked at Tommy and we burst out laughing. Tommy got in there before I did.

"What you having Sean?"

"Oh, I wonder if they do chicken and chips?" I replied. Just when I thought it couldn't get any better, the boy came over and took our orders and had the cheek to write them down. Funny old thing, we all ordered 'chicken and chips'. Even funnier was that when we had placed our order he made a point of taking the menu off us. We waited for our meal and I ordered four beers the latter were with us in seconds, the same little lad bringing them over to the table. A Bob Marley record was playing in the background which was nothing unusual, I had quickly picked up on the fact that everything was Bob Bloody Marley. It looked as if he was more of a God to these people, than a musical icon; there were photographs and drawings of him all over the place. I didn't mind the music though as I was partial to a bit of reggae and it made a change from the 'head banging' commercial crap that was being belted around the camp all day and night. We were all commenting on how cheap it was for 'chicken and chips', two dollars was nothing. It was only when the little boy brought a tray out with the four plates on it that we realised why.

Had I asked for budgerigar and chips, this lad would have got it spot on, however the fact that we had asked for chicken and chips meant he was a million miles off the mark. We looked at each other as if there had been some mistake there was a half chicken that was the size of a small frog and five chips on each of our side plates. I couldn't believe what had just been served to us. This boy stood with a big smile on his face obviously very proud of what he had just presented to us.

"You like chicken and chips, Sir?" he asked. I spoke before Tommy answered and pasted this young kid.

"Yes, when I can get it?" I replied. "Can I order something else young man?" I asked again.

"Yes, Sir," he said.

"It's okay, I don't need the menu, I will have three chicken and chips please," I said sarcastically. If I were to finish with enough food to get me through a 'heavy beer session' then this quail and chips wasn't enough to get me there. Tommy ordered another three and Andy and Ged another two each.

"What happened to the fuckin basket anyway?" Andy asked.

"It's in the same place as our chicken," Tommy said. "All in his fuckin mind."

That tickled us. It was at that point that we decided to take it on the chin, for what it was costing us, we just weren't bothered. My meal and beer still only cost me a couple of quid, and although I wasn't full, I felt as if I had eaten something at least. We decided to shoot next door to Bobby's bar and God forbid if anyone wanted a bag of crisps! The bar wasn't much different from the restaurant other than someone had splashed out big money on a table cloth which someone had spread across the bar. The bar was nothing more than two scaffolding planks sitting on two old beer barrels. There was a big stereo with twin tapes sat on an old table in the corner of what looked like the dance floor. The infantry lads who had shown us the way earlier were sitting in the corner with a shed load of beers on their table.

One of them stood up and shouted over to us with a big smile on his face, "Enjoy the scran lads?"

"Fuck off and die," I shouted back.

They all burst out laughing, they knew exactly what we had been letting ourselves in for and could have warned us about these culinary delights, but on the face of it, we would have done exactly the same thing.

By the time six o'clock came, it was beginning to get messy. I remember watching Tommy and Ged fooling around. They had both thrown ten dollars on the table in front of us.

"Watch that Sean," Tommy said.

I was confused at first but it soon became clear what they were doing. There was an old Belizean called George, drinking at the bar, he'd been there since we had come in and was fairly wrecked, our table was just behind where he sat. Tommy beckoned me to look down at his feet and when I did; I couldn't believe what I saw. It wasn't the fact that he had no shoes on, or the length of his feet, but the width must have been six inches at the widest point, they were huge! Ged took his cigarette end, and as this man was getting up off his stool he threw it under his bare foot. The man stood on the lit cigarette and never batted an eye lid. Surely he must have felt that? I thought. There was no reaction what so ever from him.

"Watch this then," Tommy said. With that he took the last draw on his cigar and waited while he picked his moment. George was now jamming away to the reggae music while he was standing at the side of his stool. At one point, he tilted backwards, grabbing at his stool at the same time and as he was falling, Tommy placed the cigar stump on the floor under where his right foot was heading. The old man fell forward stamping hard onto the cigar, we waited for the delayed reaction but it never came. George had stood on the cigar and he still never felt the effects, he was none the wiser. I couldn't believe it and Tommy and Ged had been puzzled too. When the local sat back on his stool, they both inspected the cigar stump on the floor. It had been crushed under the weight of him and was now extinguished. They looked at each other again, picked their ten dollars up from the table and called all bets off. They were obviously trying to see which one could burn this man's foot, but neither treatment had any effect.

At quarter to ten, I decided that I couldn't drink anymore and would call it a night. Ged and Andy had already disappeared, there was only Tommy and I left on our table. The bar was full of locals and the music was blasting out very loud.

"Tommy, if we make it to the clock tower, we can get a lift at ten," I shouted over the noise.

"Let's do it," he replied, which was unusual for Tommy as he would normally stay until the death but it was clear that he couldn't take anymore. I reckoned I would still be able to persuade him to come for a nightcap once we got back to camp though.

Chapter Twelve

SPIDERMAN

I couldn't remember how we had got back to camp when I woke in the morning, I couldn't even remember if we made it back to the N.A.A.F.I. or the battery bar for a finisher. Next thing I heard Dave Dawkins bollocking someone in the next accommodation block for not taking their Palludrine, how the hell he had found out someone wasn't taking their tablets was beyond me, but he did. I tried to get out of my bed but I had made too good a job of tucking my mosquito net underneath me the night before which was a good effort considering I was so drunk. It was very important to make sure your mossy net was tucked in underneath your body as the mosquitoes would have a field day if there were any gaps. Tam had slept on top of his bed the night before and was absolutely red raw with bites, he had been bitten in places where you wouldn't think it possible and as a result had spent the next day walking around covered in Anthisan cream.

By the time I broke free of my netting and walked out of the block, Dave was just coming out of the accommodation opposite and stopped for a chinwag. It turned out that someone had spoken to Dave in confidence, and told him that this infantryman had stopped taking his Palludrine as he couldn't see the point in it. Dave had warned him that unless he took this tablet there was a high risk of him catching malaria and then his last 'ace up the sleeve' was that unless he started taking it again he would be charged. The lad didn't fancy being put on a charge so he had agreed to start taking them again. Dave told him, that if he went against what had now been agreed he would 'bounce him'. Now if this was the physical version or the military version of 'bounce' then this was left to the imagination, but I wouldn't have fancied taking Dave on in either scenario.

Dave and I met up later in the afternoon at the top end of the camp and he had brought his entire 'do it yourself' Arachnophobia kit including his big jar of formaldehyde. "You lift the flag up slowly Sean and I will look to see if there's any underneath," Dave said.

"How about fuck off,' I replied. He wanted me to lift the flag up and possibly disturb all the tarantulas while he stood a million miles away and sneaked a look to see if there were any there. That was NEVER going to happen, not a chance! "I have a better idea, what about you lift the flag and I will see if there are any underneath?" I asked.

"Fucking coward," he said.

"Yes, but a living coward," I retorted. It was a known fact that the tarantulas loved this environment and the Chogies had told Dave where to find them. They had been right, he had only lifted the first flag three inches when the ground started to move. There must have been twenty spiders running in all directions and Dave dropped the flag which I didn't actually see because I was doing my Linford Christie impression sprinting down the main drag. There were at least two of the spiders that were as big as my head, they were huge! By the time I had returned to him, he was wrestling with this monster of a spider and was just about managing to feed it into this bucket with his washing tongs. If this thing broke free though I felt sure it would bite Dave, it was clear to see he was pissing it off. I watched Dave place a piece of Perspex over the top of the bucket and put a small rock on the top of it to keep it from being pushed off. This was, by far the biggest spider I had ever seen.

"How do you propose to hold that thing down on a piece of polystyrene Dave?" I asked.

"Watch," he replied as he pulled a slab of polystyrene, and the remaining kit out of his box and put it onto the ground. He slid the Perspex lid back from the bucket and pushed the washing tongues in and after a bit of a scuffle he had grabbed the spider, he picked up the large syringe with the yellow liquid in it and holding the tarantula facing forward, he drove the needle into its back. The spider went mad but only for a split second and then you could see that the juice was taking effect already as the spider was slowing down rapidly. Next he placed the spider on the polystyrene and held it with the tongs, the spider lunged its head forward and bit into the polystyrene, it was dying quickly now. Dave worked fast as he knew the effect of formaldehyde and taking each pin in turn he pinned the spider's legs out as far as he could, there was no fight left in the beast now, it was as if it was in a state of hypnosis. By the time Dave had finished pinning the legs out this tarantula was enormous, it must have measured ten inches across it looked magnificent, we would need a large case for this one.

Dave had done it completely on his own but he wasn't bothered, just chuffed that his plan had worked. Within two or three minutes the tarantula was lying still but Dave would allow a further two hours before he removed the pins from its legs to make sure it was set solid and ready to place into the case. This was our prototype ready to sell to the troops.

"Them Chogies had better get their arses into gear," he said. We needed the cases before we could start mass producing our 'stiffs' so Dave was going to kick his contact up the arse later that day. He wrapped the spider up in a bed sheet and put it into his large shoulder bag. We walked down to the medical centre where Dave had cleared an area under the counter in the treatment room which was for our treated spiders. I was well chuffed with our achievements (or should I say Dave's) that afternoon and decided to take a siesta before tea, as soon as my head hit the pillow, I was out, it felt like I had only been asleep for five minutes when I was woken by the sound of giggling. It was like I had gone back ten years and we were in the school playground laughing like children. I opened my eyes quickly and saw Big Ged standing over me with a photograph, all the rest of the troops were laughing now as well, Ged thrust the Polaroid photograph into my face again. It took me a minute to focus on it but when I did, I nearly had a heart attack, I had been asleep with my head to the left and my hands on my body, Ged had taken a bloody big tarantula and placed it on my right cheek than taken a Polaroid snap before waking me up to show me. I don't know where the spider was at this time, but it was gone.

"You Wanker," I shouted. He laughed his head off. What if this spider had bitten me? I thought. "It's okay, when you catch a weasel asleep, piss in its ear," I warned him. He looked confused at this but it was my way of telling him that revenge was going to be sweet.

Only a week had passed when I spotted Big Ged come limping into the billet. "Christ mate, what's up?" I asked him.

"Look," he replied and with that he pulled the top of his shorts down, he had a massive boil on his arse, possibly one of the worst I had ever seen. He told me that it was really painful and asked if there was anything in my medical capacity that I could do. This was heaven, I didn't know that my opportunity for revenge would come around so quickly, boils on the arse were a common occurrence here I had seen Dave Dawkins deal with two of them already, one had been on an officer's arse which I know took Dave great pleasure in removing as he hated the officer in question and the second had been on the arse of one of the 'slop jockeys', which I know Dave took equally as much pleasure in removing as this was revenge for the shit we were being fed.

"Yes mate, it's an easy procedure, it will only take us five minutes but we will need to remove the core, or the boil will come back," I told him.

"Will it hurt?" he enquired.

"Fuckin right it will," I answered. The two procedures I had watched down the medical centre had caused the victims to scream out and beg for Dave to stop. This was an old medical treatment which involved the heating up of a glass bottle when the bottle was almost too hot to hold with a cloth wrapped around it, the opening would be placed over the rancid boil and with some force initially then within a short time you would see the boil being drawn in a vacuum up into the bottle. On both occasions I had seen Dave do it there had been a loud 'pop' as the core was ripped out of its hole and slapped up against the bottom of the bottle. It was at this stage that you knew the procedure had been a success, the bottle was then removed and a solution of watered down iodine was squirted into the hole before a clean sterile dressing was placed over the wound. If the core remained in the hole, the procedure would have to be repeated. I told Ged that if he wanted I could do it after tea the next night and in the meantime I went and armed myself with the supplies.

"Can I come and watch Sean?" Dave asked.

"Too right mate, that would be good, especially if it turns pear shaped," I replied.

"No way mate there's nothing that can go wrong," he finished.

Ged got to the point when he was begging me to take it out on the Wednesday night, so I sent Tam down to the medical centre to let Dave know. I returned from tea and Ged was still in the cookhouse. I picked the six biggest lads in our troop to be my 'muscle', I briefed them to clamp Big Ged to the bed on his front and not to let him go until I gave the word, no matter what Ged said it was only me who was permitted to shout the order to free him. They all shook their heads and smiled at each other, I had Pete Sanyari and Mark Hadfield holding his arms, these were my two biggest lads and they would need every ounce of their strength to hold Ged when he kicked off. We waited patiently and I laid out my tools of the trade, I had the bottle of Iodine ready with the lid still on and the syringe at the side of it for squirting into the hole when finished.

"Where is your water mate?" Dave asked. He stared into my eyes and he immediately knew why I wasn't answering him.

"Right you lot, as soon as he comes through the door, jump him," I ordered.

Dave looked at me and I couldn't help but laugh. "You Tosser," he said.

At which point Mick McCarthy came running into the billet and closed the door behind him, "He's here lads." No sooner had he said it the door flew open, poor Ged had only entered one foot into the building and there were eight troops all over him. They dragged him to his bed and after a good struggle they managed to turn him over onto his face.

"Stick, Shorts," I ordered. Ken Browning appeared with the biggest pair of tailor's scissors you ever did see.

"No, not my new fucking shorts," Ged screamed but it was too late, they were gone in two cuts. The boil on his arse had grown considerably and it was a good job he was having it attended to. Earlier Ken had cut the bark off a really thick chunk of wood and offered it up to Big Ged to bite on.

"No, leave it lads I will give it a miss I think," Ged shouted.

"Like fuck you will," I replied. Well that was it, all hell broke lose.

"Let me go lads and that's an order," he shouted.

"Remember what we said lads," I said. Big Ged struggled with all his strength, the sweat was pouring off his forehead. "Hold him lads," I ordered. Dave was laughing his head off, I don't know whether it was because it was funny because he knew what was coming next. "You sadistic bastard," I said.

"I know, it's good isn't it?" he replied.

"Fuck off Dawkins," Ged shouted. That made Dave worse and he laughed even louder. "Last chance you Fucker, let me go," Big Ged screamed.

"Stop whinging you big girl," I shouted back.

"I'll fuckin girl you when this lot let go, you fuckin psycho."

"Promise's promises," I answered. Ged couldn't see but I was now holding my hand out waiting for John Ashton to pass me the bottle with the rag wrapped around it. As Ashey passed it to me I could feel the heat, I looked at the lads who were holding him down and I was now beckoning them to grip him tightly, I pushed the bottle hard on his arse and Ged let out an almighty scream, it sounded like a pig in the slaughter house.

"Keep the downward pressure on mate," Dave ordered. I pushed for all I was worth but it looked at first like nothing was happening and then two things occurred. I could feel the vacuum pulling at the core of the boil and secondly Ged was screaming every obscenity I had ever heard. What he wasn't going to do to me when he got free wasn't worth repeating but I think it was safe to say that he was going to kill me! Without further warning I felt a splat at the base of the bottle, I removed the rag and there were big lumps of Ged stuck to the bottom. It was foul, every bodily colour I had ever seen and a few more thrown in. He was wailing like a baby by this stage, I had been saving the best until last though and Dave knew it was coming. I repeated my look to the lads begging them now to hold him tightly. The hole in the cheek of his arse was enormous and well worth a photo and next like a well rehearsed play Ron the Rock appeared from nowhere and started to snap away. I picked up the bottle of Iodine and made sweeping hand movements for everyone to move well out of the way if they weren't involved with holding Big Ged. Dave looked at me and shook his head as if to say 'No'.

"Remember the tarantula Ged?" I whispered in his ear.

"Fuck off you idiot," he screamed back. I looked at Ron to make sure he was ready with the camera, I wanted him to photograph the iodine being poured onto Ged's arse. I stood up and removed the lid from the jar of Iodine; I could see that Dave had already started to move to the back door. I slowly poured the iodine into the spare hole. Ron stuck the 'thumbs up' to let me know that he had caught it all on camera, Ged was screaming like mad.

"Hold him lads," I said. I must have poured a quarter of a bottle in before the hole filled to the top. He was struggling like mad and thrashing like a drug addict needing a fix. "Right lads, let him go," I shouted as I was running out the back door. I looked back at Ged and truth be known he couldn't run after me if he had wanted. He was leaping around the floor in the billet trying frantically to grasp the cheek of his arse, he never placed another tarantula on my face after that!

Big Ged had started to forgive me over the next few days and the boil on his arse healed very quickly. He did say however that when it came time to change the dressing, that I seemed to enjoy causing him more pain with the iodine, perhaps he knew me better than I did but at least I didn't have to scurry around the camp hiding from him anymore. Well, that was until a few weeks later when I ran him over with a one tonne Land Rover, it's true, he was innocently walking down the main drag and thankfully, I was only doing about thirty miles an hour but I had forgotten about the width of the passenger door mirrors and I wanted to wind him up by seeing how close I could get to him with the vehicle but my plan sort of backfired and I hit his shoulder with the mirror which knocked him into the monsoon ditch. I thought I had hurt him badly but realised it couldn't have been that bad when he started throwing paving flags at me…

The Gunners' Prayer

Gunner Angel be my guide
as I climb upon my gun to ride.
Let your halo light the way
and keep me safe from harm today.

Let your wings give wind and air
and send it coursing through my hair.
Find me a peaceful and sunny place
and let it shine upon my face.

Keep the clouds and rain at bay
and keep me dry throughout the day.
Watch my brothers next to me
and keep them safe and close to thee.

Keep my gun upon the ground
so I'll return here safe and sound,
but should disaster be my fate
guide me through to heavens gate.

If I must join my fallen brethren,
please show me the way to Gunner Heaven.

CHAPTER THIRTEEN

COMMANDER OF THE GUARD

At the 'one month' point, I had kept my mouth shut and escaped all duties in camp so was feeling pleased with myself. We were getting ready to go on a fully tactical exercise with the Belize Defence Force and the Ghurkhas, so hopefully I had escaped detection until we returned from this, but no such luck, I went to read the 'Troop Orders' on the notice board on Thursday night (The 'Troop Orders' informed the troops of all the important information for events coming up). I had been stuck on guard duty as the guard commander this Friday night and I was not impressed. Chindit had put me on with a right bunch of nut cases which I didn't need on any night let alone a Friday, but on the bright side Guard duty on a Friday night started at six in the evening and finished at nine on Saturday morning, whereas Guard duty on Saturday started at nine in the morning and finished at nine the following morning. Even so, I was wondering how I was going to cope with the heat in that guardroom

On Friday night, I briefed the guards before I 'fell them out', this rabble needed keeping an eye on, they all liked a drink or six and they liked to skive off too. There was a real 'turd in the drainpipe' with this duty and that was a large artillery ammunition compound which we also had to guard. You had to come out of the camp gate, turn right and then walk down a long dusty track before reaching the tall secure gates to the 'ammo compound'. This compound had to have one of the guards locked inside it twenty four hours a day. In the middle of the compound was a very steep manmade hill with a little shelter built on the top of it. It was made out of old artillery shell pallets and had a tarpaulin sheet covering the top of it; the compound was used to keep the troops out of the sun and rain when needed. Each member of the guard staff had to complete two hours in this compound and then six hours resting in the guardroom. Then it was back up to the compound for another stint, it was very boring but had to be done. The compound was lit up like Wembley Stadium at night and I was convinced that there was little chance of the Guats breaking into this gaff undetected.

I walked into the guardroom for the first time on this duty and I remember feeling the heat of the evening, it was still blisteringly hot even though it was dark. I looked at the desk and sat on the chair as I opened the guardroom 'daily occurrence book' (D.O.B.). The D.O.B. was a must read at the start of your duty. It filled you in with all the information that you may require to make your duty a lot easier.

"Dave, up the ammo compound, Tommy, kettle on," I shouted.

"On my way Bomb," Dave replied. I continued to look through the D.O.B. and just as 'Tommy not Right' brought my brew, I noticed an entry in the book that made me laugh.

"Look at that Tommy," I said. He smiled after reading it, the entry read; 02.15hrs. 'Problem, dog barking around the camp'. Next entry read, 'Problem solved, dog shot, as simple as that'. An unlucky dog had obviously wandered onto the camp and had been caught barking and howling. The Scottish regiment didn't take too kindly to this noise so they'd terminated the dog. Killing an animal in Belize was a big thing and you had to pay big bucks if you got caught, but this regiment obviously didn't care. The evening dragged on and the lads had rotated their shifts in the ammo compound. We had a radio playing British Forces Broadcasting Service (BFBS) it was serious radio four music being played tonight, but it was all we had. It was two o' clock in the morning, time for 'Tommy not Right' to do his second stag up in the 'ammo compound' but I could see all was not right.

"You all right Tom?" I asked.

"Fine Bomb," he replied as he picked up his Armalite rifle and left the camp to head up the track. When the oncoming guard reaches the compound they have to call the guard up on the hill to come down and let them in. The guard in the compound would unlock the padlock after being given the password, then the old guard would brief the new guard coming on and handover the padlock key before securing the big gate again. The old guard wasn't permitted to leave the site until he saw the gate locked once more.

"Dave, is Tommy okay?" I asked

"Sorry Bomb, I didn't notice," he replied. "I tell you what though now you come to mention it he didn't say a word other than the password."

"Hold the fort a minute," I ordered him. I picked up my 9mm Browning Pistol and made my way towards the track, it seemed like an age before I reached the gate. I could feel something was wrong with Tom but I couldn't quite put my finger on what, he wasn't on my crew but he had a good reputation and on the whole he was a good soldier.

"Tommy," I called. It was difficult to whisper and shout at the same time. Shit, I thought, tell me the Guatemalans haven't killed him. I unclipped the press stud on my 9mil pistol. There was no answer and no sign of Tommy. I waited a few moments more. "Tommy, where the fuck are you?" I shouted a little louder, I wasn't prepared to shout again and I wasn't prepared to wait any longer. The guard commander was the only other person to hold a key to the ammo compound, so I took out the spare key and opened the padlock. All the time, I was calling and looking for Tommy, but there was nothing coming back. I walked up to the start of the steep climb up the hill, I could see the pallets on the top, just as I was about to start climbing up the hill, I looked up, I could see Tommy was at the top looking down on me. "Tommy, what's up?" I asked.

He looked right through me and raised his rifle up to his shoulder, I noticed right away that his magazine was attached to the weapon and I also knew that I had issued him ten rounds of 5.56mm Armalite bullets for that magazine.

"Tommy, put the fucking rifle down," I said quietly as I started to walk slowly towards him leaning into the hill. He now raised the rifle up with a slow jerk until it was in the firing position. His eyes had stopped focusing on me and he was now looking into the rear sights of the rifle and aiming it at my forehead. "Tommy, lower the weapon," I said again. He ignored me once more and his right hand moved to the trigger guard, I was now only seven feet away and still moving gingerly towards him. I was committed now and had I tried to retreat, I wouldn't have liked to have guessed what may have happened. As I looked down at my feet to see where I was walking, I heard his thumb push the safety catch to the 'off' position. It was a distinctive sound that I had come to know well. He cocked the rifle when I was less than four feet away from him and then he placed his right hand covering over the trigger once more. There was definitely a live round now in the chamber.

"Tommy, come on mate, put the rifle down", I begged. I slowly raised my left hand which was now twelve inches away from the muzzle of the rifle and moved forward some more. I took one more step and found myself on the same level as he was. As I touched the muzzle with my left hand his trigger finger rested on the trigger with the rifle still aimed right at my forehead. One squeeze of the trigger and it would have been curtains for me, no two ways about it.

I slowly pushed the muzzle to my right and at the same time I felt a surge of relief as the 'line of sight' was now broken. Tommy was still in a trance, there was no resistance as I moved the rifle barrel away. I clenched my right fist down by my thigh and then punched him square on the nose with all my strength, when I realised the weapon had then fallen to the ground I jumped on top of him furiously punching him anywhere I thought it would hurt him.

"You fucking idiot, what the fuck do you think you are doing?" I punched him until I was exhausted.

"Bomb, Bomb, what's happening? What are you doing?" he shouted.

"What's happening you prick?" I screamed. "You nearly shot my head off you fucking idiot, that's what's happening". It was then that it finally hit home, it was as if he had snapped out of a deep trance, he couldn't apologise enough claiming that he didn't know anything of what was going on then he started crying like a baby on the ground right in front of me.

"Tommy, what's happening mate?" I asked him. He was shaking like he had been sat on a block of ice for an hour. "Stay there a minute," I ordered him. I got up off the ground and walked over to his weapon. I removed the magazine and ejected the round from the chamber. With the round now on the dusty ground, I picked it up and placed it back in the magazine. I looked at Tommy and could see he was back to his normal self. I had mashed his face up bad, but he was adamant that he was fine. He wasn't.

"Bomb I am so sorry, I don't know what happened honestly, I am in trouble aren't I?" he asked. This was an offence which could have gone straight to a 'Court Martial', his sentence would have been two years in Colly nick and then drummed out of the army with a 'Dishonourable Discharge'. This was every squaddies nightmare, he had scared me half to death and I could easily have been killed by his actions, God only knows what stopped him from squeezing the trigger. The fact was though, I was still alive.

I sat again for a minute and told him to 'shut the fuck up' while I was trying to work it out in my head.

"Right, listen to what I am going to ask you, are you all right now?" I asked.

"Yes bomb, I am fine," he came back. "Well all except my face," he added. I had broken his nose quite badly, but I had a plan.

"Listen Tommy, if this ever happens again, I will kill you and then I will Court Martial you, is that clear?"

"Yes Bomb." He smiled. "I am really sorry, honest," he replied. I believed him and I also believed that he had temporarily cracked up. He was a good lad and needed a break as we all did from time to time. If we could get away with the story of him slipping up the hill when he was climbing up the mound then we would be home and dry, it was a believable story as he would have been holding on to his rifle with both hands when he fell forward. Anyway, the story had to be disproved first and it was his word against anyone's and as long as he stuck to the story then he would be fine. I was going to see Dave Dawkins in the morning to see if there was anything he could do. He would be the only other person to ever know about this. There were two things for sure, firstly Tommy was going to have two big black eyes in the morning and secondly he definitely had a broken nose. I regretted beating him as much as I did now, but at the time of retribution I really wanted to hurt him bad!

We stood outside the guardroom after his stag and had a cigarette, it was four in the morning and had just begun to rain for the first time since I had arrived in Belize.

"Look at that Sean," Tom said as he pointed some ten feet away.

"Wow, I've never seen anything like that before," I answered him. I walked to the edge of the rain and found that I could step out of it and then back into it again, I was dry for a moment until I stepped into the wall of rain once more and became soaked through, then I stepped back out of the rain and started to dry out again in the heat. We both stood and looked into the rain storm. It was truly unbelievable, I had witnessed the Northern Lights in Canada and that had blown me away but this came a close second.

At five o'clock, I sent Andy to start the early calls, the 'early calls book' was sitting on the side of the large table in the guardroom, anyone could come in and book an early call for the next morning and the guards were then responsible for waking that soldier. It was normally used by the 'slop jockeys' so that they could get out of their pits and start the breakfasts for camp. Andy took the book with him in order to wake the chef and get a signature from him, once you had the signature of the person you were waking you didn't give two hoots if he fell back to sleep again. I waited nearly an hour for Andy to return to the guardroom, he didn't return so I sent Tommy to find him, but in the mean time one of the Infantry Sergeants had come to the guardroom bumping his gums off about the cookhouse still being closed, the N.C.O wanted an early breakfast as he was going on a forced march with two of his troops.

"Has the chef been woken up, Bomb?" he asked me.

"Er, yes Sarge," I answered. As soon as he had disappeared back towards the cookhouse, Tommy came from the direction of our accommodation, looking apprehensive.

"Sean, Andy went to bed," he said.

"What do you mean, he went to bed?" I asked. After some preliminary investigations it turned out that Andy wouldn't go anywhere near the chef's accommodation with his room being full of tarantulas. The end result of this was not only that Andy had decided to disappear to his bed without telling any of us but also the chef was still fast asleep and the camp wasn't going to be fed early that particular morning.

I sprinted up the road to the chef's accommodation and ragged the poor lad out of his bed. "Its late mate, get in the cookhouse as quick as you can and get the breakfast on," I ordered. He leapt out of his bed immediately and started to get dressed, fair play to him he legged it out of his room and headed towards the cookhouse but it was too late, this situation had gone past being fixed. After I got Tommy in to see Dave Dawkins I decided to go and see Chindit before this sergeant from the infantry returned from his walk. If he found out from a third party I would be dead.

I stood to attention in front of Chindit. He was fuming. "You were the fucking guard commander, it was your responsibility," he shouted.

"Yes, Sir," I agreed. He was right, it was down to me and I deserved a bit of a kicking.

"Warned for Office," he barked. "Fuck off out."

'Warned for Office' was something a soldier didn't ever want to hear, it meant you were being charged under section sixty-nine of the army act and you would be marching in front of the B.C and subsequently would receive a fine and an entry onto your army record. Chindit was pegging me for something Andy Berry had done, or not done as the case may be. A bollocking would have sufficed but to charge me and put me on 'B.C's Orders' was too much.

A week later I marched in front of the B.C. and he fined me ninety quid but more importantly, there had been another entry onto my military record. Andy Berry received some heavy beastings from me for the rest of this operational tour and any shit jobs that needed doing he was the soldier that got detailed to do them. The rest of the N.C.O's lost a lot of respect for Chindit that day, he hadn't needed to go that far.

CHAPTER FOURTEEN

MAN DOWN, MAN DOWN

We received a message to tell us that the Puma helicopter was knackered and as a result there was no chance of us getting the supplies up to the lads in the Observation Post (O.P.) at the top of Saddleback Hill. The lads that were taking over from them at the end of the week were going to have to carry their own supplies up the mountain. Chindit was to pick the relief team and some extra troops who were to help carry the kit and supplies up the mountain. It would be down to the fitness and mental endurance of those men to ensure that the re-supply rations and kit got up there. I knew that I would be volunteered because of my medical skills and because I was supremely fit. We were to call on the lads with a lot of upper body strength not just leg strength to carry the supplies up this hill. It was a very steep climb through dense jungle vegetation, which would undoubtedly prove difficult and would be twice as bad if it had rained the night before or during the climb. There was no second chance or other window of opportunity here, the supplies had to go when planned and that was that.

We prepared our kit the day before the climb so we were pretty much ready to go at six a.m before the morning sun. I was guessing it would be a six hour climb and a four hour descent to crack this. We would have a quick trough from our ration pack and of course, a brew at the top, then we would be coming straight back down. There was no time for fun and laughter once we made the summit, it was serious business. There were ten fit lads in the party, six were to stay up there and four of us to come back down with the lads who had already been up there for a week. Radio contact confirmed that they would be ready to rock and roll at twelve lunch time, this being the time we guessed that we would be there. We set off bang on six in the cool-ish air of the morning. I was well pissed off, as the sergeant major who had just charged me was partnering me in carrying a twenty litre Jerry Can of water in a rucksack. Chindit led the section, with me behind and the rest of the section behind us. We would carry our load until we were knackered and ready to make the swap. I was a stubborn bastard and would make a point of carrying the rucksack until I couldn't go another step; there was no way that Chindit was going to see any chink in my armour. I wouldn't have cared if my shoulders were bleeding with the straps of the Bergen digging into me, I wouldn't stop unless I was dying. As it turned out Chindit carried it first and I was interested to see how far he would get with the load.

There was a long flat trail before we actually reached the start of our ascent. I tied my bandana around my head to stop the sweat running into my eyes, then looked up at the mountain in front of me and mentally turned the switch in my head to the 'off' position. Come on then, let's have it, I said to myself as I 'dug in' and set off. The going was slow as I was behind Chindit who was carrying the rucksack with the water in it. I didn't know what a jerry can of water weighed, but I knew it was very heavy and would be a lot heavier once we started going vertical. The first part of the climb wasn't too bad and although it was reasonably thick foliage we made some good time. It didn't make sense for Chindit to be in front of the section as he was having to do all the cutting with the machete as well as carrying one of the loads. After a brief discussion I moved to the front and Chindit 'fell in' behind me, I could cut more freely and I didn't have to worry about weight. I was in what we called 'belt order' which meant that there were only four water bottles and my ammo pouches strapped to my belt. With our new formation I set about cutting the vegetation down. There was like a semi-path that we were following which was very muddy. The vegetation on the hill was very wet, but this wasn't just a result of twenty four hours rain, but longer we thought. I called Lance Bombardier Taff Moran to the front to set about the thick twine and branches, he duly accepted the invitation and went at it like the Tasmanian devil.

We stopped at what we thought was the half way point in a level clearing, it felt good. We were well ahead of time and we reviewed our E.T.A. (Estimated Time of Arrival). There was a possibility that we would chop a good hour off our original guestimation and be arriving at the top for eleven o'clock. Chindit told me, on another attempt to take the rucksack off him, that he wasn't ready to pass it but as I looked at his face I could see a bit of dehydration appearing.

"Sir, get some more water down you," I requested.

"Bomb, I know what I am fuckin doing," he snapped back.

"Yes, Sir, but I know what I am seeing in my…" I was going to say 'medical capacity' and at that he gave me the look of 'shut the fuck up and leave me alone'. I raised my left hand as if to say 'okay, it's your call'. We tagged onto the back of the line and let the other troops lead on. Bert Bradley took up 'point'. As we set off, I took a good look at the incline and noticed that it now increased significantly we were suddenly mountain climbing, not walking up a steep hill. I was bringing up the rear being the last man in the squad and Chindit was just in front of me. We must have made another one hundred yards when Chindit started to wobble from each side of the track.

"You okay, Sir?" I called.

"No Bomb," he puffed as he fell back against the rock face, his eyes rolled into the top of his head and his skin was cold and clammy.

"Bergen, Sir, no ifs or buts," I said. He had no choice as I was ripping it off him as I was talking to him. I tilted his head back and poured water into his mouth. He kept motioning to walk forward so I stood in front of him and held him back against the rock with my left hand. This was serious, but I was sure that if I could rehydrate him, he would be fine in a reasonably short time. This man may have charged me recently, and it had crossed my mind earlier to accidentally throw him off the top of the mountain, but I still held the respect for him as a soldier and the rank he held. I had Dave Dawkins on the other end of the radio comms if I got stuck with any medical issues, but this was no problem. Within five minutes, the colour had returned to Chindit's skin and his pallor was spot on. I put him in front of me and watched him like a hawk. It was important for him to find his feet slowly at first before he picked up the pace which he did and then within another two hundred yards he was fair shifting to catch the others up. I was struggling a little to keep up but there was no way on this Earth I was going to ask him to slow down.

We battered on for what seemed like another hour before we caught sight of our team up ahead. Although we had ordered the others to keep going, we could see their concerned faces looking back to see if we were closing in on them and after another fifty yards and we had rejoined them.

"Did you miss us boys?" I shouted.

"Fuck off we were waiting for the noise as you bounced off the side of the cliff," Bert answered. "We were looking to have had a game of 'Name that Tune' at the sound of your mess tins pinging off the rocks as you were falling." He laughed.

"You heartless prick," I finished. I couldn't talk much more, I was breathless and the heat was blinding. It must have been another thirty minutes before the climb became easier and the hill levelled out a little. We were now walking through a clearing which was easier but I was on my chinstrap and couldn't go on much longer without another break, I must have nearly passed out three times myself. The troops up ahead had all stopped and were now looking back. The clearing had brought us to a natural viewing point on the mountain side which was spectacular, it looked over Punta Gorda and right out to sea, it was a picture postcard quality view. I faced to my front once more and could see the O.P two hundred yards ahead. It was a little like the ammo compound with the pallets and the tarpaulin on top (although I wanted to forget that particular location). I spotted one of our troops waving both his arms high in the air, but it was too far to see who it was.

We made it to the top of the mountain and my first thought was 'when I get down from this chuffing so called hill, I am going to look through the history books and find the name of the man (or woman) who first named this 'Saddleback Hill' and investigate the reason why they didn't call it a mountain then I am going to make it my number one priority to terrorise their ancestors before I leave Belize'. I had recently climbed Mount Snowdon in Wales and I can tell you that Snowdon was like climbing the stairs compared to this so called 'hill'.

The brew was on, I could smell it. "Give us your cup, Bomb," Steve Humphries said. First I had to get the Bergen off my shoulders and then I dug my mug out of my belt and threw it in his general direction. It came back within a minute full of scorching hot tea.

"Ah top man mate," I said. I took my combat top off and my shoulders were in bits, they were red raw and blistered. This was a 'pop and blob job', my iodine did the trick, it hurt like hell but soothed it

251

after a few minutes and more importantly, would keep it clean for the return journey. We knocked an hour and a half off our original estimated time, but it could have been at the expense of one of our team. Thankfully, we arrived just as we had set out... Together.

Sergeant Mark Norris led the way down to the bottom, we were practically running for some of the time. We made the mid-way water stop in one hour and got to the bottom in two. That was some going, I didn't think we would make it back during the hours of daylight but we found ourselves walking back through the camp gates at mid-afternoon. We were absolutely knackered but it was a good workout. Mind you, carrying the empty jerry can down the hill was a damn sight easier than carrying a full one up it. I didn't wish to make this trip again unless it was a Sunday afternoon stroll in civvy clothing and training shoes instead of uniform and boots.

What pissed us off just as our last man had walked back through the camp gates was that a Puma helicopter was just taking off having just dropped off the troop's mail. We had been under the impression that the chopper was unserviceable (U/S) and couldn't be repaired quickly enough but it had been repaired and flying literally five minutes after us leaving camp. They could have loaded the chopper and had it on top of the mountain within fifteen minutes, we were furious. Chindit was boiling mad, imagine what could have happened to him and all for nought. We had the radio and could have easily been told. Dave Dawkins was laughing his nuts off as we passed him sat outside the medical centre, it's a good job that Chindit didn't notice because he would have had *his* nuts in a vice.

The weeks passed very quickly, and before we were into our second month we were beginning to get a little more used to the raging hot temperatures and deal with all the tropical shit that went with it. The camp routine was about to be disrupted with the news of our first operational task which was called 'Operation Lion heart II'. We were to operate deep in the jungle and carry out numerous reconnaissance (recce) patrols, on foot. We would then be deploying with the Light Gun and firing some high explosive (H.E.) ammo into the sea. The latter being a show of force to let the Guats know that we had a bigger gun than them! We would be spending a total of four weeks out in the field and going deep into the jungle. Although this was serious stuff, I was quite excited as I had been in the army four years and never been permitted to play war. This was the closest I was going to come to it and it meant that we could get up to some stunts that I knew we wouldn't get away with in a peacetime scenario. What concerned me though was the fact that we had some proper psychos in our battery who wouldn't think twice about shooting someone if you mentioned it in passing. Lord only knew what they would do on a recce patrol if they were compromised. The idea of a recce patrol is purely reconnaissance and nothing more. You are supposed to gather information and intelligence and take it back to the 'powers that be' so they can work out the best plan of attack to deal with the threat. The recce patrol should never fight the enemy unless absolutely necessary. I was half hoping that we didn't come across anyone innocent in the jungle especially if our lot were to get hold of them. We did however have a real 'ace up the sleeve' and that was the use of the Harrier Jump Jets which were based at Airport Camp in Belize City. With good radio communications we could call on the 'Brylcreem Boys' to help us out of the shit a moment's notice.

At the end of the first week in May 1982 we deployed as a real force. The plan involved us being dropped in on a small road by helicopter in detachments of ten or twelve men and then tabbing (walking at speed) into a location deep in the jungle which was inaccessible by chopper. There was four of us who were to deploy first to make the ground 'safe' and clear the way for the remaining chopper loads of troops and equipment. Chindit was leading the operation and then Bombardier Bob Baker, lance Bombardier Pete Spooner lance Bombardier Taff Moran and me. We were considered as being 'in the know' as we were subject to numerous briefings and privy to a considerable amount of secret information before being deployed. It got to the point where we could have deployed during the hours of darkness and still found our way to our base location, we were that well briefed. We were all carrying a tonne of kit and I was sure that someone had loaded my Bergen with sand once I picked it up and tried it on my shoulders. I hopped on the scales and did the calculation and I had eighty pounds in my rucksack. Mind you, seventy nine of that must have been food and fags. The remaining one pound must have been essential medical supplies. It wasn't true, I had spare kit ready for a long haul. This wasn't going to be a picnic, so I took what I could carry. I even carried a spare pair of dogs (socks) which was unusual for us troops. There was always something much more important to carry, such as ammunition, food rations and water. All of which is difficult to survive without, dogs we could live without. I thought back to my days in Canada when my gun crew and I had a 'Dog Competition', it was twenty dollars in the hat from each of us and the winner took the prize. It was who could keep their boots on for the longest, thus not changing their socks and I won hands down with a total of seventeen days. My feet were like two wet loaves of bread when I finally got to them and I could hardly walk with the damage the blisters had caused. It was a cheap night in the 'Gag and Puke' that night though thanks to my one hundred and twenty dollar winnings.

All my remaining clothing was sealed in a large black bin bag and secured within my rucksack. Bin bags were always good on operations, they not only kept your kit from getting wet, but if you had to throw yourself in a river, you were guaranteed to float with the air in the bin bag, as opposed to sinking with the weight of the Bergen. They also provided waterproofing during hours of darkness when it was raining heavily.

We rubbed the cam cream (camouflage cream) into our faces and waited for the Puma. The Puma helicopter was the workhorse of the army helicopter fleet and it made light work of transporting troops and supplies and dropping them in all kinds of arduous terrains. I was stood last in our section and after passing the tube of cream up the line, I leaned forward onto my Armalite.

"Don't forget behind your ears darling," Taff Moran joked.

"Fuck off you bender," Bob replied.

Chindit, Pete Spooner and I chuckled at the remarks. These two were best friends and two very fit blokes, but more importantly, they were a couple of good lads to have with you when the going got tough as they always made a bad situation better. It was going to take me some time to get used to this weight on my back and I was hoping the base camp was only a short five 'clicks' (kilometres) through half decent ground and not as we perceived it to be on the maps during our initial briefing. Once we got to the base camp, we would be in a position to dump the big kit and patrol with our 'belt order', with just webbing, water, and ammo. The noise of the chopper broke the sound of what I used to call the 'Jungle Crickets'. We had a shed load of ammo and supplies to load on the chopper before we climbed on board, hence the small crew of only five on the first trip.

The chopper was Martialled in and landed on the 'H'. The big kit was thrown aboard with great speed by the waiting troops. As I was the last one on the helicopter I managed to book a front door seat, this had two advantages and a number of disadvantages, in the event of the Puma going to ground I would be first out the door before we all caught fire, secondly the views from high above were always stunning. I wanted to see them first hand and not be told about them from someone else. A couple of the major disadvantages were that should the chopper crash land, I would see it coming which in itself wouldn't be a big worry but the troops cutting into my headstone the words, 'Here lies Sean Connolly, during his untimely demise, he took it upon himself to wet and defecate himself' would cut deep. Secondly, if 'Gary the Guat' was firing up at the helicopter, it was more likely to be me who copped for the bullet in the head or at worse, the Loadmaster (loady).

I shouted to all our lads, "Keep an eye on your magazines."

They all looked at me puzzled and couldn't hear a word I had just said. Sound proofing inside a Puma helicopter in 1982 was about as much use as tits on a bull. I waved my hand to indicate 'forget it'. Riding through the sky in a helicopter at a gazillion miles an hour was a problem when something fell out of the door, it was difficult to pull over and retrieve it. This loss would be a double whammy should it be a magazine full of 5.56 ammunition. You could imagine the faces of the Guatemalans soldiers below listening to the sound of this magazine hitting the jungle floor and shouting 'Praise be the Lord, manna from heaven'. I decided to keep a keen eye on the exit to ensure nothing fell out.

As we landed with a loud thud our kit was unceremoniously dumped out of the chopper door and onto the ground, I turned just in time to hide my eyes from the dust cloud as it lifted off once more. I had to laugh as I heard Bob Baker shout at the top of his voice; "Oh yeah, go on throw my fucking kit why don't you, if you have broken the port glasses you are dead."

I could see Chindit wanted to tell him to keep quiet, but he couldn't. Bob's timing was superb and we all fell about laughing, if the

Guatemalans shot me now, they would wonder why in God's name I was dying with a big cheesy grin on my face. We shared the kit out between the five of us. I was going to keep a close eye on Chindit in case he took a turn for the worst again but I didn't need to as he was a different man now. He was well up for it, in good shape and like the rest of us he was keen to show the others what we could do. Remember, we were talking about a bloke who should have been accepted into the S.A.S. In addition to my large Bergen, I had tonnes of other rations and ammo strapped to me wherever I could hang it. My jungle hat was placed on my head in a way that made me keep my head up when I was tabbing. This was always good, Chindit used to say that if you looked down, you would go down. He was right and it was something I adopted and passed on to other troops throughout my career.

"Always look up and you will stay up," he would say.

We yomped (speed marched) on at a tremendous pace and made for the base as quick as possible. The plan involved Chindit escorting us into base camp then he and Pete Spooner would be making the tab all the way back to the heli pad to bring the next ten man team out at 'first light' the next day. By the time the troops arrived back by mid-morning we would be all set up in the base camp. We were all to make a judgement call to decide if it was safe for Chindit and Pete to tab it back along the same route.

We made the base camp within three hours and twenty five minutes. The going was really tough and very slow, we were all drenched with sweat and needed a break really badly. I heard Chindit call from the front.

"Just through here lads." As we came into the clearing where the base camp was we were over the moon, right in front of us stood a one hundred foot long shed and possibly thirty foot wide, it was huge. Apparently it was supposed to have been an American research centre but as a result of funds running out, the project had been abandoned. It was perfect and in really good nick. I didn't have a clue what it was intended to have researched, and I didn't care. There were no doors, windows, lights or furniture in it but it had a roof and the building was raised approximately eight foot from the jungle floor. It stood ten feet away from a really fast flowing river with a large tree standing between it and the water. There was a massive rope swing tied to one of the branches of the tree situated above the roof. It was clear that when the river was flowing slower their recreational time was spent swinging from the roof top and into the river and I couldn't wait for the river current to slow down. I needed to lean into the water and hold my combat suit while the fast water rinsed most of the sweat out of them. They would take no more than ten minutes to dry again.

The base camp was a semi-tactical location which meant we could have a bit of an easy time there. Smoke, fire and a little bit of noise were acceptable as we were some way from the border. We could strip off and clean up as long as one of us kept alert and watched the perimeters. We would then swap over, take it in turns and watch out for each other.

"I will get the brew on, Sir," I said to Chindit.

In a split second I realised I had just fucked up. I'd called him 'Sir'. This was a big no no in the tactical or semi tactical situation. The enemy would surely shoot a 'Sir' first as opposed to a private soldier, so I may as well as put a big label on his back saying 'shoot me first as I know loads' calling him 'Sir' was stupid. I held my hand up and he acknowledged he would give me this one, but I think had I repeated it he may have shot me in the head for stupidity. I lit the Hexy block and placed the mess tin of water on top of it. The 'Hexy block' was the same as a white fire lighter except that it wasn't like an oblong block one that we knew from Civvy Street it was a bit flatter but it did exactly the same job. Taff set up the water and steri tab station so we would have nice fresh water in the morning when ours had ran out. This was the area where we would end up with fresh water made from the river water. We sat and enjoyed our brew and caught our breath. We quietly discussed a few tactics and I explained what we would be doing while Chindit and Pete were gone. Chindit pointed to the thousands of rounds of ammunition and the shamuly flares, smoke grenades and hand grenades and said that we could blat a few rounds off into the river later on if we wished but we weren't to go over board with it though. Pete and Chindit left their large packs and Bergens and we all agreed that it was safe for Pete and Chindit to tab it back to the 'drop off point'. In 'Belt Order' they left the base camp with enough time for them to beat the last light. We checked the communication a number of times to cover all eventualities, we didn't want them to leave without keeping the link between us wide open.

As I watched Pete Spooner's back disappear through the jungle wall, I poured my second brew. "I'll go on stag first Sean," Taff said.

"Okay mate."

"What are we doing each? Two hours eh?" I suggested.

"Yeah cool" Bob agreed. With that I ripped my kit off and whilst keeping hold of the drawstrings, I threw it into the flowing water. The water was as clear as a bell and although, I would never do it while I had a pocket full of steri tabs, it looked good enough to drink. Taff moved to the perimeter of the clearing and built a make-shift observation post where he lay facing outwards with his rifle. I laid my combats out on the decking outside the large shed. I knew within a matter of minutes they would be dry. I needed a quick dip in the river but my training told me that there were two things I must ensure. The first was to tie a floating line around my waist and tie it off around a tree before stepping into any flowing water and secondly, be ready for the 'piranha nip'. I did both, or so I thought.

I only jumped into the first three foot of water to quickly wash the sweat off, I was going to have a proper bath here later on. I held on to the rope and climbed into the edge of the river. It was approximately four foot deep. I looked out into the centre and could see that this was very deep in the middle as, although it was very fast flowing at the moment, there were no ripples and it was very flat. I dunked my head into the cold flowing water and it felt fantastic. I had forgotten about 'the nip' and as sure as eggs is eggs it came. A fairly hard nip on the back of my thigh, I nearly leapt out of the water. The fish gave me three or four nips, hung around for a minute and then just swam off again. I could actually see the size of them around my legs but they didn't bother me after the initial nip. I could imagine the underwater conversation between these four piranhas, 'what the fuck is that, it stinks?' 'Yeah, stay away from him he smells like shit'. I had only been out of the water for a few minutes and I was bone dry, I looked at my combats lying on the decking and they looked dry too but having checked them they still felt damp on the back so I turned them over. It was amazing how soon the direct sun had dried them. Taff shouted to me, but I couldn't hear what he was saying with the noise of the river.

"What's up mate?" I asked him when I had walked over to his position.

"Any chance of another brew?" he requested.

"I'll get it mate," Bob shouted. That was good, I would be having my third pint of tea within an hour. The troops never say 'No' to a cup of tea. Bob made the brew and then went through the same process as I had, he washed his combats and placed them onto the decking next to where mine were. I pulled together all the ammunition and sorted it into types ready for issue to the troops, we had enough to start a few small battles and I remember thinking that there would be some sorry Guatemalans knocking about the jungle if it came to a situation where the rounds were flying between us. I cleaned off the G.P.M.G (General Purpose Machine Gun) and my own Armalite and kept pondering over the mountain of ammo. Chindit did say we could blat a few rounds off didn't he? I said to myself.

"Taff, Bob, over here," I shouted. Taff and Bob walked over to my 'ammo dump'.

"What's up Sean?" Bob asked.

"I have a plan," I said.

"Oh no," Bob answered.

"If we joined all the link ammo together and prepared a few grenades and thunder flashes we could have a bit of a laugh and let a few rounds go into the river," I said. Taff's eyes lit up like beacons in the night sky and he immediately agreed and so did Bob.

I made a twenty foot long bandolier of ammunition with hundreds of 7.62 rounds attached together. We had taped six thunder flashes together and tied a big stone to them. This was going to be for a spot of fun fishing. We were going to strike all six at once and then drop them into the river to see what the fish thought of it. On the bank of the river we had four hand grenades lined up and twenty magazines full of Armalite 5.56 rounds.

"Sean, what about Chindit's camera?" Bob enquired. I couldn't understand what he meant until I turned around and looked over at him. He was stood in a pair of combat trousers, his face covered with black camouflage cream and he had two bandoliers of ammo hanging over his shoulders, coming down to his waist. There were three Armalite magazines stuffed in the top of his trousers, he looked just like Rambo. It was common knowledge that Chindit carried his camera in the zip-up pouch on the top of his Bergen. I immediately knew what Bob was thinking.

"Taff, get Chindit's camera," I said.

He bent down and took his camera out of his Bergen. He aimed it over at Bob and after only a short time of working it out, he snapped two or three photos and Bob was pulling all kind of poses for the camera.

"Ere, what about this?" Bob shouted and with that he dropped his trousers and stood there holding the G.P.M.G. pointing to the sky with one hand and his private parts with the other while posing for the camera. I laughed my head off as did Taff. Taff snapped away like there was no tomorrow. I joined Bob and we both stood in various poses with our arses showing while we had weapons and ammunition hanging from all over us. We swapped so it was Bob and Taff and then Bob and I and before we knew it we had taken all twenty four photos on ' camera.

"Ooops," said Bob.

"Stick it back in his Bergen," Taff said. And with that he planted it back where it came from.

"I didn't see any spare film in his bag," Bob called. That's the last we saw of the camera. I think we must have been hoping that Chindit would think that a malfunction of his camera caused it to take multiple photos. He wasn't as stupid as we thought.

Bob found an old bucket in the large shed and walked up-stream about two hundred yards where he shouted to us then let the bucket go. He then sprinted down the river bank, picked up his Armalite and waited with us and within a few seconds the red bucket came into sight. We all let rip within a second of each other and the noise was deafening. I squeezed the trigger on the GPMG and wasn't going to let go of it until the last round of my massive belt had gone through it. I could see the spent metal links falling on the ground around my feet as I fired. I watched Bob pick up the thunder flashes and Taff picked up two grenades. Simultaneously, they struck the thunder flashes and removed the pins from the grenades. They threw them into the water approximately ten feet away from the water's edge.

"Stand Clear," Bob screamed. We moved back approximately ten feet from the bank. Three seconds later the water shook and then a second after that the river exploded with a really loud bang that was on a scale I hadn't witnessed before. I continued to press the trigger on my gun, the barrel on my G.P.M.G. was 'cherry red' with the heat. Within another five seconds my weapon stopped firing, I had expended ammunition. There was no sign of the bucket at all. I looked into the water and there was fish of every shape and size floating up to the top.

"Oh fuck," Bob said.

Taff was hysterical with laughter. "Guess what's for tea lads?" he asked.

"That'll be fish then eh?" I answered.

Taff was a brilliant cook and proved it later that afternoon as we were eating some of the fish we had destroyed in the 'fun fish'. It was beautifully cooked and he had even put a bit margarine which he took from his rations and smeared it onto it too. There was loads of it left over but it had to be eaten that night and certainly before Chindit arrived the next day. Bob and I hid all the evidence of our fun shoot, we buried all the expended ammo clips and cartridge cases so nothing could be found unless you were really searching for it, then we dug a three foot hole and poured all the evidence into the bottom of it. We covered it with jungle soil and leaves.

We tied our hammocks between the column posts in the large shed. We were sleeping by a river so the mossy presence was going to be overwhelming. No matter how much smoking I was going to do, there would be far too many mosquitoes for them to worry about it. Mosquitoes hated cigarette smoke, so if I was ever getting bothered by them I lit a fag and they soon disappeared. I made sure my net was well secured above my hammock. I took my mosquito fluid and squirted it on the string ties of my hammock and mosquito net. That way the massive ants didn't bother to try and eat you in the night. These ants were one inch in length and had a bite like a Jack Russell. When you woke during the night with one or more of them feeding on your foot, you certainly knew about it. The noise of the mosquitoes homing in on you was horrendous and this was something else I wanted to avoid as much as possible. If you sprayed the net with the repellent then it would remain in the fabric a good twenty four hours and enough to allow you some sleep.

During the silence of the night, I could hear Taff throwing something heavy through the jungle foliage while he was on stag. There was a dog barking for what seemed like hours and the bastard thing must have had a sixth sense because every time I dropped off, it would start to bark and then when it stopped and I was dropping off again, it would start barking once more. It was my stag in about an hour and, if it was still barking when I was lying down at the camp perimeter, I would be tempted to throw my machete at it. There was no way I was having the Guatemalans home into our position by a barking dog. If they wanted us they would have to do the hard work and track us like good squaddies would. I couldn't stop it barking during my two hours on stag, it would stop for ten minutes and then it would bark again for twenty minutes. I went to wake Bob for his two hour stag, but he was already awake. No surprise there then, he was fuming over this dog. Even though it was about to become daylight, I had to try and grab an hour's kip or I wasn't going to be able to tackle the day ahead. It felt as if I had just fallen asleep when I heard a loud crack, it was the sound of a rifle being fired. I leapt out of bed thinking we were being attacked.

"Sit Rep, Bob?" (Situation report) I screamed.

Bob was leaning his rifle out of one of the shed windows and I thought he was under attack. "It's okay Sean," he said calmly. "It's sorted."

"What the fuck is sorted?" I asked frantically.

"The dog," he replied.

"What"? Taff asked. Taff was leaning behind one of the windows facing out the opposite direction to Bob.

"Did you fire?" I asked Bob.

"Yeah," he replied and at that he stood up. I also stood up and walked over to where he was. I was shocked when I looked out of the window and lying down below was a dog, it was struggling for breath and writhing all over the jungle floor. It was clear even from this distance that it was suffering badly with some form of disease that resembled Myxomatosis. Its eyes were nearly closed with large solid growths of white crusts and it had large lumps around its neck and head, its body was badly deformed and that was prior to it being shot. We were guessing that this was the animal that kept us awake all night, had it been a healthy animal and Bob had shot it, I would have personally shot him, but this needed putting out of its misery. Taff saw the same as we ran down the steps of the shed. He took an aimed shot and fired it into the dogs head. It moved no more.

A few years before in Canada, I was feeding a Gopher out on the prairie, it had taken me days to get this beautiful little creature to come and take processed cheese from the palm of my hand. My gun crew used to sit and watch in awe at the bravery of this untamed animal. It was an amazing thing and looked like a white version of a squirrel. I loved animals and would only ever hurt one if it had to be done. On this particular day as the Gopher was about two feet away from the palm of my hand, a spear appeared from nowhere and shot straight though its little body. It lay bleeding in front of us and died within a couple of seconds with the massive trauma being too much for him. I was in deep shock and for a split second I couldn't understand what had just occurred. I turned to my right and saw Gunner Dave Benson from 'J Sub' laughing his head off and cheering in triumph at the results of his well aimed shot. I quickly climbed to my feet, walked over to him and head butted him bursting his nose all over the prairie, to the tune of Rab Somerville shouting 'Now that's funny'. As Benson was running away from me holding his nose, I booted him right up the arse as hard as I could. I wanted him to feel some of the pain that the little animal had just felt, I hated him for this pointless act and would never be able to get on with him throughout my army career.

The dog thing was a different situation and needed putting out of its misery. Taff and Bob gloved up and managed to get the dog in a bin bag, they placed a load of bricks in the bag with it and between them threw it as near to the centre of the river as they could. I saw hundreds of fish attacking it and the water around where it had just landed became alive with activity. I don't know why they bothered with the bricks as the fish destroyed its body and probably the bones too. We were now certain this was the dog that had been responsible for the barking all night as the jungle fell silent once more.

"Make sure you scrub down you two," I shouted.

"Not half," Bob replied. We managed to clean ourselves down, make sure all the weapons were immaculate and trough our brekky before the long wait for Chindit's troops arriving. Even though this dog was out of the game, I had visions of some Belizean farmer come looking for forty dollars because we had just killed his lovely dog!

CHAPTER FIFTEEN

SNAKE EYES

Chindit was late to the point that we made radio contact. When I finally got to speak to Chindit, I asked him who the muppet was on the line that I had spoken to first. It turned out to be Tommy Johnson who was only just learning to be a signaller. He was flapping that much on the radio that we couldn't understand a word he was saying. There was something called R.S.V.P. which was 'rhythm, speed, volume and pitch' that radio operators lived and breathed. If you spoke on the radio and applied this then you would have no problem being heard or understand. I don't think he'd reached that stage in his training as he didn't apply any of it. Eventually Chindit came on line. I was only looking for the answer to one question and that was 'is everything okay?'. They were now running very late, Gunner Sean Morrison had 'twisted his knackers' we were told. I knew exactly what this was and needed immediate evacuation as an operation was imminent. Apparently as he was climbing out of the chopper, he had fallen forward twisting his testicles. I was sure that he would have to go to Belize Hospital as a minimum or back to U.K for an operation. Being a man, I felt a twinge below and instantly felt sorry for the guy. I hoped and prayed that they could sort it very quickly for him as the pain must have been so severe.

The troops made it to the base camp by mid-afternoon and they were in the same sweaty state as we were the day before. Chindit made a little passing comment about the now reduced ammo pile, but nothing more. That was a big relief as I thought he would go mental. Had he known what we had done with all that ammo, then it may have been a different story. We were having an eventful day the troops had decided to go for a dip, the water had stopped flowing and the river was pretty much still now, so they were all swinging from the big swing which was tied to the branch above the shed roof. Chindit had decided to have a go and when it came time for him to let go of the rope and fall towards the river, he somehow kept hold of the rope and subsequently dislocated his trigger finger on his right hand. He climbed out of the water and walked towards Pete Spooner.

"Medic, Medic," Pete shouted. He sounded like something out of an American War film.

"Fuckin Hell Pete, I was waiting for you to shout 'Man Down' next." I think he had flapped a little and had gone into 'worry mode'. Chindit had only dislocated his finger and nothing more. Fair play though, it was a nasty dislocation. I thought back to my medical training for a dislocated finger, it was simple. I also thought back to when this man had charged me on B.C's orders for something I didn't do and cost me a few quid. I suddenly forgot my training and grabbed his digit then I lifted it, rotated it and pushed it back into place. I got the impression that it was quite painful, God I was enjoying this moment. It dropped back into place, but I had made a right mess of it. A 'Shepherds Crook' sprang to mind. He was very chuffed with it and he looked relieved now that the pain wasn't as intense, I on the other hand (pardon the pun) was praying that he never showed it to any other medical person because if he did I would be in the shit once more.

When we got back to Rideau Camp, I sprinted to the medical centre with Chindit close behind me. I just had time to kick the door open to the treatment room where Dave Dawkins was chilling out on the treatment couch.

"Dave, I screamed. "When Chindit comes in here to ask how his finger looks, just tell him Bombardier Connolly has done a good job of it."

At this moment the front door opened and I dived into the toilet. "Sergeant Dawkins," he shouted.

"Yes, Sir, in here," Dave answered. He must have appeared in the treatment room.

"What do you think to that?" he asked Dave.

"Brilliant, Sir. Who did that for you?" he asked Chindit.

"Bombardier Connolly. Good isn't it"? Chindit asked.

"Let me have a look then." Dave was a Tosser he knew full well that

I would be petrified in the toilet and that I wanted Chindit out of there as soon as possible. I could hear him saying, "Mmmmm, yes. Mmmmm. Yes, Sir, that's a really good job and will be as good as new in a couple of months."

"Oh that long?" Chindit asked.

"Oh yes, Sir, it can take up to six months for the swelling from a bad dislocation like this to go down."

"Oh right, okay, Sarge," Chindit said and I heard the front door of the medical centre slam in typical Chindit fashion. When I came out of the toilet, Dave asked me what the fuck I had done to his finger.

"Hang on a minute mate remember, he's just fucking charged me for something I didn't do."

"Fair point," Dave said.

At sparrows fart the next morning (early doors) we were off. It was time to get serious and do what we were paid to do. We had been joined by two members of the B.D.F. (Belize Defence Force) and one of the Ghurkhas. Now Jonnie Ghurkha was much respected by members of the British Army and we valued their jungle skills and their commitment to the task, they were awesome soldiers and fit beyond all doubt. There wasn't a man in our troop who wouldn't have fought alongside a Ghurkha and we were glad that they were on our side and not the side of the enemy. I wouldn't have liked to have fought them in a pub in Colchester, let alone on their own turf. They were special beings for which we couldn't praise them enough. The B.D.F. on the other hand were appalling, there were about six hundred of these so called soldiers who were dressed like something out of 'Dads Army', but it has to be said, they knew the jungle like I knew my bed. Their local knowledge was amazing so with the B.D.F. and Johnnie Ghurkha we were in pretty good hands.

The B.D.F. pitched up with machetes and the Ghurkha arrived with his rifle and his Kukri strapped to his side. What these guys couldn't do with this knife wasn't worth a mention. We were all issued with our normal arms and ammunition, we were dressed in belt order with extra supplies and I had my medical bag. My section comprised of some proper head cases. It was as if Chindit gave me these lads so they could have a 'run out', a bit like a football manager putting his crap players on the field with two minutes to go before fulltime, just to eat up the clock. Other than Lance Bombardier Bob Baker he had given me all the sick, lame and lazy he could find in the battery. This was going to be a challenge, but I would relish it and do my utmost to show him that these lads could do it. We were a few kilometres away from the border according to the two B.D.F. soldiers at the briefing.

"Right no worries," I said. "Do I need my map or do you know where we are" I asked them.

"No corporal, I know exactly where we are," replied the first one, all my troops looked over at me on hearing this. It was an absolute 'no, no' to call a Bombardier in the Royal Artillery a 'corporal'. Although they were the same rank it was deemed an insult but as Chindit had given me another chance when I called him 'Sir' the day before, I was willing to do the same here. I explained the reasons why he mustn't do this again and we put it to bed, subject closed.

We had the Ghurkha taking up point and walking twenty yards up ahead and then the first of the B.D.F. I was next in line and then the second B.D.F. soldier was behind. After him were Bob, Mick McCarthy, Ken Browning and Kev Dolan. I looked back and remember thinking that it looked like something out of 'Carry on Camping'. What a mob. Kev had the G.P.M.G (Gympie) at the rear of the section. If anyone sneaked up on us, they would be getting sprayed with 7.62 machine gun fire but I had to remind him that this was a recce patrol and not a fighting patrol. We were to do the coward thing and run, not pretend to be the heroes and fight if we got spotted.

Ken had the radio, he couldn't get into any trouble while he had it and his voice procedure on the net was fairly good. "Hello Alpha X-ray, this is Zero-Charlie four four Alpha, radio check over."

There was a ten second pause. His radio cracked up. "Alpha X-ray ok over," came the reply.

Ken finished with, "Zero-Charlie four four alpha okay out."

Communications were good at that moment in time and I told Kev to inform me the minute we lost communications (comms). I didn't have much faith in the PRC351 radio. Other armies were issued with far superior kit than this so why we couldn't have it was beyond me, it was like the waterproof thing, the best army in the world and they couldn't keep us dry. How poor was that? I loved the British Army, but I hated the inferior kit they issued us which became more apparent as the years rolled on and new conflicts unfolded.

267

We tramped on through the jungle foliage, it wasn't as bad as I had expected but what it did mean was that we couldn't tab on at a fast pace. We had to walk pretty slowly as we had to cut through the bushes. The two new recruits in front of me were wading through the vegetation like Edward Scissorhands. We came to a point where we had to move up a little to catch them up, I turned back to let the section know and unbeknown to me I was about to stand on a large snake slithering across our path. As I turned I just caught the B.D.F soldier as he pushed me as hard as he could in the small of my back.

"You little bastard," I called from the ground. I got off the jungle floor and headed over to him, he was getting a good chinning for this. I looked up and he was pointing to the ground, where I had fallen over a big log only it wasn't a log but the body of the large snake. It was still moving very slowly across the track and it would have been really upset to feel the weight of a smelly squaddie riding on its back. He told me that it was a boa constrictor and would have given me a nasty bite, apparently they didn't have any venom, but the bite was very painful. The boa had poor eye sight so could mistake me as its prey with no problem and before I could count to three it would try its hardest to wrap around me and suffocate me. He didn't have to sell it to me any more, I believed him one hundred percent. I could see this thing on the track. It was enormous and probably twice my length. I could have kissed this guy and told him truthfully that my disrespect for the Belize Defence Force had just disappeared. For him to see this snake in front of me was one thing, but to be looking for it was another, I was very impressed, even more so when he casually stepped over it, picked up a large bamboo and helped it across the track. He was one cool cookie that chap, total respect.

We had a good morning patrol and made it to the border for our observation post. We dug in right on the edge of a massive valley which overlooked the border into Guatemala although as the crow flies it was only two hundred yards away. I was going to get my binoculars out, but I really didn't need them. They were that close we could hear what was being said by the Guat soldiers. The two B.D.F. lads were frantically writing as much of what was being said as possible. They had split the guards in half between them so they weren't recording the same person's words. I briefed them to tell me if there was any urgent info that I should know. We made sure the radio was on silent, the last thing we needed now was to compromise our position as a result of poor field craft drills. I instructed Ken to drop back fifty yards down the track we had just come down and start the dialogue with base camp. We would use Bob Baker as a runner to take any messages to him and then he would return to us for more info. Ken slipped back through the bushes. I was bricking it at this stage as I was responsible for the whole section but if I stayed cool, we would all make it back without a round being fired. The turd in the drainpipe would occur the minute we got spotted. Looking at the Guat soldiers, they wouldn't hesitate to off load their machine gun fire onto us. Shit, we were well close enough that's for sure.

Taking into account the time it had taken us to get to this point and the time of 'last light', I worked out that we had two hours at the outside to get what information we needed before we had to retreat. We would have to be on our toes to make sure we got back through an alternative route. I was confident with my timings but ran it past the Ghurkha and the B.D.F guys. I was a little out and we decided to leave half an hour earlier to give us a buffer should anything go wrong. I confirmed with our B.D.F. chaps that all was well and they had all the information they needed, there was nothing that meant much to us at this point in time, but that wasn't our call. We would take everything and anything we could get hold of back with us. I didn't have a clue what language the guards were speaking. It was like a Spanish, Mexican, Creole Mayan twang, but it meant nothing to me, I think the B.D.F. lads struggled with it in parts too. We withdrew to an area about half a mile back from the border. Every step we took, I felt a little more relieved, the lads had done well so far for a bunch of 'non combatants' so I was chuffed to pieces. We stopped at this point to re-group and get some more water down us. I sucked on my water bottle like it was my last dying wish.

"Okay lads, all change." They knew what I meant. Kev handed the GPMG to Mick McCarthy, but I wanted Ken to keep hold of the radio I dropped back in the section with Bob Baker and Kev in front of me. I put one of the B.D.F. at the rear of the section and one behind Johnnie Ghurkha. We set off once more. I was guessing that we were only three kilometres away from base camp. After ten minutes of patrolling we came across a very wide track. I lowered my hand to let the section know that they were to go to ground. I was going to recce the track to make sure there was nobody near it and no surprises left by the Guats. I took Ken with me and within a short time we could see that it was fine and that we could cross now. We went back to fall in line again, four of the section was over the road when Kev Dolan got up on one knee ready to cross. With his hands on his knee he pushed up and immediately started wobbling around the track.

"Bob, get back here," I called ahead. Bob turned and ran back to me. I didn't have to explain what was wrong, it was clear to see. We dragged Kev onto the other side of the track where the rest of the section was now waiting. As soon as we reached them Kev hit the ground like a sack of shit.

"Who's got the hammock?" I asked.

Bob Baker started to get it out of his webbing, the army Hammock was one of the better pieces of kit the army issued and it doubled up as a brilliant stretcher. I had the choice of looking at Kev here in the open and the baking sun or undercover away from the baking sun but more importantly away from the enemy. My first thoughts were that of dehydration, but there was more to this than met the eyes. Dehydration would pass very quickly under normal circumstances but this didn't feel the same. I started my assessment trying to communicate with him constantly but it was like he had been drugged up.

As I started my text book inspection running both my hands over his head, I heard myself saying, "What the fuck is that?" On the crown of his head I had noticed a large lump identical to a table tennis ball. "Oh my God! Ken, Cas Evac Now." (Helicopter Casualty Evacuation) At the same time I was ripping my map out of my pocket and calling my Ghurkha mate to come over to me. I could see a massive junction in the track and we soon established we were at the junction of Yalbac and Yucatan Highway.

Ken blasted the radio with, "Cas Evac, Cas Evac. Request grid 554 582 junction Yalbac and Yucatan," and he kept repeating it until Chindit piped up on the net.

"Send Sit Rep over," Chindit said. Ken sent over a good description of what had happened, while I was looking at something moving under this enormous ball on top of Kev's head, his condition was deteriorating and we tried as best we could to cool him and make him comfortable. I had covered a number of viruses, tropical diseases and ailments before deploying to Belize, but I had seen nothing like this. Even when I thought I was being a 'brown nose smart arse' doing my extra studies before we came out here. We watched this lump moving for some time in his head and I began to get impatient waiting for the chopper. I was about to carryout my fifteen minute observations again on him and I heard the crack of the Puma.

I got Bob Berry to run the fifty metres to the junction and Martial the chopper in. The rest of us either carried or chaperoned the stretcher. We handed the G.P.M.G. (Gympie) to Johnnie Ghurkha who was watching the rear as we got closer to the helicopter. As soon as it landed, I saw the welcome site of Dave Dawkins. He ran over to where we had placed the stretcher, I pointed to the lump on Kev's head at the same time as saying my hello to him.

"Beef worm," he said.

"A Fuckin what?" I asked.

"It's okay, it's only a beef worm," he repeated. "Send Bomb Baker to continue with the section, you come back in the Puma with me," he said. We radioed the base camp and Chindit was fine with the arrangements. We gave an E.T.A. for the troops to make it back to the base camp and I quickly briefed Bob then I jumped in the helicopter and off we went.

We landed the Puma in a matter of minutes and there were two infantry lads waiting for us. The army ambulance was parked up at the side of the heli-pad and I could see the driver waiting to go. We offloaded the stretcher and with the help of the two troops we managed to get it into the back of the ambulance. The driver hammered it towards the medical centre where the four of us carried Kev into the treatment room.

"Beers in the fridge Sean," Dave said. "Get me one while you're there," he said calmly.

"Are you having a fuckin laugh?" I said. "Kev's fuckin dying here and we are taking about getting arseholed."

"Don't talk wet you dick, he's got a beef worm," he finished.

Apparently Kev must have taken his hat off during the patrol and caught his head on a 'Bastard Tree'. The 'bastard tree' had a two inch solid thorn and there was a possibility that every thorn had the eggs of the beef worm on the end of it, so if you caught yourself on one of these thorns it would transfer the beef worm into your head and it would then grow under the skin within hours. We called it a 'Bastard Tree', because when you caught your head on it you shouted 'BASTARD'. Dave said he had removed a few of these in his time and they were nothing to worry about. Looking at Kev, I had to disagree.

"The treatment is piss easy," Dave said as he was throwing back his beer.

"Fuckin hell, this I have to see," I replied.

He prepared the instruments on the trolley and asked me to sit Kev up in a chair. He had given him an injection while I was getting the beers sorted, so he was a little more responsive. Once Kev was sat up, Dave set about him with a pair of scissors, he was cutting the hair around the ball on his head. Once he had scalped him he turned back to the instruments on the trolley, he washed everything down with the Hibitane solution to ensure it was spotlessly clean then he placed his bottle of beer on the side. Next he picked up the scalpel in one hand and then the arterial forceps in the other.

"Watch this," he said. "Don't worry, we won't get it today, but we will have it tomorrow." And with that he slashed the lump on top of Kev's head and all the gunge and crap came bursting out. I saw this beast burrow into the skin around the wound, Dave didn't even make an attempt to get it he just drained all the gunk off and then cleaned it firstly with the Hibitane and then with some stronger liquid. He patted it dry with a piece of mellolin gauze and then reached for the large plaster he had already cut and placed on the trolley. He stuck it over the wound like it was a little pimple. "Right, bring him back in the morning, we will have it then," he said. And with that he placed the instruments into the autoclave and grabbed two more beers from the fridge.

I was in shock, "What the fuck was that?" I asked him.

"What?" he asked.

"That what you just did to Kev?"

"Oh, that was experience, you'll see in the morning, don't worry."

The next morning Kev was back to his normal self, well all bar a fucking big lump on his bonce. I took him to the cookhouse for a good trough and then I had a nice shower, but he hadn't, my God he stank like a walking turd. We reported to the medical Centre at o8.oohrs where Dave was waiting. This time there was no trolley, Hibitane or anything except a pair of forceps.

"Fuck, I was pissed last night, look at my hands they are shaking like a bastard," said Dave.

Kev's head snapped round to look at Dave's hands. "Only joking mate," Dave said. "Right Sean, I want you to rip the plaster off as fast as you can when I give you the word." I was up for that and was looking forward to seeing this thing. "Don't worry lads, we'll have it now," Dave said. "Sit down Kev," he instructed him. I stood to the left and Dave stood on the right. He got the forceps as close to his head as he could and then told me to get ready. I grabbed the corner of this big plaster with my finger and thumb and watched Dave's face.

"One, two, three," and with that I ripped the plaster back. For a split second, I saw the beast, it was disgusting. I watched Dave and sure enough, he grabbed it as it was retreating back into Kev's head. Dave raised his hand in triumph and inspected the beast, it was a big white snail looking thing that was approximately one inch in length. Dave was that confident that he already had a sputum pot waiting with formaldehyde in it which he dropped the grub into and screwed the lid on it before showing it to Kev.

"Tell me that didn't come out of my head?" Kev said.

"Yep," Dave replied proudly stitching his head back together. Dave had shaved his head like a monk.

"Don't paint obscenities on my head, Dave," Kev said.

"Would I do that to you mate?" Dave said.

"Not much," Kev answered. He didn't paint his head with dye as it was bad enough giving him the hair cut of a monk.

"You twat Dave," I laughed. He laughed to himself.

Kev was stuck in camp now for the rest of the operational part of the tour. I managed to cadge a lift from a Puma back to our original drop point where Chindit and Pete would meet me. We had a big part of the operation to plan that we were all involved with and I wasn't going to miss that for the world. It was going to be an accumulation of all our training and experience and possibly the nearest I would ever get to a scrap with a live and very real enemy. The remit however was the same, it was a recce patrol, not a fighting patrol. I wouldn't be leading this operation, but acting more as medic and watching over the troops. We would be heading towards the border as three, seven men sections and when we were half a mile from the OP's we would branch off so that we were two hundred yards apart, on the edge of the same valley as we had been on the day before. The only difference being that we were taking a two day fully tactical march to get to it over a fifteen kilometres tab. We had a lot of jungle to beat and a big river crossing in the process. There was no way the Guatemalans would expect us taking this route because the river was near impossible to cross, it was huge, very wide and was reported to be always fast flowing with a mother of all undercurrents. Our troops were looking forward to the challenge though and this was the deciding factor as to why we were patrolling this route. At the end of the two days we were to return to Rideau by Puma and pick up our Light Guns. We would then deploy and fire a few hundred high explosive shells into the Caribbean Sea over two weeks.

I was met by Chindit and Pete and we made the tab back to base camp. I was under the impression that we would go for it the next day but we had to wait for a number of factors, Belize River also known as 'The Old River' was a monster and where we were planning to cross was approximately two hundred yards, we already had two spotters camped by the river waiting to give us a day or so notice to move when the river slowed down but this wasn't expected just yet. The river took us right to the border and there was also the issue of the B.D.F. joining us. There was a section of six joining our troop, before that week I wouldn't have bothered about them but now, I wouldn't have been happy going without them. I told Chindit and Pete what had happened with the boa and Mr B.D.F. which made sure they knew just how good these jungle soldiers were. I was convinced that they would see this for themselves though but hopefully not under the same circumstances. We used the next few days wisely with a lot of organised training. I set up a first aid stand and Chindit took the troops on field craft and patrolling discipline. Pete had a small arms stand and Taff Moran covered river crossing practising on dry land and in the river for some practical experience. We did a 'Round Robin' so everyone covered all the subjects. They spent one hour at each stand and to finish, was the practical part of the river crossing. We were all involved with that, Chindit and I were the 'safety swimmers' on our side of the river and Taff and Bob were the 'safety swimmers' on the other side.

Bombardier Mark Wilkinson went two hundred yards up stream with the floating line tied to his waist and before we knew it he was making a valiant attempt to swim across to the other side. He was moving at approximately twenty miles an hour with his own efforts and the speed of the current and by the time he reached us he had made it to the other side. He took the rope off and started to pull the safety rope over. When it was on his side of the river, he tied it off around a big tree then he was straight back in the water and back on the other side. "

Well done mate," I said as he climbed out of the river. "No worries," said Mark. The first section prepared their weapons and kit for crossing. The message was very easy, 'DO NOT let go of the safety rope! Hand over hand and before you knew it you would be on the other side'.

It went like clockwork one section, then two sections and then a complete' Cluster fuck' in the way of Joe Smiley. Joe was on my crew which didn't make the blow any softer, what a fool. His section had started to cross the rope as they had been taught and all was going well with the first four troops. Then it was Joe in the water, the river was running really fast, but no faster than what it was for the previous lads so Joe thought it would be a good idea when he got to the middle of the river to show the rest of the troop how to let go of the rope for a split second and then be able to grab it again quickly.

I had been listening to Taff repeating, "Never, ever underestimate the power of a fast flowing river." All the troops had heard him and sat in front of him nodding their heads in agreement, so with that in mind I couldn't believe what Joe was doing, then when his brain told him to grasp the rope again it was too late, there was no rope to grab. He was six feet away from it and floating away from it at a great rate of knots.

"I'll get it," Chindit screamed. I knew by the line he was running in that he had predicted where he would catch Joe further down river if he sprinted and dived into the water. There was a flaw in his plan though Chindit dived from way back on the bank, not close enough to the edge, he made it into the river, but he hadn't made it into the deep water and he smashed his head on the rocks. He stood up with his head pouring with blood, certainly dazed and concussed.

"Mark, get Chindit" I screamed as I overtook the Sergeant Major stood in two foot of water. I dived as far out to the middle as I could and swam as fast as I could go, I could feel every couple of seconds the water trying to pull me under but I wasn't having it. I could see Joe and I was catching up to him, he was making attempts to swim against the current and he was exhausted and panicking. As I reached him he kept smacking my hand which was on the scruff of his neck. I quickly got pissed off with him so I pushed his head under the water for a second and then brought him back up, that did the trick and he suddenly took my lead and stopped fighting against me. I pulled and swam as hard as I could to try and reach the side, I could see five or six of our troops running along the bank and then I saw a large clump of jungle vine overhanging the river, if I pushed a little harder for a little longer I knew I could reach it.

I kicked as hard as I could and I couldn't breathe but I knew it was a once in a lifetime chance to grab the vines with my free hand. I raised my left hand and made a grabbing motion, I had managed to grab it and I wasn't letting go, I held on for dear life while our legs were being swept from underneath us. The current was still too strong for us to fight it and there was no more strength in my body but I knew I had to hang on a few seconds longer.

As I was about to let go I heard this voice saying, "Let go." It was Mark, he had tied the rope around the two of us and the lads on the side of the bank had us. When I got Joe on the bank, I beat the living daylights out of him.

"You stupid Bastard, what the fuck were you thinking of you dickhead?" He couldn't breathe and was trying to apologise in part words. It was down to sheer determination that we lived through this ordeal and as I lay on my back on the bank trying to catch my breath, I wondered how many more times during this fucking tour, I was going to cheat death. I was beginning to wish I had been shot in the ammo compound now. At least I wouldn't have known much about it. Was I living on borrowed time? I got my breath back and dragged Joe off the ground then I kicked him all the way back to the base camp.

I had forgotten about Chindit, but it was good, Taff and Mark had found my medical bag but they wanted me to see it before they covered it with a clean sterile dressing. I don't know why, it was only Chindit. It was good though and there was no deep gash as I first thought, they had stopped the bleeding and were now bandaging it after a good dose of iodine to protect it. Chindit was going to beat Joe to a pulp, but I told him it had already been done and he was now 'on stag' until further notice. He got off lightly as he was a member of my crew, it had been a stupid thing to do, but he knew that.

On the fourth day we got the nod to go, the evening of the third day we had a 'smoker' (Barbeque) at base camp. We had to catch the fish the traditional way unfortunately, then we had whatever chicken and other scraps of meat we could barby. The cooking was down to the Ghurkhas, they were brilliant at it, this was confirmed when I was lying back with another brew, picking the last bits of the fish from my teeth with my tooth pick. It was gorgeous and good to have a full belly. I pondered over the last few weeks and the patrols we had carried out and I was ready for the morning and the big one. I would be made up if it passed without any occurrences. I wanted a smooth ride over the next two days before we were to go and blow the coast of Belize up with some serious high explosive artillery ammunition.

We set off at early doors the next morning. It was fairly cool and we got a good drop on the heat. We had two of the B.D.F. lads in each section so I was feeling confident that I wouldn't be standing on any big snakes. We had a good few water breaks throughout the day and had covered ten clicks with no bother at all. I had swapped my section round lots of times, so each of the team got to carry all the kit. By the time we reached our laying up point at night, we were goosed. With the stags organised we got our head down until first light and then we were up for it again and ready to hammer the last five clicks and the river crossing. A quick brew and a bit of dry rations and off we went I was patrolling between the two B.D.F lads. When we got to the river crossing, I was shocked as to how wide it was but there was some good news in that the water was still and wouldn't be a problem for Mark to cross it with his floating line. He was an unbelievable swimmer and he took his time, within a few minutes he was over. We saw him climb out of the river and tie off around a huge tree, we warned our individual sections not to let go of the rope until they were across the river. If they did, not only would we not dive in after them, but I would personally shoot them. This time thankfully, they listened to us and the crossing went without issue. We lowered the rope into the water so we didn't have to swim it again we could just raise the rope on the return journey, after another hour of tabbing along the river bank we were at the border. I looked to my left and right and saw no sign of our other sections. This was good and it meant if I couldn't see them from here then it was a good chance the enemy wouldn't be able to see them. I knew they were there as we had left our radio operators fifty yards back and they were talking to each other.

Same drill as before, the B.D.F. lads were writing on their little notebooks like there was no tomorrow. There were at least fifty Guatemalan troops on this border post and again they were only a short distance away from us as the crow flies. It was really important that we were very careful as there were now fifty sets of eyes that could potentially spot us. We did the maths thing again and agreed to withdraw in one hour, one section at a time, we rendezvoused (R.V'd) at the river where the rope was and again made it over the river without incident. Within one hour we were flying in the chopper to pick up our Light Gun.

My crew were going to pull a 'fly one' (pardon the pun). When we hit the camp, instead of rushing to get the gun ready, I made sure that Paul O'Neil legged it to the N.A.A.F.I. for a ton of clatty bars, fags and stims. My crew had all chipped in thirty dollars each so we had a few bob to splash out for a bit of luxury to last us over then next few weeks. By the time Paul returned to the gun, we were about ready to deploy. We were minging dirty and stunk to high heaven, it would have been nice to have a shower, but we didn't have time we were off again. We dragged the Light Gun around the corner to the heli-pad and then sent the one tonne back to the camp. We climbed aboard the Puma with all our kit and then it lifted off, Ken Browning from the other gun held the hook and eye ready for the hook-up. The pilot took up the load with the help from the loady and then he lifted off with no problem. The gun was now dangling ten feet from the bottom of the helicopter. There would be someone at the other end to discharge the electricity from the gun before anyone touched it. The gun would build up a massive electrical charge while it was travelling under slung from the chopper so at the end of the flight, the pilot would lower the gun to a level that a member of the ground crew would touch it with a strop. The strop had a wire which ran to the ground and the electricity would run through this into the ground as opposed to one of the crew. Ten minutes into the flight I could sense that all was not right but I wasn't near the door so I couldn't see where we were or how far from the jungle canopy we were.

We all looked at the loady talking into his microphone and obviously he was communicating with the pilot. He looked as if he was panicking a little and he kept looking out of the side windows. First one side and then the next and then back to the first. I felt the Puma jerking from side to side and it felt as if the under slung gun was not behaving how they had expected it to. This jerking went on for another two minutes and it was getting worse and worse it seemed to be winding up like a pendulum. All of a sudden the jerking stopped and the loady sat on his little seat by the door, the frantic communication between them had stopped but the noise in the chopper was too loud so we couldn't communicate with the loady. One or two of the crew didn't have a clue but the rest of the troops knew something wasn't right. At least I was sure now that we weren't going to crash as the loady was just looking out the window at the scenery. I could see the odd tree top when he banked steeply, but I couldn't see anything else.

I felt the Puma descending. Wow, I thought to myself, there was no delay before the ground crew hit the strop and the hook was disconnected to release the gun. I was waiting for the chopper to drop that last fifteen feet before we finally landed on the ground but none of the above happened, we just fell from the sky and before I knew it the wheels of the Puma hit the ground. We all looked at each other and wondered what was going on. We scurried off the chopper and were about to start dragging our kit off when I realised we were back on the helicopter landing Pad at Rideau Camp.

We were shouted over by Chindit. "Sir, what the fuck is going on?" I asked him.

In the meantime the chopper wound down and switched off. I looked back at Chindit and Sergeant Shaky Moor had joined him. "Where's my gun?" I asked in amazement.

"Twelve miles over there Bomber, upside down in the jungle," Chindit said. He was pointing south towards the border, our signal's room had received the radio message that the Army Air Corp had dropped my gun.

"Ah sir, you are joking?" I knew immediately what had happened I put two and two together and I came up with a very accurate four.

The pilot came over to us. "Sorry lad," he said as he was looking at me. "It was the gun or us."

"I felt it, Sir, and I saw the loady flapping a bit," I answered. I knew the score and I was on his side. If it was the gun being killed or me then there was no competition. We were told at the beginning of our tour that if the gun started to move around under the helicopter to the point when it picked up more and more pace then it would be dropped at the stage when the pilot and the crew agreed that there was a serious possibility of it pulling the Puma down. It was a no brainer, it had to go.

We had returned to camp to pick up the spare gun. "Oh fucking brilliant, Sir, it's been cannibalised," I said. That meant when anyone was missing something off their own gun, they would go and nick it off the spare gun.

"It's okay Bomb Connolly, I have checked it over," Shaky said. "You will have to give it a bit of a spruce up when you get in the field." We were to try for the second time to fly out with our new artillery piece in two hours time. The crew were at a stage when they couldn't fly until they had taken this break.

"Showers lads," I shouted to my crew. "Rab, you stay with the chopper, Mickey quick shower then straight back so Rab can go and get one."

"Roger, Bomber," Mickey shouted.

We left all the kit on the chopper and legged it up for a shower. It was heaven, and I covered myself in talc then put my nice clean combat gear on. I was like a new man.

We met at the heli-pad as agreed two hours later and went through the same drill, this time the journey passed without incident. We spent the rest of the operations bored to tears firing twenty high explosive shells out to sea every day. We enjoyed the first three days but after that became bored, this 'real soldiering' turned out to be shit. We thought it pointless but had to comply with what we had been instructed to do. Once a week we took a large delivery of tonnes of rations of ammunition, food and water. That was the biggest excitement for us and at the end of the operation we safely retracted back to Rideau. We were so grateful that we had got to the end of this part of our tour. There were twelve of us flying up to Belize City on Monday and then on to a little Island or Peninsula called Placencia for two weeks in the sun and a spot of well earned R&R (Rest and recuperation). We couldn't wait.

Chapter Sixteen

Game On

On Monday morning we stood outside the accommodation block. The rest of the troops had just come back off their run and it looked like a biggy.

"What a bastard," Ron Harrison said. "I'm gutted I missed that one," he laughed.

"You sarcastic bastard," Ken Browning replied breathlessly. I laughed out of sheer relief of not having to do the run. We marched down to the Cookhouse in our civvies and had a good trough. Not only did we not have a clue where we were going, but we didn't know what was there and when we would be eating again. We all had a choice for R&R (Rest and Recuperation). The expensive option was flying from Belize City Airport to anywhere in the U.S.A. or the 'poverty plus option' which was flying to this small Peninsula on the East coast of Belize called Placencia. It had cost us thirty dollars for our accommodation and thirty dollars to fly from Belize City to Placencia on a private plane. The exchange rate at this time was four Belizean Dollars to the British Pound. For a two week holiday it was costing us fifteen quid. I noticed they didn't say thirty dollars for 'the hotel' they would only refer to it as 'accommodation' which was a worry. The lads who were flying to America were going to have the holiday of a lifetime, but for us it was just going to be a good 'piss up' and also to learn some of the many water sports that the island had to offer. The difference being that we would be taking a couple of grand home to purchase the things we had dreamed of as children. I had a photograph taken when I was fourteen years old stood with my mother next to this beautiful car. I was holding onto the driver's door handle of this Ford Capri. It had become my dream car and I had been determined from that moment in time and now after this tour of Belize, that I was going to own one.

There were eight of us travelling from Rideau to Belize on the Puma and then we would be picking another five troops up from airport camp before taking the 'crop sprayer' for the last leg of the journey which was a short twenty to thirty minute flight to the peninsula. I was chuffed to N.A.A.F.I. breaks as Dave Dawkins was joining us along with Tommy, Dave, Ron, Paul O'Neil and Brian Stafford from up north, we were sure to be getting into some trouble. This was going to prove to be a heavy session. We were only permitted to take a large pack with a few changes of clothing on the Puma, but we didn't care. A bar of soap, a pair of flip-flops and a tooth brush would have done us. It was just as well because we wouldn't have got much more in the 'crop sprayer' which was to follow the chopper ride.

We stood on the heli-pad at nine in the morning. The Puma pulled up with a jerk, the jerk got off with the mail for the troops and we got on. Lt Joplin didn't appreciate my joke although Dave thought it was very funny at the time. It was pointless us looking half decent for the journey as we were now getting blasted with dust from the downdraft of the Puma. I was gutted in my Sunday best too. It was ironic because by the time we got to Belize, we were quite chilly in the back of the chopper. Life was so different for the troops up at Holdfast and airport camps though. They had such luxuries as grass and tarmac, we landed on a lovely smooth tarmac runway which was fantastic and no dust. Even before we got away from the aircraft, we noticed what we thought were six hairy arsed infantry lads storming the helicopter. These weren't infantry and for reasons best known to me, I was able to confirm that these lads were members of the 'Hereford Hooligans' (S.A.S.). It looked like they were about to deploy deep into the jungle for a few months by the amount of kit they were carrying.

The S.A.S. had been carrying out a lot of training and exercises in the jungles of Belize. Apparently, this was one of the best jungles in the world to train and I would take their word for that! There was a jumped up Rodney who decided to challenge the SAS one day during our tour. He had parked his British war ship fourteen miles off the coast of Belize and sent a message to the S.A.S. Commander saying that there was no way the S.A.S. would be able to get on board his heavily guarded warship. The S.A.S. accepted the challenge and it was reported that at last light two days later, two squaddies walked onto a beach on the coastline of Belize, they took their large packs of their backs, took out a canoe, unfolded it and rowed away into the night. The next morning when the captain of the ship radioed through, he was gloating, he was so proud of his men. He was also disappointed with the S.A.S. as they couldn't complete the challenge.

The S.A.S. commander answered the call with, "Tell me what you find in your 'Boiler Room'. Out"."

The captain of the ship and all his senior officers made their way to the bowels of the ship. Once in the boiler room, they noticed '22 Special Air Service' Stickers stuck all over the place. It was said that the naval officer left the boiler room feeling a little inadequate and quite embarrassed. There were a lot of hard and fast rules in the forces but there was one thing that was a big 'no, no and that was not to challenge the SAS in jest or for real. You would end up looking like a certain naval officer, not Captain Pugwash, but more like Captain Mugshot.

Brian Stafford met us off the whirly bird and directed us to a Bedford Wagon. "We don't fly out from Belize Airport until two o'clock this afternoon lads. Anyone for a beer?" he enquired. We didn't need asking twice, my throat was like a Swiss angler's maggot box, I could have murdered a bottle of Belikin or three. We got to Brian's room where he opened the fridge door and showed us inside.

"Oh Brian! Well done mate," we all cheered as we sat on his bed and poured beer down our throats. By the time it was time for us to roll, I think it was safe to say that we were all 'half cut'. We were joined by the other lads and reported to Belize airport all present and correct. It was great as there were no passport checks or anything, no one even asked us our names, what planet we were on or where we were going. It was all organised and booked in advance. I looked out of the front window and wondered where this aeroplane was coming in from as it was now getting close to take off and there was no sign of it. With five minutes to spare, this big Rasta walked through the back door and into the shed they called the air terminal. He walked over to where we were all sitting in a long line on this make shift wooden bench.

"You lads going to Placencia then?" he asked.

"Not with you we're not mate," I answered.

"Well ya got a long wait for the next flight brother," he finished. Oh no, I thought. Please, just tell me that this guy is nothing to do with our flight and I will be a happy man. He was smacked off his face on weed and couldn't stand up, let alone get us on a plane. We all had to hand over the thirty Belizean Dollars that we were told to have ready at the terminal. We were a little worried though, because if this guy was on the plane and became abusive, he looked as if he could be a bit of a handful and cause a serious air incident.

"One of you is gonna have to sit up front wid me," he started again.

"Wow, wow, wow," shouted Dave Benson. "What do you mean, up fuckin' front?"

"There is fourteen seats including the pilot so one of ya have to sit in da front wid me."

Dave was standing up but had now slouched back down into his seat. He hated flying and was petrified of the big plane let alone a small one. "That's easy mate, I am most senior, so it's me," I told him.

"Okay brother, let's go," and with that he turned and headed to the rear door of the shed. To have this guy on the aircraft was a worry, but to have him flying it was suicide.

I was the first one to see the 'crop sprayer'. If you imagine a gypsy caravan covered in shiny chrome, this was the aeroplane version of it. It looked about forty years old and stank of Araldite, Polyfilla and 'Pound Shop superglue'. There was no way that I was going to mention the large crack running across the largest part of the wing to the other lads. If Dave knew he just wouldn't have got on board.

"Sean please don't fuck about will you," he shouted from the back.

"Don't worry mate, I know you don't like flying," I answered. I was half pissed and I was sitting up front, with Captain Avajoint, on an old aeroplane that looked as if it had been used as a double on the film 'Flight of the Phoenix'. If I got my way, I was going to drive this baby and there would be no doubt about that. Just because Dave Benson wasn't too keen on flying it wasn't going to stop me enjoying the start of my R&R. The lads couldn't believe the state of this plane, no wonder it was only thirty bucks. I strapped myself into my orange box right next to the pilot and noticed a photo which I was sure was of the Everly Brothers but I was wrong, it turned out to be the Wright Brothers. I think they must have been the last owners of this marvellous crate, either way it couldn't have cost more than eighty quid. In fact looking back, our thirty dollars should have given us a large stake in owning this aircraft, but then again it wouldn't have been something I would have been proud of telling my mates about. 'Oh yes lads, I own an aeroplane', I think not. That would be the same as presenting my little Hillman Imp car and telling everyone I had a sports car.

When we took off, I swore I heard Dave Benson crying on the back seat. I have to be perfectly honest and say that not only was this pilot bombed off his head on marijuana but he must have been rubbing cocaine in his eyes as well. How the hell we missed the fuel truck at the end of the runway was anybodies guess!

"Give us a cabby mate?" I asked the pilot.

"Okay brother, I take it up first," he replied. Just like that! I couldn't believe my ears, I was going to pilot the aeroplane.

Dave Benson was shouting me from the back. "Sean, please don't do it," but the rest of the lads were loving it and egging me on further. Brian Stafford was sitting directly behind me and made out that he was leaning forward to put something in the back pocket of his jeans.

"I dare you," he said under his breath. I faced my front and waited for the pilot to hand over the controls.

He levelled the plane out and turned to me, "There you go brother, it's all yours." He was as cool as a cucumber. I could hear Dave Benson at the back of the aircraft again screaming all kinds of obscenities but I took no notice, I turned the 'Stingray' steering wheel a fraction to the left and within a split second felt the aeroplane tilt left, next I did the same to the right. I turned my head fully to the rear and stared in the eyes of Dave Benson.

"Don't you fucking dare me," and before Paul O'Neil could finish saying, "Why? What are you going to do? Leave the aircraft?" I hammered the little steering wheel forward as hard as I could.

The plane dropped out of the sky, nose first like a sack of potatoes. Dave Benson was screaming like a baby and his bowels were probably doing something else besides. He had a face like a smacked arse. The lads were cheering and laughing loudly behind me and the pilot never batted an eyelid. I had been allowed to carry on with my kamikaze manoeuvre until the pilot decided that it was time to take control again. It felt fantastic as we were spearing to the ground at warp factor ten, but

Dave Benson didn't agree. After about ten seconds the pilot took control and I could feel my steering wheel being pulled back up gradually.

"Look at Dave, Sean. He looks the colour of boiled shite," said Ken Browning. I turned round and he was right, it was enough to make a glass eye weep. Dave Benson looked green, his 'sick bag' had been smudged all over his face and the nearly digested 'Belikin' was beginning to smell a little on the ripe side. Fifteen minutes later I noticed the plane was beginning to shake and shudder as we were gradually descending. Oh well, I thought, this is it. I looked out of my window and could see a beautiful island below and something that resembled a landing strip. We had been flying the right amount of time so this had to be it. When we landed on the punctured tyre, I thought we were all going to die. Dave was going on about how he was going to get so pissed on our return that he would be totally unconscious for the whole flight. Personally, I couldn't see what all the fuss was about.

As I climbed out of the aircraft I noticed that the island was beautiful and the sea surrounding was a gorgeous turquoise blue. Whoever had recce'd this place for a good 'get away' for the troops had done a really good job, maybe we had crashed and gone to heaven, I was thinking. This was nearly confirmed when I saw a bloke walking over towards us who from a distance, looked like Jesus but I wasn't sure yet. He introduced himself as 'Chicken George' then explained that he owned a lot of the island and was responsible for renting his accommodation block to the Ministry of Defence. I still hadn't heard the word 'hotel'.

"Do you mean hotel mate?" I asked.

"No, I didn't say that," he answered.

"I know, but I was hoping you did," I finished.

He was smiling as he turned away, "Follow me guys." We all chased after him. It was roasting now but there was a fantastic sea breeze. We were going to enjoy two weeks of this without a doubt.

"Are there any bars here mate?" Tommy shouted from the line.

"Yes chief. Three," he answered.

"That's me," Tommy said. "Wake me up in two weeks." I would guess that Tommy was in for some heavy sessions.

"Oh! look Sean," Joe shouted pointing at a concrete path running up the centre of the island. It was about four feet wide and looked just like the M1 at Rideau camp but a touch wider. We were told it was in the Guinness Book of World Records because the island was about sixteen miles long and this was the narrowest main street in the world measuring at over four thousand feet long. I don't know how true this was but interesting all the same. The path linked everything from the businesses on the island to the houses and the village. The point of the island was called Punta Placentia or Pleasant Point but it wasn't just the point that was pleasant, the whole island was stunning. I hadn't witnessed anything like this before, it was paradise. We were in awe at the houses these families lived in. They were shaped like large mushrooms and painted every colour of the rainbow.

We had seen a number of villagers looking at us, but they were all smiling. It was as if they had been briefed to smile at all the soldiers as they were going to be spending a lot of money on their island. I was later to find out that this wasn't the case, and that they were just very genuine people. We walked another three hundred yards and 'Chicken George' left the M1, he was walking over to this large wooden building which had been built on wooden stilts. Before I climbed the steps to what was going to be 'home' for the next two weeks, I looked around us. The Caribbean Sea was ten yards from our front door.

"What's that George?" I asked whilst pointing at this strange looking shed next door.

"Cosy's Corner. Your bar and disco, brother," he smiled. Hang on, I thought. Six hundred fags in my bag, a wallet full of dollars in my arse pocket, the Caribbean Sea on my doorstep and a bar next door this is definitely two weeks in paradise, life just doesn't get any better than this.

The building was very basic, but it was fine for what we were paying and for what we needed, which was really just somewhere to lay our head. The cost of the tuition for water sports the next day was included in our price. I fancied the 'windsurfing' lark and was looking forward to having a go, but for now I wanted a splash in the sea, an hour's kip and then a good night on the beer with the lads.

I shared a room with Tommy and Dave Dawkins. Each room had its own bathroom and toilet. 'Chicken George' showed us around and then pointed to a smart looking house behind ours on the other side of the M1. It was clear that he was well respected on the island by the way everyone was saying their hellos to him. He was a good guy to get on with and told us that if we had any problems to come and see him. After a bit of a briefing about the island he left us in peace. It was time for a dip in the sea, we had been dying for this since we landed and before you could blink, there was twelve hairy arsed squaddies destroying the piece and tranquillity of this paradise location screaming on their way into the sea. The water was verging on hot and really clear and most satisfying. We found out later that when there was a storm out to sea the water turned dirty with all the seaweed and crap coming in on the waves. It must have known that we were coming this particular day because it was fantastic. I thought how unlucky that my friends and family were not here to share this with me.

We soaked in the sea for what seemed like ages before we decided to go and get our heads down for an hour. We wanted to make the most of our first night on Placencia so a bit of a rest would allow us to do that.

I grabbed my towel and walked into our new accommodation, Dave looked at me as I walked into the room and said, "Make sure you don't swallow any water in the shower mate."

I looked over at Tommy. "You ain't seen nothing yet," he smiled. Oh no, I thought, what was wrong with the water now? I walked into the shower and put my washing bag on the stool at the side of the sink, then pulled the plastic curtain back, the shower looked in good order but when I turned it on, it looked like it had been left to stagnate in a rusty tank for twenty years it was nearly black.

"Think I'll be looking at an alternative means of scrubbing up if we can't get this sorted, it's gross," I said as I got under the shower. I immediately got the metallic taste in my mouth and that was it for me. I stepped out of the shower, wrapped my towel round me then picked up my soap and walked out of the bathroom. I took my soap into the sea and commenced my scrub down, once I had finished I walked back into the block and into the bathroom. The water in the sink was a little better so I used it to wash my hair. There was a tap with the words 'Drinking Water' above it, so I filled my cup and brushed my teeth. I would be looking to purchase water for the duration of the two weeks. What a bit of a let-down, I thought, but after all it was an island and furthermore, it was only costing us about seven pence a week to stay there, so I couldn't expect too much more for my money.

I woke from my kip with such a dry throat, it wasn't true. I noticed

Tommy was missing from his bed so I walked out onto the top of the steps which led to the beach. He was staring out to sea while smoking his cigarette.

"Fuck me Sean," he said. "If I never see another thing in exchange for this moment I will be a happy man. This is paradise at its best." I didn't know how he knew it was me that was coming to join him, but he did. There was a little bench at the bottom of the steps just on the beach.

"I have to agree mate, you could never forget this, could you?" The view was amazing in the late afternoon and we both sat there for a further fifteen minutes without saying a word to each other. I can remember my thoughts to this day.

"You coming to find a shop mate?" I said after a while.

"Yes defo, I need a load of stuff," he replied, as he got up to walk back inside. We collected our wallets and put our flip-flops and T-shirts on then headed for the M1. We hadn't passed a shop on the walk from the airstrip, so we took the calculated chance of walking the other way. We had only walked approximately two hundred yards when I saw three young lads having a kick around with an old plastic football on the soft sand, I noticed they were all bare footed, but thought to myself that it would be impossible to play on the sand like this and not burn the soles of your feet. I bent down and felt the sand while Tommy asked them for directions to the shop. It was scorching, but they didn't even acknowledge the heat, let alone anything else.

"Straight down the M1 and keep looking left mate," Tommy said.

We walked another three or four hundred yards at a slow pace whilst taking in the scenery and looking at all the local people. I hadn't yet seen another person wearing any footwear. There was one thing for sure, we wouldn't be going barefoot, certainly not in the daytime anyway. There was something else that we were very conscious of and that was the heat of the sun, there may well be a nice sea breeze on Placencia, but we knew all too well about the sun bouncing off the sea's waves. It would burn our fair skin in no time so we were careful to cover up after about ten minutes even though, we were fairly well tanned at this stage. Our holiday could easily be spoilt if we became complacent and we would bollock each other if we had been uncovered for too long.

About one hundred yards off the M1 there was a rotten old shed with a couple of dusty Frisbees and a long string of flip-flops tied together outside. "Tell me that's not it Tom," I said pointing at this derelict building. Tommy laughed and the little old lady who was sitting outside must have heard him because she looked up from the machete she was sharpening with a stone. "Have you seen what she's doing mate?" I asked him.

"Oh shit," he replied. Once inside we discovered that it was equally as bad on the inside as it was on the outside, but it had everything we would need from the first glance. Tommy was buying everything he could see whereas I was buying beer, beer and more beer.

"Hang on a minute mate," Tommy said. "How the hell are you going to get that lot back to the block?"

"Watch me," I replied. He had a fair point because by the time I got back to the accommodation, I was on my knees. Thinking I was being smart and walking right by the waters edge wasn't too clever either, I was sinking in the hot dry sand or the wet muddy sand where the tide had come in and back out again. This was a double kick in the teeth because by the time I had got the warm beers back to the accommodation, I couldn't even drink one until I had been able to cool them down. We had a small fridge in the kitchen that would hold twelve beers but that was it. I was gagging for cold fluid so begged Tommy for some of his coldish water.

It was pretty much as the main land in that the day turned into night as if someone had turned the light switch off. Placencia fell suddenly into blackness. All of a sudden there was a loud bang of a generator backfiring and when it kicked in and fired up, the dim electrical lights lit up the island. It looked so fantastic in the day and as equally great at night, however as soon as the generator kicked in everything was like a military operation. The 'Swingfog' started up and before we knew it the island was covered in the thick smog we had grown to know and love. I thought that this island with its sea breeze would never suffer from mosquito and other annoying insects, but obviously it did. The next thing that happened was a number of the small sheds and houses lit up for the people that could afford it and then finally, the music from the disco next door. It was very loud, but inviting all the same. We were going to save Cosy's Corner for later and make our way to the top end of the island where we were told by the mad machete bird earlier that there was a very nice bar called the 'Creole Bar' which was famous for its seafood and good beer. We needed to eat somewhere before we went on the pop and this sounded like as good a starting place as any.

All twelve of us walked into the Creole Bar. It would be difficult to miss as it was lit up like a satellite at the end of the island and was as loud as a seventies disco. We decided that if reggae music stopped playing forever, the whole of Belize would disappear. The bar wasn't as bad as I had first thought and certainly a star higher than Bobby's Bar on the ratings.

"Look at the size of her Dave," Tommy said. He had pointed to this girl stood over by the D.J. propping up one of the speakers.

"Shit, if she says jump, you ask how high," he replied. She was enormous and must have weighed in at over thirty stone. She seemed to have a really bubbly personality. This bar had a few sets of tables and chairs and we were impressed as it had a proper sprung dance floor. What was clear to see was that a lot of pride had gone into looking after this place as everything in it was old but looked immaculate. The big girl came over and introduced herself as Brenda, she didn't own the place but helped her friend out when it got busy and we were chuffed to pieces with her hospitality. She knew we had arrived on the island and was expecting us. These Chogies didn't miss a trick, the Jungle Drums would have been speaking to the Mad Machete Bird too, which would have also given the game away.

We split up into teams of four to keep some sensibility in the beer rounds etc. "Twelve beers love please," I got in first.

"No problom man," she replied in a heavy Caribbean accent. She turned and screamed at the top of her voice to a set of double doors on the back wall of the bar. "Sheila." Within three or four seconds another girl appeared and it had now become apparent as to why there were double doors on the back of the bar. This woman made Brenda look like Twiggy! She must have been another eight to ten stone heavier.

"Shit," Brian said. "I bet they don't make any fuckin money here then." Obviously referring to her eating all the profits. She walked over to a massive chest freezer and took a key out from between her enormous boobs then unlocked a padlock which secured the lid on the freezer and put the key back where it came from. Dave Benson stared in amazement.

"I will give you ten dollars if you produce that key in the morning," Paul O'Neil said to him.

"I'll have some of that too," Andy said throwing his ten in.

"I'll throw ten dollars in as well Dave," I said. Next thing we knew, we had all bet him ten dollars. Here we go, I thought. B.A.O.R. (British Army on the Rampage).

I clenched my teeth as I asked for the menu and waited for something to come back written on the back of a fag packet but I was pleasantly surprised when Brenda appeared with a two page menu. It didn't just say chicken and chips in a basket ten times either. Most of us ordered the large fish platter which looked really appetising from the photo, it cost two dollars and when it arrived, I was surprised for a second time. If it tasted as good as it looked, I would be a very happy man. It did as well, the 'Belizean slop jockey' in the back of this bar had it well sorted. It looked like this was going to be my eating 'gaff' while I was on here. Had I purchased seafood as fresh and as well cooked as this in the UK, the cost would have been at least ten times as much. No sooner had we finished our meals the DJ turned the music up. Brenda kept bringing bottles and more bottles of beer to the tables and I was getting more and more pissed. We wanted to go onto the third bar on the island, but we were having such a good time here, we decided to give it a miss until the next day.

At about ten o'clock the front door opened and in walked two more large girls, not as big as Brenda or Sheila, but still big. I wouldn't have fought any of them to be honest. We couldn't understand why the girls on this island were so large, with all the fish and good sea air around them, but when we spoke about it, they were probably sitting around bored most of the day and eating as part of the habit. There were only two girls in the bar who might be under eighteen stone.

By the time we left the bar we were too drunk to make it anywhere else. We would have to be more organised in future or we wouldn't be seeing anything else. The evening had cost the four of us on our table thirty dollars each which was nothing for getting bladdered and having the opportunity to eat all this superb food. Tommy, Dave and I left and the rest stayed out for the duration. They were either going to get as pissed as they could, try to end up with one of the local beauties or in one case, try and retrieve a key. The thought of trying to retrieve that key made me feel a bit sick to be honest, but it brought back memories of when we went to the Reeperbahn in Hamburg Germany.

Back then we had come to an alley which was blocked off at each end with big steel partitions, it was called 'Five Mark Alley'. Five marks as in 'Deutch marks' which was the equivalent to one pound twenty five pence and if you managed to get into 'Five Mark Alley' without the bouncers stoving your head in, there were rows of windows on each side of the alley. In the windows were prostitutes sat on little wicker chairs dressed in all kinds of provocative lingerie. If you picked one of these prostitutes it would cost you five Deutch marks to go and do the business with her. Very reasonable you may think and you would be right to think that too, the only drawback being that the youngest one of these prostitutes was probably seventy and I couldn't even imagine how old the oldest one was but she was cleaning the inside of her own window and it wasn't with a chamois leather. If you couldn't score There, you couldn't score in a brothel with a fiver stuck out your ear. We all bet one of our lads that he wouldn't go in with one of the prossers. He refused until thirty five of us chipped in ten Deutch marks each, then he was in there like a rat up a drainpipe, he never gave it a second thought. When he came out, one of the sergeants asked him what it was like and I will never forget his answer as he was collecting his bounty from all the troops.

"It was like flicking a fag end through that doorway."

"Enough said," we'd said.

That troops would take on any sexual challenge once they had an audience and a belly fool of beer.

The next morning we were woken by a British Army P.T.I. (physical training instructor) My heart sank, that's all we needed.

"It's okay lads," he started. "My name's Corporal Allen and I'm here to teach you the water sports, but only if you want to, and if not I will go and leave you all to it. It's entirely up to you," he finished. It turned out that this lad was on Placencia for six months just to look after the British troops when they came to stay here. He had to spend the weeks teaching willing troops the water sports. It was a free service but if we didn't want any sport it meant that he had a free week to chill out and do nothing. What a life he had, we thought, but fair play to him. His accommodation was in the only proper hotel on the island. Jammy sod,

I thought. With my heart attack over, I told him that I wanted to learn how to windsurf. A couple of the lads wanted to do snorkelling and three lads sea canoeing.

"You can shove that canoeing up your arse," I said to Joe. I'd nearly drowned in Wales and I ripped all the tops of my legs open trying to get out of the bloody thing upside down. I think I must have panicked and I'd suffered dearly for it, never again! Two of the lads hadn't returned from the night before and we later learned that Dave Benson was still trying to retrieve the key and he was successful, also before lunchtime Ron Harrison had scored with one of the two under eighteen stone girls.

We agreed that we were going to do this water sports thing until lunchtime or just after and then bin it and do our own thing. I was right into this windsurfing job, but as soon as I thought I had it, I would fall off the board again. The corporal showed me time after time and he made it look so easy. Bloody smart arse!

Dave was trying to make me feel better by saying, "Yes but think of it this way, he couldn't fire an artillery gun."

My reply was smooth and swift as I was falling of my board once more, "Fuck off Dave."

The lads were all laughing, including the P.T.I. I stuck at the windsurfing all morning but still couldn't get the hang of it. The corporal told me that I had to stick at it as one morning it would just click and I would be able to do it. I couldn't wait for that day. My stomach muscles and arms were aching with holding onto the boom and fighting to stay on the board. I was going to do one hour snorkelling with the lads and that was it for the day.

No wonder they were all telling me to snorkel, I couldn't believe how many colours of fish and plant life were under the waves, it truly was a spectacle. Ron Harrison had joined us for the last hour and all the lads were ribbing him about his sexual exploits from the previous evening. One of the lads threw an old scrubbing brush at him as he was walking into the sea with his snorkelling gear.

"Don't forget to give the crabs a good scrub, will you?" We all fell about laughing.

"Fuck off," he replied. "If I could afford the wood, I would have your mouth boarded up."

I fell about laughing as the timing of his delivery was spot on. Two things happened in quick succession while we were snorkelling which made me think. Never underestimate the sea, it's as simple as that. Tommy and I were snorkelling and swimming together heading out to sea. We must have only been thirty yards out from the shore when we noticed Ron approximately ten yards in front, but swimming towards us. I checked to my right and noticed Tommy was still there and then looked back at Ron. I could see a grey shape to the right of him which was about six or seven feet in length. I felt a tap on my arm and looked at Tommy he had stopped in the water and pointed to the opposite side of Ron, I looked and then pointed to the other side at what I had seen. We waited one second and it became clear, there were two sharks about fifteen feet away from Ron and they were swimming right towards the left and right of his head. They must have only been eight feet in length at the most and I started waving to the left and right of him in the hope that he looked up at us by this stage Tommy was off doing his impression of 'Jesus' and was now running on the top of the water towards the shore. Finally Ron looked out in front of him and saw me frantically pointing. The second he turned his head to the left, I had done my good deed for the day and I was gone. I was swimming as hard as possible to get back to the top for some air.

The second I broke through the water, I turned and crawled as if I was racing Mark Spitz in the Olympic one hundred metre crawl. I think I would have beaten him too. As I was about to put my feet down to run out of the water for the last few yards, Ron came sprinting passed me. All the lads were on the beach laughing their heads off. They didn't know at this point what had happened, but they knew something wasn't right.

"Fuckin' sharks! Two of the bastards," Ron screamed between breaths. The P.T.I. came over and asked if everything was okay and Ron told him that he was never going back in the water because it was shark infested and someone was going to get eaten.

"Don't be soft," said the P.T.I. "Look," he was saying as he was walking into the water. We could see the two sharks quite clearly and they were just swimming around approximately four feet from the corporal which made me feel a little better, but I don't know if I was completely happy about this. Tommy said he was going back in, so we all agreed to join him. Ron decided at this point to sit this one out for a while.

The second thing that freaked me out after the shark incident was when I was snorkelling fifty yards away from the shore. Most of the other lads were now back in the water behind me and I was looking down at all the fantastic colours and enjoying the warm sea water. There were thousands of beautiful little fishes swimming all over the place and then all of a sudden as I was swimming further out, I noticed that the colours under me had dropped off a shelf below. So much so I couldn't see the bottom and I was looking into complete blackness. The worst part of this strange happening was that the water turned from really warm to freezing cold. I suddenly felt alone, strange and very vulnerable. I turned in the water and hurriedly made my way back to the shore. It was nothing more than the strange sensation of the deep blackness and the cold water but it was enough to remind me of the utmost respect I would keep for this water. I climbed out of the water and decided to call it a day.

That night, we decided to try the other bar at the opposite end of the island. There was a problem with this as our 'food stop' was down one end of the island and the third bar we wanted to go to was at the opposite end up near the air strip. We were going to have a few pints in there and then make our way next door to Cosy Corner later in the evening. I decided to step outside and wait until one of the locals passed me on the M1. I was going to ask about this third bar; I needed to know what it was called, what it was like and if it sold food. I didn't have to wait long before an elderly lady with a face like a melted welly came out of a house some two hundred yards up the M1 and headed my way. It took an age for her to reach me, to the point where I found myself edging up the path towards her.

"Excuse me luv," I started. She looked up at me.

"What can I do for ya boy?" she asked. "

The bar at the top of the-"

"The Pit," she snapped.

"No, the bar," I repeated.

"It's called The Pit," she snapped again. I thought to myself that this was going to be another experience that I just couldn't miss.

"Do they sell food?"

"Yes," she snapped again and barged me out of the way leaving me standing alone again. She was about as helpful as piles and made me feel as welcome. This was the first witch I had spoken to on this island and I was pretty relieved when she walked away from me, I was just hoping that she hadn't cast a spell on me, the miserable hag.

The lads were overjoyed when I told them the name of the bar. They were more up for it than they initially were. Same routine as the night before, twelve of us marched up the M1 in search of food and drink. It was dark but there was a lovely sea breeze so we all took our shirts off. There was nothing worse than walking into a bar feeling hot and then having to sit all night in a sweaty shirt. This way we would be cooler whilst walking and still have a nice fresh shirt on arrival. We made a point of asking directions from a few people on the way up the M1 but as it turned out it would have been difficult to miss. We weren't taking any chances though as we had all been in the water for a long time that day and were starving.

We reached this shed with a single light above the entrance. There was a sign above the door which said 'The Pit'. I think it had been drawn on a piece of drift wood with a black crayon, but there was nothing new there. We walked inside the bar and it wasn't as bad as I thought. Its name didn't do it any justice. It was no better and certainly no worse than the Creole Bar. We did the same as the night before and split into our tables of four, it took a little shuffling around as there were only two chairs at each table. A smart looking young man came to the table to welcome us he introduced himself as George and informed us that his business partner was Bobby. I asked him what the business was and he smiled at my sarcasm. Our table asked for the customary twelve beers and then asked if they had a menu.

"No problem sir, I'll fetch it for you," he replied.

Another man appeared who was a little older than the first my guess was that this was Bobby. Belize was a strange place, I hadn't met any local guys who weren't called George or Bobby. Originality was obviously not their strong point. The music was Bob Marley for a change, but at least it was an album that most of us knew this time. It had to be said that the food menus were improving and if The Pit could produce what the menu was suggesting, this was going to be very interesting. It was a toss up between a steak and chicken again. I had visions of George and Bobby butchering a small cow out the back and taping its mouth up so we didn't hear it. I had the same vision of them smacking a chicken all over the place and plucking its feathers as quick as they could before serving it up to the half pissed squaddies. I ordered two portions of Chicken and Chips because I was thinking back to my experience in Bobby's Bar in P.G. Paul O'Neil and Brian ordered the steak, this I had to see. When the food turned up I was well impressed, my portions of chicken and chips were enormous. It was only costing two dollars and fifty cents which was sixty two pence for one portion. I looked at Brian's steak which was equally as inviting and it came with all the trimmings too. I went from thinking this was going to be a total 'train wreck', to it being amongst the best food I had tasted in months. Brian said the steak was to die for, really beautiful. We all paid for our food separately and I gave Bobby a five dollar tip. He couldn't believe it and was very grateful.

"No listen mate, credit where credit's due, that was spot on," I said. They deserved every penny and we would all be looking forward to eating here again. An hour later, we learned that they could probably rustle up something like an English breakfast as he had bacon and baked beans. Fuck me, I thought, we were half way there, all we needed now was for a chicken to walk through the bar with an egg hanging out of its arse.

"Oh Bobby, I forgot to ask you," I started.

"What is it, Sir?" he asked.

"This place looks ok, so why do they call it 'The Pit'?" I enquired.

"It's short for 'Snake Pit'," he answered.

I thought for a brief moment and then it clicked, "Oh fuck, you are joking? Tell me there are no snakes here?" I asked him.

"Yes, Sir, we have had this bar full of snakes for fifteen years and we can't get rid of them, it's okay though they won't bother you," he finished. Apparently when they bought the bar it was called 'The Peninsula Bar' but due to the fact that they were continually bombarded with snakes which they couldn't get rid of they changed the name to 'The Snake Pit'. Now everyone just knew it as The Pit.

"Listen Bobby, will you do me a big favour please?" I begged.

"Yes, Sir, anything," he replied.

"Don't tell the other lads the reason behind the name. If they ask just tell them the bar was built in a hole or something okay?" I suggested.

The food was out of the way and it was time to get pissed, I was feeling more up for it than the night before and the beer was going down a treat. I was going to make it to Cosy's Corner tonight. We drank in The Pit until eleven o'clock, then made the decision to head over to Cosy's. We thanked Bobby and George and told them that we would see them in the morning.

"What a nice gaff to go and relax and have a good scran," Brian said. I nearly swallowed my tongue, if he had known about the snakes the word 'relax' may not be one that he would have used so readily.

Unfortunately Cosy's Corner was the worst out of the three bars. To say this was a 'den of depravity and it stunk like a lavatory' would be an understatement. I couldn't believe how many people were in there, I counted between thirty and forty but there were no chairs or tables, just a thin shelf that ran around the inside walls, just big enough to rest a couple of bottles on. There were three large wooden pillars which I was guessing, were holding the roof up.

"Sean look," Dave said pointing to the bar. There was the Belizean 'Stick Rum' sitting in the demijohn on top of the bar.

"Fuck it, go on then," I said. He came back with a half pint tumbler full of this rum and it was as neat as it could possibly be with its eleven poisons to boot. Dave Benson had been to the toilet and Andy Berry had been for a quick recce out the back. Dave came running back into the bar.

"Sean," he waved me over. I walked into the bogs behind him and I walked over to the urinal which was a deep hole disappearing into the ground. It didn't take me long to see what he wanted me to see. There was a big Rastafarian guy with the Jamaican multi coloured tea cosy on his head, selling joints for one dollar. When I say joints, I mean joints, they were ten inches in length and easily a good one inch in circumference. As I looked to my left I could see Dave buying the biggest spliff I had seen in my life and handing over his dollar.

"You getting one?" he asked me.

"Fucking right," I answered as I pushed my dollar bill into Bob Marley's face. We left the toilets with our spliffs and raced over to tell the others who then filed into the toilets like kids in a sweet shop and returned with their joints. Andy said there was an area directly out the back door which was laid out with four big railway sleepers. We should buy a shed load of beer and go and try our spliffs. The area had been set out so folk could sit in a big communal area, drink beer, smoke joints and chew the fat. This area was approximately ten feet from the sea and only twenty yards from our back door, this just couldn't get any better.

With my 'Stick Rum', my spliff and my beer, I was on a hiding to nothing. Dave Benson walked round with his new Belize Zippo lighter and we all lit our joints. There were twelve of us sitting around dragging on our humongous cigarettes and then looking at the ends to see if something was happening. Within three or four drags, it hit me like my old maths teacher smacking me on the back of the head with the board rubber. This was my first joint so I wasn't too sure what was supposed to happen, but I watched all the other troops to make sure I was dragging it right and I quickly realised that I wasn't going too far wrong. Before I knew it, I had epilepsy of the lips and could hardly speak, we were all laughing at everything and everybody. One of the last things I remember was the DJ announcing a new record by a woman singer, it was Bob Marley's daughter, Rita Marley and the song was called 'One Draw'. As soon as we heard this come over the mic we all fell about laughing. Had any military police been stationed on the island it would have it the fan big time. All twelve of us would be charged with serious breaches of the 'army act' and we would be being whisked back to Colchester Prison for 'Misuse of the drug act'. At the time, it was great but when we woke the next morning we were all appalled. We had tried it, done it and it was never to be repeated. Thankfully, we never got caught as this would have undoubtedly ended our military careers.

My head felt as if someone had been carrying out the 'Monkey Taps' on my forehead for a couple of hours the next day. Dave Dawkins was just throwing a few Brufen tablets down his throat and offered me the jar.

"Oh yes please mate," I said swallowing four as quickly as I could in the hope that this hangover would disappear. I could hear Ron Harrison in the next room moaning at first and then panicking as he ran to the toilets to pray to the 'water gods'. He was retching for ages before we heard him washing himself down. We spoke very briefly about the night before and in particular the joints we had all smoked we all agreed that it was to be a quick chapter in our lives and was never to be repeated.

The night after, Tommy Baker, Dave Dawkins, Ken Browning and I all went out early. I don't know how it happened but we managed to get split up. I know Ken went with this Belizean girl in 'The Pit' so he stayed in there, but where the rest of the troops went I would never know. I had that much rum and beer inside me I can just remember staggering into Cosy's Corner ordering two beers and after downing the first one staggering onto the dance floor and holding onto the post running up to the ceiling. I grabbed the post with one hand and tried in vain not to fall over, I was absolutely bladdered.

After screaming at the top of my voice, "WHO THE FUCK IS BOB MARLEY?" Which went down like a sausage roll in a synagogue, I can't remember much else that happened apart from when I was flying through the air and passing over the threshold of the window sill. I must have thanked my lucky stars that there was no glass in the window at the time. I don't remember landing on the beach and I certainly don't remember getting rolled and all the contents of my wallet being stolen from me. I was guessing that some of the blokes in the bar were appalled by my Bob Marley comment and took umbrage by it, to the extent that they saw fit to throw me through the window. After all, if God was the God of Earth then Bob Marley was God of the whole universe and I had just committed the ultimate sin by bad mouthing him. Having woken up on the sand some hours later and gathered up what was left of my wallet, I sheepishly walked the ten yards back to the accommodation. I don't know exactly what time it was, but it was beginning to become daylight again.

CHAPTER SEVENTEEN

SHARK ATTACK

After a few more days had passed, I was sitting on the beach with Tommy and Joe Smiley. We had completed the morning water sport session and the windsurfing lark was starting to get me down. I couldn't understand why it hadn't yet clicked. I wasn't going to give up on it but it was trying my patience that was for sure. We were down at the bottom of the island at the rear of the Creole Bar. I was wearing a 'black coral' necklace which I had bought on the way, it had cost two dollars and it looked stunning although it was only threaded on a piece of thin leather rope around my neck. The 'Mad Machete Woman' told us that black coral was special and if you were to purchase it from anywhere else in the world it would cost you a pretty penny. Well, she would say that, we were seeing kids all over the island polishing the stuff as it looked to be a good source of income. The amazing part about it was that these kids, must have only been around twelve years old, would dive from these tiny boats just off the coast. This must have been close to seventy five feet in a free dive, with no tanks right down to the sea bed. They would rip this black coral up, fasten it to their waist and then swim the seventy five feet back up again. An almost impossible task by my reckoning, then they would pass it on to their other family members who would sand it down and polish it until it was ready for sculpting by the next member of the family and then it would be buffed to a high gloss before being sold to the locals or visitors to the island. It was a beautiful product and made fantastic jewellery. This part of the beach was particularly beautiful and very quiet but we were in a good spot because Brenda had the bar open and we could put our hands on freezing bottles of coke and Fanta in a matter of a few minutes. Tommy came out of the bar and walked back over to us with a big smile on his face.

"You will never guess," he said.

"Go on, tell us," I replied.

"The girls have challenged us to a game of softball tomorrow afternoon outside the school." I nearly fell off my chair. The girls were enormous and this was going to be so embarrassing for them as we would run rings around them. Brenda was coming over shortly with some snacks that Tommy had ordered for us and she wanted our answer as to whether we were up for the challenge. I was a little concerned that one of these girls could suffer a heart attack due to the weight they were carrying. We had become really friendly with them and we didn't want to see them come to any harm. I watched Brenda wobble over the sand to where we were sitting, it must have been only forty yards and she was knackered when she reached us.

"There you go boys," she said as she laid a tray of food on the old coffee table in front of us.

"Thanks Brenda," Joe said.

"Brenda, about this baseball match," I started.

"Yes are you up for it then?" she replied.

"Er yes, if you are okay with it."

"Oh yes no problem, shall we say a slab of 'Belikin'?" she asked boldly.

"Shall we say two?" asked Tommy.

"Good idea," Brenda said.

"Can you do two o'clock tomorrow at the school?" she asked as she was turning away.

"We'll be there," I finished. We watched her wobble back over the sand towards the bar, she was a big, big girl. This game was going to be a walk-over.

At 6pm the four amigos were sat in Cosy's Corner making plans for the rest of the night. Joe Smiley and I had decided that we needed a quiet night, so we would walk up to the top of the island to the American bar. We had never visited this bar because we had never ventured that far up the island, but two of our lads who had been up there said that they had seen more life in a tramp's vest, which sounded like the kind of night we needed.

We left the hooligans to get pissed and walked the twenty minutes along the coastline. As we approached we could see a large boat tied to the jetty that we guessed belonged to the bar. It was beautiful and must have been at least a ten berth motor boat cruiser which would have cost a pretty penny.

As we walked through the front door, I looked to where there were four people laughing and joking. I only recognised one and that was 'Big Brenda'. The black girl we had been speaking to earlier when we were arranging the game. My interest however was not on her but on the white girl that she was sat opposite and having a laugh with. The other two were clearly a couple and by the way they were holding hands, I would have thought that they were either seriously in love or they hadn't been together that long.

Brenda climbed off her tall stool and turned towards us waving us to come over and join them. I led the way through the chairs and tables and Joe followed me. Other than the five of us there was only a small girl approximately twenty-five years old working behind the bar. Brenda introduced us to the three guests and I felt a little special as she remembered my name, but also felt a little embarrassed when she'd forgotten Joe's.

"Don't worry Brenda, I've spent years trying to forget his name," I said. Everyone laughed including Joe. He knew the score and that it was nothing personal.

The young American girl was called Amelia and it turned out that she was the daughter of this couple, who had been married for thirty-seven years. Bob and Marie owned the bar and the three of them were only visiting for one night as they had just stopped off on their way to Mexico. They were leaving early the next morning.

Amelia was well fit and probably about the same age as me. I remember thinking that if all went well, then there was a good possibility I could score. What also helped my cause was the fact that Brenda was all over Joe. It was her night off, so she didn't have to rush back to her own bar, which meant that if she kept him occupied, I had a free reign to direct my efforts on the American girl.

Joe looked over Brenda's shoulder and straight at my face. He knew exactly what I was thinking. I don't however know what he was thinking at the prospect of spending a night with 'Big Brenda'. Mind you, I once heard someone ribbing him after he spent a night with a scrubber in Colly. They shouted across the N.A.A.F.I. bar 'that he would fuck the crack of dawn if he could get up early enough'.

Turning and looking once more at Brenda's figure, the comment wasn't a million miles away from the truth. I would be so grateful to him on this occasion though.

Within the space of an hour the older couple had said goodnight and made their way to the front door. Bob made it perfectly clear that they were sleeping in the luxury of their four hundred thousand dollar boat. Typical fucking yank, I thought. Full of shit and full of money.

I seized the day and pulled my stool in front of Amelia. I could see a little smirk appear on her face. Joe was happy sitting face to face with Brenda and every so often, I could hear them talking about how beautiful the island was.

After a few drinks, I felt myself getting pissed. It was at this point that Joe stood up off his stool and called over to me.

"Sean, see you later. We are off to the beach." It was late at night and I knew I wouldn't be seeing either of them again until tomorrow. I was chuffed to N.A.A.F.I. breaks.

"Okay mate, see you later," and at that he gave me a nod and an undetected wink as he walked out of the door.

Within fifteen minutes Amelia had led me through some curtains at the back of the bar and down a long dark corridor. She turned to the right and I followed. There was the distinctive click of a light being turned on followed one second later by a dimly lit bulb springing into action in the middle of the ceiling. Right in front of my eyes was a massive double bed draped with a finely meshed mossy net and the mattress was covered with silk sheets. I couldn't believe it; I hadn't seen a bed like this for a long time.

She pulled me over to the bed and then down on top of it. As I went to grab her she was up off the bed and heading hastily towards the door. I was just starting to think, was it something I said, when she turned off the light and returned to the bed. It was only when I felt her body next to mine that I felt a surge of relief rush over me.

The early morning sunlight was bursting through the four large windows. There was no one next to me in the bed. I looked at my watch. It was only 6 a.m. so I lay still for a moment and thought back to the previous evening. What a night. I had only been asleep for two hours, but didn't care how tired I was feeling.

A quick thought came to my head and then I leapt from the bed looking in the direction of the sea. I immediately focused on the jetty only to see the boat had gone. This girl had arrived on the island the day before, used and abused my body and then in the dark of the night had sailed off over the horizon. I smiled to myself. Fair play, I thought as I sat on the bed to pull my jeans on.

As I left the bar, I headed directly to the shore line. It was chilly at that time of the day, but for my night of passion, I could live with that. I tried to re-live the events of the night before but due to the alcohol, I could only remember parts of it. What was clear though was how alive and spent I felt.

As I opened the back door to the accommodation, I sneaked into my room. Tommy and Dave were fast asleep and there wasn't a sound coming from the block anywhere except for one of the troops snoring gently next door. No sooner had my head hit the pillow and I was out like a light.

At two o'clock in the afternoon and after continuous barracking from the lads, we arrived at the school. Dave and Paul O'Neil were carrying our beer and up until this point we believed that this was going to be an easy return on our beer. What met our eyes made me feel sick right in pit of my stomach. These girls were warming up on the baseball field and they looked as if they were a professional team. They had all the 'roper' baseball gloves and were launching the ball to each other at a speed and precision that I had never seen the likes of before. I looked over to the other lads, Andy was stood with his jaw resting on the sand.

"What the fuck?" Ken said. They were launching these balls to each other and catching them with one hand behind their backs and not even breaking the conversation they were having with a mate. This was ridiculous, but they wouldn't be able to move on this very soft fine sand and we would fly when we hit the ball.

"Just play it cool lads and leave it to me," I said. Brenda came over to us. For some strange reason she couldn't look me in the eye.

"Do you want to bat or field?" she asked. With no hesitation I told her that we wanted to bat first we needed to get some points on the board and scare these girls. They may be able to throw a ball to each other and catch it well, but that wasn't enough to beat us.

Sheila shouted over to me, "Sean what's your team called boy?"

"Helmet and the Throbbing Robins," I called back.

She chalked it on the blackboard behind her head and the game began. This girl stepped up to pitch at Dave Benson. Dave had a look of determination on his face that said prepare to be humiliated girl. She rooted her body to the spot and launched this ball at Dave.

The only reason Dave knew he had been pitched at was because Tommy shouted, "Dave, turn round." Dave snapped his neck round and saw this large girl picking the ball out of her glove. At this point that I knew we were in for a pasting, I hadn't seen a man pitch as fast and ferocious as this, let alone a woman. She was an out and out animal and she was taking no prisoners.

"You have to run this time mate," Andy shouted. It was too late, the ball had been pitched, caught in the glove of the girl behind Dave, onto the girl who was standing on first base and back to the pitcher before Dave raised his bat. He dropped his bat and walked over towards where we were sitting. No wonder they weren't worrying about running on the sand, they had no intentions of doing so. Normally at this stage the troops would be shouting obscenities at Dave, but we knew there was absolutely nothing he could have done about what had just occurred, we were shell shocked. Paul Tommy and Ron went in much the same way except Tommy managed to touch the ball. This was ridiculous and if it hadn't been for our pride we would have thrown the towel in. They may as well have allowed the rest of their team to sit down and enjoy the show because they only needed three players, the pitcher to bowl, the girl on first base and Brenda to captain them. I took up the bat reluctantly but on my lonely walk up to the batting point I decided I was going to give it my all. I never took my eye off the ball in the girl's hand, or so I thought. This situation was impossible, the ball travelled at an amazing pace. Where on Earth had they got this girl? I went without even stepping one foot closer to first base. That was five of our team gone without scoring one run and if Brian ended up walking the line as well; this was going to be a whitewash. These girls were taking every opportunity to throw the ball around the field to each other and all we could do was watch in amazement at how skilful they were and how easy they made it look. It wasn't them that were looking inadequate, it was us and I am sure they were relishing their moment. I am sure we would have done the same had it been the other way round.

307

"That's my mummy," said this girl sat to my left. She was pointing at the pitcher. "She is good isn't she?" she asked.

"Yes, very good," I replied. "Does she play much?" I asked her.

"Oh yes, every day and even on Christmas." We had been conned, hook, line and sinker. After a little more probing it became apparent that this team met three hundred and sixty five days a year to play or practise. If they missed one day, they would have to forfeit their place on the team and a queue of islanders were waiting to take their places. It wasn't just a passion to these girls but more of a religion. It turned out that on this particular day we were the ones who had been 'preached' too. Things didn't improve for us at the change over point, our team were out for a golden duck and now it was their turn to bat. If they could field and pitch as good as this then it was obvious that they could also strike the ball. Brenda went first and received a fast ball from her new boyfriend, Joe Smiley. I was quite impressed by his speed and technique it wasn't a million miles away from the girl who had pitched earlier. Brenda hit the ball, holding the bat with only her right hand while smiling at Joe. The ball flew way beyond the boundary which meant they had hit a run in the first strike and had won the game. Brenda didn't even have to move out of her circle except to walk the ten yards back to her seat in the shade. Sheila was next but she wasn't as good, don't get me wrong, she still hit the ball beyond the boundary but she had to use two hands on the bat. This was crazy! Their hand/eye coordination was unreal I don't think there was one occasion in the game when one of their players only just connected with the ball, they all smashed it into next week. One of the smaller girls hit a magnificent strike causing the ball to stop just short of the sea which was a long way. By the time Brian had jogged back with the ball he was knackered and sweating like there was no tomorrow, it wasn't just the fact that it was raging hot, but also that the ball ended up miles away. The score got to seventeen runs to our zero, we conceded under embarrassing circumstances and ran off with our tails between our legs.

Not only did we give the girls the two crates of beer, but we also had to make our way to the Creole Bar and buy them rum. I would like to say that they played a blinder, but truth be known they probably didn't. They were just well practised and took us apart. They deserved a 'toast' and we were going to make sure they had one. Later we headed down the M1 to the bar and when passing the school on our way, I think we all made some remark or excuse about 'not being used to the weather' or 'not enough time to practice' and so on. It was Tommy who stopped the lame excuses.

"Come on lads, we were destroyed," he said.

"Agreed, we were taken apart," Paul answered. We walked on briskly in the hope that none of the locals were still around to laugh at us and after another ten minutes we were sitting in the Creole Bar. I was starving and decided to go for the sea food platter again, we only had a couple of days left on the island and I was going to savour the dish. We were sure that it would prove difficult to find food like that anywhere else on this tour so I was going to take full advantage of it and five of the other lads joined me. The food arrived not long after ordering and it tasted equally as good as the first time. Afterwards we had a toast to the girls before leaving for Cosy's Corner, I looking forward to getting pleasantly pissed as I knew there couldn't possibly be a repeat of the previous evening's events. I smile to myself once more.

There were only a couple of locals in Cosy's Corner, but we noticed 'Rasta man Bob Marley' was doing a roaring trade in the toilets with his 'ganja'. We weren't playing tonight though, we had done it once and got away with it and that was enough. We ordered plenty of 'Belikin' and a few 'Stick Rums' between us then went to sit on the sleepers outside. We were talking and having a laugh over the highlights of the last week and a half. I think we all knew that we would never be given an opportunity to revisit Placencia unless something drastic occurred and we all felt very privileged. The general feeling about the Caribbean was that Belize was the arse of the world, but it had some very nice dimples on it. Brian said that if he were to be posted here again he would do a runner so he didn't have to come. We would be entering into the last two months of our tour soon and although it had been made difficult due to the climate and other difficult restrictions, it wasn't quite as bad as what I had expected. It was a hole but not unmanageable. I hadn't spent a sober night in my room since coming to Placencia and tonight was going to be no different. I was well on my way to getting hammered, my plans of saving my head for the morning fast fading away. I was going to crack this windsurfing if it killed me.

State Normal, I thought the next morning with no clue how I had got to bed or even what time. One minute I was in the bar, the next I was in my bed. It was the effects of this 'Stick Rum', it was a killer. The ten mile runs were going to kill us when we got back to camp, I was dreading them. There was one bonus for me and my crew though, we would be having the last two months in Salamanca camp. Chindit would be staying up at Rideau and we would be moving away from him for the last part of the tour. Lieutenant Brannagan was at Salamanca and he was a pretty laid back officer. I threw the Brufen down my neck and sucked on a full pint of water and within half an hour I was ready for windsurfing once more.

"Come on you lazy bastards," I shouted around the accommodation. "Hands off yer rocks and on to yer socks."

"Fuck off you psycho," came a noise from Dave Benson's bed space. I grabbed my bar of soap and headed to the water's edge on the beach, no sooner had I got there and the lads were behind me. They knew that I wouldn't leave them to sleep, so because they couldn't beat me they would have to join me. I had a good scrub with my bar of Camay, it was really weird that there were hardly any bubbles due to the salt but it was better than using these showers. It was a sprint back inside to wash the hair and brush the teeth and within fifteen minutes Corporal 'brilliant at all Sports' would be there to help the lads. This gave me enough time to get my windsurfing board and life jacket sorted.

The troops slowly filtered from the block and into the water. Dave shouted over to me, "You're a noisy bastard you." When I looked over at him I noticed he looked like a vagrant.

"I do try," I answered.

He walked to the sea with the speed of a striking slug then when it was deep enough he just fell forward. This sudden feeling of the sea on his face must have woken him up because when he came back up he looked much better. Joe grabbed his canoe and jumped straight into it. Other than a bit of snorkelling, that's all he had done over a week Fair play to him, he really did give it some welly and would be still at it when everyone else had called it a day. The only downside to this was that we all had to take it in turns to watch him when he was out on the water on his own. The PTI arrived looking smart and bright as usual. We hated him for that and asked him if he ever got bladdered, to which he said there wasn't much chance as he didn't drink. My old sergeant had told me never to trust a man that didn't drink, but this guy was all right.

"Today's the day Sean," he said.

"Fuckin' right, I've had enough of this," I answered. The conditions were fantastic, there was just the right amount of breeze to help me but not enough for it to keep throwing me off the board. After an hour of Corporal Allen shouting orders to me from the shore I was up. I could hear him cheering from the beach, I was over the moon. After all this time I was bombing along the waves at twenty miles an hour, sorry I mean knots. It came time for me to turn around and although I knew in my head what to do, I didn't know if I was going to be successful. I carried out the manoeuvre as slick as he had shown me and before I knew it I was travelling back the opposite way. I was made up; I practised another half hour and then went in for a cigarette. I was showing off a little now as I took the windsurfing board right to the edge of the water and just stepped off it onto the beach.

When I had finished my cigarette I was straight back to my board. I didn't want the know how to leave my brain and I had to confirm that it wasn't just a fluke. After another hour of tacking up and down the waves and not leaving visual contact of the accommodation block, I did find myself approximately four hundred yards out to sea. It was no problem to me now though as I could stay up on the board and I knew how to steer the bloody thing too. With that in mind I aimed at the beach, it was clear that there was a bit of a current but it wasn't going to bother me on my board, I was cutting through the water with ease now. When I had cut the distance down by half I looked up at the accommodation hut and I could see all the lads lined up on the water's edge. I would have thought that the bastards were winding me up, but Corporal Allen was with them and they were all pointing frantically and shouting at me. I turned my sail into the 'Luff' position so I was now stationary, the sail remained upright but ineffective and I was still holding onto the mast. I looked up at the troops once more and then looked around the board. I couldn't believe what I was looking at, I counted between twelve and fourteen fins swimming through the water. Some of them were big enough to convince me that these were very big sharks. All the reassurances about the sharks a few days ago had now gone from my head and my concerns about Bull Sharks started to worry me. They were all as unwelcome as a bag of chips at Weight Watchers, the Bull shark was a nasty piece of work and wouldn't think twice about attacking a human being. It was considered the third most dangerous shark in the water around Belize and also as having a bad temper. I immediately dropped my mast and froze. I was still standing up and as a result of this my legs began to tremble. I was absolutely shitting myself.

"Try and paddle in," I heard Dave shout from the shore.

"Very good, Marjorie Fuckin Proops," I screamed back at him. "Not the type of fuckin agony Aunt I had in mind," I finished. I sat down on my board and tried with my finger tips to paddle and steer myself back to the shore. I was constantly trying to work out little calculations in my head of how long it would take for a shark to remove my finger tips? It was clear I wasn't thinking straight, so much so that every few seconds I was hammering my arms and hands through the water in the hope that they didn't see me. I made it to approximately one hundred yards from the shore and still I paddled when I thought it was safe. I was exhausted, I stopped and took a look around the board and could only see five or six fins remaining but they were still large and now wasn't the time to stop. I started to paddle again but didn't dare make the effort of picking my boom up and trying to windsurf again, this just wasn't an option. It would mean standing up again and there was no way I was going to do that.

It took me an hour or so before I looked round again and saw no more fins in the water. They were gone and I was only ten yards from the water's edge. I gave it one more minute and then jumped off the board and practically sprinted the last few yards out of the water. The lads had now decided as a result of me not dying, they could laugh but I wasn't feeling as jovial at this point and told them to go and boil their heads.

This occurrence had really knocked me back and although I would do the odd bit of snorkelling, that was it for most of my water sports and certainly my windsurfing. I found out many years later that there was the possibility of a windsurfing board coming out that resembled a seal and attracted certain sharks to the board. Stuff that for a game of soldiers. I had wanted to learn how to windsurf but not at the cost of a leg.

We had a few beers that night but not enough to be blind stinking drunk again. We all went up to The Pit for our evening meal and I decided to chance the steak, which was as good as my last meal if not better and I was wishing I had tried the steak a lot earlier in the holiday. I was surprised none of our lads said anything as to why I was looking about the floor in the bar all the time we were there. I didn't mind them getting bitten by a coral snake, but I for the sake of a bit of peeping around the floor wasn't going to. Bobby was going to come out to the rear jetty to teach me to fish with a single line in the morning for an hour if I could be there at ten o'clock. We didn't know about this rear jetty, apparently it was the grotty side of the island. If we came out of our accommodation and crossed over the M1 and carried on walking we would come across the rear jetty. Bobby did warn me that it wasn't nice and I pondered over this for the remainder of the evening, but I was also looking forward to it.

I was up at 'sparrow's fart' in the morning and tried not to wake the others up. I went out onto the top of the steps and looked out to sea. We were to leave this paradise the next morning, but there was one thing for sure. We had done it all and a lot more besides during our visit. We had agreed the night before that we all wanted to get the next two months out of the way and get back to Blighty even though at this time I had no spouse back home as most of the lads did, the best alternative for me was to leave me there for the rest of my days, but I didn't think the British Army would entertain my request. I laughed at myself as I hadn't told the lads why The Pit was called The Pit. I couldn't wait to tell them on the plane on the way home, they were going to freak.

I met Bobby at the jetty on the east of the island and I have to say, he was right. It was where all the sewage was pumped and there was even a 'thunder box' (toilet) just plonked over the end of the jetty that went straight through to the water, it was disgusting. He pointed to another jetty which was two hundred yards away and we both started to walk towards it, he had a few tiny lead shots, a couple of hooks and some bait which he'd brought from his bar. He gave me a stick with some twine on and told me to copy what he did. He set his hook up and I did exactly the same then we moved to the end of the jetty and lowered our hooks into the water. I didn't have a clue what we could catch but he seemed to know everything.

"Hold my hook a minute," he said as he ran towards the other jetty. It became clear that he had left his bag leaning up against the far jetty. No sooner had he gone when I felt a tug on my fishing line, I threw

313

Bobby's on the jetty. If something had have bitten on his line now, it would have disappeared to sea along with his rod. There was only approximately ten feet of my line in the water so I started to pull it in. Whatever it was I could feel the power of it pulling against me. When I got it to the point were I couldn't take anymore twine in I knelt down to look at it, it was an amazing fish. I leaned right over into the sea to pick it up when I felt this big pair of hands on my shoulders.

"No," this voice said and with that he threw me back along the jetty.

"What the fuck are you doing?" I shouted.

"Scorpion fish," he replied as he lifted the fishing wire from the sea to lift the fish onto the jetty. He looked around and picked up a three foot long piece, of three by two wood and started to beat the fish. I was sure that if the fish had fingers it would have stuck two up at him and if it could speak it would have said 'Is that the best you can do mate?'. The beating seemed to have no effect on the fish for what appeared to be an age. Bobby stuck to the task though and carried on until the rapid movement of the fish started to slow down. I would guess it took a full five minutes of severe beating until the fish finally died, I couldn't believe it.

"Look," Bobby said as he lifted the fish up to eye level. "See these," he carried on as he pointed to the spines lying down on its back "When you go to grab the fish, these stand up and stick into your hand, it injects you and you are dead."

"Oh fucking brilliant George, thanks mate," I said sincerely.

"No problem," he finished. He was as cool as a cucumber obviously he had dealt with this sort of thing more than once.

CHAPTER EIGHTEEN

ONE MAN AND HIS BOAT

We arrived back at Rideau Camp mid-afternoon that Friday which we were pleased about as it gave us two days to sort all our kit from Placencia, then pack our personal kit ready for leaving early Monday to Salamanca. We had heard good reports about the place and were ready to go there by the time Monday came round. I was hoping that Chindit wasn't going to be there to wave me off just in case that tear drop in the corner of my eye spilled over onto my face and ran down my cheek, I think not. It had been long overdue for my crew and him to be separated for a short time. We were over the moon now as we were on the downward slope and hopefully life was going to be a lot easier at our new home for the next two months. This Chinditless environment was going to suit me and my gun crew down to the ground.

"Look at this Sean," Ron Harrison said as I was walking over to the notice board.

"What is it?" I asked as I noticed Ged appearing from the accommodation block. "How's your bum for blackheads Ged?" I said before he could speak.

"Same as your belly for spots mate! How was your R&R?" he asked.

"Fantastic mate, forget mainland USA get your arse to Placencia," I said.

"Brilliant, I'm going in two weeks," he answered.

"Cool mate! It really is the place to be," I finished. At that he made a punch in the air, he was happy now he knew that he was going to have a good holiday. Ged nodded towards the notice board.

"You going? There's only four places left" he said. A Cayes trip had been laid on for the troops leaving in the morning. Twenty places had been available and we were just about to fill the last four spots. "

Twenty bucks is a bit steep isn't it? We've just had *two weeks* in Placencia for thirty dollars," I growled.

"It is, but apparently these islands are something else," Ged said. Tommy, Dave and Ken made up the other numbers so we were going with a full compliment of troops. Twenty raving squaddies sat on a small island off the coast of Belize, eating fresh fish and chicken and drinking copious amounts of beer. We had to meet Bobby the Belizean on Punta Gorda Jetty at nine in the morning. I was hoping that his Cayes trips were better than his 'Chicken in a Basket' or we were right in the shit.

The word 'Titanic' kept springing to mind. I had another two missions to carry out before the trip though, firstly Dave and I were going to catch some tarantulas and mount them in their cases. Then as a result of collecting the cash for them we would go and get hammered in the N.A.A.F.I. I had been asked by at least five lads and Dave at least double that, for the 'spiders in boxes' so it was, as Dave had predicted, a good money maker. As Dave wasn't going to Salamanca, his role was to get as many tarantula orders as possible for the last day of the tour and when I returned to Rideau for the last day we would work every hour to make sure we filled those orders. This would make us some extra dollar to take home with us. Dave and I were walking up to the top end of the camp to go tarantula hunting when Shaky Moor shouted us over.

"Listen lads, I thought you should know," he started. I didn't like the sound of this and I looked at Dave. "Chindit has pegged Dolan."

"Oh no, what for now?" I asked. It turned out that Chindit had gone a bit loopy and was charging everybody and anybody for whatever trivial reason he could get them on. For stuff that he would normally punch you on the back of the head or kick you up the arse for. This was disastrous, we would have a mutiny on our hands if he carried on like this.

"What the fuck has that got to do with me?" said Dave. He was in the Medical Corps not the Royal Artillery.

"Well, Dolan fell asleep in the sun and burned his legs, he blistered so badly that he had bags of plasma hanging from his thighs and the tops of his legs. Seriously, there must have been two pints of plasma in the eight bags of skin hanging off him," Shaky went on.

Chindit had caught him and said if he didn't make the early

morning run the next day he would charge him for self inflicted wounds. Technically he was right, for example, if you had a tattoo done and it impeded your duties the next day then you could be charged with self inflicted wounds. This was very harsh on Gunner Dolan as it was difficult to stay awake in this heat especially when you had been working hard early in the morning. Dolan's punishment was enough for him to be suffering the agony of these giant blisters but to peg him too would serve no purpose. Apparently Chindit told him that if he couldn't get a pair of shorts on the next morning and join in the run, he would go ahead with the charge. The run was up Saddleback hill, and Chindit also said that if he stopped at anytime, he would go ahead with the charge. This sucked, it was starting to sound a little more than Chindit disciplining a soldier.

The next morning just before the run, the troops tried to help Dolan. Everyone did what they could to avoid him getting charged. They treated his legs with all sorts of lotions and creams and even helped him on with his shorts. All the troops felt sorry for him as he was being hard done to. Shaky said that Dolan had been doing a decent job on the run, but after a while his shorts began to rub into the blisters and although he was in a lot of pain, he carried on. By the time he had gone a further three or four miles, two of the bigger blisters underneath his shorts' line had started to bleed allowing the salt to get in and rub on them causing the pain to become unbearable, he had to stop.

Chindit had apparently turned his head and casually shouted, "Warned for office Dolan."

"It was heartless and unforgiving," Shaky said.

This was really bad on its own, but he then made him walk back to camp. Something was happening with Chindit while we were in Belize but I couldn't put my finger on it. It was only later that I found out that as a result of the B.S.M's absence Chindit had had the B.S.M's responsibility dropped on his lap at a moment's notice, the whole episode may have been a little too much for him. Had he been able to plan his more superior role in Belize a few months ago then it may have been a different story but charging the troops left right and centre was certainly not the answer.

Dave and I left the tarantulas and headed straight to Dolan's bunk where we found him lying on the top of his bed. Dave looked at the wounds and they were particularly bad but they were on the mend. Dolan's pride had been damaged more than his legs. There were some nasty comments being bandied around referring to Chindit, but these troops weren't seeing the bigger picture.

"Cut it out lads and keep your comments to yourself. I don't want to hear it," I shouted down the block. It fell silent, but I knew what they were all thinking and it was now my ears that were burning but I didn't care, I had broad shoulders. Dave and I had missed our opportunity now as it was about to go dark. There was no way on God's earth I was going to catch tarantulas in the dark. I had a shower and arranged to meet Dave down at the Cookhouse, I wanted to tell the 'slop jockeys' how good the food was on Placencia in the hope it may shame them into producing something a little more appetising than dung.

Tommy and I walked down the M1 towards the Cookhouse. "I wonder what's been going on here Sean while we've been away?" Tommy said.

"I don't know mate, but I am glad we are off to Salamanca, at least I will be out of it," I replied as I walked through the Cookhouse doors. "Dave have you told this shower what we have been eating over the last two weeks?" I shouted.

"Yes, and guess what?" Dave shouted back.

"Go on surprise me," I said. The sloppies were cooking a steak for Dave as a means of showing them what they were made of. "Yeah, if they are showing you what they are made of, I hope they don't slip on it," I said. Tommy laughed at this because he knew where I was coming from. In all fairness though, the food wasn't too bad on that particular day. I had gotten into a habit now of expecting the worst case scenario, therefore, if I expected a shit meal and it turned out half decent, I was happy. If it turned out a nice meal which was as rare as hen's teeth then I was mega surprised.

Dave's steak was an all time accident by the chefs. It must have taken a team effort to make this steak as good as it was. I suspended my abuse on that occasion and would save it for when the food went back to normal. I wouldn't be having that many more meals at the Rideau cookhouse now as we would be dining in 'Restaurant a La Salamanca' in a few days. No worries Tommy and Dave would still be there to throw as much abuse as would be required.

We met in the morning as arranged and Ged had detailed various groups of lads to go to the cookhouse and pick up as much swag as possible. There were big ice boxes containing chicken and sausages and then something similar with water, juice and ice in them. We were warned numerous times to ensure we took some long trousers and long sleeved cotton shirts to cover our skin after ten minutes. A hat was an absolute must, even if it was the army issued jungle hat. Ged and I sat in the front of the Bedford nursing a pair of hangovers, but I had noticed when we were securing the tailgate at the rear of the wagon that the vehicle was carrying tonnes of beer, Fanta and coke. I got 'Tommy not Right' to throw us a few bottles of Fanta to the front to put us on. They didn't last long, I was just finishing my last bottle before we pulled up at the jetty. We were running an 'honesty bar' during this trip which meant that whatever you ate or drank, it was your responsibility to put the money in the box. If all the troops were honest when paying for their refreshments there would obviously be enough money in the pot to pay for everything that had been consumed. Most of the troops would round it up to the nearest dollar when paying, so more often than not there was more than enough to pay the bill. Any extra that was made went to the battery barman as it was he who arranged all the swag for the trip. If the funds fell short of what the total bill should be at the end of the trip then each person on the trip would have to pay a portion of the outstanding balance, this however was very rare, especially after the verbal warning from Big Ged.

"Where's Bobby then Ged?" Dave shouted.

"How the fuck should I know, it's only quarter to nine," he answered. This was our first Cayes trip so no one knew how it was supposed to work. All we knew is that we had pitched up on the side of a jetty with a vehicle full of supplies and ready to go. We made sure that all the food and drink remained undercover on the back of the Bedford Wagon at that time so the sun's rays weren't shining directly on them. With approximately five minutes to spare we heard the putt of a motor board engine.

I turned quickly as I heard Andy Berry, "What the fuck?"

I looked out to sea and couldn't believe what I saw. There was Bobby, sitting at the rear of a tree trunk with a small boat engine stuck on the arse end of it. When he pulled alongside the jetty we were all

319

staring at this burnt and cut out tree trunk with planks nailed across every few feet which he claimed were seats.

"Morning lads," Bobby shouted to us. He was standing at the back of his tree trunk with his chest stuck out proudly showing off his boat.

I turned to Bobby and said, "Bobby, it was a good morning until now." He looked confused. "Let me help you Bobby, your boat is shit," I said.

The troops were laughing their heads off but Bobby looked dejected, "Wot wrong wid it boy?" he asked.

"Fuckin hell, where do you want me to start? Has Arthur Negus seen it?" I answered.

Ged ordered the lads to get the supplies onto the boat, most of which were stored up at the front. For the size and shape of this log, it was unbelievably steady. We were jumping into a cut out tree trunk to be transported to this island for a barbeque and beer. Had it not been for the issue of needing this tree for the return journey, I would have strongly suggested that we carry on burning it on the barbeque when we got to the island. What the fuck were we letting ourselves in for? We had no life jackets and would definitely have drowned and/or been eaten by sharks had this thing decided to do a Titanic on us, and we were paying twenty dollars for the privilege. Bobby was taking four hundred dollars off us and he did the Cayes trip three times a week. With this kind of wedge behind him and the price of boats in P.G. he could buy every one in the harbour. We really couldn't understand why we were floating out to sea looking like Robinson Crusoe in a burnt out tree. I am glad that none of my mates back home could see me.

It was so hot even at this time of the morning and we made sure everyone covered their shoulders and kept their hats on while we were on-board The Titanic. The last thing we wanted to deal with was one of the troops burning before we had even got to the island. With the supplies stored at the front and two people on each plank of wood that Bobby called seats, it evened out pretty well. I still wasn't convinced however that we were going to make it to the Cayes, but it would be a laugh trying. Dave and I were sitting on the last seat at the rear. The only person behind us was Bobby who reached under his plank and pulled out a few fishing lines wrapped around some sticks. There was a small hook on the end of each one. He passed the lines to Dave and me to pass out amongst the troops, then he produced a small tin with bits of freshly cut meat inside. I didn't dare ask him what this meat was but it looked like a child's tongue. We threw the rest of the lines up to the middle of the boat and the troops caught them. After taking a few pieces of bait we sent the tin up to the other end. Within two minutes we had our lines set up and thrown over the side of the boat. We were now trawling a considerable amount of fishing lines and hooks behind as we bounced gently on the waves. I was still hungover and had decided to throw some more stims down my neck. I was gulping Fanta like it was going out of fashion and Dave was leathering the coke.

"Bobby, would you like a drink mate?" I asked him.

"Thanks man, I am really thirsty," he answered in his broad Rasta accent. Within a short time, I had a Fanta in one hand, a fag in my gob and I was trawling my fishing line in my other hand. Dave was doing the same and Bobby, who didn't smoke was grasping his cold drink whilst twisting the accelerator grip on his Honda 5 horse power engine. The engine was chugging away to a steady putt, putt, putt, putt. Bobby informed us that if we caught anything on the way out to the island we would be eating it on the barbecue as long as it wasn't poisonous. I was just hoping I wasn't going to catch another Scorpion fish. If I didn't see another one of them in my life it would be too soon, however I was prepared to be a smart arse and inform everyone of the dangers if we caught one on our boat.

We had been travelling for about forty minutes when a commotion started, it was clear that one of the lads had got a bite on his line. Everybody around him was really excited, but he remained calm and started to wind it in. He had brought in most of the twine to the point that the fish couldn't have been too far from the boat when I heard him shout.

"Bastard! It's gone."

The fish must have been having a lucky day, as in another thirty minutes there would have been twenty rough arsed squaddies ripping it to pieces on the barby. Within fifteen minutes it was my turn and it felt as if my right arm was being ripped out of its socket. I had dropped my bottle of Fanta and my arm was now was being pulled towards the back of the boat. Something had bitten my hook and it wasn't small. I could see all the troops trying to get a look in and see what all the fuss was about. I tried to pull it in a little and then wind the twine on the stick but it was very difficult and it wasn't practical. I had to hold it a little while until it had tired a bit. Bobby shouted to me to get winding or I would lose my fish as well. That's all I needed to make me put maximum effort in. I wound the twine and before I knew it I could see the shape of the fish under the water.

"Fantastic, it's a barracuda," Bobby shouted. That was it, everyone in the boat except for me and Bobby abandoned their positions and made their way up to the front of the boat.

"Thanks lads," I shouted.

"Fuck you," came the shout back.

"Cowards." I laughed.

"Fuckin live cowards," Ged shouted. That was it, I was on my own or so I thought. As the fish came to the top, I noticed that I only had about six feet of line to wind in. It wasn't needed, the fish jumped from the water and landed on the boat about six inches away from my feet. I jumped up onto the seat and felt Bobby, who had now released the motor accelerator, push past me. He grabbed the fishing line and pulled it towards his feet, this shark was approximately four to five feet in length and had the strength of a lion. It was in beautiful condition and provided we could contain it, was going to look well on the barbecue. Once I was sure Bobby had control of the fishing line, I went to join the rest of the cowards at the front of the boat. I turned in time to watch Bobby ram a coke bottle into its mouth in the hope that it may subdue it, he then picked a Fanta bottle off the floor and rammed that into its throat as well, then a third and finally a fourth. This fish slowed right down and eventually became motionless.

"Is it dead Bobby?" I shouted.

"It won't cause you any harm now," he replied.

"That wasn't the question, is it dead?" I shouted again. He was never going to say it was dead, but looking from the bottle hanging out of its mouth, I guessed it was never going to bite anyone again. We all regained our seats, but the troops sitting near the back never took their eyes off the fish.

"Well done friend," Bobby said. "Have you ever had Barracuda?"

"No," I replied.

"You are all in for a treat, trust me," he finished. Within a short time we landed at this beautiful island. It must only have been one hundred yards by one hundred yards but it was like Placencia in that it was paradise. There were a number of palm trees and other trees I didn't recognise and evidence of previous barbeques. All the kit was unloaded, including tonnes of snorkelling equipment, flippers, float boards and goggles. The sand on the beach was out of this world, but it was also very hot. The sea breeze was fantastic but it was the kind that would burn your skin in a heartbeat, so it was important that we had to watch the troops while they were in 'sun bathe mode'. It was only a couple of steps after leaving the water's edge before I had to put my flip-flops on. I remember noticing how warm the water was as I helped to unload the wets, which we placed out of the sun and under the trees for now. Later we would place them in a little crate in the sea. The sea was fairly warm, but once all the ice had melted around our drinks, it would be the coldest place for our beer to go. Bobby directed operation around where the food was going. He was going to be the 'chief cook and bottle washer'. It was said that these Chogies could cook a five course meal from a cockle so this was going to be interesting to say the least. I could see that portion size was going to be an issue though thinking back to when I last dined in his restaurant. Saying that, most of the food had been supplied by us.

It was time to hit the beer so Tommy did the honours but his usual twelve bottle shuffle was not to be carried out while we were on the Cay. The bottles of beer would be warm before we knew it and although I would drink beer in any condition under normal circumstances, this wasn't normal circumstances, it was roasting hot. Drinking beer in these temperatures was dangerous, we would be closely watching the lads. I would have a couple of beers and then go back on the stims and Dave was doing the same. The last thing we wanted was to be out the game after only a couple of beers. Bobby was well in control of the food and I couldn't wait to taste the barracuda, everyone who had tasted it before had commented on how fantastic it was. At our end of the island there were a number of fruit trees and we had prepared numerous coconuts and bananas. We had Don Robinson who was really good at climbing the banana trees so I could imagine that he would be sick of the sight of those trees. By the time Bobby had prepared and cooked his food on the barby, we were all drooling. We got the nod just on lunchtime and after thinking there wasn't going to be enough, I was proved wrong. There was tons of food and there was no reason why Bobby wouldn't be taking some back for his millions of kids.

Dave and I sat under this large coconut tree in the shade. We tucked into the barracuda and I had to agree that it was every bit as good as what people had told us it would be. It melted in our mouths and it was a dish that I would be eating time and time again. I'd had far too much chicken and bread with all the rest of the barby food and by the time we had all finished we were all wobbling around the beach like pregnant mums, moaning as if we were about to give birth. We had to let all the food go down and think about snorkelling as soon as possible. There was no way that I had come to that island just to have some food and not be able to swim in the sea. I would give it an hour then I would be in the water come what may. I checked the ground around me for beasts first and then lay down on the sand. Thinking about Ken Dolan, I didn't want to fall asleep in case I was up with burns like he had sustained. I had plenty of respect for the sun and even when I was hiding under a large tree I was fully covered.

It wasn't long before we were in the water, I had to do something before I fell asleep. It was Tommy who had gone in first and started to scream at us to come in too. There were some pretty abusive comments thrown back at him, but it was only banter that we had heard thousands of times. It tickled me how the troops always rose to it and I was no different but I used to give as good as I got. I climbed to my feet and went to grab a pair of size twelve flippers before they all went. This size was rare but there were loads of other sizes. I armed myself with snorkel and mask and I was in the water, shortly followed by Dave. Ron turned the 'Boogie Box' on and it was REO Speedwagon blasting out, he must have turned the volume right up because I was under the water and could hear how loud it was. It was only the fact that there was no other Cayes close to our location that we could have it blasting out like that.

The troops had a marvellous afternoon, one that some of them would remember for a long time. Some of us were doubly lucky as we had Placencia to remember too. We spent a couple of hours in the water and had a little walk on the island, it really was a postcard picture whichever way you looked at it.

It came to the point when it was time to get back and on the boat.

We only had a small window before it started to get dark and we all knew what happened at witching hour. It was like the lights had been turned out, there was no way I wanted to be looking for P.G in the dark when we could get back in daylight. However, I was sure Bobby could find his way back in the dark or the light. The boat was somewhat lighter on the return journey, with all the beer and stims having taken a severe battering, but this didn't help the speed of the boat. Bobby must have been trying to save on his fuel but he had collected all his money before we left the Cayes so he should have had enough money to buy the fuel station! When I saw P.G in the distance my heart began to race. If the log tipped over now, I could still swim for it. It may have taken me a good hour or so, but I would have stood more of a chance than hanging onto the boat.

I was so relieved when the boat pulled alongside the jetty and my feet were planted safely on the ground. It was no good travelling with anyone else on the Cayes trips because as I looked out to sea, I could see the infantry lads returning from their Cayes trip in a similar boat to ours but a lot longer and carrying more troops, at the end of the day a Chogie was making five hundred dollars out of a log. Enterprise at its best.

CHAPTER NINETEEN

JOHNNIE GHURKHA

Somewhere to the South West of Punta Gorda and Rideau and to the East of San Antonio lies the camp called Salamanca. It was built primarily by the Ghurkha Regiment and the Royal Engineers in the seventies. We pulled out onto Southern Highway and drove for an hour and a half, we were covered in dust and the heat was unbearable. With the gun hooked on the back it was difficult to take the speed up to twenty miles per hour. The roads were appalling and I could hear the moans from the troops. At the two hour point I could sense that we were close, I had followed the map well and picked up all the reference points. The troops told me that when you cross a recently repaired road bridge with red handrails you are two hundred yards from Salamanca camp, carry on driving down Belmopan Road and Salamanca is on the left hand side. The directions were spot on and we had made it in one piece. Lt Brannagan and 'K Sub' were waiting for us to arrive, before 'K Sub' were allowed to set off. As soon as we drove through the camp gates I could see all their crew looking pissed off. It was pretty clear that they didn't want to spend the last two months up in Rideau with Chindit and the regime he had set up there and we were glad to be away from it.

"Get your crew over there Bombardier and I will come and talk to you all," Lt Brannagan said.

"Yes, Sir," I replied.

We parked at the side of the road, the camp itself was on a hill and buried deep into the dense jungle. This was the closest that the army could put a camp to the border, so it was always good should the shit hit the fan, for us to go and cause some damage. They said that if we deployed one of our Light Guns outside the camp gates we could shower the Guatemalans with high explosive artillery shells and easily reach the border and beyond. It was a much smaller camp but it had a good feel about it.

"Under the atap lads," I instructed my crew. I pointed to this new atap that someone had obviously taken a long time building, it was fantastic. There were real benches made from all jungle materials and it had Johnnie Ghurkha written all over it. The Rodney came over to the atap.

"Stand up," I ordered the lads.

"It's okay Bomber you can cut all that shite. You are in 'Sunny Salamanca' now so just relax."

I couldn't believe what I was hearing. He went on to say that he had heard what was going on in Rideau and we were lucky as it would probably get a lot worse there over the next two months. We could enjoy our time here and look forward to some proper 'work hard, play hard' times. I had never heard a Rodney talk like that, but if he was true to his word then I was definitely up for it. Sergeant Dave Norman was at Salamanca now too and we were with all the O.P. (Observation Post) boys. The O.P's had some right nut cases amongst them so we were in for a few lively sessions.

"Right, Sergeant Norman will show you around and where to park and I will expect you all in the N.A.A.F.I. for a beer tonight," he finished and then walked away. I was in heaven, a lieutenant in the British Army was coming into the N.A.A.F.I. to have a pint with the O.R's (Other Ranks), it was unheard of and we were chuffed to N.A.A.F.I. breaks. While the crew were sorting all the gun kit out, Dave Norman showed me to my pit. It wasn't much different from Rideau except that I had a lot more bed space, it was a bed on its own and not a bunk bed and the fan above it worked a little quicker and better. Sergeant Norman had been up here a few weeks and I could see by picking his brains that he was relieved to be here now. The camp was very clean and had to be kept that way, it was the army's way of keeping the rats, and all the other beasties down. They had 'Swingfog' the same as they had in Rideau, twice a day, all over the camp.

"Yeah if we keep Brannagan happy then he will leave us in peace." I got the picture.

There was no way my lads were going to rock the boat, certainly after I had briefed them later. I got Joe Smiley to pull all the rifle barrels through as a last little clean before they were secured in the armoury. He poured tons of oil over them too to make sure they didn't rust. Dave showed us around the camp and it felt strange, but good that we could just throw our combat tops off and walk round with a civvy T-shirt on. It made life a lot more comfortable as it was hotter than Rideau camp by a mile. The fact that we were entering a very hot time of year in Belize certainly had something to do with it. Mick McCarthy showed us to the cookhouse which was so much cleaner than at Rideau. If the food matched the standard of hygiene then we were in for some good trough here.

"Oh believe me Sean," Mick started. "The sloppy sergeant here is right on it and his standards are very high. The food is amazing and he won't let his lads cook anything less than perfect." I was excited by this and was looking forward to trying it. He was right and although I didn't have anything cooked at lunchtime, the food was so much better, fresher and so well presented. I complimented the chefs and gave them the credit that was due, I was looking forward to something cooked later on.

We had a cracking Siesta before we played Basketball, Lt Brannagan was right into it as well. He was on my team and although I didn't know at the time, he wasn't half bad. More importantly for us though was the fact that he had taken part. That meant a lot to us and was clearly evident because the troops didn't kick the living daylights out of him as they would have normally done. There is no rank on the sports field, everyone is at the same level, so soldiers always took the opportunity to beat the officers to a pulp for any grief that they may have previously caused them. No it wasn't like that at all, it's because they could get away with it, even the referees turned their backs when the Rodneys were getting twatted.

If I had a pound for every time I heard a referee say, "No, sorry, I never saw fuck all, Sir." I would be a millionaire.

After a fantastic meal in the Cookhouse it was back to the block for a sort out and a quick shower before the N.A.A.F.I. I was over the moon that I didn't have another bunk above me, I could feel the benefit of the fan above my bed. It was heaven in that I had to pull a towel over my shoulders earlier on in the day, because I was getting a little bit cold. I finished my unpacking and only threw in my locker what was needed, the rest stayed in my suitcase. This was a slightly different heat than we had grown used to at Rideau, it was much more humid.

"Do you have a dobbie walla?" I asked Steve Humphries in the bed opposite.

"Yes mate and she is shit hot," he replied.

That was good news because to have nice clean clothes was a big plus here. It amazed me how they could receive them in the morning and have them on the bottom of your bed all nice and clean with your bill by early afternoon. This wouldn't be a problem if it was one or two soldiers, but it was for the whole camp. There were only about four women doing the dobbie so it was a well organised operation they had going. The boot boy was a lad called Sam. 'Sam, Sam the boot boy man' which made no sense at all, but it fitted quite well. He was another one of the hard working Chogies that I became impressed with. The Chogies were amazing people, they kept themselves to themselves, worked as hard as they possibly could and never stopped, they loved people and loved to make them happy. I always gave them credit as they thrived on it, give them the odd extra dollar and they would have gone to war for you. Their outlook on life was in a different league to ours and we could learn so much from them had we taken the opportunity.

Steve and I entered the N.A.A.F.I. at eight o'clock. I was impressed as it was a little more refined than Rideau Camp N.A.A.F.I. What I meant to say was that there was no one pissing up the wall in the corner, or having a bare knuckled boxing match in another. There was no one throwing bottles or food at each other so it looked good for the time being. How foolish was I? The troops had only just walked through the door and they were stone cold sober. The squaddies were the same, it was only the location that was different. In fact, as far as the Royal Artillery was concerned, we had more mental cases situated here at Salamanca than we did at Rideau, by a mile. I couldn't answer for the infantry lads, but I would surely find out in a few hours' time. The building itself was in a lot better nick and the staff weren't bombed out of their heads on cannabis, yet.

We walked up to the bar and ordered four 'Belikin' each. Most of the lads here were drinking Schlitz beer but I didn't like it as it went through me like an Intercity 125. I was going to stick to what I knew best. I was a little disappointed though as we couldn't get 'Stick Rum' and that I would miss. We grabbed a table which just so happened was the nearest to the bar, Steve could actually hold his arm out and touch it. The boogie box was playing some girlie music from the seventies and I distinctly remember hearing Sister Sledge 'We are family' being played for the third time since we'd walked through the door. We always threw all our crap on the table in front of us when we were on the beer. I would stack my lighter on the top of my cigarettes and then just throw my dollar bills next to them, we all did the same it was an unwritten law that you never ever touched another persons 'table swag'. Even in the event that you were pissed off your face you would never go near the property of another soldier if it was on the table where he sat.

It wasn't very long before the Lieutenant came in the N.A.A.F.I. with Sergeant Dave Norman. It was looking to be a good night as we all got on really well with each other. I liked Dave Norman because he was a top soldier, the experiences that he had gone through over the years were amazing and I'd learned so much from him without him even knowing. Lt Brannagan was a well respected officer and had never done anyone a bad turn just for the sake of showing who was boss, that wasn't his style. He was however very keen on his job and when out in the field he was renowned for being a first class soldier. There was one other thing too, he'd forgiven me for blowing him up.

A couple of years before he'd been taking a dump in one of the 'thunder boxes' on an exercise in Soltau. A 'thunder box' is like a small shed with a large box inside it with a hole cut into the top like a toilet. A six foot hole was dug by the naughty boys in the regiment and then the 'thunder box' was placed over the top of it. A roll of bog paper was put inside and that was it. When the hole was nearly full of shit the 'thunder box' was then moved to its new hole and the naughty boys had to fill the hole in.

It was when the hole was nearly full to the top and one of the lads whispered, "Rodney's on the shit house," that I flew out of my tent and ran around the back of the 'thunder box', took the flash, bang from my pocket, struck it up and dropped it down and into the back of the hole. I wasn't aware that it would have quite the effect that it did. It blew Brannagan out of the door and picked the shed up and threw it ten feet away. There was 'Richard the Third' all over the place and including all the way up his back. It was just as well that the hole was full of turd as he would have suffered serious burns. The medics confirmed that it was the shit splattered all over him that saved him. This was good as it took the focus off me nearly killing the guy away from it all. It was one of those occasions when I could have been booted out of the army and looking back it wasn't as funny as what I was hoping.

He did forgive me, though even years later when he was in my company and had to be excused to go to the toilet, he would always stare into my eyes and say, "Stay there Bombardier and that's an order."

I would always drop my head and reply, "Yes, Sir."

The night was going fairly well and I could sense the rivalry between the infantry troops and us. There was one problem in that we had our officer with us so we were on best behaviour, the infantry only had a corporal with them, so it was a little easier for them to let their hair down. This became evident at ten o'clock when one of the infantry lads disappeared for a short time and reappeared with this young Chogie. I didn't know for an hour or so, but it turned out to be Sam Sam the boot boy's man's younger brother. He had ten dollars in his hand and was sniggering loudly to himself.

Steve looked at me and asked, "What the fuck are the grunts up to?"

I couldn't work it out. "I haven't got a clue mate, but I think we're about to find out," I replied.

We then watched them place two tables together and one more table on top of them. Two of the infantry lads climbed up before a third one passed the young Chogie up to the top of this pyramid, he must have only been nine years of age and three stone, he couldn't put a fag out. Another one of the lads standing by, passed a roll of 'Bungee Tape' while another turned the switch on the wall to stop the fan.

"Oh no, please, tell me they aren't?" I said.

Steve looked at me. "What?" he asked.

And with that another one of the infantry troops joined the other two on the tables. Two of them passed the Chogie up even higher and held his back as close to the blade of the fan as they could. The other lad with the tape started to wrap the tape around him and the fan blade. It was never going to work unless they evened up the weight on the other side but they hadn't sussed that out. I wasn't going to tell them with our officer sat next to me. They tried and tried but couldn't get the distribution of the weight right, so there was no way that we were going to see the end effect. The Chogie didn't mind as he had his ten dollars and was never going to give it up. After about ten minutes of trying they cut the tape and let him down. The lads involved climbed down from the tables to lots of booing from their own troops.

The evening passed without any further occurrence and we managed to behave, due to being suppressed by having a sergeant and a lieutenant with us. No worries on that score, we would have our day. I reported to Brannagan the next morning even though I had a head like a robber's dog.

"Bombardier Connolly," he said.

"Yes, Sir. What can I do for you?" I asked.

"Well, it's more of what I can do for you," he added. It turned out that the infantry needed a medic to go on one of the O.P. border patrols and they were wondering if I wanted to go.

"Fuckin hell, Sir, does a bear shit in the woods? Are Abba number one? Too right, I want to go, Sir."

Their medic had joined 'The Sick Lame and Lazy' so they were left short. There was no way that a patrol could go into the jungle without the presence of a medic, I was chuffed to N.A.A.F.I. breaks as I could join an infantry patrol but in my medical capacity.

"What about my crew sir?" I asked.

"Don't worry about your crew, I'll sort them out. You'll be back in a week and a bit," he finished. I saluted him and marched out chuffed to pieces. I immediately went to see Corporal Dymond from the infantry who briefed me and gave me all the gen on the patrol. It was good for me and, as I thought, like a Sunday outing as I didn't have to carry the kit the lads carried. As long as I carried my rifle and my medic bag they didn't care what else I took but my hammock was a must as was my mosquito repellent. I didn't mind getting shot, as long as I wasn't covered in mosquito bites when they laid me to rest in the ground.

The next morning at six o'clock I was walking out of the camp gates with the infantry, it was much the same as our previous patrols. 2 of the B.D.F. joined us and one of the Ghurkhas who took up the front. The infantry valued these B.D.F. soldiers and didn't need me to tell them how valuable they were as they had carried out many patrols with them.

When I had the conversation with the infantry corporal later, he was well impressed about my snake story when I believed the B.D.F. guy had saved my life. He would be happy not to experience the same. The Infantry troops set off at a pace I wasn't used to, they were like gazelles. I thought that there was no way they would be able to keep that pace up through the jungle, but they did for hours. I was praying for the thick jungle so we would have to slow down while Johnnie Ghurkha cut through the foliage. It may have been my only relief from this relentless pace, I just didn't know when the next water break was, but it couldn't come quick enough for me. I thought our lads were super fit, but these infantry boys were mental, on a different level of fitness.

We hit a wall of foliage and it was going to take some time to cut through, we had been patrolling for three hours by this point and I was fit to drop. I threw the water down my neck and wiped myself down like a sweaty racehorse. I had rested well by the time we were ready to carry on and I knew from the briefing that we only had a couple of hours until we would hit the base camp. I remained at the back of the patrol and that was only so the infantry troops didn't see me suffering. They had now slowed the pace and it went a lot better for me. It was nearly the end of the first days patrolling and I hadn't even issued a plaster, which was good. I was looking out for the unusual injuries like Beef worm and 'Twisted Knacker Syndrome'. Dave had taught me a thing or two and it was a case of what you could see was not always the worst injury. He was a good teacher as well as a good medic.

We pulled into this base camp which was occupied by seven Ghurkhas. It was unbelievable, it looked as if M.F.I. or B&Q had been out here and helped build the kitchens and all the bedrooms, but they hadn't it was all made out of atap, bamboo, sticks and jungle vine. It looked as if they had made good use of their spare time too, as they had dotted around the perimeter approximately two hundred Pungee Stakes. Pungee stakes were nasty, they were two foot long, sharpened sticks stuck in the ground, facing outwards on the perimeter of the camp. They were designed for when the enemy charged the position, the sharpened stakes would stick into the shins of the attacking force causing great injury. You had to ensure that everyone who was classed as 'friendly forces' knew about these Pungee stakes or life could turn pretty embarrassing when you had caused multiple stab wounds to one of your own sections coming into your camp at the end of a long night patrol. I had been worrying about sleeping on the jungle floor, but there was no need to because these lads had not only built beds which were raised off the deck but also a really crude version of a thick mattress, which was more comfortable than my mattress back at camp. There was an area for me to tie my ground sheet up so I could have light on at night without breaking the camp night routine. To think I could have a brew in the middle of the night was quite exciting and if this was roughing it, then I wouldn't have minded roughing it for the rest of the tour.

It turned out to be like a holiday for me as the infantry lads would come to me in the morning and ask me if I wanted to go for a patrol with them. If I said no, that was it, I didn't have to go. They treated me like royalty throughout the time I was with them and I couldn't believe the respect they showed me, I felt like a king. I did go on a few patrols through the week, but the one I wanted to make sure I didn't miss was the one on the penultimate day which was a high visible patrol right on the border at Sastoon. There was a huge valley looking over into Guatemala just short of the Sastoon River and from our O.P we could look right over and into the town of Sastoon. The tab was only about three kilometres from the base camp so if the infantry lads had one of their mad moments and sprinted to the O.P, I may not be able to keep up with them but I wouldn't be far behind. I would make sure one of the B.D.F. lads stayed with me to ensure I made it in one piece and didn't arrive with a boa constrictor wrapped around my fat arse.

"We are moving out at five in the morning if you are up for it Bombardier," the lance corporal informed me.

"Too right mate, just give me an early call," I replied.

True to form, they woke me with a pint of hot tea, I laid there for a minute and had a cigarette while I savoured my brew. These lads couldn't only march at a fast pace but they were on the ball when it came to making a good 'Scooby Doo' (brew). I climbed out of my scratcher (bed) and had a good scrub down with cold water. I knew it would be a waste of time as within two hundred yards of leaving the camp I would be soaked through with sweat. At first light we moved out, the jungle light was turned on, as in two minutes it became light which I was relieved about as there was no way I was patrolling in the dark after my snake scare. There was my B.D.F. guy and me at the rear. I made sure I walked in front of him as he was the one who would be saving my life if push came to shove (pardon the pun). It was as predicted, the infantry lads sprinted off and I had trouble keeping up. With clear tracks in front of us it wouldn't take us long to cover three clicks. No water stop or anything, we hammered it to a point fifty yards behind the observation post. The infantry lads stopped and waited for us to catch up. As we caught the other lads up, I turned behind me and said to the B.D.F lad.

"Come on lad, catch up, you are making me look unfit here."

The B.D.F. guy looked confused, but the infantry lads laughed, they knew the score and I smiled. I wasn't trying to bluff them, it was only a joke. They had ample opportunity to see that I couldn't keep up with them, even if I was at the fittest time of my life. They really were fit lads, we had the briefing and I hadn't even got my water bottle out of my webbing and these lads were ready to move forward. There were two trenches fifty yards apart. Two of the infantry troops were manning one and me and a Private Metcalfe in the other. Metcalfe was only a young lad, I guessed about twenty one and certainly no more then twenty three. It was weird as we normally had to sneak up to these trenches and carry out a covert observation, but the brief for this was the opposite. We were to stand up in the shallow trench and show ourselves to the Guats across the border. We were there for five hours in the trench and there was no let up from the blazing sun.

We had only been in the trench for one hour when I could have killed the idiot who had placed the 'slit trench' where it was. There was an opening in the jungle canopy above us and the sun was beating directly onto the jungle floor where our trench was. Everywhere else around our trench was in the shade. Me and my infantry mate were well pissed off. We spent some time talking. He came from a place called Weoley Castle in Birmingham and I just spent the time taking the piss out of his Brummy accent. I did however tell him that if he called me 'duck' one more time, I would bury his head in the ant's nest which was directly in front of our trench. I hope he understood that I was joking as he was carrying the G.P.M.G. and had two hundred rounds of 7.62 ammo with him. We had been in the trench for three hours and we were both sweating like pigs. I have to admit we were both in a bit of a state as we couldn't get the water down us quick enough. We still had two hours left.

"Look at that Bombardier," Tony Metcalfe said as he pointed on the other side of the valley into the town. There was a little girl approximately seven years of age. She had a beautiful red dress on that looked as if she had just taken it out of the packet. She was waving at us from the side of a large shed that looked as if it was someone's home. She jumped onto a track that led down into the valley. We thought no more of her.

"Bless her," I said. We chewed the fat some more and had all the banter about which was the better regiment, I outranked him so I won that discussion. Within twenty minutes the girl from across the valley was stood right in front of our faces.

"You want coke English?" she asked. "Dollars. Dollars," she added. I discussed it with Anthony and although he had no money with him, I did. I could get him some drinks and he could pay me back when he got back to base camp.

"How much? How many dollars?" I asked her in slow English.

"Cold drink? Cold," she said. I took my cig packet out and folded into the crease at the front of it were two twenty dollar bills. I had no choice but to give her a twenty dollar note as I had nothing smaller. I held the note in front of her face and said to her.

"You bring coke and I give you more money." She looked at me and smiled. She took the money and dropped down into the valley once more before our eyes, I felt confident that she would return. We faced the valley once more and I think we both lay there imagining the cold coke pouring down our throats. We waited and waited for what seemed like ages until we watched the girl climbing up on the other side of the building where she originally started from. She stopped at the side of the building without turning around for a second until all of a sudden she turned and lifted the twenty dollar note in front of her face and then lifted it in the air as if she had won the world cup. She started laughing and jumping around like a Jack in a box. It became clear now that we had been 'had' and there was nothing we could do about it. Diplomacy and morality wouldn't let me shoot the girl, but I have to say that the temptation was certainly there. Suddenly my throat felt a lot drier. Tony and I were gutted as we both agreed that we thought she would come back. This girl wasn't stupid. Why did she have to work for a tip when she had my money in the first place? I wondered how many times she

336

had pulled that stunt and gotten away with it. My worry was that if she tried it with some of the mental cases I knew in the paras then she may come unstuck. This was a right kick in the teeth for us as we still had an hour to push. Now normally we would just turn the 'head switch' and then grit the teeth and crack on with it, but this heat was pushing us to the limit.

All of a sudden, someone purposely coughed right behind our heads. I turned as quick as I could. I couldn't believe what was in my face. It was half a playing card. A joker. There was a joker on the other end of it too. It was Dave Dawkins.

"What the fuck are you doing here?" I said to him. "You should be sunning it up in Rideau Camp." It then dawned on me that I didn't have my half of the joker and he knew damn well I wouldn't have it with me. He had done me proper, guess who was going to be paying for the next beer night? He was laughing his head off.

"I have been detailed to come and check on the patrol medics to see if they are doing okay and also to make sure the medical centre is stocked and ready for handing over to the next battle group," he explained. "I am here for two weeks mate."

"Swaraaaay, fuckin bargain pal." This meant that I was glad to see him and we were going to have a good session when I got back the next day. The bastard had asked the infantry where I was and exactly which trench I was hiding in and he found me. I hated him for this and I was determined to have the last laugh.

"Dave, have you got any water with you?" I asked him.

"Yes too right," he replied and at that he passed me one water bottle and Anthony another. His water was cold, I was in heaven and must have sucked the guts out of it. He was going directly back to Salamanca which wasn't far as the crow flies and didn't need the water. We had to take the long trek back to the base camp so it was a must to take this on board. I supped it a little more before passing it back to him.

"Thanks mate, I thought I was going to die." He knew I had 'Steri-tabs' with me and if it came to it we would have taken water from the river, but even after treating it with Steri-tabs I didn't really want to take a chance. Dave had taken another water bottle off his mate and swapped it for one of our empty ones. "Cheers mate. Just have the beer on the table at seven tomorrow night and yes, I know, I am paying," I said, to which he smiled like the smug bastard I knew he was and he got up and walked back to the single track at the rear of our O.P. position.

"Keep your arse down won't you?" he said finally as he disappeared into the jungle. By the time we made it back to base camp, I was so exhausted I felt like dropping to my knees. The only thing that stopped me was the fact that all these infantry lads were watching me. Head up, chest out, I thought to myself. Don't let the bastards see the pain. As soon as Johnnie Ghurkha walked over to me with a pint of tea I was fine, all had been forgiven and I was in heaven once more. A cigarette and a cup of tea, this was nothing compared to the pan of stew they served me, it was amazing. I sat down on my mattress afterwards with a full stomach, my feet soaking in hot water and another pint of hot tea. I thought to myself that this was as good as jungle life gets, surely. I scrubbed myself down with a large bucket of cold water just before last light and settled down on my mattress. I covered my body in my 'non smelly talc' and rubbed Mycota powder into my feet. Mycota was a brilliant fungicidal powder for your feet and squaddies, although hated the smell of it, loved what it could do. I remember having my last cigarette and wrapping myself in my mosquito net and even before the jungle lights turned off, I was gone. 'Boogie Wonderland'.

I was woken up at 'sparrow's fart' by Johnnie Ghurkha with my pint of brew. "Bombardier Doctor, I bring you breakfast. you stay here," he said to me. This guy was ace, he couldn't do enough for me. I would miss him when I left later in the day. I could smell baked beans and fried spam and if I wasn't mistaken I was sure I could smell eggs too. Johnnie Ghurkha opened my ground sheet screen and passed me a plate with about ten slices of buttered bread sat on the side of it. I was right, it was the nearest to an English breakfast I had seen out there. The fried spam replaced my bacon but there were mushrooms, eggs and beans. Just like the night before, I couldn't move when I had finished. It was out of this world.

At three o'clock that afternoon, we arrived back at Salamanca. I stank like a Sumo Wrestler's jockstrap. There was sweat coming from every pore of my body. I needed a cold shower, a quick power nap, a good scran in the cookhouse and then twenty bottles of cold beer. As I said my goodbye to the infantry corporal, I headed off to my accommodation. I couldn't wait until he was out of sight so I could drop my shoulders and limp off into the block like I wanted to but there was no such luck, as I could see Lt Brannagan coming towards me.

"How did you get on Bomber?" he started.

"Piece of piss, Sir," I replied.

"I knew you would eat it, there is nothing the 'grunts' can do that we can't."

"Fuck all, Sir, fuck all," I answered.

When he turned and walked away, I fell into the accommodation block. If only he knew that the infantry lads had surely gained my respect. They were amazingly fit soldiers and equally as good at what they did as we were at what we did. I would always take every opportunity to give those lads the credit they deserved in the future. I got arseholed in the N.A.A.F.I. that night, I couldn't get the beer down my neck quick enough. I stuck to our 'joker pact' and bought Dave's beer all night. I didn't have a clue how much money I'd spent and I didn't care. I was doing well and saving a lot of money while I was in Belize. I couldn't even remember how I got back to my bed that night but it was the weekend so it was no problem that I was in a complete mess in my pit the next day. Had the enemy attacked our camp that particular morning then I would have gladly let them shoot me with no remorse.

"Are you coming to brunch Sean?" Steve Humphries asked.

"No mate, do the honours will you? My cup is on my chair," I said. The 'slop jockeys' often put a brunch on at the weekend. This was their idea of breakfast and lunch at the same time. It was good in the sense that you had a bigger window of opportunity to get something to eat during the morning and it was available from six until two. An added bonus was that we had a thing in the army where we would bring each other food and or drink when we came back from the cookhouse for whoever was still in their pits and requested it. Steve would bring me some scran and a brew back. The 'sloppies' didn't like this because we robbed all the plates and never took them back to the cookhouse.

We played some serious volleyball over the weekend and I got pissed on Saturday night for a change! The infantry were on form on Saturday night and ended up throwing one of their young lads through the window, except the windows in Salamanca N.A.A.F.I. had glass in them. He was very lucky that he didn't sustain any serious injuries as there

339

may have been some serious come back for those lunatics. We had a good run on Monday morning and I rejoined my crew afterwards, I was so relieved to see them.

The next week saw us preparing the gun for exercise. It was good to get back out into the field for two weeks and blast the hell out of Belize. I felt as if I was where I should be, at home looking after my crew, directing then and training them to be good gunners. It was a bloody good exercise and we did what we loved to do best. We had expended all the training ammunition and remapped the face of Southern Belize, I knew that somewhere seven miles from our gun position there must have been a hole big enough to put Rideau camp in. We had bombed that particular area like there was no tomorrow. It was a good show of force for the Guat forces had they been watching.

We were well into the last month of the tour now and although, I wasn't impressed with Belize as a whole, there were parts of it where I would rather be. I carried out a couple of guard duties within the two months and I could live with that, but the way of life there was so much more relaxed than at Rideau Camp. They had it well sorted, the officers off the camp decided to initiate a big clean up which was a good idea at that time. The infantry and our officers decided that as it wasn't far away from leaving Salamanca and of course Belize it would be good if they split the areas of the camp up for each of the N.C.O's, and then once cleaned by them and their teams of men, the Rodneys would go and inspect them. The Anglian Regiment and the Royal Artillery Regiment N.C.O's had a meeting in the small N.C.O's mess once we had received our areas of responsibility. It looked like I had drawn the short straw as I got the 'bin compound'. This sounded easy enough but it was a huge compound filled with all the 'pig bins', swill bins and general waste bins for the camp. It was minging. It wasn't too bad for me though as I had a lance Bombardier and a lance corporal from the infantry to help and then we had ten blokes from both regiments to do the heavy stuff. I was lucky in that I had Lance Bombardier Andy Berry working under me and he was as keen as mustard. I knew when we were on the job that I would be able to sit back and just watch him kick all the arses.

We went up to the compound to have a look at what was required of us and it soon became clear that we needed the 'brute force' approach to this one. We would have to remove everything from the secure compound and then get the hosepipe on it and scrub with some heavy duty commercial disinfectant. The infantry guy said he would get hold of all the kit from the stores and that included ten bass brooms. Bass brooms were big heavy duty yard brushes that were good for this type of clean up. We went and detailed our men that were on the list and met at the location at nine the following morning. It was at this point that I realised that it wasn't the best idea to get pissed the night before as I was now stood inhaling all the waste from the camp and it wasn't going down too well. I was throwing cold water down my neck as well as my tablets, but it wasn't having any effect as yet. The temperature at this time of the morning was unbearable so we had to act fast and that's what the lads were doing. The two 'lance Jacks' had briefed them well. They turned up in any kit they wanted as long as they didn't mind it getting ruined. The 'slop jockeys' had sussed what was going on outside of the rear door to the cookhouse and approached one of the lads asking if we wanted an urn of tea. The first I knew about it was when I saw two chefs carrying an urn of tea towards us with a brown paper bag on the top of it and some plastic cups.

"Sugars there lads," the corporal from the Catering Corps said.

"Hey, thanks mate. You don't know what that means to these lads," I said.

"Oh listen mate, if these lads like a brew as much as me then believe me I really do." I smiled knowing that he understood. He was over the moon about us cleaning this compound as it fell under his remit and he was always worried about how he would never be able to free enough men up to clean it nearer the time of handover. The lads grabbed a quick brew and then got stuck into the job again.

The R.A. lads worked hard but the infantry lads were amazing. They were like the English version of the Ghurkhas. They were relentless even in this heat and burning temperatures. At ten o'clock they had dragged everything from out of the compound, I thought we would still be removing the bins an hour or two later so that was good going. Mind you I did tell them that it was 'Job and Knock'. They knew as soon as they had finished and I'd been given the authority to knock them off if the standard was as it should be. I could see that all twelve lads were in one corner of the compound shouting at something and as I went to investigate I could see three or four of them prodding with their broom handles, I was sure it was a snake but when I cleared the troops out of the way I couldn't believe what was in the corner on the ground just sitting looking up at us. It was the biggest frog I had ever seen anywhere in the world and it must have measured the size of a human head and weighed a couple of pounds easily. It was frightening to look at and would have scared any child but frog or no frog it had to go. Some of the troops wanted a photo of it and others were trying to move it with their brushes. Either way, it just looked at them as if to say 'piss off and leave me alone'. The lance corporal brought in the water hose and got behind it.

"The fucker will move now," he said and he was so sure of his plan. "Turn it on Tim," he shouted.

I could hear the water blasting through the pipe and then all of a sudden it smashed through the end of it and hit the frog directly in the mush. The frog was not impressed but never batted an eye lid. It didn't move a muscle. We could all see that the corporal then changed his tact and started to squirt the water underneath its body in the hope that it would lift off the ground so we could sweep it away, but there was no chance. The temperature was at its highest now and I was beginning to lose my temper.

"Turn the fuckin' water off," I shouted impatiently as I stomped over to the frog. I couldn't believe we were being held up by a blasted frog of all things. There was no hesitation on my part and I pulled my right foot back like a cocked weapon and then let rip with an almighty right boot. I connected with the frog right in the left hand side of its body. Not only did I feel the instant pain, but I heard my big toe crack. I knew right away that I had broken it. The frog looked up at me as if to say 'is that the best you can do big boy?'. I made a hasty retreat to the wall outside the compound I had been downed by a frog.

The lads were all laughing their heads off, but funnily enough I wasn't. As I was taking my boot off to inspect the damage to my foot, the lads just casually moved the frog onto a piece of cardboard then carried it out of the compound and let it go in the undergrowth at the side of the monsoon ditch. Rab walked passed me as he was re-entering the compound and he had a big grin on his face.

"Bombardier Kermit, shall we scrub out now?"

"Fuck off dick head! You'll be scrubbing out your cell in a minute if you don't get out of my sight" I retorted.

All the other lads giggled to themselves but they didn't understand that I was in agony and now had to report to all the officers that I had been taken out by a frog. Brilliant, I thought to myself, that's all I need. I managed to get back to my bed space where I took my porous tape out and strapped my toes together. There was nothing more I could do with it now.

When I reported to the officers' mess, they were all sitting out on the veranda shouting, "Ribbit, Ribbit, Ribbit, here comes Kermit."

"Okay, Sir, at least I don't have to explain what happened as it appears that you already know."

I gave my salute, 'about turned' and hobbled off, back down the hill to the sound of rapturous laughter. This was one of those times in my career that I wished I could have told an officer to 'fuck off'. I would give the Rodneys that one. I wondered what may have happened had this been at Rideau, would Chindit have pegged me for 'Self Inflicted Wounds', as I kicked the frog and had no real need to? It made me think, there would be no more running and physical activity for me for the rest of the tour now with my broken toe.

Over the next week, I was used in the supervisory role to detail groups of soldiers to clean certain areas of the camp with a view to handover to the new battle group in the next couple of weeks. Their 'advance party' was due to arrive on Monday so we had the remainder of that week and the weekend to ensure the place was tip top. On Friday morning we received some shocking news regarding the Falkland Islands, Lt Brannagan told us that it had kicked off big time and 66Battery who were from our regiment and should have been coming out to relieve us had now been redirected to the Falklands. Before our minds started to work overtime with the thoughts of us having to spend another six months in the 'arse-hole' of the world, Brannagan put us out of our misery. They had already detailed another battery to relieve us and there would be no problem with the handover. I felt a little sorry for 66Battery as they had done all this warm weather training and were now on their way to the Falkland Islands where it was freezing. They would be using the same gun, the good old Light Gun.

We had a good break at the weekend and binned all cleaning until early Monday morning. The whole of the camp was looking fine and we had cleaned it to a much higher standard than Rideau was when we arrived, that's for sure. I wasn't at Salamanca when our troops landed there, but I bet it was cleaner now than when our lads arrived. There were no incidents to report over the weekend except for Steve Humphries losing it a little, he got so drunk on Saturday afternoon that he took the machetes out of all the troops webbing in our room. He then lay on his bed with all eight of them and while we were all lying on our beds too, he decided to throw them up into the fan one by one. The fan was on very fast and just picked the machetes up and threw them wherever it wanted.

"Steve, pack it in you dickhead," Mick shouted.

"Fuck off," he shouted back.

We never tackled him when he was pissed to the point of us stopping him doing anything, as he was a hard lad and it would end up in a fight if you were to pursue it. He threw the next one and it embedded itself in the back of the steel locker which was up against the left hand side of my bed. It missed my legs by twelve inches, I didn't wait around for the next one and dived under my bed onto the concrete floor. It was here that I could shout my commands to him although I knew it was all going to be in vain.

"Steve, put the fucking machetes down you blimp," I screamed at him. "You're going to kill someone."

Back came the same answer as before. "Fuck off."

It was pointless me telling him that I would 'charge' him as he knew I wouldn't so I would just end up looking a fool. If you 'warned someone for office' it was important that you followed it through. If you failed to peg that person then not only would you be treated like shit by the other N.C.O's but no one would take you seriously. It was no good and we had to sit it out. After a couple of minutes the next one went up. I heard the noise of the two metals coming together. Then the clanging and the smash as the machete went through the window and the mosquito net above his own bed. He let rip with three in quick succession and I heard two of them hitting the Nissen hut walls and then one hitting the end of someone's bed. The last couple landed on the concrete floor after whirling around the fan a couple of times and fortunately, by the time he threw the last one, he was unconscious. It was just as well as I was sure big Dave would have knocked him out for being such a fool, someone could easily have been killed. He didn't

344

know anything about it on the Sunday morning when the troops were telling him what he had done. We agreed that machetes should be locked away in lockers from here on in. We knew we only had days left to go, but should Steve get leathered like that again then it may be a different story.

On the Sunday night, I chose to stay sober with the rest of the troops. They were all attending the 'Ten Miler' in the morning but due to the injury the frog had caused me, I wasn't going to be attending the run. Not only would I be able to have a 'lie in' but I would get first dabs on the showers and I would be first in the cookhouse. I think the whole camp had an early night and by ten o'clock we were all in or on top of our pits. It was roasting hot and pouring down outside the hut. We were now coming into the rainy season so we didn't know whether this was a shower or if it was in for the evening. Either way it was coming down very hard and fast. I didn't have a clue what time I drifted off, but I do know I tossed and turned for at least a couple of hours. I must have got to a point when I was so tired I just flaked out. I was the first person to wake in the morning and the reason I knew that was simple. Had anyone else woken before me they would have probably been running around the camp like a headless chicken. It was 'first light' now and the reason I woke was my mattress was soaked. Having first thought that I had 'lagged my chariot' (pissed the bed), it quickly became clear that we were right in the middle of a flood. I jumped off my bed and the water was up to my knees. I started shouting the troops to get everyone up.

"Tommy, get your arse up," I shouted.

He looked over to his right and spotted the water. "Fucking hell!" he screamed.

By now everyone was out of their beds, there was kit floating all over the room. I started to wade towards the door and remember kicking someone's webbing with my broken toe. Now was not a good time for sympathy and I had to stick to the task in hand. I looked out of the door and noticed that the rain had stopped, but all the accommodation blocks were under water. The water was pouring very fast down the Monsoon Ditches, but it wasn't enough to take all the water away that was obviously running from the hills. I could hear Tommy and his troops screaming at everyone to get out of their pits and for them to get around their own men to make sure that everyone was accounted for. I set up a command post in the atap at the top of the hill and told all the N.C.O's to come up and report to me when they had accounted for all the troops in their charge. At first glance I could see that this was one of the only dry places in camp. I sent Joe to get the officers and ask them to report to this location ASAP. He sprinted off up the hill, theirs would be the only accommodation block not to be affected by the water as it was high up near the top of a very steep hill. The officers were horrified at what they saw. I could see at first that they were about to offload on me as they would be pissed off that we had dragged them out of their pits, but as they approached the atap they saw the water level first hand.

"Are all the men accounted for Bombardier Connolly?" one of the infantry Rodneys asked.

"Yes, Sir," I replied. "We are just carrying out a tec check, Sir,'" I explained. The 'tec check' was a check of all the weapons and operational equipment to ensure nothing was missing first of all and then secondly that it was all in a place where it wouldn't sustain any further water damage. If we were missing any operational equipment like a weapon for example, then we would organise a massive search until it was found. It wasn't long before we found out that the armoury had not been affected and all the weapons were safe. The Light Gun had been covered with water but only to the point of the gun trails receiving a good soaking. The barrel and breach were all fine and the water was a good twelve inches away from them. This would have been a pain in the arse if it had turned rusty prior to us handing the guns over to the incoming battle group.

It was some four hours later that the troops from the new battle group pitched up at Salamanca and they couldn't believe the state we were in with all the available troops trying to cope with the excessive water. There was tonnes of kit ruined and a very heavy claim was to be submitted on our return to Blighty. The new soldiers understood our plight and were very sympathetic with our situation. It took a further two days for the water to fully subside before we could start the big 'clean up' operation. What was brilliant about this was the incoming troops helped us to clean the camp ready for us to hand it over to them, classic move. The plan was for us to clean all the kit down and have it completely handed over to the new battle group by 'close of play' on

Thursday ready for our leaving party in the N.A.A.F.I. that night. The troops worked really hard towards that goal and it was good to see everyone rallying around to help each other. We spotted the new troops from time to time all over the camp. It wasn't difficult to spot that they had just arrived due to the milk coloured skin that they all had. The new teams were now checking all the kit and signing it off whoever had owned it for the previous six months. My handover of the Light Gun and one tonne Land Rover was first thing Thursday morning. The lads had put some extra hard graft in on the gun and it was immaculate when I turned up to the atap.

"There shouldn't be any problem Sean," Paul O'Neil said.

"I hope not mate, I think we've had our bit of bad luck with that flood," I replied.

Paul was right, the handover went like clockwork and we now had nothing except our own small arms to worry about until we got back to Colchester and they were locked in the armoury until we left in the morning.

The officers had paid for our piss up in the N.A.A.F.I. and I think I spent no more than five dollars of my own money. We had very little left to do before starting the long journey back up north to Belize City. I had a few tarantulas to sort out with Dave for the remaining orders and then my last job of the tour was to get drunk, for the very last time in Belize

Chapter Twenty

Chickin Lickin

We drove into Rideau Camp for the last time and we were covered in dust having roughed it in the back of a Bedford Wagon. I thought I would be able to ride up front but the sergeants had the luxury of that, they called it 'privilege of rank'. I felt like a camel coming out through the desert after a two week trek, I was that thirsty. The one tonne Land Rover and gun had remained at Salamanca ready for the next detachment so it wasn't as if I could have had the comforts of the Land Rover. I jumped out of the back of the wagon and removed the towel that I had used as a filter covering my mouth. We looked like something out of 'Lawrence of Arabia' and I would be relieved to see the back of these roads, if I had to swallow another mouthful of this dust I think I would cry. Dave Dawkins was there waiting for me as I climbed off the back of the wagon.

"Sean, you look like shit. See you in the Cookhouse at lunch," he said.

"Oh hello to you too mate, but what about the tarantulas? Don't we need to get stuck in?" I replied.

"Don't worry, I have done them all and I have five spare already in cases if any of your lads want them," he explained.

"Yes mate I will need three," I finished. This was brilliant as I was dreading coming back on my last day to go searching around the camp for tarantulas. The last three would go to some of the lads who had just come back from Salamanca. He took a big wad of dollars from his pocket, took some notes from one pile and placed them onto another pile and then passed me the first pile.

"You take the sixty bucks off the other lads then and that's us straight," he said

"Hang on mate I can't take that, I have hardly done anything," I protested.

"No mate, take it we said we would go halves and besides that, I've had a right laugh." With that he hurried off to the medical centre to operate on some poor sick soldier.

"Okay see you lunchtime," I shouted after him.

If the food was shit we could have a joint ripping session on the 'slop jockeys'. I counted the money when I got to my old bed space and there was three hundred and eighty dollars and I still had sixty to come back from the other three sales. I felt a fraud though as I had done nothing to earn this money, I would have to speak to Dave later and get him to take most of the money back.

When we left Salamanca I can remember feeling really pissed off about all my kit that had been left in my suitcase, it had rotted away and practically turned to dust. I couldn't believe I had lost some of my new clothes as a result. The flood had taken a lot of my stuff which was stored under my bed and now the climate and conditions had claimed a load more. When I tipped all the dust out of my suitcase onto the floor, the troops would normally have laughed their heads off but they had been caught out in the same way and knew what a blow this was.

"Bollocks to this for a lark, it's all going on the insurance claim," Rab said.

"Too true mate," I replied. Having let it go out of my head I decided that I would get my laundry done so that I didn't have to travel home with a load of stinky kit in my luggage and it would leave me less to do when I got there.

We had been on an exercise called 'Lion Heart' a few years ago in Germany for three weeks and when we'd returned we'd stashed all our contraband in our large packs and stuffed all of our dirty washing on top of it. When the customs had asked us if we had any extra duty free we told them that we didn't, then they told us to open our packs and they soon told us to close them again. This wasn't one of those opportunities so therefore I was going back with as much clean kit as possible. I took my dirty clothes bag out of my large pack and placed it outside the door. By the time I had stripped off and made my way to the shower block, it had all been collected. I would get it back later that afternoon, nice and clean and ready to go straight back into my suitcase.

I took a cold bottle of stims into the shower with me but it looked as if Taff Terry had beaten me to it.

"How you doing Taff?" I enquired.

"Hey up Sean, how was Salamanca mate?"

"It was fantastic Taff. I am just so glad we had the last two months down there that's all."

"Yes I must admit it's been hard up here, with Chindit getting worse as the days went by," he added. He told me that Chindit had cracked up and totally lost it now.

"You should have shot him," I said. Taff just laughed but everyone was just relieved to be getting back, knowing that they didn't have to be around him too much, as we were due three weeks leave when we got back.

"Did you hear about the B.S.M. Sean?" he asked me.

"No mate and I would love to know where the fuck he got to," I said. It turned out that the B.S.M had been done for shoplifting in the UK the day before we'd flown out. We didn't know if this story had been confirmed and we had no further details concerning it. "No way Taff, he was a lot of things, but he wasn't a 'tea leaf," I loyally replied. I wasn't having this story and for whatever reason I felt that someone was making this up.

"That's what I heard," Taff said as he was about to leave the shower. I shook my head and disagreed totally with what he was telling me. The B.S.M. was a first rate soldier on a good wage, he didn't need the money or the hassle that went along with the possibility of getting caught shop lifting. I wasn't buying it (pardon the pun once more). I sat on my plastic chair now alone pondering on the information Taff had just left me with and I could still see no truth in it.

After getting dressed and sitting on my bed waiting for lunch, I thought about the good times we'd had during our stay in Belize. Although the place was as we had been warned the 'The Boil on the Buttocks of the world' we had met some good people whilst we were there and had some really good laughs. We hadn't lost anyone, all but a couple of injuries and one casualty evacuation back to England. Okay I hadn't got to kill anyone but hey ho, that's life. It had been a brilliant opportunity to get stuck into some good training and put some good soldiering under our belts. Johnnie Ghurkha and the BDF had played a big part in that. I suppose during all the slagging off which we aimed

350

at this country, it hadn't been as bad to us as one may have guessed. Like most of the troops now, I couldn't wait to get home to some good old English draught beer, a nice English lass and my own pit. I stood up as Tommy was standing at the bottom of my bed.

"Come on miserable arse, we have got an appointment with 'the king' after lunch," he said. Tommy knew I liked Elvis, but he wasn't on about that king, he was taking the piss as we had one more Chindit parade to attend and that was after lunch. It was supposed to be a happy event when Chindit and all the Rodneys thank us for all our efforts and they were to tell us that there was going to be one almighty 'humdinger' of a piss up in the bar later and not to be late. I had forgotten about the parade, but that was one of the good things about being in such a big 'family' there was always someone there to remind you should you forget. Once the parade was out of the way we were going to have a quick siesta followed by a few games of volleyball and then our final piss-up in the evening. It was all down hill from now on.

Tommy and I met the rest of the mob down at the cookhouse. Taff was sitting with Rab and Steve Humphries. "Don't worry if you haven't got a knife for your steak Taff, Steve has got eight," I shouted. They all laughed except Steve.

"All right, all right, I know," he shouted back embarrassed. "Wankers," he added before lowering his head.

Had he been a little quicker to react, a little mention of 'frogs' may have put me in my place and prompted a reaction but he had missed his golden opportunity. Tommy and I went over to where Dave Dawkins was sitting and I put my plate on the table to reach into my pocket for some cash.

"Don't even think about it mate," he said.

"Fuck me! You don't miss a trick do you?" I answered.

"If you try and pass money to me again, I will burn it," he finished. He wouldn't accept any of the money he had given me earlier even though I felt I had done nothing to earn my share of it. Dave had chewed and swallowed a twenty pound note once that I had persistently tried to sneak into his pocket in the Robin's Head in Colly. He did warn me not to but I'd wanted to be the smart arse and slip it back to him without him knowing. He'd chewed it and then swallowed it with a quarter of a pint of cider. He'd never batted an eyelid.

"Fuck you two, I'll have it," Tommy said.

"Like fuck you will, go and boil your head you scrounging git," Dave answered.

So on this occasion I knew I was stuck with the money although I wasn't complaining, I would be taking a minimum of two grand back to the UK with me which at the time was a lot of money and this would just add to that figure. I told Dave to meet us all in the N.A.A.F.I. later on as it was as much as his leaving 'piss up' as it was ours and the infantry boys.

"No problem," he said as he walked out of the cookhouse.

The 'slop jockeys' had been very clever and cooked a meal fit for a king (not Chindit and not Elvis). I think there may have been two reasons for this. The first was they were getting used to cooking in this ruthless environment now and secondly they were frightened to death of the rest of the camp hanging them from the flagpole if they continued to serve up the shit they had previously served us. There had also been earlier threats from Big Ged which I didn't catch fully but the words 'tarantulas' and 'bollocks' were definitely said to the chefs so either way, it was in their interest for them to keep it at this standard until we left camp. The A.C.C. (Army Catering Corps) had certainly outdone themselves. After a pint of the cold jungle juice we all left the cookhouse at the same time and headed back to the block.

At one o'clock we all stood in the baking sun on parade out in the road. If this had been six months earlier then we would have been dropping to the floor like flies but we were used to this heat now so it wasn't too much of a problem. I heard someone shout that Chindit was on his way up the road, we looked to the right and sure enough he was marching up the road on his own. We were all dressed in our sports kit, but he was dressed in his jungle combats and jungle hat. A trooper to the end, I thought to myself as he reached us.

He brought us up to attention and then stood us at ease, he never even blinked until he shouted, "Connolly, Moran and Baker, out here now."

"Oh fuck," I heard Bob Baker say from behind me as he was falling out. I turned to the right and marched out to the front, as did Taff Moran who was at the left hand side of me.

"Turn and face the squad you three," he ordered us. We were still puzzled as to why he had brought us three in particular out to the front of the troop. My mind was working overtime and for a brief moment I thought to myself that it couldn't be something I've done. How wrong was I? Next thing I was falling to the ground clutching my sternum. In the blink of an eye Chindit had thrust a photograph of me with my pants around my ankles, my left hand holding my plums, a machine gun in my right hand and tons of ammunition strapped to my shoulders and waist. I had a smile on my face not dissimilar to the Kray Twins walking free from court for murder. It was one of the photos from the jungle shed when Chindit left us alone and allowed us to fire away some ammo, the photos that we had taken from the camera that we had removed from his Bergen and then stashed back in the hope he didn't notice. He was not too happy at all.

"Fucking Hell, Sir" I said clutching my chest.

"Got something to say Bomber?" he asked.

"No, Sir," I replied. As I was slowly climbing back to my feet, I noticed another photo on the ground but this one was Bob stood in an ungracious pose, he had a thunder flash planted deep between the cheeks of his arse and two rifles in his hands and all the ammo hanging from him with his head turned and beaming at the camera. He was now on his way to the ground, Chindit had dropped him in the same way, like a sack of shit. I heard the thud as his fist connected with Taff Moran's chest and again I noticed a photograph falling to the ground. I failed to see what was on this one but I had a good idea. I was now wondering how he had managed to get photographs developed in Belize but I didn't have to wonder for much longer, he was holding the photos up and showing the troops. I could see on their faces that they were dying to laugh but didn't dare because Chindit would have killed them.

"These three Wankers decided while I was away from camp during the tactical phase to remove my camera, on returning from the jungle, I decided that I would put a new film in my camera and send my old film home to my wife to have it developed. I told her to keep the photos in Colchester until I got back as it was pointless sending them back out here, but she couldn't resist sending me these seven photos."

I couldn't believe what I was hearing, Chindit had sent the film back to his wife who had now seen us three with our plums out in various poses, but also with a grenade stuck up one of our arses. I nearly died.

This wasn't turning out the way we had planned and we certainly didn't wish to be receiving such a degree of corporal punishment for something that started as a bit of a laugh and ended in total disaster. This went down as another 'cluster fuck' by the troops on the 'rampage'.

He fell us back into the squad clutching our chests before the Rodney arrived to address us. We were brought up to 'attention' once more before being ordered to 'stand at ease' and then 'stand easy' (which meant relax). The officers took it in turn to address us and thank us personally for all the hard work we had put into the tour. It was an extra hard climb due to the conditions and the climates.

We played our last games of volleyball and every time I jumped high in the air for a smash at the net I got this little reminder in my chest that told me not to nick our sergeant major's camera, if we did we should remember that showing our private parts may not come across as funny when his wife developed the photos! Our team won the competition which brought in another twenty dollars. I couldn't do any wrong where money was concerned on this tour. My team hit the showers as the victors and this time it wasn't stims that we were drinking it was cold, refreshing 'Belikin' and Schlitz beer. We had no more work and no more running to do until we arrived safely back in Colchester. We all made sure that we had packed everything away so that in the morning if we got out of our pits late, we would be able to get up and go almost immediately. I went to our last evening meal in my 'going out' clothes and made sure that everything else apart from my clothes for the morning and my washing and shaving was safely locked away. I had even given a big tip to the girls when they handed me my clean washing.

I walked into the cookhouse with Ken Browning. "I am going to miss this place Sean," Ken said.

"Fuck off! You'll be the only one then, I will miss this and the 'slop jockeys' like a hole in the head mate," I answered.

Ged shouted from over in is usual seat, "Fuck off Browning, they're about as much use as a cardboard leg in a monsoon."

Ken was off his head and if anyone was to come out with a statement like that then it had to be him. A while ago in Germany when I was taking Ken out driver training, I'd told him to go and jack the wagon up, while I got the paperwork sorted but when I came out, he had a trolley jack under the Land Rover and he was literally jacking it up.

When I'd said 'jack it up', I meant for him to check the water, oil, lights and tyres etc, not literally 'jack it up'!

We had hit the jackpot with our last evening meal and it looked like we would be leaving without ripping the 'slop jockeys' to pieces, we would see if we made it to breakfast in the morning.

Approximately ten or fifteen of us walked into the N.A.A.F.I. at seven o'clock and it was packed. Even the troops from the incoming battle group were in there and were half pissed already. This looked as if it was going to be a good night. The TV was switched off and the infantry lads had one of their own private soldiers who fancied himself as a bit of a D.J. set up in a corner with a really big 'Boogie Box' and by the amount of tapes he had on the side of the table, it looked as if we were in here for the week let alone for one night. His choice of music was good though, late seventies and early eighties.

"Look Sean, Bob fuckin Marley's on the turntable again," Mick shouted.

"Hey he's all right this kid, listen to that," I shouted back to him. There were a couple of groups of the local Chogies in two of the corners and the odd Chogie sat with some of the troops they had become friendly with over the six months. It was really good to see them mixing and I would be sure that it would be worth their while near the end of the night. The 'boot boy' was doing all right even now with a pile of notes on the table in front of him. This would prove to be the equivalent of months and months of hard graft wages for him, he was a good lad though and it was good to see him enjoying himself. The kid knew already that no one would touch his money on the table in front of him, so he wasn't behind the door, by the end of the evening with this daft lot, he would have enough wedge to retire on a British island somewhere with his feet up but I would be advising him against the Falkland Islands.

Taff Terry, Mickey Hill and Steve Humphries walked in. Steve was already off his face and had clearly made the most of an afternoon hidden away on the beer it wasn't good to see him so pissed this early on in the evening, but we would all keep an eye on him to make sure he didn't snot any infantrymen and start a mass brawl or cause injury to himself. With a bit of luck on our side, he may 'flake out' in one of the comfy chairs in the corner of the N.A.A.F.I. after a couple more drinks.

Dave and Rab went and got the wets in and I grabbed a large table near the front wall where I could see everything and everyone in the bar so if anything funny was to happen I wouldn't miss it. That was of course, until I got pissed.

The night was going well and the infantry were up to some silly, but harmless games that they had got the Chogies involved with. It was really funny as the Chogies were fleecing them at all their own games, it was costing these troops a small fortune, but they didn't care. The rest of the N.A.A.F.I. were cheering the Chogies on and laughing loudly. It really was fun and the more pissed everyone got, the funnier the games got. Some of the lads were that pissed-up, they were just stood jamming away on the make-shift dance floor.

The troops had been at the games for two hours and lost a lot of money so it was time for a break. Everyone retreated to their tables and replenished all the beer bottles. I scoured the N.A.A.F.I. and looked at all our boys, everything looked on form, there was no sign of any trouble and the atmosphere was fantastic. It's at these times that boisterous or pissed up individuals within either of the two regiments can sometimes spark off a fight, but this was not that type of atmosphere, everyone just wanted to have a good laugh. No one had even been thrown through a window yet!

At around eleven o'clock I saw this Chogie woman walk into the N.A.A.F.I. She was followed by what looked like her daughter who only looked about eight years old. The girl was walking with a chicken on a piece of string as if she was taking it for a late night walk.

"Dave, look," I said pointing towards the girl. "

You have got to be kidding me," Dave replied. She was soon spotted by the rest of N.A.A.F.I. and everyone was laughing. I knew that the Chogies had some unusual pets but I hadn't quite seen anything like this. A few months before I'd seen a Chogie cuddling an anteater but this took the biscuit. The mother looked round at some of the Chogie groups and spotted someone she knew, they were sitting on a table at the opposite end of the bar to us. She started to walk along the walkway in the centre of the N.A.A.F.I. towards her friends followed by her daughter and the chicken. I was watching the reactions of all the troops as she passed them, they were all laughing in a gentle and friendly way. She came level with Steve Humphries and carried on walking, I could see that Steve had looked across at the girl and showed no emotion at all. I could feel that this wasn't good as he was absolutely 'shit faced'.

The mother was now at the table where the friends were and the daughter was three yards away when I noticed Steve turn to his left as fast as he could. He grabbed the chicken around the neck in one foul swoop, he brought the chicken's head up towards his own. He opened his mouth and placed the chickens head into it, at which point I tried to stand up and make my way towards him, but it all happened too quickly and I was too late. It was only then that the little girl had turned round and seen what was happening. The look in Steve's eyes was like something I hadn't seen for a long time, he looked as if he wanted to take someone's life. It may not have been a bad thing that he settled for a chicken.

He removed the chicken minus its head and placed it on the ground in the standing position, there was blood everywhere. The little girl began screaming hysterically. Steve made a loud spitting noise and spat the chickens head on the ground. The headless chicken was now running around in circles and would not lie down.

"Andy, Bob, get him the fuck out of here now with no questions," I shouted. With that they jumped over the table and grabbed Steve by the arms. Most of the people in there were still in shock with what they had just witnessed and we used this to our advantage. "Joe, Brian, get some 'clean up' from behind the bar quick," I shouted over to another one of our tables. I grabbed a number of twenty dollar bills off my table. I ran over to the mother who was clutching the child and trying frantically to calm her down. "Brian get some stims for the girl."

"On it Sean," he called back. I looked at the mother and started to apologise profusely. She was really good about it and considering that if you killed a Chogies animal by mistake in Belize, it would normally cost you forty to sixty dollars I knew I had to do better under these circumstances. If this got back to the powers that be then Steve would be Court Martialled for this stunt for sure. It was a good job that the senior ranks and all the officers were having their own piss up in the 'senior ranks' mess' down at the bottom end of the camp. There was only Taff Terry with us and he was too pissed to even spell chicken let alone remember this incident.

I quickly passed her one hundred dollars which instantly made the girl stop crying, for two dollars she could buy a new one. Furthermore I had just given the mother approximately one year's wage so she was more than happy. Mr Humphries would be coughing up some money in the morning before I ripped his head off. My next task was to go around and apologise to the infantry lads. We knew that now the shock was gone they would want to sort Steve out for this callous act and I was now worried that they would send a team of lads out to, lets say 'have words' with Steve so we wanted this to end now. I went over to their most senior corporal, I knew this guy as he had the same surname as me. Connolly. Corporal Daniel Connolly was built like a brick shit house and I knew he was the man to see. I didn't have to explain what had just happened as he had just witnessed every bit of it. I apologised for Steve's actions and told him I would personally deal with it. I informed him also that we had just slipped the Chogie one hundred bucks and she was more than happy with that. Corporal Connolly disappeared into a group of his soldiers on the opposite side of the N.A.A.F.I. and judging by the finger wagging and pointing at their more mental troops he managed to contain what looked like could have been a nasty situation.

"Sean what the fuck, are you going to do about him?" Dave asked me.

"Nothing mate, he will be discharged the week after we get back but I will be giving him a bollocking and a half in the morning," I replied.

Steve had finished his twelve years and wasn't even meant to be going to Belize until the numbers fell short, he had a week left as a soldier when we got back and then he was away. God help Civvy Street, I thought. Dave shook his head. We had done some mad things but this took the biscuit. I was going to be bollocking him for this stunt, but he probably wouldn't even know about the chicken he was that pissed. My priority now was to ensure I got my money back off him.

Well the ceremonious removal of the chicken's head virtually put the mockers on the evening as I think everyone was still in shock for some time after. A couple of the infantry lads came over to me and said that even though they had done some sick things in their careers, they had never done anything even remotely like that. They would never forget the sight of the chicken running around the N.A.A.F.I floor with no head. I was fairly drunk at the time of this incident and was feeling pretty good. I had now started to sober up because for the last thirty minutes I had been running around like '*a headless chicken*' trying to keep a lid on it before Steve got himself 'filled in'. The lads from both regiments started drifting away from the N.A.A.F.I. shortly afterwards and either went to carry on with their parties elsewhere around the camp or they had just had enough and decided to call it a night. I could see me now having another beer, then calling it a night. By the time I hit the sack I had the sound of the little girl's screams ringing in my ears. It was unfair that Steve was now flaked out fully clothed on the top of his bed while that little girl was probably still being comforted by her mother.

I made it up in the morning just in time to get breakfast. I had quarter of an hour to spare so decided that I would shower when I returned from my scran, I threw my clothes on and noticed the lump on the bed still curled up across from me. It looked as if Steve Humphries hadn't moved from the night before but for now, I ignored him, I would speak to him later after my shower. I legged it down the M1 and when I arrived I was surprised to see so many of our lads in the cookhouse. Dave Benson came over to my table.

"Do you mind Sean?" he asked.

"No mate be my guest," I nodded towards a seat. "I thought it would be empty in here this morning," I started.

"Fuckin' hell, you are joking aren't you? Humphries made sure the troops got an early night after Steve's stunt last night, so it was no problem for us all to get up this morning."

Steve had a lot to answer for, he had not only upset the infantry troops, but also our own lads, which was not good. I could only re-affirm that I would be speaking to him, I needed him to know the extent of damage he had caused last night. For the next thirty minutes our lads were coming and going from the cookhouse, most of them looked over at me and shook their heads, it felt as if I had bitten the chicken's head off and not Humphries. By the time Tommy crawled into the cookhouse, a surge of relief passed over me, I really needed the support of a mate now. The odd infantry man looked over at me but they didn't pass any comment, they were being pretty reasonable about the incident but I did get the feeling that they wanted to tear Steve apart. Tommy came over and we discussed the events of the night before. Tommy commented on how this was Steve's worst stunt to date and how it was just as well he was leaving the army because if he had he stayed in the army, we couldn't imagine what he may do next. He really was a basket case.

By the time I returned to the block, I noticed that Steve Humphries' bed was empty. Joe said he was in the shower.

"Wait until you see his 'boat' Sean," Joe Smiley said (Cockney rhyming slang for his 'boat race', face). I immediately thought that someone had come into the accommodation and filled him in on his bed while I was at breakfast.

"Ged, come with me mate."

I didn't have to say anymore, Ged got up off his bed and walked over to me. We left the block and headed towards the showers, just as we arrived at the shower block Steve came out with his towel wrapped around him.

"Steve, a word," I said pointing back to the shower block. His face was swollen with bites, I remembered that he had laid upon his bed with no mosquito net over him and the mosquitoes had bitten him all over, I would put this down to 'rough justice'. Taff Terry had beaten me to it and Steve was now fully aware of what he had done, but as I'd suspected he didn't remember a single thing about the previous evening, let alone the chicken. Ged and I told him that this went beyond 'fun' and he acted in a really irresponsible manner. He was a lance Bombardier in the Royal Artillery and this was not the way an N.C.O. should behave. It was clear he was ashamed and it wasn't going to serve any purpose me standing there ripping another strip off him. He told me that Taff had informed him that he owed me one hundred dollars and to think himself lucky it wasn't more. Taff had also told him that he was a lucky boy because the infantry were looking for his blood last night and had it not been for Daniel Connolly from the infantry then he may have been taking his shower in the medical centre this morning and nursing more than a hangover.

We got back to the accommodation block and the first thing Steve did was go to his locker and take out his wallet, he took out one hundred dollars and passed it over to me. As I took the money from him, he lowered his head in shame and said, "Thanks Sean."

I thanked him for the money and packed the remainder of my kit.

As the troops finished packing they all took their cases outside the accommodation. They knew the drill; we would detail a number of groups to clean certain areas of the camp. I think everyone knew that Steve Humphries detail would be destined for the toilets. Although the shower block had cleaners, we needed to leave it in a condition decent enough for the cleaners to clean. Most of the lads were detailed to clean the accommodation block as it was minging. Most of the remaining troops who were sat outside with the luggage were called back into their block as nearly everyone had forgotten their 'shrapnel'. There was a little plastic drawer that was screwed to the inside of the locker door which is where the troops would throw all their loose change when they came in off the beer at night, we referred to it as shrapnel. We all planned to give it to the little kids before we got on the RPL at the harbour in downtown Punta Gorda.

"See you on the boat Dave," I shouted to Dave Dawkins as he was walking back towards the medical centre.

He turned around and shouted. "No worries, I will keep you a cabin."

I waved while I was chuckling to myself, I remembered the twelve hours of torture on the boat on the way here and I was not looking forward to it on the return leg. However, I could handle it a little better now we were going home.

We carried out a final inspection and arrived at the conclusion that we could clean and clean all day long, but as the saying went, 'you can't polish a turd'. I handed the block over to the incoming artillery boys who looked totally dejected, it was no different to how we'd looked when we first arrived. We were sitting under the shade now waiting the fifteen minutes until the Bedford pitched up. We had plenty of time to make it to the harbour at P.G so I was going to brief the driver that he had to drive really slowly. All the troops were looking clean and thinking about the dust in the back of the wagon, it was the way we wanted to remain. I was sure that the rest of the lads would have agreed with me and preferred to have taken longer to reach the harbour. There were four Land Rovers with the Rodneys and Chindit in them, two of which would go up ahead to make sure that everything was ready for us arriving at the harbour.

The minute the wagon arrived I placed my suitcase and my large pack at the back of the tailboard. I asked Mickey Hill to make sure it went on the wagon. The driver was someone I had not seen here yet and judging by the colour of his skin, I could hazard a guess as to him being a new boy.

"Listen mate, can you drive as slow as possible? We have eaten the dust for six months now and we are really pissed off with it, we don't want anymore," I said to him.

"No problem Bombardier, I will go as slow as I can," he replied. I walked to the back of the wagon and climbed on board, the front seats were occupied by the sergeants. The driver came to the rear of the vehicle and secured the tailgate then within another minute we were waving goodbye to Rideau Camp for the very last time.

We turned left out of the camp gates and I waved at one of the little Chogies who worked in the 'pan scrub' in the cookhouse. He was a hard working guy who was probably being paid a tenner a month from our government, but I had grown to know him during our time here. The driver stuck to his word and took it very slowly. I was planning on this journey taking approximately forty minutes but nobody cared, we were just pleased we weren't getting covered in dust.

Bob Baker started singing loudly, "A yellow bird," and the troops repeated "*a yellow bird.*" Then Bob once more, "With a yellow bill". The troops again, "*With a yellow bill*" and so it went on. Taff and I were exchanging information on how much we had made on our 'side lines'. Taff made more than Dave and I on his empty stims bottles. He made nine hundred and thirty dollars, which was amazing for collecting empty bottles. It was worth all the heartache of not having a bed space in the end everywhere you looked around his bed, there were empty bottles but for that kind of money it was well worth it. We got to the harbour with ten minutes to spare, but more importantly we were still clean. All the lads commented on the fact that they had remained dust free as they climbed down from the wagon.

With all the kit now off the wagon and stood under the shade of a large atap tree, I could see one of our Land Rovers driving up and down the road in front of the jetty. It was only approximately two hundred yards away but it had possibly thirty kids chasing after it. I could see two blokes in the back of the Land Rover and they were holding something. Don Robinson was driving the vehicle.

"Sergeant Norman, what are they doing?" I asked Dave who was standing next to me.

"I am fucked if I know, go and ask them," he ordered. I walked over to the Land Rover at the same time as I saw some of the kids biting something. What the hell? I thought. When I was about ten yards away from them the penny dropped.

"You lot, get your arses here." Don Robinson, Mick McCarthy and Mark Hadfield stood in front of me. "Hadfield, tell me the truth, what are you doing?" I asked. I didn't need to ask the question, but I was that shocked as to what I had seen that I wanted to hear it from the horse's mouth.

They had taken some Hexamine Blocks which were the white flat fire lighters we used on our small camping stoves and covered them in strawberry jam from the compo rations then made a hole in the centre and tied a piece of string to it then towed it behind the wagon. The little Chogies saw the jam and chased them to the point of being fit to drop. The idiots in the back would then let the string go and the Chogies would beat the living daylights out of each other to get to the jam then the victor would pick it up and bite into it. It would take only a couple of seconds of frantically chewing the block to realise that they were eating something poisonous.

"You bunch of twats, are you stupid or something? You will kill them," I said.

"Get rid of that jam and pack it in now." I had to turn and walk away quickly as I was pissing myself laughing. The consequences of their actions could have been a lot different, but it was funny at the time. I arrived back at Dave Norman. How the hell would they think of doing something like this? I thought to myself.

"What they up to Sean?" he asked.

"Nothing Sarge, they are just fucking about, I have told them to pack it in," I finished as I turned towards him. He nodded his head and carried on smoking his cigarette.

Just before the Sergeant from the R.P.L. called us over a considerable amount of the locals had come to wave goodbye. "Look at that Taff," Tommy shouted. "It's like a scene from the fuckin 'Railway Children', is there a tear in your eye yet?"

"There'll be a tear in your fuckin eye in a minute if you don't shut up."

Everyone fell about laughing. There were a few faces I recognised as we started to walk towards the boat with our luggage. If we were due to sail at twelve o'clock, we only had a few minutes to get aboard this crate. There were no vehicles to take onboard so it was just a case of walking the gang plank. It only took us a couple of minutes and we all made our way down to the large square hole that awaited our arrival. It felt as hot as it did the first day we arrived and the steel on the floor of the boat was scorching hot, which meant we couldn't lie down on the hull.

"What about our shrapnel lads?" Mickey Hill shouted.

"Shit, yes," I called.

Our luggage was left where it was and we all made our way up to the narrow gantry which ran around the top of the boat. I reached deep into my pocket to make sure I had every single coin in my grip. All the little Chogies were waiting by the back of the R.P.L, standing on the jetty. I threw the coins as hard as I could so that they landed near the shore in three or four feet of water and as soon as they hit the water, the kids started punching and slapping each other in the face as they were diving into the water. They couldn't pick the coins up from the bottom of the sea quick enough. All the time they carried on battering each other in the hope they would be able to collect more of the spoil. As the boat now started to move the rest of the lads let rip with their shrapnel. There must have been hundreds of coins flying through the air and landing roughly in the same location. It was unfortunate that some of them actually hit the kids. There was so much coinage flying through the air that it looked like a plague of locusts in flight. What was good about this was that there was enough money to go round and even the thinner smaller kids were collecting some of the money. All these kids mangled up in the water in front of us reminded me of a few years ago when we were stationed in Mansergh barracks in Gutersloh, West Germany.

For years the troops would go down town into Gutersloh and get bladdered as well as stealing everything else in sight to serve as a souvenir. We would always start off with the best intentions and fold twenty Deutch marks up and stash it in our back pocket for our taxi home, the problem was that we would end up getting pretty arseholed and spending the twenty marks thus leaving us the problem of how we would get home at the end of the beer drinking night, but that was easy, we would do what every law abiding British squaddie stationed in Gutersloh at Mansergh Barracks would do and that would be to steal a German's push bike. It could take you a while to get your hands on one but as a rule they were relatively easy to get your hands on. In 1982 there was no C.C.T.V. to watch you so stealing a bike off one of the Germans was easy pickings. I know that this was S.O.P. (Standard Operating Procedures) for some of the lads. They wouldn't have any intentions of getting a taxi back to the barracks and would steel a bike every single time they went out, one of my mates must have stolen, in excess of fifty bikes. The River Dalke ran right past our camp, this meant that we could pick our pushbikes up from outside most bars in the town then ride like mad down the main drag, stop on the bridge outside the camp, pick the bike up and lob it into the river. Then you would walk the last one hundred yards into camp. Bargain! A free ride and you would have built up a good appetite for some trough when you got into your flat.

During our last summer in Gutersloh, 'Herman the German' decided to drain the river to carry out some cleaning operations. I would imagine, the sight of three or four hundred rusty push bikes in the river must have really pissed them off but we found it quite amusing and it kept the troops talking until the day we left Germany.

The remaining time upon the steel gantry was spent waving at the residents of Punta Gorda. The kids were still killing each other in the shallow water splashing around like a shoal of piranha fish. I would imagine that they would be there until the early hours of the next morning searching for the last five cents. The troops let out a long cheer as we finally pulled away. I don't think we would be totally relieved until the wheels of the V.C. 10 left the runway at Belize International Airport in thirteen hours time. We were now made to climb down into the hole of the boat and stay in the hull. No one was permitted to stay on the gantry while the boat was sailing and this was a great shame as the sea breeze was fantastic. We had come prepared on this occasion though as not only did we have a freezing cold tea urn filled with jungle juice, but we each had our four water bottles filled with cold water. The 'slop jockeys' had made us all a nice packed lunch and with our water, and juice we would do okay until we finished on this tug. The only unfortunate thing was that there was no brew.

The midday sun was scorching and the lads had already started to whinge. There was nowhere in the hole to take shelter from this direct sunlight so that made the troops restless. We waited and waited as patiently as we could and hammered the cold water and juice. We all agreed that we would wait until dark before we troughed our food as it would be a lot more comfortable.

"I would give my high teeth to be in one of Bobby's cut out logs now Taff," Dave Norman shouted.

"Hang on a minute, there is a limit I'll go to, and that's crossing it," Taff Terry replied.

As soon as the 'Belize lights' were turned out I could hear the squaddies' sigh of relief coming from all directions. It went something like, "Thank Fuck for that," and, "There is a God." It would only be a few hours before we were moaning that it was too cold with the direct sunlight now gone, we thought the hull of the R.P.L would soon turn cold but it didn't.

Within an hour we could hear the troops tucking into their ration packs, so then everyone was into them. Chindit was sat next to me and he was the only one on the boat that I could see who wasn't tucking in to his food. He was just staring into the wall of the boat. I was getting a little concerned for him because since he walloped me in the sternum, he had been very quiet. Not half as quiet as I went when he hit me, but nevertheless. This was out of character for him, it was as if he had lost interest even before we got to Blighty. The day he dived into the river and smashed his bonce on the bottom in the shallow waters could be taking its toll. Although we were due to go on leave shortly after our return, I would be interested to see how he was when we returned. Something was amiss, we had our ups and downs with Chindit, but I think deep down we respected him. It was clear though that he was going through a bad patch at the moment.

At ten o'clock I lay back on the deck of the boat, it was cool but certainly not as cold as I had expected it would be. It was when I heard Dave Dawkins choking on his cigarette and I shouted, "Chuffed to fuck," and he replied with, "Eat shit and die," that I closed my eyes and thought of how he had stitched me with his joker while I was in the trench on the border. It was a good one and I had to hand it to him that he'd got me good and proper.

I must have nearly drifted off to sleep as I was one of the last to react when the RPL lads were calling, "Prepare for landing, prepare for landing."

This was the moment that the front of the R.P.L ran itself aground and was quite a normal thing for it to do. As the boat stopped with a small jerking motion, we were all chuffed to pieces, which was evident when the loud cheer sounded. For most of us, this would be the last time that we would have to ride on one of these things, but what an experience. We all considered this to be the worst part of the journey. The flight on the V.C. 10 after this would be a doddle. We all gathered our kit and carried out a final check of the area before leaving the boat. We said a jovial goodbye to the crew and walked onto the shore. It was only a short journey to the Belize City International… Shed, or better known to the locals as *the airport*. I still believed that the Belizeans could be prosecuted under the trading standards for calling that location an airport. The front porch of the average three bedroom house in the U.K would prove bigger in most cases.

As I walked round to the entrance of the shed, sorry terminal, I could see a massive RAF Tri-Star aircraft. I had travelled on a Tri-Star before and they were fantastic and so superior to the V.C. 10 by a mile. I wished at this point that we were flying on it back to Brize. I spotted one of the 'R.A.F. Movers' (Ground crew).

"Where's our V.C. 10 mate?" I asked him.

"Fucked pal," he answered.

"Is that ours?" I asked him while pointing at the Tri-Star.

"Yep, it is that," he finished.

"Oh you beauty," I shouted and walked into the shed. I was quick to tell our lads, but it was pointless as they had never been on a Tri-Star. All I knew is that I had learned a little about this baby before I flew on it last time.

I can remember vaguely that it had four hundred seats, so we could all count on a few extra seats each on the way home. I couldn't remember the amount of fuel it carried, but it was somewhere around eight tonnes and it used one tonne on take off. It had three large engines, each one costing a million quid. It could easily carry on flying or land if one of the engines blew. It was a magnificent aircraft, but I wasn't going to be fully convinced that this was our flight home until it took off the runway. I had been in situations before when the troops had been turfed off one aircraft only to be shoved onto a smaller less superior one. We were waiting anxiously in the shed for someone to come and give us the 'Is this your bag? Did you pack it yourself' etc but nobody came and no one looked at our passports. No one issued us boarding cards or anything. We came out of the shed (departure lounge) and dumped our cases on the pod trolley prior to 'the movers' loading them on the Tri-Star. I was getting more and more excited as we got closer and closer to the plane. We were all still shocked at the lack of customs control. There was a member of the aircrew counting with a 'hand clicker' and another was directing our troops to climb either the front or rear steps. I climbed up the steps at the rear of the aircraft with Tommy walking in front of me. I could hear the troops as they entered the aircraft and they were made up with their new ride home.

"Wow," Tommy said.

The seats were ten wide, so I made sure I had the four in the middle. I told Tommy where the best place to go was now he was on board and he took the four seats in the row in front of me. It was like having a single bed to go to sleep on all the way back to England, we had never had it so good.

I crossed all my fingers and toes and a lot more besides as the plane was taxiing down the runway. The air-conditioning was a little cold, but we had all brought warm gear with us ready for when we landed at Brize. Just as I went to cover my shoulders I felt the aircraft wheels lift off the ground. Yes, I thought. This was a relief in itself as the last time I was on this particular aircraft it had had a blow out on two of its tyres but it hadn't been a problem as the ground crew only took thirty minutes to change them and we were battling down the runway at Brize Norton once more.

No sooner had the captain gone through his safety talk it was onto the crew to start shoving food down our necks. We never said no to free food, so there were no complaints from the troops. It was the cup of tea I needed to get my hands on and when it came, I was in seventh heaven. Especially when I found out that it was P.G. Tips. By the time I had finished my third cup, I started wondering how many times it would disturb my planned kip when I needed to go to the toilet five times an hour. I decided not to make it a fourth even though the 'trolley dollies' offered more. The food wasn't too bad for a cardboard meal and the minute my rubbish was removed from my little table, I was out like a light. I had rolled up my pullover which I had removed from my large pack along with my coat earlier and placed it under my head that was it, I was gone. The earlier trip on the R.P.L. had really taken it out of me along with the heat, so it was time for some serious sleep.

I was woken by the safety belt warning bell and the crew asking everyone to fasten their belts as we were about to land in Washington. We were all made up as most of us could have a smoke there, and for the non smokers, at least they could stretch their legs.

"Tam, ask Sean for his camera," said Rab sarcastically.

"Yes very good children," I replied. There was one thing for sure, my camera was safely packed away in my case and that's where it would stay until I got home to Colchester. If there was an A.W.A.C. aircraft on the pan then I know one person who wasn't going near it. Mind you, I wouldn't mind meeting up with Sergeant Smart Arse of the American army again in a dark room during my short stop. I owed him a bit of verbal as a minimum. 'No, I reminded myself, I needed to stay out of trouble. Well that was until I got back on terra ferma anyway.

When we were sitting in the terminal I made sure I stayed in the smoking area and drank my cup of coffee from the machine. I kept myself to myself and remained that way until the aircraft had been refuelled and I was sitting back in my seat on it. Taking off from Washington I noticed we were a good half hour ahead of time, so if the Tri-Star flew at a similar speed then we may arrive back in the U.K. a couple of hours early. I watched approximately half an hour of the in-flight film on the back of the seat in front of me, but I couldn't hear the volume at all. It didn't matter because I turned over, spread out on my four seats and then flaked out.

One of the air crew was shaking me on the arm. "Wake up Sir, can you put your seat belt on please?" she asked. I sat up and rubbed my face. This was it we were landing back in England for the first time in six months, it was Friday 1 October 1982 and not only did we have some serious leave coming our way, but we had the added bonus of the weekend upon us. There would be some serious partying this Friday and Saturday down town.

I made the adjustments to my watch and realised that we had made approximately two and three quarter hours up during the flight due to the extra speed of the Tri-Star. This was fantastic, but I don't think the buses would be there waiting for us, it would have been far too easy for someone to radio ahead with an E.T.A. so they could adjust the times of the buses to match. It would mean that we were going to have to sit around the terminal for a few hours while we waited for the 'mess tins on wheels'. It was quarter past four in the afternoon and if the buses arrived soon we could be in Colly by half eight. The aircraft pulled up at the terminal and we waited for it to stop completely before we released our seatbelts. It was freezing on the aircraft so it would be interesting to see what it was like outside.

"Don, Ken, where are your coats?" I asked.

"We won't need a coat just to get inside the terminal Bomb," Ken replied. I thought that they would be eating those words in five minutes and guess what? I was right. As soon as the front and rear doors opened, I could feel the cold weather blowing in to greet us and a severe through draft between the front and back door. Don and Ken were directly in front of me as we stepped off the aircraft and immediately started to rub their arms with both hands.

"Oh shit," Ken said as he turned around and looked at me.

"Don't say it Bomb," Don said. I didn't need to really and in all fairness I didn't care. I had a pullover and a coat on and I was still cold, so there was no way that these pair of Muppets could have hidden it. There is a saying in the army, 'any fool can be cold', and this pair epitomised that saying.

By the time we entered the terminal, I could see that it was not only Don and Ken that were cold but most of the other troops were ill prepared for the return trip too, they were absolutely freezing cold. I was further amazed as we walked in from the aircraft pan end and straight through the terminal and exited out of the front door, ending up at the front of Brize Norton Terminal building, which was fine for me, but not for the troops without coats. As I was level with the exit, I looked ahead of me on the bus park. There were five army buses all parked side by side. If these were our buses we were made up, we could be in Colchester by eight-thirty and in the bar shortly after that.

We had just walked through the terminal carrying our bags and again, no one had stopped us, challenged us or searched us. This would have been a drug dealer's paradise. I couldn't believe that they would let us return from Central America without someone looking in our bags. How strange, I thought. One of the coach drivers walked over to where we were all standing smoking outside the terminal, he looked like Manwell from 'Fawlty Towers' at first glance but I was wrong it was one of our drivers and I recognised him as he got closer.

"Colchester?" he shouted.

"Yes, mate," I shouted back.

He turned round and waved the other drivers to bring their coaches over. I didn't know at this time which coach I was travelling on, but it certainly wasn't going to be the one that I came on. Although I would never know the registration, I knew it was a green one so if I stuck to the colour white I couldn't go wrong, or so I thought.

I sat as far away from where I thought the engine was and by the time we set off I realised it just didn't matter where you sat on these buses it was still a very loud experience. A Tri-Star blasted out 160 decibels on 'take off', a pair of disco speakers blasted out 140 decibels, an army bus blasted out 240 decibels on 'tick over'. My question is, where was 'where there's blame there's a claim'? In 1982! Because we would have been minted. There was no talking on the bus as not only could we not hear each other but we just couldn't be bothered shouting that loud.

We arrived in Colly at ten minutes past eight on Friday night. The artillery troops fell in on parade. The 'slop jockeys', mechanics, engineers and medics all went their separate ways.

"Give us a shout in the morning Sean," Dave shouted to me.

"Yes mate, no worries," I shouted back.

Unfortunately for him, he would be seeing me a little earlier than that. The B.C stood out in front of the troops and reiterated what the Rodneys had said in Rideau. He was over the moon as to what had been achieved and all the troops that went out there had returned. Except for Sean Morrison, who came back from his tour a little early and less one testicle. The B.C. dismissed us and told us to report for battery parade at nine o'clock on Monday morning. We were given the weekend to rock the town and go and get pissed. He didn't even mention the fact that he didn't want anyone fighting this weekend, as it would have served the same purpose as the military police telling us not to drink Green Stripe.

When we fell out, I could see two bodies slowly making their way over to us but it was very dark at that time which made it difficult to make out who it was. Then I noticed that one of them had a walking stick and I knew who it was. It was Pat Walters and Sean Morrison. I was about to shout hello to Charlie Chaplin, but I was too late.

"Oh look, it's the wobbly brothers," Tommy shouted. "
Fuck off," Pat shouted back.

Ged joined in the banter. "The last time I saw you; you were fuckin' about and squirming on the running track," he said.

"Fuckin' about? I was in agony honestly Ged there is one thing you never want to do and that's to break your femur," Pat answered.

"I have no intentions of doing so, anyway what happened to gritting your teeth you big tart?" Ged finished.

"Hey Torvill and Dean, can you show us your twirl?" Rab then shouted from the back.

This was followed by another, "Fuck off," from Pat which made us all laugh, but Pat didn't find it so funny. When Pat showed me the scar, I thought that the ambulance driver must have got lost on his way to the medical centre and ended up at Colchester Abattoir, I had never seen a longer scar on a human body. It was a broken femur, so why the scar started on the back of his head was anybody's guess. It looked as if this surgeon was trying to beat a record of the longest scar and Pat was going to be the winner whether he liked it or not. It was good to see them both on the mend though especially Sean Morrison, because at the time of the Cas evacuation he looked as if there may be irreversible damage that could have threatened his future in the army.

"Sean. Are you coming over to the N.A.A.F.I for a quick pint?" Rab shouted.

"Yes mate, I'll have a quick one and then I have something I need to take care of," I replied.

Rab looked puzzled but he didn't ask what because he knew me better. Rab placed a pint of draught bitter on the table in front of me. The girls behind the bar knew him and let him put it on 'the tab' as he had no English money with him. I raised the glass up in front of my face.

"Lads! Here's to a good tour, you can keep Belize and shove it were the sun don't shine, but we did it, we wrecked the place and made it back safely," Ged shouted. And at that we all raised our glasses and knocked back our ale. I stopped when there was an inch left in the bottom. "Nectar," I said. Tommy and Rab smiled. "See you later lads," I said as I gulped the last swig of my bitter.

"What are you up to?" Tommy asked.

"Never you mind, I'll see you later," and with that I left the N.A.A.F.I.

I sprinted over to my room and dumped all my kit just inside the door, checked my back pocket to make sure I had my wallet and left the accommodation, running in the direction of the 'training wing'. I was so excited and prayed that my plan would work. If this panned out as I hoped, it could prove to be the proverbial icing on the cake and a job well done.

Within five minutes I arrived at number fourteen, Hornbeam Close. The house was in total darkness. It had been no more than thirty minutes from us arriving back at Colly to me being outside the front door. I took my wallet out and opened it, lifted the little flap and removed my joker, then placed it in my mouth and clenched my teeth over it. I returned my wallet to my back pocket at the same time as I was checking round to make sure I hadn't been rumbled. I licked my left hand, rubbed my right hand against it then placed both hands on the drainpipe at the side of the porch. With a little jump, I started to shin up the drainpipe. It was hard work, but with the determination and excitement of what I was hoping would happen, it made it an easier task. I climbed past the porch and continued up the drainpipe until my head was just lower than the top bedroom window. I pushed once more, making sure I kept my head lower than the window sill. I gripped the drainpipe as hard as I could with my right hand, taking the Joker out of my mouth with my left.

I quickly lifted my head above the sill and looked through the window, I could see Dave and he was about to climb on top of his wife, his hairy arse now winking at my face. They were both lying on the bed and he was stark bollock naked. It had to be the first thing he was going to do after six months away from his wife. My timing was impeccable, I banged hard on the window and he reacted quickly by turning round. I poised myself hanging from his drainpipe with my joker card now facing him. He panicked and looked on top of the two bedside cabinets for his wallet but it wasn't there. His head slowed as he lowered it onto his wife's chest, then he turned and stared at me.

He knew he'd been beaten by a better man as he mouthed the words, "YOU FUCKING BASTARD."

ACKNOWLEDGEMENTS

So to the serious part of the book. Without the help, support and encouragement of a certain group of people, there would be no serious part to this book and indeed there would be 'no book'.

To all the lads who I had the great pleasure to serve with and the troops who disbanded with the regiment June 2012. Thank you for many years together and the opportunity to re live some of those memories. The troops who didn't make the final tour, R.I.P comrades.

Thanks must go to my daughter Lisa, all my family and especially my brother Bill who has believed in me right from the word go. Our 5.am talks over the phone every morning have certainly paid off. I owe so much to David Lewis Richardson from Dreamwolf Films. His continued interest, encouragement and assistance in the military and the Belize trilogy has brought out the best in me. One of the best and most current authors of our time, Caroline Smailes. Her delivery of the 'right between the eyes' criticisms will be remembered by me and taken into my next book and without who's help I couldn't have made it thus far.

Thanks to Dave at Benridge and Anthony Metcalfe who became my two top test readers once the book was completed.

Jean Clarke (M.I.L) Senior Tactician and Proof Reader. Her attention to detail and post chapter comments have encouraged me no end.

And nearly finally, Petal (Naomi) my wife. Whose initial idea to write the book came at a time when it needed to be compiled. She has pushed me and supported me every step of the way. Not only has her final proof reading managed to retain the structure of the book but she as also kick started the young heart in it too.

And really finally. A Big, Big thanks to my baby boy. I have enjoyed all the extra playtime sessions with my little soldier Daniel, as a result of his mummy having to carryout extra 'Proof Reading Duties'. (I still say the little red car is mine and you can have the yellow one).

I love you all so much and thank you for your belief and faith in me. I hope you are not too tired for 'round two'.

ALSO BY SEAN CONNOLLY

'GUNNERS & GRENADES'

Sgt. Sledge is rough, tough and bad, a man of principle – his own principles. A man with no respect for authority – so what the hell's he doing in the Army? – He's about to be thrown out – that's what! Think Jack Reacher meets Frank Gallagher and you're getting close to Sgt. Sledge – which is probably the last place you want to be…

TO FIND OUT MORE ABOUT SEAN CONNOLLY
AND HIS FORTHCOMING NOVELS VISIT:
www.armynovels.com